STENDHAL
The education of a novelist

COMPANION STUDIES

Odette de Mourgues: *Racine: or, The Triumph of Relevance*
Ronald Gray: *Goethe, a Critical Introduction*
R. F. Christian: *Tolstoy, a Critical Introduction*
C. B. Morris: *A Generation of Spanish Poets, 1920–1936*
Richard Peace: *Dostoyevsky, an Examination of the Major Novels*
John Bayley: *Pushkin, a Comparative Commentary*
Dorothy Gabe Coleman: *Rabelais: a Critical Study in Prose Fiction*
W. E. Yates: *Grillparzer, a Critical Introduction*
John Northam: *Ibsen, a Critical Study*
Ronald Gray: *Franz Kafka*

Other volumes in preparation

STENDHAL
The education of a novelist

GEOFFREY STRICKLAND
Lecturer in French, University of Reading

CAMBRIDGE UNIVERSITY PRESS

Published by the Syndics of the Cambridge University Press
Bentley House, 200 Euston Road, London NW1 2DB
American Branch: 32 East 57th Street, New York, N.Y. 10022

© Geoffrey Strickland 1974

Library of Congress Catalogue Card Number: 73-91619

ISBNS:
0 521 20385 6 Hard covers
0 521 09837 8 Paperback

First published 1974

Printed in Great Britain
at the University Printing House, Cambridge
(Brooke Crutchley, University Printer)

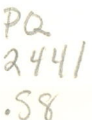

In memory of my father
Reginald Bertram Strickland (1887-1965)
Royal Engineers

Contents

Acknowledgments ix
A note on the quotations and references xi

1 The life and times of Henri Beyle
Introduction   1
An age of cant   8
The childhood of Henri Beyle   18
Coming of age in post-Revolutionary France   21

2 Le Beylisme
Beylisme and 'de-Rousseauisation'   27
Beylisme and Utilitarianism   33
De l'amour and *D'un nouveau complot contre les industriels*   44

3 Beyle the critic
Beyle and heroic drama   52
'Le style est ceci'   63
The discovery of a 'natural' style   72
'Le plus grand plaisir possible'   79
'Le beau idéal' in painting   89
'Le beau idéal' in music   94

4 The chronicler and historian
Beyle and Napoleon   99
Italy and the eruption of energy   107
The chronicler of contemporary France   114
History and truth   121

5 *Le rouge et le noir*
    The problem of form   126
    'Apprendre à vouloir'   135
    'Scènes probantes' and the historical revelation   145
    The mind of the assassin and the language of the author   149
    Two kinds of heroism   156

6 *Lucien Leuwen* and autobiography
    Souvenirs d'égotisme   165
    Lucien Leuwen, part one   171
    Lucien Leuwen, part two   190
    Lucien Leuwen and the critic   208
    La vie de Henry Brulard   212

7 *La chartreuse de Parme*
    Le rose et le vert and *Les chroniques italiennes*   220
    Fabrice and Clélia   224
    Mosca and Gina   237
    Lamiel and *Suora Scolastica*   254

8 Some conclusions   259

  Notes to the text   267

  Chronological table   288

  Index   293

Acknowledgments

I originally planned to write an account of the relation between Beyle's novels and his criticism as a doctorate thesis for the University of Paris. The fact that I never completed it is not entirely due to my indolence – the more I came to enjoy his poise and intelligence, the more daunting my chosen subject came to seem; nor can I pretend I was not encouraged. Mr H. A. Mason, my supervisor at Cambridge, communicated to me some of his own enthusiasm and gave me my first copy of *La vie de Henry Brulard* and his own notes on Beyle and his contemporaries. Professor Vittorio del Litto, the late Pierre Moreau and Professor Robert Escarpit gave me their valuable time and attention and both the Office des Universités in 1954 and the Centre National de Recherche Scientifique in 1964 gave me generous grants enabling me to spend two periods of uninterrupted study in the Bibliothèque Nationale in Paris and the Bibliothèque Municipale in Grenoble. I have also been helped considerably by the students with whom I have discussed Beyle's work in the University of Reading, in Scripps College, California and the University of California at Los Angeles and by the comments on what I have written by various colleagues and friends. I should like to mention especially Mrs Marie-Pierrette Allum, Mme Gaynor Bartagnan, Mr Michael Black, Dr Margaret Davies, Mr Norman Henfrey, Professor B. C. J. G. Knight, Professor Haydn Mason, Dr Walter Redfern, Mr Ian Robinson, Mr Morris Shapira, Professor Colin Smith, my brother Edward Gale Strickland and Professor Stephen Werner. I wish to acknowledge my debt to all those who have helped me and not least of all to Philothei for her encouragement, advice and patience.

Part of chapter 3 appeared originally in *The Human World* and I should like to thank the editors for permission to reproduce it here.

GEOFFREY STRICKLAND

Department of French Studies
University of Reading
April 1973

A note on the quotations and references

There is no standard edition of Stendhal's writings. The most reliable and the most carefully annotated – also the most sumptuously bound and most expensive – is that published in Geneva by the Cercle du Bibliophile under the direction of Vittorio del Litto and Ernest Abravanel. Many of the volumes in this collection, I gather, are to be reprinted in the Gallimard Pléiade series, while a new edition of *Lucien Leuwen* is being prepared by Professor del Litto for the Gallimard Livres de poche. This may also be the appropriate place in which to recommend the very inexpensive edition of *Racine et Shakspeare* published by J.-J. Pauvert in their admirable 'Libertés' collection and the edition of *D'un nouveau complot contre les industriels*, presented with an accompanying 'dossier' by P. Chartier and published by Flammarion.

Not all libraries can afford to keep up to date with new editions and not even collectors of Stendhal own all those that have appeared in the last fifty years. I have therefore decided to refer wherever possible to chapters of works by Stendhal and to the dates of letters and entries in his diaries and travel books. I refer to specific editions, usually Martineau's Divan or Pléiade editions, only where this is unavoidable.

All quotations are given in English, or in French, followed by a translation, in places where a tolerably adequate translation is impossible or where I wish to draw attention specifically to the language of the original. The translations are my own.

I
The life and times of Henri Beyle

Introduction

The reader of Stendhal who feels curious to know about his life and personality will find that there is no lack of easily available information. Few men have left a more minute record of their thoughts and sensations from one day to another and few lives have been studied with closer scholarly attention. Much of what he committed to paper over the years in letters, diaries, notebooks and in the margins of books, as well as in his unfinished autobiographies, has survived and can now be read in the carefully annotated editions of the late Henri Martineau and Professor Vittorio del Litto. Many of the enigmas with which biographers have been confronted have now been solved, though fresh information concerning Stendhal himself and the influences on his work still continues to be published regularly in *Stendhal Club,* the journal edited by Professor del Litto in Grenoble, Stendhal's birthplace.

My purpose in writing this book has been not to provide a summary of all that is now known about Stendhal the writer and Henri Beyle the man, or to add to this any new information, but to consider one particular aspect of his life and literary career. My subject, briefly, is the education of Stendhal: not merely the schooling which he underwent during his early years in Grenoble but the education which ended only with his sudden death in 1842. My argument is that the education took place and that Stendhal's writings, particularly in his later years, are those of a genuinely educated man. The phenomenon is not a common one and it is for this reason, I wish to argue, that

Stendhal's life and writings are of general interest. They illustrate what education can mean.

One of my reasons for saying this is that Beyle – as it may be more appropriate from now on to call him – seems to have belonged to the class of human beings for whom an education is never complete. Nietzsche, who was to describe himself as Beyle's 'posthumous son', has talked of those writers who are 'seekers' and of the irony of their being transformed into 'classics':

> But how has our Philistine culture judged these seekers? As if they had found what they were looking for. It forgets that they never thought of themselves as anything other than seekers. 'We have a culture of our own', we then hear, 'because we have our classics. And not only have we the foundations of a culture. We have also the edifice and *we* are the edifice.' On which the Philistine proudly taps his forehead.[1]

One may be reminded here of what Beyle himself said towards the end of his life of his own literary talents: 'If there's another world, I shall certainly go and see Montesquieu. He may say: "My dear fellow, you had no talent at all." I shall be vexed if he does but not at all surprised. This is something I often feel: what eye can see itself?'[2] and of his letter to Balzac thanking him for his article on *La chartreuse de Parme* and replying to the criticism that the novel suffered from certain faults of construction: 'I see only one rule: *to be clear*. If I am not clear, *my whole world* is annihilated.'[3] These two quotations provide, I believe, one of the essential clues to Beyle's genius and to his art as a novelist.

Since the days of Nietzsche, Beyle too of course has become a 'classic'. (Nietzsche had found that few of his fellow academics were capable even of spelling Beyle's name.) Much of what has been written about him during the present century corresponds perfectly to what Nietzsche has said of the homage and attentions of the Philistine. The twentieth-century Stendhalian scholars differ in this respect from the nineteenth-century 'Beylistes' who established his present reputation, acknowledged gratefully what they had learned from him as men and who spoke of how he had opened their eyes to the world around them and its past. They differ, that is to say, from Taine, who spoke of Beyle as a *maître à penser* and a pioneer in the study of art and society, from those who saw in him the exponent of a way of life based on a revolutionary moral code, and above all from Nietzsche himself. No French critic that I know of has said more, for example, to suggest why Beyle should be thought of as an educated man. I quote from one of Nietzsche's few passing allusions to Beyle, allusions which have a Stendhalian quality in that they are tantalisingly brief and yet go straight to the point:

In contrast to the German lack of experience and the German innocence *in voluptate psychologica*...and as the most perfect expression of a truly French curiosity and inventiveness in the domain of delicate sensations and emotions, there is Henri Beyle, that remarkable precursor and pioneer who, with Napoleonic impetuosity, made his way through *his own* Europe, through several centuries of the European spirit, exploring this spirit and submitting it to his scrutiny; it has taken us two generations to catch up with him, to become aware of some of the enigmas which tormented and thrilled this strange inquisitive Epicurean, who was the last of the great French psychologists.[4]

I have set out in writing this study to follow some of the implications of this passage.

The evidence on which my argument is based is to be found principally in the writings by which he is now best known, in *Le rouge et le noir*, in *La chartreuse de Parme* and in the unfinished *Lucien Leuwen*. It is to be found also, however, in the copious letters and notebooks published since his death, and in the journalism, criticism and popular travel books published during his own lifetime. These are practically the only documents from which a biographer can hope to draw any conclusions about his mind and character. Among his acquaintances there was no Boswell or Eckermann, and the French custom of publishing the table talk of famous men had gone out of fashion before he was born. Consequently there are no accounts of his conversation anywhere near as detailed as those that survive of Boileau's, Dr Johnson's or Goethe's. Even Mérimée's little memoir, *H.B.* tells us disappointingly little of Beyle the talker and what we are told is related in a tone of amused if affectionate superiority which may have dictated the choice of reminiscence. The main impression one gathers from Mérimée's anecdotes and from those of others who know him is that Beyle's conversation was witty and outrageous, though Lamartine also tells us that it was learned and instructive whereas he was expecting it to be blasphemous.[5]

From Beyle's earliest years, the education he acquired was one that he saw as serving one particular end. 'Few men have prepared themselves to write with so much effort and conscientiousness as the young Beyle', wrote Jean Prévost.[6] Beyle's literary ambitions date apparently from the age of twelve or thirteen when he began the habit of voracious reading which was to last throughout his life and wrote a comedy based on the *Nouvelles* of Florian. The comedy was never performed and none of the plays which he planned and worked on for the next twenty-five years was ever completed, even though the manuscript of one of them, *Letellier*, which was to have been a satirical drama of the intellectual world under the despotism of Napoleon, accompanied him on his many travels through Europe and even on the retreat from Moscow. In 1826, at the age of forty-three, he began work on his first novel, to console himself, he writes, for the separation from his mistress, the comtesse Curial. The novel, *Armance*, was completed and published in a few months, and from then on he wrote quickly, and without any of the inhibitions he had known as a dramatist, the stories and novels for which he has since become famous. Beyle's long 'apprenticeship', as Prévost calls it, was continued under conditions and over a period of time that would have discouraged almost any other man. Even when he finally found himself as a writer, he enjoyed little popular success except as an amusingly outrageous pamphleteer and he was forced to console himself with the thought that his novels would perhaps be read in 1935. Most of his comments on his lack of success are made, however, with stoical cheerfulness and he appears to have suffered far more from the miseries and frustrations he experienced as a lover than from those of disappointed ambition. For one thing, his ambition involved far more than merely 'being a writer' and enjoying the prestige which goes with the rôle. Nor is it easy to think of him as a martyr to his art. The patience and stubbornness with which he pursued his apprenticeship were not those of a dedicated craftsman wrestling with an intractable subject or medium. In this respect, as in many others, he was very different from

Gustave Flaubert. 'What is my aim?', Beyle wrote at the age of twenty. 'To be the greatest poet possible.' (With characteristic precision and realism even when writing in a mood of exaltation, he does not say, for example, 'the greatest poet of my time'.) 'For this I must know man perfectly. In poetry style is of secondary importance.'[7]

Beyle's single-mindedness lay principally in the way he set out to realise the second of these ambitions, 'to know man perfectly'. The oddity of the phrase to the modern reader is a reminder of how much he was influenced by the fashionable psychology and philosophy of his early years. ('What is general grammar? What is its purpose? What is man?' were questions to which the boys were expected to find an answer in one of the newly-created Ecoles Centrales in 1799.[8]) Beyle outgrew the optimistic belief that he would ever understand human nature 'perfectly', but the ambition to understand it as well as it was humanly possible never left him. Nor did his preoccupation with a small number of 'principal ideas'. 'By instinct', he wrote towards the end of his life in *La vie de Henry Brulard*, 'my whole moral existence has been spent in considering attentively five or six principal ideas and in trying to understand in what ways they are true.'[9] And again:

Madame Le Brun, today marquise de la Grave, told me that all those who attended her little salon were astonished by my complete silence. I was silent by instinct, I felt that no one would understand me...It was the only way in which I could maintain a little personal dignity. If ever I see that very wise woman again, I must question her closely to find out what I was like in those days. I myself haven't the least idea. I can only tell the degree of happiness which my organism experiences. As I have gone on ever since penetrating deeper into the same ideas, how can I tell what stage I had reached then? The shaft was only ten feet deep, each year I have added another five. Now that it is a hundred and ninety feet deep, how can I have any conception of what it seemed like in 1800 when it was only ten?[10]

Beyle's writings over the years confirm this impression. So too do the concentration and ease of his major novels written in a prose which, as Prévost puts it, 'conveys in a few hastily thrown off pages the long progressive refinement of his mind'.[11] It is easy, however, to mistake the originality and independence of Beyle's mind for an imperviousness to external influences, to think of him as habitually unobservant, self-preoccupied and given to introspective reveries. This has been the tendency of many of Beyle's modern critics. It is even implied by Prévost, though perhaps unintentionally, for his book on Stendhal was finished hastily during the Second World War shortly before his death in action and, by a tragic coincidence, fighting with the Resistance in the mountains above Grenoble. Beyle, as he points out, was essentially a critic, though he leaves us with little idea how fine a critic. Because of this Beyle was not only able to see through or ignore what was merely fashionable. He was also able to respond whole-heartedly to all that appealed to his finer instinct, to follow his instinct without misgiving, and to learn in this way from the experience of others. There is a passage from a review by the young Henry James of A. A. Paton's life of Beyle which puts what I am trying to say far better than I am able to myself:

> In repudiating Mr Paton's assumption that he is a light writer, we would fain express that singular something which is fairly described neither as serious nor solemn – a kind of painful tension of feeling under the disguise of the coolest and easiest style. It is the tension in part of conceit – the conceit which leads him with every tenth phrase to prophesy in the most trenchant manner the pass to which 'les sots' will have brought things within such and such a period – and in part of aspiration, of deep enjoyment of some bold touch of nature or some fine stroke of art. This bespeaks the restlessness of a superior mind, and makes our total feeling for Beyle a kindly one. We recommend his books to persons of 'sensibility' whose moral convictions have somewhat solidified.[12]

Prévost's study gives us little idea of Beyle's capacity to learn and enjoy and it tells us little of the influences by which he was formed. It is true that these influences have been much exaggerated and that scholars who dwell on them rarely show us the ways in which other men's ideas became his own. The task of deciding what Beyle learned, whether or not he was conscious of learning, is extremely delicate. But it is also indispensable if we are to understand more than a little of what he wrote and became. T. S. Eliot's well-known remarks on 'tradition' are made with specific reference to poetry but their relevance here will, I hope, seem obvious:

We dwell with satisfaction upon the poet's difference from his predecessors, especially his immediate predecessors; we endeavour to find something that can be isolated in order to be enjoyed. Whereas if we approach a poet without this prejudice we shall often find that not only the best, but the most individual parts of his work may be those in which the dead poets, his ancestors, assert their immortality most vigorously. And I do not mean the impressionable period of adolescence, but the period of full maturity.

Yet if the only form of tradition, of handing down, consisted in following the ways of the immediate generation before us in a blind or timid adherence to its successes, 'tradition' should positively be discouraged. We have seen many such simple currents soon lost in the sand; and novelty is better than repetition. Tradition is a matter of much wider significance. It cannot be inherited and if you want it you must obtain it by great labour. It involves, in the first place, the historical sense, which we may call nearly indispensable to anyone who would continue to be a poet beyond his twenty-fifth year... This historical sense, which is a sense of the timeless as well as the temporal, is what makes a writer traditional. And it is at the same time what makes a writer most acutely conscious of his place in time, of his own contemporaneity.[13]

Nietzsche has described the nature of Beyle's 'historical sense' in a passage which I have quoted already. I wish to show in the following chapters some of the ways in which Beyle acquired it and at the same time became aware of his 'place in time, of his own contemporaneity'.

In order to do this it is necessary to distinguish between the various influences which Beyle underwent and resisted. And it would be absurd to argue as if these were merely philosophical or literary. Beyle was very much a man of the world, a role he cultivated conscientiously despite his liability to attacks of shyness. Few men have observed more attentively the customs and beliefs of the society they lived in, and few men have been more affected by these beliefs, more acutely aware of the ways in which they resembled or differed from their own. He was born in 1783, during the last years of the *ancien régime*, the son of a lawyer and landowner of royalist convictions, served under Napoleon as a civil servant travelling with the Imperial armies and died under the 'bourgeois' monarchy of Louis Philippe, whom he represented as consul in the port of Civita Vecchia. The 'ideas' he talks about in *La vie de Henry Brulard* and which occupied his thoughts throughout most of his life owe much to the influences of his boyhood and youth. It is partly because of this that in later years his writings had little popular success, while he himself was famous chiefly as an eccentric. The profound political and social changes which Beyle witnessed went with an inevitable transformation in customs and beliefs of the most ordinary-seeming kind. Beyle refused, or was perhaps unable, to change with his contemporaries, to conform merely for the sake of conforming to new moral and religious codes or to follow new fashions in philosophy. In order therefore to understand his evolution, it is necessary to consider, if only briefly, certain of the widespread popular beliefs of his boyhood and youth. These beliefs may have influenced his mind far more profoundly and permanently than much of the literature and philosophy he read. Often in fact they help us to understand why he read with enthusiasm writers whom today it is difficult to imagine being read even with sustained attention. The beliefs are in themselves simple enough and easy to summarise, so much so that it may be difficult to understand why they were held by men who, like Beyle himself, were far from simple-minded. Their strength and, despite this, their rapid widespread decline can easily be traced though far less easily explained. We may succeed in understanding them more clearly perhaps if we take them in the right order and consider first among the changes between the France of Beyle's childhood and that of his later years the changes in the function of the Catholic Church and in the attitude of wealthy citizens to organised religion and to the traditional Christian virtues.

An age of cant

'...all our words, manners, religion, morals, and our whole mind and existence in modern Europe, turn upon one single hinge, which the English in one expressive word call cant.'
(Byron in a letter to the Rev. C. Bowles quoted by Beyle in an article in *The London Magazine* for October 1826.)

Beyle was a child of six when the newly constituted National Assembly ordered the seizure of the enormous properties belonging to the Catholic Church in France and placed them 'at the disposal of the nation'. In the following year the Civil Constitution of the Clergy was approved, according to which bishops and parish priests should henceforth he appointed by the elective assemblies of each department and paid according to a fixed salary by the state. The Reign of Terror, which followed the invasion of France by the armies of the Duke of Brunswick and the royalist revolts in the south and west, was directed partly against the Church, which in 1793 was virtually disestablished, though many of its priests had refused in any case to accept their new role as elected functionaries. Grenoble remained calm during the Civil War and the Terror but Beyle's father was a royalist and devoutly catholic and Beyle recalls how during this period there would always be a priest or two living in hiding in their home. One of them revolted him by the bolt-eyed way in which he would wolf his food.

The Terror ended throughout the country after a series of military victories had ensured the survival of the new régime. Yet the régime, as we know, was to undergo what may have seemed like a wholly unexpected transformation. The decisive victories of Desaix in Italy and of Moreau at Hohenlinden and the conclusion of the Revolutionary Wars might have been expected to lead to a consolidation of what had been achieved ten years earlier: the creation of certain democratic institutions and the abolition of hereditary privileges or of the special privileges of any one religious sect; to the establishment, that is, of a social order like that which exists in France today. Instead of this, Napoleon was created Emperor of the French 'by the grace of God', the ceremony taking place in Notre Dame only ten years after the ceremonies in the same cathedral in honour of the goddess Reason. Priests were once again paid from the public exchequer (as well, it is true, as Protestant ministers) and Roman Catholicism recognised as the religion, if not of the state, 'of the majority of French citizens'. Napoleon's own relations with the Vatican were clearly not always of the most amicable. Yet in a decree of 1808 he stipulated that the 'basic principles of education' in the Empire should be 'firstly the precepts of the Catholic religion and the maxims on which are founded the organic laws of different creeds; secondly, fidelity to the Emperor, to the Imperial monarchy, guarantor of the people's welfare...; thirdly, obedience to the statutes of the teaching profession', etc. The Church honoured the new *entente* in its own way; in its catechisms, for example, in which fidelity to the Emperor and the Imperial dynasty was included among the duties of the Christian, failure to comply with which might lead to eternal punishment.[14] The fall of Napoleon and of Charles X were not, in either case, accompanied by fundamental changes in the relationship between Church and State and the Church continued to enjoy most of the privileges granted to it under Napoleon until its final disestablishment in 1904.

The religious and educational policies of Napoleon and his successors received the support of large sections of the middle and upper classes including many whose support had rendered possible the anti-ecclesiastical policies of the various Revolutionary governments. The rationalistic and deistic anti-clericalism which had inspired these policies survived, but generally in a more subdued and conciliatory form. Voltaire, Diderot and Helvétius continued to be read but their influence was counteracted by that of the most powerfully influential work of the first half of the nineteenth century, Chateaubriand's *Génie du christianisme*, published two years before the coronation of the Emperor. Chateaubriand had been an officer in the émigré armies which fought against the Republic, and though *Le génie du christianisme* is couched in terms that will appeal to the religious sceptic whose main concern is not with dogma but with the state of 'civilisation', it is an apology for orthodox Catholicism and an attack on the 'sophistry' of the eighteenth century. Voltaire, he writes, 'had the fatal talent, writing as he did for an amiable and capricious nation, which enabled him to render fashionable incredulity in matters of religion...His destructive system spread throughout France. It became established in the provincial academies, which became so many sources of faction and bad taste. Fashionable ladies and grave philosophers occupied chairs of scepticism.' His own intention was to prove that 'of all the religions which have existed, the Christian religion is the most poetic, the most human, the most favourable to liberty, to the arts and to literature; that the modern world owes to Christianity everything from agriculture to the abstract sciences, from the shelters and almshouses for the poor and indigent to the temples built by Michaelangelo and adorned by Raphael'.[15]

No work did more to determine the form taken by French Romanticism during the first three decades of the century.

Lamartine and the young Vigny, Victor Hugo and Sainte Beuve often seem like versifiers of Chateaubriand's noble declamatory prose. Yet the reasons for Chateaubriand's success and influence were almost certainly far more fundamental than his own obvious genius and Celtic powers of persuasion. And to understand Beyle's career and his general dislike for Chateaubriand's prose and for French – as opposed to either English or Italian – Romanticism, it is necessary to consider what these reasons may have been.

One reason for the decline of anti-clerical feeling after the Revolution is offered by Professor Charles Morazé in his sketch for a study of the French middle classes. The widespread popularity, Morazé argues, of anti-religious ideas in the eighteenth century and of an idealistic secular humanism, can be explained partly in economic terms. For the middle-class merchants and their dependents, the Church and the monastic orders, because of their enormous wealth and their commercial and fiscal privileges, were an obstacle to their own enrichment. If Voltaire and the Encyclopédistes were read with enthusiasm, it was because '...a century of philosophy had gilded the aspirations of the productive classes with a number of doctrines'.[16] If the same classes after 1804 tolerated the revival of the Church, it was again because this was, to say the very least, in no way against their own interests. After the seizure and sale of Church property and the abolition of its commercial privileges, the Church ceased to function as a major economic rival. And in agreeing to the terms of the Concordat with Bonaparte, the Vatican had wisely refrained from pressing for a restitution of either. There is no reason to believe then that the Catholic revival coincided with a revival of genuine faith. On the contrary. Under the Empire and the Bourbon Restoration '...the church and the temple are forsaken and if they are attended at all, it is for the sake of fashion or good form and as a result of the influence of the old nobility whose prestige in matters of everyday behaviour is all the greater since it has become harmless. Fundamentally, however, Christianity is no more now than a form of art. It is no longer a faith.'[17] Morazé's analysis of the conventional religiosity of the early nineteenth century is corroborated by some of the more perceptive writers of the day, by Gérard de Nerval, for example, who is not usually credited with insight of this kind, a comment perhaps on the survival until recently of the nineteenth century's own conventional view of itself:

There is certainly something more terrifying in history than the fall of empires; the death of religions. Volney himself experienced this sentiment when visiting the ruins of edifices which had once been sacred. This impression is perhaps unknown to the true believer, but a man who shares the scepticism of our times shudders occasionally when he sees so many sombre doors opening on the void.

There is one door which still seems to lead somewhere – the pointed doorway whose Gothic ribs and broken and defaced statuettes have been piously restored and through which can still be seen the elegant nave lit by the magical stained glass of the rose-windows. The faithful surge forward over the marble flags and past the whitened columns on which can be seen the coloured reflections of saints and angels. The incense burns, the voices resound, the Latin hymn and its accompaniment are raised high to the vaulted ceiling. But beware of the unhealthy breath rising from the feudal tombs where so many kings are heaped together! They have been disturbed from their eternal rest by the irreligion of the last century and piously re-interred by our own.

Why should one care about the shattered tombs and desecrated bones of Saint-Denis? The hatred of the desecrators was a kind of homage; their restoration today is the work of indifference. They have been restored out of a love of symmetry, as if they were mummies in an Egyptian museum.

However, what creed is there which when it has triumphed over the forces of impiety has not more to fear from simple indifference? What Catholic would not prefer to think of the crazy orgies of Newstead Abbey and of the drinking companions of Noel Byron setting drinking songs to parodies of plain chant, dressed as monks and drinking claret out of skulls, rather than see the ancient abbey turned into a museum? There is true religious feeling in the wild laughter of Byron and in the materialistic impiety of Shelley. But today who would deign even to be impious? One wouldn't dream of such a thing.[18]

The pervasiveness of the conventions which were to identify poetic feeling and moral decency with religious observance and belief can be seen in the work of those who in everyday life were to confess their own religious scepticism. It is seen, for example, in Vigny's extraordinary and in its own time popular allegory, *Eloa*, the story of a tear shed by Christ, transformed into an angel and at the end of the poem seduced by Satan. Of Eloa's influence on the terrestrial sphere as she passes through its orbit, Vigny tells us:

> Tous les poignards tombaient oubliés par la haine;
> Le captif souriant marchait seul et sans chaîne;
> Le criminel rentrait au temple de la loi;
> Le proscrit's s'asseyait au palais de son roi...

[All daggers dropped, forgotten by hatred; the smiling captive walked alone and without chains; the criminal returned to the temple of the law; the condemned man sat down in his king's palace.]

The modern reader may be reminded here of the ethos of Dr Frank ('Love thy Boss') Buchman, as the *Daily Worker* used to call him, the founder of Moral Rearmament. *Eloa* is a fairly extreme example.[19] Reviewing it in *The New Monthly Magazine* for December 1824, Beyle had to assure his English readers that the author of 'this strange quintessence of absurdity' was 'not actually mad; for a great portion of his verses are well turned and most elaborately polished, so much so as to render obvious the great art and labour employed upon them'. Furthermore, 'this incredible amalgam of absurdity and profaneness is most enthusiastically admired by a great city containing 80,000 inhabitants and called the Faubourg St. Germain...'. He might have added that the young Victor Hugo had praised *Eloa* in the most extravagant terms in May of the same year in a review in *La muse française*.

The widespread religious scepticism of the first half of the nineteenth century and, going with this, the popular cult of religious sentiment as opposed to religious belief, may explain why Beyle was to write in one of his unfinished lives of Napoleon of the 'formidable progress' made 'in the art of lying'.[20] And seven years earlier: 'Today in 1822 men nearly always lie when they speak of the true motives of their actions.'[21] It may explain too why Nietzsche was to admire in him 'a sincere atheism rarely to be found in France'.[22]

The question of Beyle's 'atheism' is one to which it will be necessary to return. For Beyle can disconcert us by the respect with which he writes of the honest Christian. His judgment in ethical matters may equally strike us as enigmatic unless, like his beliefs concerning religion, they are seen as a response to the real and feigned beliefs of his own contemporaries.

Beyle habitually addresses his readers, and it is one of the most striking singularities of his prose, as if he were perfectly aware that we may or may not share his own feelings of admiration or disgust. It was this that struck Bussière, the author of his obituary in *La revue des deux mondes* for January 1843:

M. de Stendhal does not seek to establish his success on the kind of embellishment which is achieved when the reader is taken unawares and his good faith abused. He is so little concerned to earn this strange distinction that rather than that the latter's vigilance should grow dull, he takes care himself to hold it in suspense and constantly maintains him on his guard. He makes few assertions which are not followed by a warning which he repeats in every conceivable form: 'I invite the reader to mistrust everyone, even myself...Only ever believe what you have seen, only admire what has given you pleasure and assume that the neighbour who addresses you is a man paid to lie.'

In this he differs from those of his contemporaries who, like Vigny in *Eloa* – despite the thrilling and conveniently vague implications of the ending of the poem – write of virtue and vice as a simple matter involving few problems of identification. Balzac is in the habit of referring to the fallen women, of whom many varieties appear in his novels, as *cette sorte de femme* or *ces créatures*. ('Monarchist and catholic', his friend Gautier wrote of him, 'he defends authority, exalts religion, preaches duty, lectures against passion and denies the possibility of happiness outside marriage and outside the family.'[23]) And Musset's Count uses the same expression at the end of *Il faut qu'une porte soit ouverte ou fermée*, when clearing up the misunderstanding between himself and the young widow on whom he has called (Musset, unlike Beyle, succeeded in writing successful stage comedies):

La Marquise. What? Really, I'm losing patience. Do you imagine that I'm going to be your mistress or another of your women in rose-coloured hats? I warn you: not only do I dislike the idea, I find it repulsive.
Le Comte. By all that is mighty, if I could, I would lay down all that I have and all that I shall ever be at your feet. I would give you my name, my possessions and even my honour. Do you think that I would dream of comparing you for a single instant with those creatures whom you mention only in order to wound my feelings – or for that

matter, with any woman in the world? You must think I am out of my mind!...You told me just now that you don't altogether dislike my company and that you even perhaps feel a certain affection towards me. I believe that is what you said, Marquise. Do you imagine that a man who had been worthy of such a precious, such a heavenly favour would ever be capable of disrespect? Do you think I am blind or mad? You my mistress? No, my wife.
La Marquise. Ah! Well, if you'd said that when you came, there'd have been no need to argue.

Musset, of course, was himself a confessed sinner. The 'confession' – and the word is entirely appropriate – is elaborated in *Les confessions d'un enfant du siècle* in which the sins receive appropriate psychological retribution. They resemble, in this respect, those alluded to in a contemporary best-seller, Byron's *Childe Harold*. Childe Harold too sins and suffers and it is for this reason possibly that his adventures were regarded both in France and England as morally edifying, certainly more edifying, in any case, than those of his unrepentant Don Juan, a spiritual descendant of Fielding's Tom Jones, in the poem which Beyle himself considered to be Byron's masterpiece. However, as far as questions of morality were concerned, Beyle was not, according to another contemporary, Sainte-Beuve, the most reliable of guides: '...he lacked in writing our own sense of moderation in moral matters; he saw hypocrisy where there is only a sentiment of legitimate conventionality and a reasonable and honest observation of nature, such as we wish to find even in the midst of passion'.[24]

The reader of the present study may find, of course, that he agrees with Sainte-Beuve. Yet he will also agree, I hope, that there are certain periods of history in which the moral sentiments to which Sainte-Beuve refers will seem familiar to a majority of those who regard themselves as reasonably civilised and other periods in which this will not be so. It is doubtful, moreover, whether, holding the views he expresses, Sainte-Beuve would have felt the same moral solidarity between himself and his readers during the eighteenth century. The common meaning of a word like *virtue* seems to have changed during the intervening years and to have been associated less with service to one's country or a dedication to the betterment of mankind that with the cultivation of a blameless private life, the kind of life evoked by Sainte-Beuve himself in *Les Consolations* or led by Balzac's virtuous heroines. It seems to have been thought of, in other words, as Christian virtue rather than the *virtus* of Republican Rome.

The change in conventional ideas of morality is described by De Tocqueville, among others, in *L'ancien régime* written in the 1850s:

> The men of the eighteenth century were on the whole unfamiliar with that passion for well-being, if one can describe it in this way, which engenders servitude, which is feeble and yet tenacious, which readily mingles and becomes, so to speak, inextricably confused with the private virtues: with the love of one's family, with moderation of behaviour, with respect for religious beliefs and even with the lukewarm but assiduous practice of the established religion; which allows respectability but prohibits heroism, which excels in forming men of regular habits and at the same time cowardly citizens. They were better than that and also worse.
>
> The French in those days loved gaiety and adored pleasure. They were perhaps wilder and more undisciplined in their passions and ideas than we are, but they knew nothing of that well-tempered and seemly sensuality that we witness today. In the upper classes it was considered important to render one's life distinguished rather than comfortable and to gain merit rather than riches. Even in the middle classes life was never absorbed entirely in the pursuit of well-being; this was often abandoned for that of higher and more delicate pleasures; there was no class in which money was considered to be the only desirable end...[25]

If the Frenchmen who made the Revolution were more prone to incredulity than we are in matters of religion, they possessed one admirable belief which we lack: they believed in themselves. They had no doubt of the perfectibility and power of man, they had faith in his virtue. They had proud confidence in their own powers of the kind which often leads to error, but without which a nation is only capable of servility; they had no doubt whatever that they had been called upon to transform society and regenerate our species...[26]

This account is corroborated in an undeservedly little known essay by a young critic who was to become one of Louis Philippe's ministers, Charles de Rémusat's *Des moeurs du temps*.[27] Ideas of virtue in the nineteenth century can be summed up, according to Rémusat, by the single phrase: *Je suis bon père*.

These quotations inevitably simplify what happened over a period of half a century. And to quote De Tocqueville out of context is to give a very incomplete notion of his awareness of the complexity of social change, since his characteristic method of writing history is to advance a series of bold clear generalisations, all of which in effect qualify one another and together leave us with an impression of the many-faceted nature of the society he describes; meanwhile, and this is one of the many virtues of the method, each generalisation corresponds to the way in which we actually think of a society, which is usually in simple terms and as a result of mood, circumstances or the particular facts on which we are concentrating and which determine our view of the society as a whole. It is obvious that eighteenth-century ideas of such matters as religion and virtue varied to a considerable extent from one man and one moment to another, as did those of the Empire and Restoration. It is also obvious that the two contrasting *codes*, for want of a better term, were not altogether peculiar to any one phase of history. Most of the ideals of the French Revolution have survived throughout the nineteenth century and into our own time. (Flaubert's Homais, the apothecary in *Madame Bovary*, voices them parrot-fashion.) So too has the tendency, described by De Tocqueville and Rémusat, to confuse private and domestic morality with public and even political morality. After the dissolution by the National Assembly of the Third Republic in 1940, the Republican motto, *Liberté, Egalité, Fraternité* ceased to appear on coins and official documents and was replaced, in what may seem a significant order of priority, by the words, *Travail, Famille, Patrie*.

However, when all these necessary qualifications have been made, Beyle's sense of isolation from his contemporaries is no less comprehensible. Nor is his tendency to see the changes described by De Tocqueville in what to many of his critics have seemed like exaggerated and perversely simple terms, his tendency to sound like a nineteenth century version of Molière's misanthropic Alceste, one of his numerous *noms de plume*. However, in order to understand it, it is necessary that we should know how discerning or how obtuse a critic he was of his own contemporaries; how often, in other words, he was right. It is also necessary to appreciate the extent to which he was himself a man of the eighteenth century, and the extent to which he was formed by the same ideals and the same influences which made the Revolution possible.

The childhood of Henri Beyle

The origin of Beyle's attachment to these ideals is described in *La Vie de Henry Brulard*; and so are the circumstances which made him a precocious rebel and which turned his childhood into a 'constant period of misery, hatred and perpetual impotent desire for vengeance'.[28] His mother, with whom he tells us he was 'in love' and whom he would sometimes kiss so passionately that she was forced to leave him, died in childbirth when he was seven years old. His mother's elder unmarried sister, Séraphie, who took her sister's place in the home and whom he could never recall in later years without intense loathing, reproached him after the funeral for not having shed enough tears. The influence which she and his father exerted on him for the rest of his childhood explain to a great extent the hatred he felt throughout his life for false piety and false sentiment of every kind as well as for the compulsory pleasures on which the puritanical mind insists. He was never to forget the long walks on which he was taken by his well-meaning aunt and father 'for a treat'. His Jacobinism, he admits frankly, was partly inspired by their own devout royalism, as was his joy when the news came of the execution of Louis XVI:

The house shook as the mail-coach from Lyon and Paris drew up outside. My father rose to his feet: 'I must go and find out what those monsters have done.'

I thought to myself: 'I hope the traitor will be executed'. Then I began to reflect on the extreme difference between my own feelings and those of my father. I felt a tender love for our regiments which I would watch from my grandfather's window on their way through the Place Grenette. I imagined that the king wanted the Austrians to beat them. (As you will notice, although barely ten years old, I was not far from the truth.) But I must confess that the concern for the king's fate shown by the vicar-general Rey and the other priests who were friends of the family, would have been enough to make me wish for his death. I considered at the time, on the strength mainly of the verses of a song which I would sing to myself when there was no danger of being heard by my father or Aunt Séraphie, that it was one's *strict duty* to die for one's country when this was necessary.

What did I care for the life of a traitor who, by means of a secret letter, could slaughter one of the fine regiments I saw go through the Place Grenette? I was passing judgment on my family and myself when my father returned. I still see him in his white flannel frock-coat, which he had not bothered to take off, as the mail office was only a few yards away.

'It's all over', he said with a deep sigh. 'They've murdered him.'

I experienced one of the most intense moments of joy I have ever known in my life. The reader will perhaps think I am cruel, but I am still the same at the age of fifty-two as I was at the age of ten... I could fill ten pages describing that evening, but if the readers of 1880 are as feeble-hearted as the fashionable circles of 1835, both the scene and the hero will fill them with deep aversion and even horror, as those *papier mâché* souls would say. As for myself, I would always feel a great deal more pity for a man condemned to death for murder without entirely conclusive proof than for a king who found himself in the same position. The death of a guilty king is always useful *in terrorem* to prevent the strange abuses into which such people are driven by the *extreme folly* produced by absolute power.[29]

Beyle's precocious Jacobinism was accompanied by an appropriate veneration for the heroes of Roman antiquity:

One cold evening as the sun was setting, I had the audacity to escape on the pretext of joining my Aunt Elizabeth at the house of Mme. Colomb and I plucked up the courage to go to a meeting of the Jacobin Club, which held its meetings in the church of St. André. My mind was full of the heroes of Roman history and I thought of myself sometimes as a Camillus, sometimes a Cincinnatus and sometimes both at the same time. Heaven alone knows what will happen to me, I thought, if one of Séraphie's *spies* (this is how I thought at the time) should see me here.[30]

He was disconcerted by the disorder which reigned throughout the meeting and by the vulgarity of his fellow Jacobins, and found himself experiencing one of the contradictions of his later years. He 'loved' the common people, he tells us, and hated their oppressors – but would do anything rather than have to live with them.

The young Beyle's ideas of nobility, and particularly nobility inspired by Roman models, were shared by many older and more active revolutionaries throughout the country. The 'classical' inspiration is seen in the speeches of the period and in the noble theatrical gestures of the revolutionary politicians in the paintings by Louis David, the same nobility and often the same gestures as in his paintings of conventional classical subjects. It is even seen in the Greek and Roman names given to children born during the Revolution, which Edmond Schérer has compared with the Old Testament names given to English children during the English Civil War.[31] Beyle, like many of his contemporaries, read Plutarch's *Lives of Illustrious Men* (probably in the sixteenth-century translation by Amyot) and in his letters to his younger sister Pauline, written from Paris before joining the Republican armies in Italy, he recommends Plutarch enthusiastically and scolds her for not having followed his advice. His taste for Plutarch and for Roman virtue explains too his early enthusiasm for the tragedies of Corneille and Alfieri.

Beyle's brief period of formal schooling, from 1796 until 1799, confirmed these heroic and patriotic influences, while at the same time awakening his interest in philosophy and painting and his liking and respect for mathematics. The twelve-year-old Henri was a willing pupil, for school meant release from home and from the tyranny of the priest who was his private tutor. The subject matter of the lessons, moreover, and the way they were taught seem to have suited his mind and his temperament. The Ecole Centrale in Grenoble, which Beyle attended on the day it opened, was the creation of the law of 1795[32] which established similar institutions throughout the country and sought to apply the educational theories which had been debated over the past five years by men such as Condorcet, Talleyrand, Siéyès and a thinker to whom Beyle was to owe a great deal, the former Count Destutt de Tracy. The innovations of the Ecoles Centrales included, partly on Talleyrand's insistence, an extremely flexible system of optional courses, as opposed to the rigid identical syllabuses of the old Jesuit college and the future lycée. They included also instruction in the natural sciences, painting and drawing – Beyle's first duel was fought with another pupil who had obstructed his view of the model – and, perhaps most important of all, the philosophy or 'general grammar', as it was called, which it was hoped would provide the future citizens with the same basic, rational and non-metaphysical notions of the nature of man. Destutt de Tracy's own major philosophical work, the *Eléments d'Idéologie*, was conceived as having a pedagogical function and it was as a result of his own optimistic influence on the Committee for Public Instruction that schoolboys throughout France were expected to answer such questions as 'What is general grammar? What is its purpose? What is man?' With other pupils, Beyle read Condillac's *Logic* and was thus initiated into the philosophical tradition running from Locke to Tracy himself. Literature and the study of French and Latin occupied a relatively unimportant place in the syllabus, which may account for his notorious departures in later life from normal grammar, usage and even spelling, though he was fortunate in having in Citizen Dubois-Fontenelle, author of the tragedy of *Ericie ou la Vestale*, a master of *belles-lettres* who taught his pupils to look out for and despise pedantry, to look to other countries, including England, for inspiration in the theatre, and to appreciate the relevance of the thought of Locke and Condillac to the study and practice of literature itself.[33] The implications of these lessons, which for Beyle were very far-reaching indeed, are something to which we shall have to return.

The Ecoles Centrales were abolished by order of the First Consul in 1803 and replaced by the more highly organised lycées, with their quasi-military discipline and rigid syllabuses as we have known them up to the present day. (It is questionable whether Beyle would have been so apt a pupil had he been born ten years later.) Destutt de Tracy, who had helped prepare the coup d'état by which Bonaparte seized power, was dismissed from his post on the Committee of Public Instruction and the philosophy syllabus in schools altered to exclude the thinkers whom Tracy favoured. Beyle, whose admiration for Napoleon was never, even in later life, to remain unqualified, always deplored these two decisions. In this respect and on account of the terms of the Concordat, he was to regard the Revolution as having been betrayed.

Coming of age in post-Revolutionary France

The story of Beyle's education from the time he left Grenoble a few days before Bonaparte's coup d'état, can be traced more easily than during his childhood and youth, for it is a matter simply of reading the copious diaries, letters and notebooks that have survived. The story belongs to the following chapters of this study which are concerned with these and his other writings. This study will, needless to say, exclude much that is crucial to an understanding both of Beyle and the age he lived in and this is due not only to its brevity but to the nature of the subject itself. 'I wrote biographies in my youth', he was to note in the margins of a copy of *Le rouge et le noir*, 'which are a kind of history, lives of Mozart and Michelangelo.[34] I regret it now. With the biggest just as much as with the smallest things, it seems to me impossible to get to what is true, at least to what is true in *some detail*.'[35] Many of the details that would enable us to understand the important truths about the life of Beyle and the facts of his everyday existence are missing from this study and many more, of course, are lost irretrievably.

I have chosen so far to stress the early influences which helped to determine Beyle's feelings towards the world he knew as an adult and in doing so to offer one of a number of possible explanations of his development. Yet I do not wish to argue, even if I may seem to imply, that Beyle virtually never grew up or that he closed his mind – which would be the same thing – to anything other than the remembered influences of his childhood and adolescence. Unfortunately, this is what certain of Beyle's finest critics have not only suggested but seemingly believed, among them the young Léon Blum in the book in which, during the first years of the present century, he tried to rescue Beyle from his more cynical admirers and portray him as a human being:

> Beyle's early character remained intact beneath his borrowed manners and deliberate attitudes. It remained, one might say, like something fresh and subterranean in his inner life and gushed out freely in his written work. Chronologically his books are those of a mature man; psychologically they belong to his youth, in so far as they are governed by his early ideas and nourished by his first impressions...[36]

Blum continues, in a passage which may tempt us to ponder the significance of the fact that this was written at the same time as *A la recherche du temps perdu*:

> A poet has defined happiness as the realisation in the years of manhood of the dreams of youth. For Stendhal these dreams, with their con-

comitant disappointments and interrupted aspirations, continued throughout his entire life and never came true. His inner life is one of a constant youthfulness expressed or rather confessed to in his writings with a clarity of insight which owes almost nothing to experience and age. M. Paul Bourget expresses this admirably: 'After his eighteenth year he acquired nothing other than an amplification of his early tendencies.' He acquired nothing and, what is more significant and rare, he lost nothing. When we try and envisage Stendhal, or when we imagine Julien Sorel, a process which is not very different, we should take care not to give too much thought to the fact that the novel appeared in the Paris of 1830.[37]

(Beyle himself had something to say about this kind of extrapolation. 'The resource of envy', he wrote to Mme Alberthe de Rubempré, who had found the same familiar traits in Julien Sorel, 'is to say, when the author depicts an energetic and hence somewhat scoundrelly character: "The author has portrayed himself!" What can one possibly say to that? A man sees himself only from the inside, as one sees the Georama in the Rue de la Paix.'[38]) As Blum points out, there is a remarkable similarity between the prose of Beyle's youth and that of his mature years. The early prose is often startlingly fine. But there is a simple test to which Blum's further claims should be submitted and this is to compare Beyle's letters to his sister Pauline written during his early twenties and his letters of twenty-five or more years later. The following extract is fairly typical of the former:

What the devil are you up to? Are you in love? So much the worse for you if you are. Take care not to marry a man you love; unless you marry a man who is very intelligent, you will be unhappy. If I were you, I should choose some decent fellow with plenty of money who is not as clever as you are.[39]

So too is the letter of three weeks later when Beyle realises to his alarm that Pauline may have been responding to years of his highly unorthodox advice and is thinking seriously of running away from home:

Remember this. Who would ever want to marry a girl, even if he were in love with her, if she had run away from her parents? I can think of no one with fewer prejudices than I have and I assure you that even I wouldn't marry such a girl. If I were in love with her, I would *debauch* her and then have nothing else to do with her.[40]

The Beyle who wrote these letters has certainly something in common with Julien Sorel and, as in Julien, there is something both comic and frightening in his fierce affectation of wordly wisdom. They would seem more amusing still if we could be sure that Pauline was capable of taking them light-heartedly herself. Unfortunately, it seems that she took her brother very seriously and that this did not contribute to the future happiness of her life.[41]

These extracts may be compared with a letter written in March 1830, when Beyle was still working on *Le rouge et le noir*, to the young Sainte-Beuve, who had just expressed his own views on domestic virtue and happiness in his collection of poems *Les consolations*. Beyle had just gone through them at a single reading:

> If there were a God, I should be delighted, for he would pay me for being the gentleman I am by sending me to his Paradise.
> Thus I would not change my conduct in the least and I should be rewarded for doing exactly what I do now.
> One thing, however, would diminish the pleasure I feel whenever I think of the warm tears which a fine deed brings to the eyes: the idea of being *paid* by a reward, a paradise.
> This, Sir, is what I would tell you in verse if I could write verse as well as you. I am shocked that those of you who *believe in God* imagine that to be *in despair* for three years because a mistress has left you, you have first to believe in God. In the same way, a Montmorency imagines that to be brave on the battlefield you have to be called Montmorency.
> I believe, Sir, that you are destined for the greatest of literary careers; but I still find a little affectation in your verse. I wish it were more like La Fontaine's. You talk too much of glory...La Fontaine once said to La Champmeslé, 'We shall both achieve glory, I for writing, you for reciting.' He had guessed the truth. But why talk of such things? Passion has its own modesty. [*La passion a sa pudeur.*] Why reveal these intimate details? It looks like sharp practice, a kind of *puff*.
> These, Sir, are my thoughts and all my thoughts. I think you will still be spoken of in 1890. But you will do better than the *Consolations*, something stronger and purer.

Les consolations were written in Sainte-Beuve's earlier, more conventional manner, in which the combined influences of Chateaubriand and Lamartine were predominant:

Mais comme au lac profond et sous son limon noir
Le ciel se réfléchit, vaste et charmant á voir
Et déroulant d'en haut la splendeur de ses voiles,
Pour décorer l'abîme y sème les étoiles,
Tel dans ce fond obscur de notre humble destin
Se révèle l'espoir de l'éternel matin;
Et quand sous l'oeil de Dieu l'on s'est mis de bonne heure;
Quand on s'est fait une âme où la vertu demeure,
Quand, morts entre nos bras, les parents révérés
Tout bas nous ont bénis avec des mots sacrés;
Quand nos enfants, nourris d'une douceur austère,
Continueront le bien après nous sur la terre;
Quand un chaste devoir a réglé tous nos pas,
Alors on peut encore être heureux ici-bas...

[But just as the vast sky, which is so delightful to contemplate, is mirrored in the deep lake and beneath its black slime, just as it draws aside the splendour of its veils to adorn the abyss by sowing it with stars, so is the hope of eternal morning revealed to us here below in this dark place of our humble destiny; and when one has placed oneself early on in the sight of God, when one has formed a soul in which virtue can dwell, when our revered parents dying in our arms have blessed us with quiet holy words, when we know that our children nourished in austere sweetness will continue to live worthily after us on earth, when a chaste duty has commanded our every step, then we can still live happily down here...]

Sainte-Beuve grew out of it, as Beyle hoped that he would, but the latter's comments may explain why in later life Sainte-Beuve was to write that Beyle was a poor judge of style and poetry.[42]

If we consider only Beyle's deeper formative and dynamic beliefs, it is true that, as Blum says, he changed very little. Yet 'psychologically' there is a world of difference between his adolescence and his mature years. One thing that has happened is that Beyle has learned to live, if not happily at least without 'impotent hatred', in a world which is not of his own choosing, a world in which the language of *Les consolations*, for example, is what passes for the language of poetry and ethics. And the effect on his character of events obviously explains to some extent why he evolved in this way: the effect of the years spent as a high-ranking public servant travelling with the Imperial armies and then as a *dilettante* subsisting by means of a small pension on the fringes of distinguished society; the effect too of a lifetime spent in the way he describes in *La vie de Henry Brulard*:

> I see that I have been constantly occupied with unhappy love affairs... And what is strange and unfortunate, I was thinking this morning, is that my *victories* (as I used to call them with my head full of military ideas) never procured me a pleasure half as great as the profound chagrin caused by my defeats.[43]

A longer study than this would have room to describe the various adventures into which Beyle plunged, according to his own account all too eagerly, in the course of his protracted bachelor life, as well as the joy and liberation he experienced on discovering Mozart, Cimarosa, the southern slopes and valleys of the Alps and the social amenities of the city of Milan, of which he wished on his tomb to be remembered as a citizen. If Beyle evolved as he did, it was partly because of such accidents of good fortune. It was not, however, I should like to suggest, due only to these or to a natural 'mellowing' of character. Characters do not usually mellow naturally, even when their owners are lucky enough not to be plagued, as Beyle was, by poor health, an unattractive physique and repeated humiliating disappointments. The charm, frankness, urbanity and wit of Beyle's later writings may seem 'natural' in the sense of seeming unaffected. But this does not mean that they are the product of circumstances over which he himself had no control. The character and style of the mature Beyle were the result in part of years of self-interrogation and self-discipline and of the cultivation of a personal philosophy – one could also describe it as an art of living – of which the art of his novels was perhaps the most perfect expression. It is this personal philosophy, to which Beyle himself gave the name of 'Beylisme', that I wish to consider now.

2

Le Beylisme

Beylisme and 'de-Rousseauisation'

To describe Beyle as a man of the eighteenth century is, of course, all very well. The eighteenth century speaks to us with many discordant voices. We may understand 'Beylisme' a little better if we consider how he responded to them at various times in his career and why he found some more congenial than others.

'I have never enjoyed the writings of Voltaire', he recalls, looking back to his childhood. 'At the time they seemed to me childish only. I think I can say that nothing by that great man has ever given me any pleasure. [When I was a boy] I was unable to see that he was the legislator and apostle of France, our Martin Luther.'[1] And in the *Racine et Shakspeare* of 1823: 'Foreign critics have noticed that there is always something *malevolent* behind the gayest of the jokes in *Candide* and *Zadig*. The rich Voltaire amuses himself by directing our gaze on the inevitable misfortunates of poor human nature.'[2] We tend to forget that during Voltaire's lifetime and for years after his death, he was thought of not only as a satirist and philosopher but as the brilliant successor in the theatre to Corneille and Racine. Beyle, however, even in his early twenties, considered him to be an inferior dramatist and incapable of a true understanding of the heroic.

I feel that, as he had never conceived the idea of a great republican, he knew almost nothing of those whose lives have reflected honour on the human species; he judged mankind by the kings and courtiers he had frequented. He knew nothing of true greatness, he often talks about it but he doesn't feel it, he doesn't talk about it well. He lacked *the comprehensive soul*, [in English in the text] a quality necessary in any poet. This is why all his characters resemble one another.[3]

He admired Voltaire's use in his prose works of what in the eighteenth century is known as *le style coupé*, the equivalent in writing of conversation between witty and intelligent equals, but he found him, none the less, inferior to Montesquieu. Voltaire 'flatters the reader's self-esteem by leaving him to guess a great many things; but in Montesquieu the veil is less thin'.[4]

Montesquieu receives warmer and more consistent praise from Beyle than almost any other French writer and it is obvious that his interest in the ways in which notions of the good, the true and the beautiful can *vary* from one culture to another accounts to some extent for his appeal. Yet his appeal for Beyle seems to have been not so much that of his ideas as such, but rather that of a congenial temperament and of a refined generous civilisation which speaks to us in the very rhythms of his prose. After the fall of Napoleon and during the years when Beyle, despite his earlier Republicanism, was ready to express what seems to have been a sincere allegiance to the new constitution imported from England,[5] he read Tracy's *Commentary* on *L'esprit des lois* and agreed completely with Tracy's strictures on Montesquieu's excessive Anglophilism and failure to understand the need for practical safeguards to protect individual liberties.[6] The science of politics, Beyle concluded, had advanced considerably since Montesquieu's day. Again, if he learned something from Montesquieu's study of the moral and cultural differences between nations, he learned even more from Mme de Staël,[7] though he never admired Mme de Staël's prose and never wished to imitate it.[8] Yet something remarkably like Montesquieu's formal, though often quietly mischievous decorum is evident in Beyle's mature writing, together with the rhythms of his prose. Compare, for instance, the two following passages from *L'esprit des lois* and *De l'amour*:

Avec cette délicatesse d'organes que l'on a dans les pays chauds, l'âme est souverainement émue par tout ce qui a du rapport à l'union des deux sexes: tout conduit à cet objet.
   Dans les climats du nord, à peine le physique de l'amour a-t-il la force de se rendre bien sensible; dans les climats tempérés, l'amour

accompagné de mille accessoires, se rend agréable par des choses qui d'abord semblent être lui-même, et ne sont pas encore lui; dans les climats plus chauds, on aime l'amour pour lui-même; il est la cause unique du bonheur; il est la vie.

Dans les pays du midi, une machine délicate, faible, mais sensible, se livre à un amour qui, dans un sérail, naît et se calme sans cesse; ou bien à un amour qui, laissant les femmes dans une plus grande indépendance, est exposé à mille troubles.[9] [Because of the delicacy of the human organs in hot countries, the soul is moved, above all, by everything related to the uniting of the two sexes: everything leads to this end.

In northern climates the physical concomitants of love have hardly the strength to make themselves felt; in the temperate climates, love, accompanied by a thousand accessories, is rendered agreeable by circumstances which at first seem to be, but are not yet love itself; in the hotter climates love is loved for its own sake; it is the sole cause of happiness; it is life.

In the countries of the south, a delicate, fragile but sensitive organism abandons itself to love which, in a seraglio, is ceaselessly aroused and calmed; or else to love which, when women are left in greater independence, is exposed to a thousand torments.]

Voici ce qui se passe dans l'âme:
1. L'admiration.
2. On se dit: Quel plaisir de lui donner des baisers, d'en recevoir, etc.!
3. L'espérance.

On étudie les perfections; c'est à ce moment qu'une femme devrait se rendre pour le plus grand plaisir physique possible. Même chez les femmes les plus réservées, les yeux rougissent au moment de l'espérance; la passion est si forte, le plaisir si vif qu'il se trahit par des signes frappants.

4. L'amour est né.[10]

[This is what takes place within the soul:
1. Admiration.
2. One thinks to oneself: how very delightful it would be to kiss her, for her to kiss me, etc.!
3. Hope.

One studies the perfections of the person one loves; this is when a woman should surrender to the advances of her lover in order to enjoy the greatest possible physical pleasure. Even the eyes of the most reserved women are red during the moment of hope; the passion they feel is so strong and the pleasure so intense that it is betrayed in the most strikingly obvious ways.

4. Love is born.]

The stylistic resemblance may seem even more obvious if one compares these accounts of the sexual love experienced both by men and women with the following passage from Rousseau's *Emile*:

L'Etre suprême a voulu faire en tout honneur à l'espèce humaine: en donnant à l'homme des penchants sans mesure, il lui donne en même temps la loi qui les règle, afin qu'il soit libre et se commande à lui-même; en le livrant à des passions immodérées, il joint à ces passions la raison pour les gouverner; en livrant la femme à des désirs illimités, il joint à ces désirs la pudeur pour les contenir. Pour surcroît, il ajoute encore une récompense actuelle au bon usage de ses facultés, savoir le goût qu'on prend aux choses honnêtes lorsqu'on en fait la règle de ses actions. Tout cela vaut bien, ce me semble, l'instinct des bêtes.[11]
[The Supreme Being has chosen to treat the human species honourably: while giving the man leanings without limit or measure, he has at the same time given him the law which regulates them, so that he may be free and his own master; while abandoning him to immoderate passions, he has combined with these passions the reason which governs them; while abandoning the woman to limitless desires, he has combined with these desires the modesty which contains them. Over and above this, he has added one more immediate recompense for the good use of our faculties, that is the pleasure one takes in worthy considerations when one allows them to regulate one's acts. All this, it seems to me, has at least as much to be said for it as the instinct of the beasts.]

The differences in sensibility, in vital rhythm and in the implicit assumptions of the prose are so obvious as to require no comment.

Rousseau's influence, none the less, on Beyle and on most of Beyle's older and younger contemporaries can be seen as powerful and pervasive. His way of thinking and feeling, with its startling paradoxes and *voltes-face*, is in fact common to many of those who made not only the Revolution possible but also the Concordat, the Empire and the constitutional monarchy of the Restoration, men whose minds were far simpler than that of Rousseau and who were fired by one or other of the many contradictory-seeming arguments he so passionately expounded. Both Robespierre and the royalist Romantics of the Restoration were in varying ways and degrees Rousseau's disciples. The full extent of his influence on Beyle is difficult to estimate, for after worshipping Rousseau as a boy and a young man, he embarked in his early twenties on what he was to describe as a process of 'de-Rousseauisation'. It is clear when one compares the three passages I have quoted that the cure was conducted with some success. Yet in the very process of reacting against Rousseau, he was defining, in a way that might not otherwise have been possible, what it was he wanted to be. He was working out what he begins to refer to, with mock pomposity, in his diaries and letters, as the philosophy of 'Beylisme'.

The Rousseau he admired as a boy was the Rousseau of *The Confessions* and *La nouvelle Héloïse*, and in *Henry Brulard* he recalls his impressions in the spring of 1800 on his first journey to Italy when he passed through the landscape described in the letters of Rousseau's Saint-Preux and Julie d'Etange:

...drunk with joy at having read *La nouvelle Héloïse* and at the thought of being about to pass through Vevey – I may have mistaken Rolle for Vevey – I suddenly heard the majestic peal of the bells of a church on the hill a quarter of a league above Rolle, or Nyon, and climbed towards it. The lake stretched out before my gaze, the peal of bells accompanied my thoughts with their ravishing music and gave to them a sublime physiognomy.

This, I would say, is the nearest I have ever come to a state of *perfect happiness*.[12]

However, in reliving the past Beyle forgets, characteristically, the superlative in the last sentence. A few days later in the opera house in Ivrea he heard the music of Cimarosa for the first time:

Straight away, the thought of my two great exploits: firstly, having crossed the Saint-Bernard Pass; secondly, having been under fire, became as nothing and seemed merely common and vulgar. What I experienced was something like my enthusiasm by the church above Rolle, but an enthusiasm which was far purer and more intense. The pedantry of Julie d'Etange made me uncomfortable, whereas everything in Cimarosa was divine.[13]

Beyle often confesses in his letters and diaries how much he had been formed by Rousseau and how much Rousseau had influenced his ideas of what it would be like to fall in love or meet noble and virtuous men and women; how much Rousseau had also prepared him for the inevitable disappointments by his romanticising of self-pity and of a noble self-pitying aloofness from the world.[14] It was for this reason that he began to 'de-Rousseauise' himself. In the little treatise which he sketched out in 1812 with his friend Louis Crozet and to which they gave the title *Du style*, he takes the process further by analysing the tendency in Rousseau to dominate the reader and tell him exactly what he should think and feel:

We think that the style of Fénelon (the *Dialogue des morts* and the *Contes pour le duc de Bourgogne*) is far superior to that of Rousseau, in that it holds up a faithful mirror to nature and leaves it with its *infinite variety*; whereas the style of Jean-Jacques gives everything a certain colour.

In Jean-Jacques, a cool grove of trees is a lesson in virtue; in Fénelon it leads one only to feel a certain voluptuous delight, which is its natural effect in hot countries.

Since the style of Fénelon is perfectly natural, it allows both for comic and tragic effects and for everything else in nature. Rousseau's has a certain dose of exaggerated tragic affectation and hence cannot be employed humorously...[15]

While conforming entirely to the style of Fénelon, one can describe the feelings of the heart as successfully as Jean-Jacques; but one can't say what the reader is to think of them; one can't produce his feelings for him, one can only leave him to himself. Rousseau tells us what we are to think of everything he describes.

Not only does Rousseau expose himself to the ridicule of having his assertions denied, often he provokes his readers by abusing those who might be merely tempted to deny them. For example: 'This state of mind [i.e. the refusal to take anything on trust recommended by Descartes at the beginning of the *Discours de la méthode*] is scarcely made to last; it is disturbing and painful; it is in the interests of vice alone and spiritual sloth that we should be left in such a state.'[16]

To begin with, we know first-hand examples which strike us as evidence that the state of mind in question is neither disturbing nor painful. Also, insults put us in a bad mood. This passage is as unlike Fénelon as it is possible to imagine.

Rousseau would have upset no one and would not have departed from the style of Fénelon had he said: 'This state of mind, it seems to me, is scarcely made to last; I found it disturbing and painful and I have always noticed that vice and spiritual sloth alone rendered it tolerable.'[17]

In Moscow, after his arrival in the city in the early autumn of 1812, Beyle re-read Rousseau's *Confessions* in the intervals of working on his *History of Painting in Italy* and gave the following impressions of them in a letter to Félix Faure:

> I was reading Rousseau's *Confessions* a week ago. It is only for want of three or four of the principles of *Beylisme* that he was so miserably unhappy. His mania for seeing duties and virtues everywhere made his style pedantic and his life wretched. He gets to know a man for a few weeks and then, before you know where you are, he's talking about the *duties of friendship*, etc. *Beylisme* would have told him that two bodies approach one another, that this produces a certain heat and fermentation, but that all phenomena of this kind are ephemeral, that it's a flower to be enjoyed voluptuously, etc. Do you follow what I mean? The finest things in Rousseau, for me, have something over-heated about them. They lack the Correggio-like grace which the least shade of pedantry will destroy.[18]

The differences of outlook were by now fundamental. The implications of the error he ascribes to Rousseau are profound and tragic. The differences are inevitable, moreover, if one considers the eighteenth-century philosophy he did admire and the principles to which, throughout the rest of his life, he was able to give his entire allegiance.

Beylisme and Utilitarianism

At the age of nineteen, Beyle began to study intensively the writings of Claude-Adrien Helvétius, the farmer-general, philanthropic reformer and author of *De l'esprit* and *De l'homme,* together with the philosophers who acknowledged his influence, the *idéologistes* or *idéologues*, the term used disparagingly by Chateaubriand and Napoleon and which has since passed into general usage. This was after Beyle had resigned his commission as a lieutenant of dragoons and settled in Paris on a small private income provided by his father who, as a devout royalist, preferred that his son should remain unemployed rather than serve in the armies of a Republic. It was the moment too at which this school of philosophy began to fall into general disfavour and to undergo the effects of the eloquent criticisms made by Chateaubriand and Mme de Staël,[19] though Beyle seems to have been undeterred by the new official and fashionable views. In settling down to study the *idéologues,* he planned to further his ambition to 'know man perfectly' and hence to become a great dramatic poet. He was encouraged in this by the example of 'the divine Alfieri' who had proved to him that 'a man whose mind is full of Helvétius can be a sublime poet'.[20]

A man whose mind was full of Helvétius could not very well find room for Rousseau as well, at least not for the Rousseau of *Emile* or *The Social Contract*. In 1837 Beyle was to remark that the principal merit of the latter work lay in its title,[21] and it is obvious that, despite his lifelong interest in the *Confessions* and his sympathy for the persecuted Rousseau, he gained little from Rousseau's ideas. Beyle took sides early in life, as we can see from his notebooks and letters, in one of the main philosophical controversies of his day, one in which few, if any European thinkers remained altogether uninvolved. The main issue and some of those related to it may be familiar to students of the history of ideas, for they involve perennial philosophical problems, but the late eighteenth and early nineteenth centuries were a period in which their practical implications were widely recognised and discussed. Broadly speaking, the issues were whether the mind and its experiences were to be thought of as the adventures of a specially constituted body in the world or as subject to other than material laws; whether there is a known or knowable human nature; and whether any man is capable of behaving in a purely disinterested way – that is, of seeking and gaining gratification of something other than his own desires. Helvétius, like Condillac and Locke, accepted a physiological explanation of the mind's experiences. (*Esprit*, of course, means not only 'mind' but 'soul'; Condillac, as a priest of the Church, had overcome one obvious disadvantage of this explanation by distinguishing between the immortal *esprit* and the *esprit* that thinks, remembers and wills.) Helvétius accepted this explanation as alone constituting limitations on the nature of man, for the mind of any man, he maintained, is liable to the same degree to degradation or perfection according to whatever influences he will have undergone in the world; and he asserted categorically – the assertion for which Beyle was always to express particular gratitude, though Helvétius was by no means the first to say it – that all living creatures in all their actions, and by the mere fact of being alive, are seeking their own interest, whatever this may be, even if it is often with a mistaken idea of where their true interest lies.

Helvétius's influence in France has been traced by Picavet in *Les idéologues*, which, though it was written at the end of the last century, is almost the only study of its kind, for the *idéologues* have never come back into fashion. Helvétius's influence in England has been traced by Elie Halévy in *The Growth of Philosophic Radicalism*. (I quote the title of the English translation, as the original French text is also out of print.) Helvétius influenced Bentham directly and through Bentham the English Utilitarian school. In France, during his own lifetime, however, Helvétius was condemned not only by the Parlement de Paris, which in 1757 ordered the public burning of his second major treatise *De l'homme*, but by Rousseau himself in that section of *Emile* which is entitled *La profession de foi du vicaire savoyard*, though it can easily be taken and usually has been for Rousseau's own personal credo. The allusions to Helvétius are clear, even though he is not mentioned by name, for when Rousseau heard of the persecution of Helvétius he burned his own explicit refutation in order not to join in the general hue and cry.[22]

For Rousseau there emphatically *is* a soul, immaterial in its origin and perceptions, which makes itself heard through the voice of 'conscience' and exercises itself through 'will', the most difficult human attribute to explain if consciousness is seen in simple Lockean terms as the combined effect of passively experienced sensations. Where Helvétius had written, at the opening of *De l'esprit*, that 'to judge is to feel', the vicaire savoyard asserts: 'To perceive is to feel; to compare is to judge; to judge and to feel are not the same thing.' And where Helvétius had insisted that judgment of value is judgment of where one's true interest lies, Rousseau's country priest speaks as follows:

Conscience! conscience! divine instinct, immortal and celestial voice, the sure guide of one who is ignorant and limited but intelligent and free; the infallible judge of good and evil rendering man akin to God, it is to you that the excellence of man's nature and the righteousness of all his acts is due; if it were not for you, I would feel nothing within me to raise me above the level of the beasts, nothing but the wretched privilege of wandering from error to error with the aid of an understanding that knows no rules and a reason that knows no principles.

We have been delivered, thank Heaven, from the clutches of philosophy: we can be men without being learned; we have been spared from having to sacrifice our entire lives to the study of morality, and we have a less expensive and more certain guide to lead us through the labyrinth of human opinions. Yet it is not enough that this guide should exist, we need to know how to recognise and follow it. How is it that so few understand it, if it is true that it speaks to every heart? Because it speaks to us in the language of nature which everything has conspired to make us forget. Conscience is timid, she loves solitude and peace; the noises of the world appal her: prejudices, from which men claim she is born, are her cruellest enemies and she flees or is silent before them; their noisy voices drown her own and prevent her from making herself heard; fanaticism has the audacity to borrow her garb and to dictate crime in her name. In the end, she is disheartened as the result of so many rebuffs; she speaks to us no longer, she no longer replies and after despising her so long, it costs as much to recall her as it once cost to banish her.

Belief in this natural goodness, expressing itself in 'natural religion' and a 'natural law' is indispensable to Rousseau's ethical, pedagogical and political systems. 'The general will' of society in which sovereignty alone can be found, a concept which has mystified generations of students of *The Social Contract*, is explicable perhaps only if we see it as an expression of natural goodness, for like 'conscience' the 'general will' can never be wrong.

Beyle's rejection of Rousseau's main premises and their implications seems to have been conscious and over the years consistent. It is significant, for example, that if he showed little interest in Rousseau's ideas, he was unimpressed also by Descartes, whose theory of clear, distinct and infallible ideas, non-material and ultimately divine in origin, has obvious affinities with Rousseau's notions of conscience and consciousness. Beyle recognised Descartes' historical importance and in particular because he led to Pascal,[23] but on one of the few occasions when he mentions him at all, he describes him, together with Plato, Aristotle, Leibnitz and Spinoza, as a 'great genius' who wrote 'boring poems'.[24] The word Cartesian has been somewhat over-used in accounts of French intellectual history and it would be wrong to assume that when Beyle insists, as he so often does, on the virtues of 'clarity', he is using this word in the Cartesian sense.[25] As for the Kant whose daily walk through Königsberg was delayed, according to legend, because he had started to read *Emile* and was unable to put it down and whose ideas of ethical judgment were strongly influenced by Rousseau's own, Beyle professed to find him unreadable.[26] For that matter, despite his choice of a German pseudonym, his knowledge of the language was never more than rudimentary, while German philosophy in general remained for him literally a closed book.

In politics too, for all his revolutionary sympathies, it would be difficult to think of him as a Rousseauist or as a fervent admirer of the Robespierre and Saint-Just who regarded themselves as Rousseau's heirs and who, as well as resisting the enemies of the Republic outside and within her frontiers, followed the teachings of *The Social Contract* by endeavouring to suppress any institution or faction which was independent of the central authority of the state. His political thinking was far closer to that of Helvétius himself and Helvétius's friend and admirer Montesquieu, if only because of their readiness to admit the diversity of human needs and their freedom from any over-riding preoccupation such as Rousseau's with the possibilities of a natural law springing from natural human goodness. At the age of twenty-two, Beyle also read the essay *On Human Nature* by Thomas Hobbes, which he described anachronistically as 'an edifice built on the foundations of Helvétius'.[27] And though he did not go on to draw the conclusions of *The Leviathan*, there is no reason to think that he disagreed with Hobbes in regarding natural law as 'the natural law of the power of the strong over the weak'.[28] 'There is no natural law', Julien Sorel reflects in the penultimate chapter of *Le rouge et le noir*. 'The word is only an antiquated piece of humbug worthy of the advocate general who hunted me down the other day and whose ancestor was enriched by property confiscated by Louis XIV. There is only *law* when a man is prevented from doing something by fear of punishment. Before the *law* exists, there is nothing *natural* at all except the strength of the lion or the need of any cold or hungry creature...' Beyle goes on to question the conclusions that Julien draws from this belief. He says nothing to suggest that the belief is mistaken.

Beyle's debt to Helvétius must not be exaggerated, for there were large areas of contemporary intellectual discussion in which his attitude seems to have been one of indifference or the philosophical equivalent of agnosticism. He did not seriously question, for example, as William Blake had in England, the epistemology that Helvétius derived from Locke. Nor, however, did he seriously attempt to defend it. It was Helvétius's version of the basic Utilitarian premiss that particularly won his admiration and this was a principle he could easily have found stated elsewhere. 'Every man regards the actions of another as *virtuous, vicious* or *tolerable* according to whether they are *useful* to him, *harmful* or *indifferent*...', he wrote to Pauline in 1803. 'You will be able to see as a consequence of this luminous principle that men have described as *great* someone who has rendered them an important service or who has given them much entertainment. Henri IV is known as Henry the Great because Frenchmen hope, by paying him homage, to encourage other kings to follow his example.'[29] What is striking and curious is that, from this time onward, Beyle should have attached such importance to the principle in question and that he should not, in any of his surviving writings at least, have considered the obvious objection that when problems of value and ethics are reduced to such simple terms they merely become easily solved problems of definition. Everything depends simply on what one happens to mean by interest or pleasure.

One of the advantages of using such language, however, and one of its attractions possibly for Beyle, is that it disposes of certain problems which to those in whom conscience has been carefully nurtured may seem insoluble and inescapable. It is no longer necessary to ask oneself: *what right* have I to do this or that or to judge others or myself in a certain way? To judge is simply, from the point of view of Helvétius, to observe one's own and other people's behaviour and to find out that they are acting in a way which gives some degree of satisfaction or is harmful or offensive to oneself or to them; to judge behaviour, in other words, in a way which is unavoidable, whether or not it can be justified in other ways. In his article on Helvétius in *The Paris Monthly Review* for April 1822,[30] Beyle illustrates the attractive and frightening simplicity of the philosophy he is defending by quoting from Book II of Virgil's *Eclogues*:

> Torva laena sequitur; lupus ipse capellam;
> Florentem cytisum sequitur lasciva capella;
> ...trahit sua quemque voluptas.

[The lioness with the bloodshot eyes pursues the wolf; the wolf the goat; the goat seeks out fresh clover...each one is drawn by his desire.]

Another of the attractions of the 'luminous principle' described in the letters to Pauline was almost certainly that it reconciled two apparently contradictory tendencies in Beyle's own nature: his hatred of false sentiment and of the dutiful affectation of certain feelings – such as those he was scolded for not exhibiting at his mother's funeral – and his own extreme emotional susceptibility, shown in what he tells us of his passionate adoration of his mother, his loathing of his father and Aunt Séraphie and his correspondingly ardent 'Roman' patriotism. It is natural, if one considers the implications of the principle, for men to admire actions they regard as conducive to the general good, which includes their own. In the same way, the desire to serve the interests of others can be seen either as a wish to be admired or a desire to improve or safeguard one's own interests, that is, to improve or safeguard the world one lives in. Saying this in no way obliges us to use words like 'materialistic'. The world will seem a better place to live in, arguably to anyone, if certain things have been said or done in it. The Helvetian standpoint, in other words, enables us to distinguish in principle between moral feelings which are simulated in a desire to persuade oneself or others of one's own respectability and moral feelings which are unfeigned.

For the pursuit of one's own interest and pleasure is seen even in the most heroic deeds. In one of the illustrations of this theory which Beyle borrowed from Helvétius himself, we are asked to consider the motives of Regulus, who, after his capture by the Carthaginians, was sent back to Rome to convey terms of peace, having sworn on his honour to return if he failed, though this would mean, as he knew, certain torture and death:

> A man of ordinary character and intelligence, such as Prince Eugene of Savoy, if placed in the same position as Regulus on his return from Carthage, would have calmly remained in Rome and laughed at the credulous simplicity of the Carthaginian Senate. Prince Eugene would have been following the dictates of his own *interest* in remaining and in the same way Regulus was following his by returning to be tortured.
>
> In almost all the circumstances of life, a generous mind will perceive the possibility of certain actions, the idea of which a commonplace mind is incapable of understanding. The moment that the possibility of accomplishing these actions becomes apparent to a man of generous instincts, it is immediately in his own interest that he should carry

them out. If he fails to, he feels the sting of self-abasement and as a result becomes unhappy.[31]

In distinguishing between the conceptions of honour of a 'generous' and a 'commonplace' mind, Beyle touches on a further principle which he had found in Helvétius: the simple axiom according to which ideas of the public and general good vary from one man to another. It was for this reason that Helvétius insisted that 'In matters of integrity one should only consult and have faith in the public interest, not in the men among whom we live, who are too often deluded by personal interest.'[32] The truth of this axiom had almost certainly been brought home to followers of Helvétius such as Destutt de Tracy during the Revolution and the Reign of Terror. (Tracy, one of the most active legislators both of the early years of the Revolution and later of the Directory, who, at the age of seventy-six, wearing his green eye-shade and carrying a long staff, joined the insurgents of 1830 on the barricades, had been imprisoned and condemned to death for treason during the rule of Robespierre's Committee of Public Safety and saved only by the execution of Robespierre himself.) It was an axiom for which Beyle too was to be permanently grateful and which helped him to tolerate in later life his own lack of success as a writer and the unpopularity of most of what he believed in. Characteristically, he refers on a number of occasions to literary success as a prize in a lottery and to his own books as lottery tickets. 'What distinguishes me', he writes in *Henry Brulard*, 'from the conceited fools...*who hold up their heads like a holy sacrament* is that I have never believed that society owes me a single thing. I have been saved from such immense foolishness thanks to Helvétius. *Society rewards the services it sees.*'[33] These remarks should be read together with those on Rousseau in the letter from Moscow to Félix Faure (quoted on page 33). They explain as clearly as is at all possible what Beyle himself meant by Beylisme.

An American admirer of Beyle has defined Beylisme in the following terms:

Livy tells us how the ideal of behaving in a manner worthy of the name of Fabius inspired the Fabii to tremendous exertions; and Shakespeare's Romans are particularly eloquent on the subject. Antony will do nothing unworthy of Antony; Caesar must live up to a public idea of Caesar which he has himself created. Perhaps it was this notion, that a man owes a duty to his own definition of himself, which furnished to Stendhal the seed for his concept of Beylism; a 'philosophy' which actually provides not only obligations and guidance but immunities and liberty, based upon one's consciously defined relation to a self one is in effect creating.[34]

This is not only less clear than Beyle's own explanations. It also introduces abstract considerations which are, I would suggest, unhelpful if we are to understand either his behaviour or his philosophy. Beyle may not have read the passage in the *Treatise of Human Nature* in which Hume confesses his inability to find anything in his perceptions or feelings that corresponds to the notion of 'self' and that is thus 'constant and invariable'.[35] (He seems to have known and admired Hume only as the author of *The History of England*.) It is unlikely, however, that he would have thought that Hume was talking nonsense. He speaks with scorn, for example, when writing as a journalist for the English reviews, of the contemporary French philosophers who claimed to have succeeded in an operation similar to the one in which Hume had failed:

They assert that 'consciousness is a feeling in itself, and is not felt through the senses'. They pretend that to hear the revelations of consciousness, it is necessary to wrap oneself in silence and obscurity, so as to be free from the operations of the senses. In a word, one must 'hear oneself think'. The philosophers of this new school allege that, after being long accustomed to these reveries, they discern an immeasurable perspective extending from man to God.[36]

The 'self', whether it is to be thought of as consciousness or a sense of identity, is not something in which he seems to have been greatly interested *as an idea*, though it is true that he was concerned to more than a normal degree with the impression he himself produced on others and that he was far more than usually introspective. The Helvetian idea of the perfectibility of each individual, given the right education and environment and provided that the individual wishes to be perfect, also aroused his enthusiasm for a time and it encouraged him in the course of self-training and self-observation which he underwent as an aspiring successor to Molière. In this respect, furthermore, he shared the enthusiasms of many of his older contemporaries.

For the eighteenth-century belief, as De Tocqueville puts it, in 'the perfectibility and power of man' and their assurance that 'they had been called upon to transform society and regenerate our species'[37] can be seen in the discipline and education which certain of them imposed on themselves. Tracy's close friend and collaborator the physician Canabis met, in the salon of Helvétius's widow, Benjamin Franklin, who presented him when he returned to America, together with his sword and the stick he had used in his experiments on calming waves, his own meticulously kept journal. In it, as Cabanis wrote in his essay on Franklin, the reader could follow 'the chronological history of Franklin's mind and character'. He could see 'how both had developed, strengthened and been adapted to all the acts in which their perfection consists'. What the journal offered was an example of 'the art of life and the art of virtue, learned as one learns to play an instrument or to fashion weapons'.[38] Beyle's own intimate journal, which he kept regularly for fourteen years, had a similar purpose, one that is apparent as well in other intimate diaries of the day:[39] 'If an indiscreet reader should find this journal, I wish to deprive him of the pleasure of laughing at the author by pointing out that what he sees can be nothing other than a mathematical and inflexible report on what I have been. I neither flatter nor slander, but state purely and severely what I believe to have been the truth. It is written with the intention of curing me of all that is ridiculous in my character when I read it in 1820...the best moments I have known, what I felt when listening to the music of Mozart, when reading Tasso, when waking to the sound of a street organ or offering my arm to my mistress, are not mentioned.'[40] Beyle's abandonment of his journal may correspond to an outgrowing of his original belief in his own or anyone else's perfectibility[41] and, as he grew older, in the possibility even of self-knowledge in the sense of seeing oneself as others see us.[42] 'With the exception of his *omnia possunt omnes*', he wrote in the May of 1818 to his friend Mareste, 'everything in Helvétius is divine.'

Helvétius may well be divine and the greatest philosopher of whom the French can boast, as Beyle describes him in *The Paris Monthly Review*. It is disconcerting, none the less, how little Beyle ever wrote to substantiate such a claim. According to Mérimée, though he was always recommending Helvétius's writings to his friends, he could never be persuaded to re-read them himself. This could be taken as one of his many notorious inconsistencies, though there are two good reasons at least for thinking that, as far as Helvétius was concerned, he was perfectly serious. For the discredit into which Helvétius had fallen was not merely one of the periodic wanings of the reputation of an honest and intelligent man. There is every reason to believe that the simple truth of his teaching was unwelcome in the society that succeeded the Revolution, a society which often preferred not to say or know where its own true interests lay. The young Karl Marx, while seeing in the theory of economic exploitation sketched by Helvétius a poorer version of the middle-class ideology of the English Utilitarians,[43] admired Helvétius's contribution to the development of materialist thinking and saw him as a forerunner of socialism.[44] And it is significant that during the first decades of the nineteenth century, Helvétius was not so much forgotten as periodically resurrected for the purposes of vehement refutation. 'There is no means of proving', Mme de Staël writes, 'that virtue is always in accordance with interest, unless one comes back to thinking of man's happiness as lying in the repose of his conscience.'[45] According to Benjamin Constant, 'The natural effect of this system of philosophy is to make every individual his own centre. Now when everyone is his own centre, all are isolated. When the storm comes, the dust is turned to mud.'[46] And the most influential academic philosopher of the 1820s in France, Nerval's examiner in the *baccalauréat*, insists that 'the human race' is unable to believe when it thinks of Regulus 'voluntarily encased in a coffin sprouting with upturned spikes', that he chose this fate 'from a love of pleasure'.[47]

It was partly because of the dangerous mystifications that can arise when the propositions enunciated by Helvétius are denied – as opposed to being dismissed on certain occasions as of little relevance or use – that Beyle chose to remain their champion. It was almost certainly too because they provided the starting point for what was to become a lifelong preoccupation. In his letter to Balzac thanking him for his review of *La chartreuse de Parme* and telling him how the novel was written, he uses a phrase which has become notorious – unfortunately, since it is usually taken out of context:

I first take someone I know very well; I let him keep all the habits he has formed in the art of setting out every morning on the pursuit of happiness (*la chasse du bonheur*); and then I make him more intelligent.[48]

It has often been assumed that Beyle is writing here as a mere hedonist and advocating or stating his interest in one particular kind of happiness, rather than describing the pursuit in which, as in Virgil's *Eclogues*, every living creature is engaged. What do men 'find to live *for* – what kinds of motive force or radical attitude can give life meaning, direction, coherence?' Our most distinguished living critic sees this question as one to which each of the main characters in Conrad's *Nostromo* 'enacts a particular answer...'[49] And it is a question that is by no means irrelevant to *La chartreuse de Parme* itself. How is it, to use Beyle's own language, that men so often 'lose their way on the road to happiness?' We may be disconcerted by the deliberate simplicity or nakedness of Beyle's language in the letter to Balzac, in an early essay entitled, significantly, *Si la comédie est utile* or in his early notebooks where he will formulate for his own guidance working principles such as the following:

Since every comedy is an indictment of something harmful, it ceases to have any interest for us as soon as whatever this is is regarded as harmful and ridiculous and, as such, is banished from society.[50]

If the principles he enunciates appear simple, however, he was too intelligent not to realise the difficulties and improbability of their being successfully applied. He failed ever to write the comedies on which he brooded in vain for so many years and his writings on literature reveal as he grows older a growing refinement and subtlety in the expression of what remains, none the less, a very conscious Utilitarianism.[51]

De l'amour and *D'un nouveau complot contre les industriels*

What is positive and original in Beylisme, or rather in the thought and outlook implicit in his writings, is particularly apparent in his critical notes and essays and even more so in his three major novels. It can be seen also in *De l'amour* of 1822 and in his polemic of three years later directed against the new Saint-Simonian doctrines, works which belong to one of the most wretchedly unhappy and yet spiritually formative and intellectually fruitful periods of his entire career. In the summer of 1821 Beyle had left his beloved Milan, partly because of his fears of the Austrian police who may have suspected him of Liberal and *carbonaristo* sympathies but also because of the hopeless state of his passion for Mathilde Dembowski, the Milanese wife of a Polish-born general, whose portrait we may be glimpsing at times in all three of Beyle's major novels. This proud, idealistic and beautiful woman, who had been loved also by the poet Foscolo, found Beyle's attentions increasingly importunate. Beyle contemplated suicide and then returned to France taking with him the unfinished manuscripts of the book in which he was attempting to analyse and universalise his own experiences of love.

De l'amour, the first of his books not to be published at his own expense, enjoyed a certain notoriety during Beyle's lifetime. It is still a work that needs little introduction. In any case, it almost defies introduction. One can point out that in it Beyle categorises and illustrates four of the varieties of sexual love: *passionate love, love arising from enjoyment and the satisfaction of taste (l'amour goût), physical love* and *the love inspired by vanity*. One can point out also that in defining love, Beyle introduced into the European languages a new term: *crystallisation,* corresponding to a slightly less original concept, that of the emergence of real or apparent facts as the result of unacknowledged hopes or fears. It is impossible, however, to suggest the actual scope of Beyle's thinking in this work except by quoting it more lengthily than there is space for here.

One of the problems which Beyle tried to overcome in writing it is suggested in the ninth chapter, which consists of the following three sentences:

> I make every possible effort to write *drily*. I wish to impose silence on my heart, which has a great deal, it believes, to say. I am always trembling at the thought that I may have only written a sigh, when I believe that I have noted down a truth.

Beyle wrote *De l'amour* partly as a contribution to the pursuit of truth as envisaged by the *idéologues* and partly too in the spirit in which Petrarch had composed the poems addressed to and inspired by Laura:

> Ove sia chi per prova intenda amore,
> Spero trovar pietà, non che perdono.
> *Sonnetti e canzoni*, 1.

[Wherever there may be someone who understands love from experience, I hope to find pity and not just pardon.]

The two forms of inspiration were not incompatible, for in describing such directly personal experience and in telling the reader that he would be able to understand him only if his experience of love were similar, Beyle was simply taking the methods of proof and description that had been adapted by the followers of Locke a step further towards true precision. It has often been said that the psychological theories and the epistemology of Locke and the French *idéologues* depend on large unproven assumptions concerning the nature of our senses and the external world and on evidence that can be revealed and corroborated only by introspection. And a modern critic of Locke (whose thought in this respect and in a number of others is akin to Beyle's) has seen the way forward from this position in two alternative kinds of psychology:

> One unobjectionable sort of psychology is biological, and studies life from the outside. The other sort, relying on memory and dramatic imagination, reproduces life from the inside, and is literary. If the literary psychologist is a man of genius, by the clearness and range of his memory, by quickness of sympathy and power of suggestion, he may come very near to the truth of experience, as it has been or might be unrolled in a human being.[52]

De l'amour has no pretentions to being anything other than psychology of the second kind and it is perhaps for this reason that Destutt de Tracy was unable to believe that it was meant to be taken seriously.[53] It consists almost entirely of fictitious anecdotes and Beyle's own painfully recent memories, while its characteristic form of argument is by analogy rather than deduction from general principles. The precision that Beyle achieved in writing it is that of the minutely noted fact or *le petit fait vrai*, a term that appears repeatedly in his writings. The test of the truth of each fact lies in its compatibility both with the reader's own experience and with facts observed in different moods and circumstances. The passionate lover, for example, may, during his first conversations with the woman he loves:

let slip any number of things having no meaning or meaning the opposite of what he feels; or, what is even more agonizing, he may exaggerate his feelings, so that they become ridiculous in her eyes. As one is vaguely aware that she is not paying sufficient attention to what one says, an automatic impulse leads one to address her in carefully formed, heavy, declamatory phrases...During the first moments of love I ever knew, this peculiarity that I felt within me made me wonder whether I was really in love after all.

I understand now how a man can be a coward and why it is that conscripts try to overcome their fear by throwing themselves recklessly into the line of fire.[54]

De l'amour is not a novel, though it is obviously the work of a novelist of unusual inventive powers, for the illustrations which well up on every page contain the essential material for much longer stories. Nor is it, obviously, a poem in any ordinary sense of the word, though the disconcerting form of many chapters has something akin to a poetic structure. It is a work that makes its own shape – understandably, since, as in genuine poetry, the effort to understand and identify an experience has arisen from and is part of the experience itself, rather than an interpretation made in terms of a dominant preconceived idea. The prose of *De l'amour*, as in genuine poetry, conveys the swiftness and sudden reflective pauses of actual thought animated by a developing and hence constantly changing mood. Beyle will even momentarily on occasions (as in chapters 3 and 5) fall into a kind of free verse.[55] However, it would be wrong to conclude from this that *De l'amour* is a 'lyrical rapture' in which Beyle 'ventured far down the path of imaginative sensibility towards a world of private values...', to quote one fairly common view.[56] Mme Simone de Beauvoir has found in Stendhal's work in general and in *De l'amour* in particular one of the most humane and realistic accounts in literature of women's character, intelligence and needs and, like George Eliot(whose praise is admittedly more qualified[57]) admires him for seeing in female frivolity or stupidity the effects not of an inherent biological weakness but of particular social conventions and rules and particular forms of female education.[58] Beyle advocates in *De l'amour* opportunities and an education which, as far as possible, will be the same for men as for women and he replies to the objection that women would then become the rivals and not the companions of men:

Yes, they would, and as soon as love had been banished by decree. Until such a law is passed, the delights and transports of love will be redoubled and that is all. The foundation on which crystallisation takes place will grow even wider than before; the man will be able to enjoy all his thoughts together with the woman he loves, the whole of nature will take on new charms in their eyes and, as ideas always reflect certain shades of character, they will know each other better and commit fewer acts of imprudence; their love will be less blind and produce fewer misfortunes.[59]

He is, needless to say, an advocate too of matrimony as a result of love and free choice, rather than the usual business arrangement of the times and, like Helvétius, of divorce in the case of obvious incompatibility. *De l'amour* is inspired not only by the desire to note down certain 'truths' and to enjoy the luxury of addressing unknown kindred spirits but by the passion for social reform which makes him an authentic as well as a professed Utilitarian.

It is as a Utilitarian also, believing in what is 'useful to the greatest number' that he appears in his pamphlet of three years later, *D'un nouveau complot contre les industriels*, though the term has also been used to describe the doctrine against which it is aimed, and Beyle himself in using it points out the obvious truth that the greatest good of the greatest number can be envisaged in many different and conflicting ways. The issues with which Beyle is concerned in the pamphlet are both political and economic, which may explain partly why it has been so long neglected, for it is only in fairly recent years that his wide reading and insight as an amateur economist have been noticed by readers capable of appreciating them, notably M. Fernand Rude in his *Stendhal et la pensée sociale de son temps* and M. Lucien Jansse in an article in which Beyle is depicted as a forerunner of Keynes.[60] Between the ages of twenty and thirty, Beyle studied carefully and pen in hand Jean Baptiste Say's *Traité d'économie politique*, Adam Smith's *Wealth of Nations* and Malthus's *Essay on Population*. After 1814, he seems to have read also, soon after they appeared, the works of Ricardo, James Mill, the French statistician Baron Charles Dupin[61] and Count Henri de Saint-Simon together with the members of the school which was to bear his name. It is against these latter that the pamphlet of 1825 was directed.

The theories of Saint-Simon have often been confused with those of his self-professed disciples and with those of modern socialism. Yet Beyle's polemic may be all the easier to follow when we recall that the Utopia envisaged by Saint-Simon himself in works such as the *Système industriel, Le catéchisme des industriels* and *Le nouveau christianisme* is authoritarian and hierarchical. Saint-Simon, like Joseph de Maistre, whom he and his younger collaborator Auguste Comte both admired, looked on the French Revolution as merely destructive and deplored Jacobin egalitarianism. What Saint-Simon advocated was 'industrial inequality' in which the 'captains of industry' (to use Carlyle's consciously Saint-Simon phrase) would assume the rôle and functions of the old priesthood and feudal aristocracy. What is new and may seem socialistic in Saint-Simon's works and in the writings of the contributors to the Saint-Simonian journals is the condemnation as merely parasitic of all but the productive members of society, that is the *industriels*, and the belief that the latter should exercise supreme authority. The highest degree of productivity, according to Saint-Simon himself, was that which was apparent in capital investment, and the natural leaders of society therefore necessarily included the bankers.

Elie Halévy has pointed out how much of Saint-Simonianism survives in the ethos and practice of modern capitalism, in the fascist corporate state and in modern Marxian socialism.[62] Napoleon III himself, who in 1838 had produced his Saint-Simonian pamphlet, *Idées napoléoniennes,* was to think of himself after his seizure of power as a Saint-Simonian on the throne. Beyle's own pamphlet does not prophesy these developments, but the prophetic insights that it does contain may be appreciated if one reads it together with Halévy's analysis of Saint-Simonian economic doctrine. For the assumptions that the pamphlet exposes with deadly accuracy of aim and yet apparent flippancy have been current for many years along the whole range of the political spectrum.

The text on which Beyle's pamphlet is a commentary is taken from *Le catéchisme des industriels*:

It is industrial capacity that has to take the first place and adjudicate between the value of all other capacities, while making them all work for its own greater advantage.

The modern cult of productivity, the orders of nobility conferred on the directors of chain stores, and the exaltation of labour in

Soviet art, are all foreshadowed in this unusually candid affirmation of belief. What Beyle questions is the equation between a man's productive capacities and his claims on our admiration or his claims to be an infallible judge of what is admirable:

> I am willing to believe that a thousand *industriels* who, with no sacrifice of probity, each gain a thousand écus, add to the strength of France; but these gentlemen have contributed to the general good *only after* contributing to their own. They are all fine honest men, whom I honour and whom I should be pleased to see elected as mayors or deputies; for the fear of bankruptcy has led them to acquire habits of suspicion and, what is more, they can count. But what I look for in vain is what is *admirable* in their conduct. Why should I admire them more than the doctor, the lawyer or the architect?...
>
> The *industriels* lend money to those who govern and often oblige them to make a reasonable budget and not to waste the taxes. That probably is all one can say of their *usefulness* to the public at large; for they care little whether with the money they lend, help is sent to the Turks or the Greeks...
>
> Industrialism, which is a not too distant relative of charlatanism, pays for the newspapers and, without even being asked to, assumes the responsibility for the defence of the cause of industry; moreover, it allows itself a little error of logic: it proclaims that industry is the cause of *all* the happiness enjoyed by the brave new world of America. If it will allow me to say so, industry has merely profited in America from excellent laws and the advantages of not having frontiers that can be attacked. The *industriels*, by means of the money they lend to a government, that is *after they have guaranteed themselves against loss*, momentarily add to the *strength* of that government; but they care little about the actual direction in which the strength is exerted...

The relevance of these observations to the contemporary world calls for no comment. It is by the standards of a truly general usefulness that Beyle condemns mere productivity.

Already in 1810, before Sismondi and Fourier[63] and before the first of the great industrial slumps in England, Beyle had questioned in the notes for an unwritten treatise on 'wealth, population and happiness', the widely accepted theory of Jean-Baptiste Say, according to which under normal conditions, each product will naturally find its own market. The only justification of productivity, Beyle argues, lies in the enjoyment of what is produced and it is because of the variation in men's capacity for various kinds of enjoyment that markets are so often saturated or unexploited. How then can the general good be either measured or foreseen? To begin with, at least, he argues in *D'un nouveau complot*, by not confusing fundamental issues. We should, for example, distinguish between the good which is done as an indirect consequence of some other aim and the good that is directly intended. We should remember too – and here certainly take a lesson from Saint-Simon – from what point of view and with what interests in mind the arbiter of the general good speaks for us. Beyle himself speaks as a member of the class of those who possess a private income of 6,000 livres:

They alone have the *leisure* to form an opinion which is their own and not that of the newspaper they read. To think is the least costly of pleasures...

The thinking class accords its consideration to whatever is *useful to the greatest number*. It recompenses by its esteem and sometimes with glory the William Tells, the Porliers, the Riegos, the Codrus, those, in other words, who risk a great deal in order to obtain what, rightly or wrongly, they believe to be useful to the public...

For to deserve a high esteem, it is on the whole necessary that there should be a *sacrifice* of interest to some noble end.[64] What sacrifices have Zamet, Samuel Bernard, Crozat, Bouret, etc. ever made, that is the richest *industriels* whose memory is preserved by history? God forbid that I should conclude from this merely historical observation that the *industriels* are without honour. All I mean to say is that they are not heroic...

What is heroism? Is it possible in the modern world? Beyle's experience of armed encounter, gunfire and perilous adventure was limited – possibly even more so than he wished posterity to believe.[65] It is in his own novels and his comments on the poets and dramatists he admired that we can best hope to find an answer to these questions.

3

Beyle the critic

Beyle and heroic drama

During his own lifetime, Beyle seems to have been best known as the habitué of various salons, as a pamphleteer writing under a somewhat absurd German aristocratic pseudonym and as a connoisseur of music and the arts. After the publication in 1823 and 1825 of his two brochures on *Racine et Shakspeare*, he also achieved notoriety for a time as a literary critic given to amusing polemic, and a defender in theory of the new Romanticism. With the discovery since his death by the general public of his three major novels, his critical writings have been neglected, for they have long since lost their *actualité* and their claims to permanent interest have still to be recognised. I myself have been taken to task by a well-known authority on French literature[1] for suggesting, what I wish to argue here, that if Beyle's work as a whole were better known he would be recognised as one of the great French critics.

Beyle's critical writings – those that he himself published and those that survive in letters, notebooks and diaries – are, to use T. S. Eliot's term, those of a 'practitioner', an aspiring dramatist who, after the age of forty, resigned himself to the rôle of a not very fashionable novelist writing mainly for posterity. His interest in literature was in no sense academic. In reading he was guided by his deep and volatile enthusiasms, by his need to understand human nature and history and by his desire to learn from writers of the past how to speak to a contemporary audience. Beyle's 'interest' in writing criticism is plain – if we use 'interest' in its Helvetian sense – and it is this which accounts for its unusual clarity and its freedom from such affectations as those of academic impartiality. If Beyle so often hit on the actual truth about those he read, it was precisely because of this all-embracing need to learn from his predecessors rather than judge them.

Beyle's critical writings give us the principal clue to what Prévost has described as his apprenticeship (see pages 5–6 above) and one can trace in his comments on what he read over the years certain major preoccupations which presumably correspond to the 'five or six principal ideas' he had spent his life 'considering attentively', preoccupations which are apparent also in the subject matter and technique of his novels. To avoid confusion, it may be necessary to consider these singly and therefore once again, while considering the history of Beyle's education, to avoid an exact chronological sequence.

Beyle's preoccupation with the heroic and the possibilities of heroic action in the modern world dates, not surprisingly, from his early childhood. It is of course normal for any small boy to dream of acts of heroic daring and sacrifice and to grow up realising that these were nothing but dreams. But Beyle was unusual in that he grew to consciousness during the great adventure of the Revolution and the Revolutionary wars when many responsible-seeming adults spoke of themselves as re-living the annals of the Roman Republic. He would exult in secret not over the exploits of warriors remote in time but over the heroes of the daily news, and the thought that men might actually live through such days again was never to leave him. The 'tender love' he felt at the age of nine for the regiments he would watch from his grandfather's window riding through the Place Grenette in Grenoble was to remain with him throughout his life and survive the disillusionment of his serving as an officer in the very same army only seven years later. The same regiments were to appear, if only briefly, in his novels as the embodiment of some supreme unfulfilled possibility.

Epic and heroic drama understandably exerted an enormous appeal over Beyle's imagination as a youth and, for that matter, throughout his life. Ariosto's *Orlando Furioso*, Tasso's *Gerusalemme Liberata* (and *Don Quixote*) were to remain lifelong favourites, though in middle age, he decided regretfully that Ariosto's heroes had too much of the 'ostler'[2] about them and that it was Tasso who was the superior genius of the two. The heroic drama of Corneille seemed to him for several years the most sublime achievement of the theatre and undervalued only because there were so few capable of understanding the character and behaviour of Corneille's heroes. 'Since the eyes of petty men are too weak to bear the light of true greatness', he wrote in an early notebook,[3] 'they prefer Racine to Corneille and Virgil to Homer.' And again: 'It is in his depiction of character that a poet has always been great; this is why Homer, Corneille and Molière are superior to Virgil, Racine, etc.'[4] In his admiration for Corneille, moreover, he was encouraged by Helvétius, who, in *De l'esprit*, defines the hypocrite as 'someone who, not being sustained in his own study of moral qualities by a desire for the happiness of humanity, is too much absorbed in himself...' and who recommends Corneille for his 'depiction of great heroes and statesmen'.[5] Not surprisingly, the hero of his own unwritten comedy *Les deux hommes* was to have received a proper philosophic education, unlike his decadent and affected rival, and the effects of his education were to have been apparent in his generosity, integrity and realism. Beyle's admiration for Corneille and, after his first stay in Italy, of the plays of Vittorio Alfieri, seems to have waned only after his discovery of Shakespeare.

Beyle's comments on Corneille and Alfieri, like those on Rousseau, are of interest not only for what they tell us of these authors themselves but as an indication of the kind of man he became in the process of growing older. For his various comments over the years on the pride and honour which Corneille and Alfieri exalt in their plays remind one of what he wrote both about his own precocious Roman Republicanism and about the influence on his character of his beloved great-aunt Elizabeth Gagnon. Mlle. Gagnon, when he knew her as a boy, was a tall thin elderly lady with a dignity which had something Spanish about it in its refinement and scrupulosity: 'In this respect, she formed my character and it is to my Aunt Elizabeth that I owe the absurd would-be Spanish dignity of which I was the dupe and victim for the first thirty years of my life.'[6]

One has only to read one of the few works by Alfieri which can still be read as living literature, his superb autobiography, to realise why Beyle found him congenial as a young man and in later life a somewhat dangerous influence. The description of Alfieri's lonely childhood, in the Piedmont of the 1750s, during which he rarely saw his own family and was left to the care of servants and priests, resembles Beyle's in the impression it leaves of an acute spiritual malnutrition, though the deprivations from which Alfieri suffered were probably more cruel than those of Beyle after the death of his mother. It is impossible to tell whether Beyle exaggerated the miseries of his own childhood in *La vie de Henry Brulard* but if he did, it is arguable that he was influenced unknowingly by the *Life* of Alfieri. Brought up as he was, Alfieri developed the fierce proud independence of character which is seen in his account of the duels he fought, in his passion for hard dangerous horse-riding, in the terseness of his prose and verse, and in his hatred of political tyranny and admiration for Plutarch's *Lives*. It is also seen in the determination with which he set out to learn the Italian of Florence (which, for a Piedmontese educated in Turin, was almost a foreign language) and to become the author of tragic masterpieces written in the Italian of Dante. His conception of tragedy is also what one would expect from what he tells us of his life. Despite his Republicanism, his admiration for England and his contempt for France; despite also his dislike of the French classical alexandrine and of the classical convention of the *confident*, his conception of tragedy is essentially close to Corneille's. 'When Alfieri wrote one of his immortal tragedies', Beyle wrote in a letter to Pauline, 'who could afterwards rob him of the infinite satisfaction he had found in giving utterance to the minds of those men who have come closer to being divine than any others before him or since, to men like Brutus, Timoleon, etc.?'[7]

Feeling or at least imagining he felt a close kinship with Alfieri, Beyle became increasingly conscious as he grew older of the penalties of the proud independence which is achieved at the expense of an awareness of different ways of thinking and feeling and which is hence fatal in a dramatist. He became aware also of a curious emptiness behind Alfieri's terse magniloquence. In December 1804, after seeing Talma act in a version of *Macbeth* by Jean-François Ducis, he noted in his diary that 'there is no sensibility *without detail* [my italics]. Their failure to remember this is one of the principal failings of French dramatists. I felt this too when reading the other day Alfieri's *Oreste* in which I found the same defect...Shakespeare is much closer to the kind of tragedy I have in mind but shall probably never write.'

And seven years later, after seeing *Oreste* performed in Florence, he noted: 'Full of rapidity, vengeance; but completely without interest. It seems to me too sublime...there is not enough of the *human* to make sympathy possible.'[8]

A similar evolution is seen in Beyle's attitude to Alfieri's politics. On the day of Napoleon's coronation, in the year following Alfieri's death, after seeing 'religion come to sanctify tyranny and all this in the name of human happiness', he had read some of Alfieri's prose in order, he writes, 'to rinse out my mouth'.[9] His admiration for Alfieri's Republicanism waned, however, after he had read the latter's denunciation of all that had happened in France since 1789. He found himself wondering in what sense, if any, Alfieri had ever cared about human liberty.

Beyle's early enthusiasm for Alfieri and his subsequent misgivings explain perhaps why, after he had discovered *The Edinburgh Review*, a journal he was to describe as a revelation,[10] he paid special attention to an article by Francis Jeffrey on Alfieri's life and writings which appeared in January 1810. Long passages from this essay are translated and introduced into *Rome, Naples et Florence en 1817* and the extracts are attributed to the fictitious Count Neri of Bologna. (Where Beyle has translated directly from Jeffrey the text here is in italics.)

*Though professedly a Republican, it is easy to see that the republic he wanted was one on the Roman model – where there were Patricians as well as Plebeians, and where a man of great talents had even a good chance of being one day appointed Dictator...*Boredom, together with a hatred for those who are happy, was the dominant feature of his existence and on the throne he would have been a Nero.

As it is the great excellence, so it is occasionally the chief fault of Alfieri's dialogue, that every word is honestly employed to help forward the action of the play, by serious argument, necessary narrative or the direct expression of natural emotion. There are no excursions or digressions – no episodical conversations,– and none but the most brief moralizings. This gives a certain air of solidity to the whole piece, that is apt to prove oppressive to the ordinary reader and reduces the entire drama to too great uniformity. The intelligent reader anticipates far too easily what is going to be said. There is nothing striking, nothing stirring; when one has read three or four of his tragedies, the others leave no surprises. One reads him as one reads Milton out of a sense of duty and leaves off without regret.

I say this speaking as a learned man of letters; as for my own particular feelings, *I believe that those who are duly sensible of the merit of*

Shakespeare will never be much struck with any other dramatical compositions. In these respects he disdains all comparison with Alfieri or with any other poet. Alfieri, Corneille and all the others consider a tragedy as a poem; Shakespeare saw it as a presentation of the character and passions of men, which, if it is to move the spectator must do so by arousing his sympathy and not because of a vain admiration on his part for the poet's talents...

Alfieri was incapable of seeing things from this point of view and of distinguishing between the actions of men and the different ways of portraying them which have given rise to the various dramatic schools. He took as his guide the French school, the only one he knew. He mistook his memories for the result of his observations. With a little more intelligence, he would have recognised that he had never really observed anything...[11]

The change in Beyle's attitude to Alfieri coincided, as the above extract suggests, with a reassessment of Corneille. 'Racine is often perfect in his depiction of love...', he had written in his early twenties. 'His style is nearly always perfect. What is perfect in Corneille is often the thought rather than the style. From which it follows that Corneille will be enjoyed by those who look for the substance rather than the shadow and enjoyed far less by the common herd.'[12] The latter judgment was one which he had come to modify as time went on and as he came to realise how baffling the thought of Corneille can be, despite the superficial clarity of his style.

During Beyle's periods of leave from 1811 to 1813, he had sketched out with his former school friend, the engineer Louis Crozet, character-studies of mutual acquaintances and notes on the books they read together. Their notes on Corneille's *Cinna*, which survive in the handwriting of Beyle and Crozet, were never intended for publication, though they constitute perhaps one of the finest commentaries on classical drama to have found its way into print. The notes are an analysis of the first act of *Cinna*, beginning with Emilie's opening tirade, in which she tells us of her 'impatient desire' to avenge her father condemned to death by her own protector, the Emperor Augustus:

> Impatients désirs d'une illustre vengeance
> Dont la mort de mon père a formé la naissance,
> Enfants impétueux de mon ressentiment

> Que ma douleur séduite embrasse aveuglément,
> Vous prenez sur mon âme un trop puissant empire...
>
> [Impatient desires of an illustrious vengeance, engendered by the death of my father, impetuous children of my resentment that my seduced grief blindly embraces, you hold too powerful a sway over my soul...]

Beyle and Crozet comment on these lines:

The main fault of this monologue is that Emilie talks to herself with all the clarity and eloquence of a woman addressing a stranger. We feel that Shakespeare would have made this scene altogether more natural by giving Emilie the simple authentic language of a troubled soul. He would have shown her, for example, at two o'clock in the morning leaving her bed and walking agitatedly up and down in her room to the great astonishment of one of her maidservants. What a difference it would have made to the interest of the drama if Cinna were to enter her room at two o'clock in order to talk to her of the conspiracy! Otherwise, if the risk were too great, Emilie could have been made to form some decision of which she informed Cinna the following day in the course of a hunt.

The style is not suited to Emilie's character, but if we assume for a moment that it is, we find that it is noble and passionate (or tragic); it is clear, and it has the terseness which is that of a mighty soul. To prove this, one has only to imagine the four lines ('Vous prenez sur mon âme', etc.) spoken by a character like Voltaire's Amenaïde and the disconcerting effect they would produce.

Imagine that the dialogue is a portrait. Imagine, that is, that the poet claimed to be repeating what Emilie herself had said in his hearing. If this were the case, we should blame the poet for everything that struck us as contrary to nature... The problem we wish to raise is the following: what would our conception of Emilie be after we had heard this monologue? We would imagine her as a woman of firm character, lacking consequently in grace (in the charms of weakness), a little in love with Cinna and unable to distinguish between her vengeance and her love. It is difficult to imagine (still with reference to this one monologue) one of these two passions, love and vengeance, completely overcoming the other; or, in other words, which is the stronger of the two.[13]

The speeches of Cinna himself are also disconcertingly out of character and give no hint of his subsequent eager gratitude to the forgiving Augustus. Beyle and Crozet analyse his account of the propaganda of the conspirators preparing to overthrow Augustus and his henchmen:

> Je les peins dans le meurtre à l'envi triomphants,
> Rome entière noyée au sang de ses enfants:
> Les uns assassinés dans les places publiques,
> Les autres dans le sein de leurs dieux domestiques;
> Le méchant par le prix au crime encouragé;
> Le mari par sa femme en son lit égorgé...
> (act I, scene iii, lines 195–200)

[I depict them striving to outdo each other and triumphant in murder, the whole of Rome drowned in its children's blood; some assassinated in the public places, others in the bosom of their household gods; the evil man enticed to crime by gold; the husband's throat cut by his wife as he lies in bed...]

This is a perfect model of the tragic style. There is a certain seeking after effect, but this is in no way cold or vulgar...nor, we may add, is there any hint that the speaker is a man without character, momentarily exalted.

The ending,

> Demain j'attends la fin, etc.,

announces a mighty character and induces in the reader the quivering of a proud smile; the reader admires himself and imagines himself to be capable of sentiments as elevated as these.[14]

What in fact is the play about? Beyle and Crozet admit their bafflement:

> In general, in what we have seen of the play, we do not acquire an *intimate knowledge* of the characters. Basing our judgment merely on what they say, we are able to form three or four totally distinct impressions of their character.
>
> Is Emilie moved by the sheer love of liberty, by filial piety or by a proud desire not to remain unavenged?
>
> After five minutes, we see at once what sort of a woman Lady Macbeth is or Desdemona...[15]

This analysis of Corneille resembles in more than one respect Beyle's and Jeffrey's analysis of Alfieri. In the writings of both poets, we are shown the inhibiting effect of the desire to 'appear noble'. To quote once again from the fictitious Count Neri:

> ...the correct gravity of the sentiments expressed in these tragedies, the perfect propriety and the wise moderation with which the author depicts passion are exactly the opposite of what might have been expected from his fiery and independent character...Not even the most inattentive reader can fail to notice the immense labour he devoted to his style. Faithful to his patrician character, Alfieri imagined

that by writing in this way he would be *more respected*. He would have been much greater and certainly more original if he had been himself.[16]

One of the advantages of this approach to Alfieri and, in so far as he resembles him, to Corneille as well, is that it explains not only why their plays can seem so baffling and unsatisfactory but also why they can seem the opposite; why it is, for example, that *Cinna*, despite what Beyle and Crozet say, has gone on appealing over the centuries to readers and playgoers. The spectator or playgoer to whom the play appeals responds presumably to the pride and joy in living of Corneille's characters, to their passionate even if simple sense of justice and to the serene courage with which they are able to confront inevitable and appalling dangers. To quote Beyle and Crozet once again:

> The ending,
> *Demain j'attends la fin*, etc.
> announces a mighty character and induces in the reader the quivering of a proud smile...

Yet it is possible for the reader or spectator who finds the play inspiring in this way to allow such moments as those to dominate his impression of the play as a whole and not to notice how much he is seeing in it only what he wishes to see. What Beyle and Crozet criticise in *Cinna* is not the fact that it arouses a response of this kind, but that because of something inhibited in Corneille, it fails to satisfy it, all the more so if one wishes to learn from the play and find in it something more than a reflection of what one knows, feels and believes already. The conclusions they reach are all the more eloquent in that they confine their comments to the first act, saying nothing of the capitulation of the proud Emilie and the intrepid Cinna when their conspiracy is discovered or of their effusive thanks when the Emperor Augustus decides to forgive them.

As Beyle himself makes perfectly clear, the fact that he became increasingly demanding in his reading of Corneille and Alfieri is explained to a great extent by his discovery of Shakespeare, whom he read both in English and in the translation of Le Tourneur. 'He is like a flowing river', he wrote in 1805 after re-reading *Othello*, 'a river which sweeps over everything and carries everything with it. His sheer vitality is like a river. He is nature itself...'[17] And a few days before this, in the mixture of languages of which he had already grown fond: 'O *divin Shakespeare*, oui thou art the greatest Bard in world!'[18]

The Shakespeare of whom he speaks most often and with most enthusiasm is not, however, the Shakespeare who was able to show heroic idealism in the most bleakly cynical and withering light. If he soon came to prefer him to Corneille, it was not because he had come to hold the views of Thersites or Falstaff on 'honour'. Beyle's ideas of honour and heroism changed over the years, it is obvious. They ceased to be of the kind one associates with adolescent hero-worship. One could say perhaps that he came to be more imaginative and perceptive and hence more prone to scepticism in his thoughts concerning the kind of life in which survival is only tolerable when consistent with self-respect and the demands of principle. Beyle's increasing proneness to scepticism, however, went with a deepening of his admiration for what he saw as acts of genuine rather than merely self-dramatising honour and heroism. ('For to deserve a high esteem, it is on the whole necessary that there should be a *sacrifice* of interest to some noble end.'[19]) In this respect, as in many others, there is a continuity of feeling between the mature and the adolescent Beyle.

Much of what he has written on Shakespeare suggests that he found in his plays a satisfaction not unlike that which he had formerly derived from those of Corneille and Alfieri. There is little sign that he recognised that it is also far less obviously heroic. His commentary on *Julius Caesar*, which he wrote with Crozet at the same time as the notes on *Cinna* is in this respect very revealing. The commentary tells us virtually nothing of the ferocious irony of the play, the irony, that is, on Shakespeare's part, of such lines as the following:

> Stoop, Romans, stoop,
> And let us bathe our hands in Caesar's blood
> Up to the elbows and besmear our swords:
> Then walk we forth, even to the market place,
> And waving our red weapons o'er our heads,
> Let's all cry, 'Peace, freedom and liberty!'
> (act III, scene i.)

The subtle hypocrisy of Shakespeare's Brutus (what Mr Morris

Shapira has described in a lecture as 'the leak in his nobility') is something also of which they say nothing:

What we are shown very vividly is the purity of Brutus's character: the character of a sensitive and affectionate man who loves Caesar and who realises that it is necessary to kill him. He says
> We shall be call'd purgers, not murderers...[20]

What they criticise in Brutus and Cassius is that they are too magnanimous and too much addicted to philosophising:

They should never have hesitated to sacrifice Mark Antony. Instead of this, when Caesar is dead, they amuse themselves by giving lectures in philosophy...Moreover, if these two Romans were to come back to life and read Plutarch themselves, I think they would have been annoyed with him and amused at us for seeing in a conspiracy only what an old sweet-tempered philologist had imagined...[21]

These comments were made in 1811. Beyle's tendency, however, to attribute to Shakespeare's heroes motives of an unequivocally noble and virtuous kind is seen twelve years later in his comments on *Othello*, one of the plays which he seems always to have considered among the finest. In *La vie de Rossini* of 1823, he criticises Rossini's Othello who, from the moment of his first triumphant entry, is made to seem far too proud: 'For pride is the one thing in Othello one should avoid suggesting.' Rossini's Othello lacks also 'the tenderness which would have made it clear to me that it is not vanity which places the dagger in Othello's hand'. In Shakespeare's Othello, the love we are shown is a love like Werther's, 'a love which can be sanctified by suicide'.[22] One is tempted to add: a love like that of Julien Sorel in *Le rouge et le noir* for Mme de Rênal.

The temptation is one which it is better to resist, however. It is quite likely that the inspiration for Julien's attempted murder of his former mistress came from the tragedy Beyle most admired as well as from the newspaper account of the shooting by Antoine Berthet of Mme Michoud in 1827. Julien's motivation is complex, however, and is shown as such, far more than that attributed by Beyle to Othello. It is possible too that the subtlety of insight which we find in *Le rouge et le noir* is a consequence of his reading of Shakespeare even though his comments on the psychology of Shakespeare's characters may sometimes disappoint us by their simple-mindedness. What is certain is that his notions of the heroic were no longer as simple as when he sat down at the age of twenty with the intention of becoming 'the greatest poet possible'.

'Le style est ceci'

There is one other conclusion which can be drawn from Beyle's comments on Corneille and Alfieri: his interest in these writers is invariably, as in his comments on the prose of Rousseau, an interest in the language they use. The point of view from which he writes is always that of the literary critic, whatever else this point of view may involve.

Since ideas both of the function of language and of the nature of criticism are always changing, it is necessary, however, to be more specific. I should like therefore to quote two rather disparaging accounts of Beyle's qualifications as a literary critic and then to explain why I find them unjust.

The first is taken from Sainte-Beuve's essay on Beyle in *Portraits contemporains*:

It is to be noticed that, as far as style is concerned, through wishing it to be limpid and natural, Beyle seemed to exclude from it the poetry, the colour, the images and those expressions of genius which clothe the passions and enhance the language of dramatic personages, even in Shakespeare – and I would say, above all in Shakespeare.[23]

This judgment has been echoed by most of Beyle's critics ever since and I feel a certain temerity in describing it as nonsense. It is echoed, for example, by M. Georges Blin in his recent study of *Stendhal et les problèmes du roman*. In the second of the two passages which I wish to consider, M. Blin talks of the contradiction or 'tension' between Beyle's insistence on truth and realism in drama and the novel and his interest in the various kinds of sheer beauty to be found in painting and in sculpture:

The tension is such between the realistic end which he ascribes to all works of literature and the criteria of which he approves as an aesthetician, that one wonders whether he thought of literature as art at all, as something, that is, corresponding to the same conditions and liable to the same kind of judgment. One's doubts are all the more legitimate since he tended to expel from the realm of letters all poetry, that is to say, the form of literature which achieves the highest degree of insubordination to any meaning.[24]

Neither Sainte-Beuve nor M. Blin explain why if Beyle wishes to exclude from literature all poetry, he should have found in the poetry of Dante and Shakespeare the qualities he had looked for in vain in Corneille and Alfieri. ('No man has ever been *more himself*', he writes than Dante. 'Alfieri was not himself in his language and much less than he thought in his ideas.')[25]

However, it is Beyle's conception of poetry and style in general to which Sainte-Beuve and M. Blin take exception and in taking exception, they each invoke an alternative view of how language works. Sainte-Beuve's analogy with clothing is a familiar one. It is used, for example, by Alfieri himself when talking of his first attempts to write verse in the Italian of Florence while thinking still in the half-French dialect of his native Piedmont. The substance of his *Cleopatra*, he writes, when given expression in French was altogether excellent. Rewritten in Italian verse, it was worse than mediocre: 'So true is it that in all poetry the clothing is half the body, while in some kinds of poetry, in the lyric, for example, the clothing is everything.'[26]

The comparison between clothing and literary style is as familiar in English as in French or Italian and because of this it is very easy to believe that one understands it. Yet the distinction that Sainte-Beuve and Alfieri have in mind is not between the words themselves and what they stand for; between what contemporary linguisticians describe, that is, as *le signifiant* and *le signifié*. If it were, they would be referring presumably to all forms of language, even that used in railway timetables. It is by no means certain what they mean but it is likely, none the less, that they are distinguishing between what can be understood and adequately conveyed in different words when one is reading poetry (or prose that has a poetic quality) and what is conveyed to the reader without his understanding what he is experiencing or why. They may have in mind, that is to say, what we mean when we talk of the 'magic' of someone's style or what critics such as the Abbé Bouhours in the seventeenth century described more clearly and unpretentiously as the *je ne sais quoi*, a phrase which has unfortunately become trivialised beyond redemption.

The analogy between style and clothing is one which Beyle himself, as far as I know, never used. The one comparison which resembles it and which he did use on a number of occasions is a comparison with varnish. 'Style ought to be like a transparent varnish: it must not alter the colours or the facts and thoughts on which it is placed', he and Crozet remark when writing of the style of Rousseau.[27] However, in his more rigorously precise definitions of style, he avoids altogether simile and metaphor. In the same notebook he and Crozet assert roundly:

Le style est ceci: 'ajouter à une pensée donnée toutes les circonstances, propres à produire tout l'effet que doit produire cette pensée.[28]
[Style is this: to add to a given thought all the circumstances liable to produce the total effect which this thought must produce.]

'Thought' here, as in general in Beyle's vocabulary and that of the idéologues, is a term which covers not only 'ideas' and 'memories' but also 'sensations' and 'emotions'.[29] 'A given thought' is here a deliberately comprehensive phrase, as is also 'circumstances'. The attention given to style when reading is, according to this view, nothing more than the detailed attention to what is implied or betrayed by the use of words. Style is seen as a function of meaning. The definition is, in other words, perfectly consistent with one's experience of the *je ne sais quoi* and with the view that there are forms of literature which, in the words of M. Blin, achieve a 'high degree of insubordination to any meaning.'

There is a difference, however, between the insubordination to meaning which appears to be a consequence of what is unfamiliar or mysterious in what is communicated (in certain passages of Shakespeare, for example) and the meaninglessness which is merely the result of self-deception, obscurity and incoherence on the part of the author. According to Beyle, the poetry of Alfieri is of the latter kind and he reproaches him, together with other Italian poets born and educated outside Tuscany, for forcing himself to write in the Italian of Florence rather than in his native dialect: 'You will acknowledge, I think, that a man can be a poet in that language alone in which he talks to his mistress and his rivals.'[30] There is an analogy, in this respect, between the Tuscan of Alfieri and the conventional *style noble* used by Chateaubriand in his novels. Speaking, for example, of the latter's *Le dernier des Abencérages* in the *New Monthly Magazine* for September 1826, Beyle writes: ... 'The author has not observed that extreme loftiness is only attainable in French by the rejection of words degraded by common use. Now this rejection casts at once a *veil of obscurity* [my italics] over the language, which is a deadly fault in a novel.'[31]

These two quotations may not invalidate the point M. Blin is making but the injustice of his argument is apparent when one reads other general pronouncements by Beyle on the nature of language, style and poetry. By 'high degree of insubordination to any meaning' one may assume that he is referring to what Sainte-Beuve and Alfieri presumably have in mind when they talk of the 'clothing of style', to what in genuine poetry, that is to say, defies paraphrase or translation. And to say that Beyle was blind to poetry in this sense of the term is to ignore his comments over a period of forty years on the poets he most admired.

His preoccupation with what is unique and irreducible to other terms in genuine poetry is seen in the importance he attaches to *detail*:

...there is no sensibility without detail. Their failure to remember this is one of the principal failings of French dramatists. I felt this the other day when reading Alfieri's *Oreste*...[32] Surely a poet would benefit greatly by particularising far more his comparisons; 'I go up a majestic river'. Why not name either the Rhine or the Rhône? It seems to me that this is Ariosto's way of writing.[33]

'Detail' or 'the little true fact' is a term which recurs constantly in Beyle's writing throughout his career. (One is reminded of Blake's dictum that 'Truth lies in minute particulars.') For Beyle, as also for Destutt de Tracy, it is that which precedes all thought, or rather on which thought, reflection and memory depend. According to Tracy, it is our general ideas which are incorporated in particular perceptions and memories rather than the other way round.[34]

If Beyle learned from Tracy in this respect, he learned also from the poetry he admired. The actual detail and observation which he found in Shakespeare he found also in La Fontaine, the only poet, he once wrote, 'who touched his heart in the same spot as Shakespeare'.[35] And what he also noted and admired was the tact and delicacy of their appeal to the reader's imagination. I quote from the entries in his diary for 23 August 1804 and for 5 February of the following year:

The poet is someone who arouses the emotions of his reader; there are two ways in which this can be done.

One can depict perfectly things capable of giving a very small quantity of emotion. By this means, one can make them convey the whole of this emotion:

La Fontaine, for example, when he portrays the weasel trying to get out of the granary [see Fables, Book 3, Fable 17].

Or one can depict more or less successfully something capable of arousing a great deal of emotion:

As Voltaire does when he shows us the situation in which Mérope finds herself and what she does in the tragedy of that name.

I believe that if I were to read attentively (and with a well practiced feeling for what is bad and false in feeling, if I were to read as a poet would) *Mérope* and then the fable of the poor woodcutter burdened with faggots, the first fifteen lines of the fable [book 1, fable 16] would move me far more than the entire tragedy.

One way of moving the reader is to show the *facts, the things themselves*, while saying nothing of the effect they produce. This method can be employed by a person of sensibility who is not a philosopher...It is a method which Mme de Staël seems completely unable to use herself. Her book *Delphine* is wholly lacking in moments of repose like those which the great Shakespeare offers the reader in his tragedy of *Macbeth*. In this play, in which terror is carried to the utmost pitch, one of the gentlemen who is accompanying Duncan as he enters the castle of Macbeth points out, at a moment which is terrifying for the spectator and perfectly ordinary for him and his companions, the sweet pure beauty of the site of the castle where the 'temple-haunting martlet...Hath made his pendant bed and procreant cradle.' It is one of the most divine strokes of this great man and one which I feel is more profound that the 'Qu'il mourût' of Corneille[36] and the 'Qui te l'a dit?' of Racine.[37]

The conscious delicacy with which Beyle notes the precise degree and kind of enjoyment he experiences when reading La Fontaine and Shakespeare reminds one of how much he shared the preoccupation with 'taste' and 'sensibility' of a number of contemporary French and, more particularly English philosophers and critics, especially those who had found in David Hartley's theory of the Association of Ideas the foundation of an aesthetic theory justified both by common sense and by what was revealed in flights of imagination. Beyle read and admired not only the *Discourses* of Sir Joshua Reynolds[38] but also the far more interesting and now undeservedly forgotten *Analytical inquiry into the principles of taste* of Richard Payne Knight.[39] His interest in the *effect* of poetry is an interest in what John Stuart Mill has described as 'not an illusion but a fact' and his writings from his earliest years make it seem more than likely that he would have endorsed Mill's arguments in favour of 'the cultivation of the feelings' through the imagination. Mill describes in his *Autobiography* his defence of Wordsworth in a debate with his friend J. A. Roebuck, a man 'of very quick and strong sensibilities', though 'like most Englishmen who have feelings, he found his feelings stand very much in the way'.

> It was in vain that I urged on him that the imaginative emotion which an idea, when vividly conceived, excites in us, is not an illusion but a fact, as real as any of the other qualities of objects; and far from implying anything erroneous and delusive in our mental apprehension of the object, is quite consistent with the most accurate knowledge and most perfect recognition of all its physical and intellectual laws and relations. The intensest feeling of the beauty of a cloud lighted by the setting sun, is no hindrance to my knowing that the cloud is vapour of water, subject to all the laws of vapours in a state of suspension....[40]

There is some significance in the fact that Mill, like Beyle, was formed to some extent by the reading of Helvétius.

Beyle's debt to Helvétius is considerable and a study of Helvétius himself and the other philosophers and critics by whom he was influenced can help the reader to appreciate, more readily than he might have otherwise, the kind of thinking that lies behind Beyle's often misleadingly laconic remarks on the style of other writers.[41] Beyle was fortunate in being able to read some of the best eighteenth-century philosophy and criticism and differed from his contemporaries mainly in the quickness with which he came to realise the truth of its finer insights and the whole-heartedness and pertinacity with which he continued to learn from them. In making these insights his own he was, of course, following not only the spirit but the letter of a philosophy for which personal experience and judgment are the beginning and the end of knowledge. As Helvétius wrote in a passage which Beyle copied and commented on in his early notebooks:

> In every *genre* and in particular in those which seek to give pleasure, the beauty of a work varies according to the sensation it arouses in us. The more clear and distinct this sensation is, the keener the beauty.[42]

What is true of 'the beauty of a work' is true equally of the feelings and experiences of a fictitious character. The following is another of the principles which Beyle noted as a young man and which helped to form his idea of literature:

> ...one can never depict the passions and feelings convincingly unless one is capable of experiencing them oneself. Suppose that a character is placed in circumstances which are liable to set in motion the entire activity of the passions within him. In order to depict them in an authentic way, it is necessary that one should first be susceptible to the feelings whose effects one has set out to show. One's model must be within oneself...[43]

Yet Helvétius's comments on language and style, or at least language and style considered as such, are more cursory and less original than those of Condillac or Destutt de Tracy. They are interesting partly because of what he fails to say – because of his freedom, that is, from many of the beliefs and preoccupations of his own contemporaries, and in particular from those which we associate with the name of Voltaire.

Chief among these is a belief not only in the desirability but the feasibility of what amounts to a perfect language, in other words of a language capable of expressing all that we ever need to say and of conveying this, without loss or distortion, to any normally intelligent educated adult. Expressing oneself with perfect accuracy, according to this belief, should be merely a matter of knowing and finding *le mot juste*.[44] A perfect language for Voltaire is also one in which the meaning of words has been established for all time. He speaks of the period when English poets learned to write 'correctly'[45] and when criticising a turn of phrase used by Corneille, he objects to it on the simple grounds that it is no longer in use. 'It is shameful for the human spirit', he writes, 'that the same expression should be found good at one period of history and bad at another.'[46]

A 'perfect' language for Destutt de Tracy is an impossibility, '...for we have seen', he writes in his *Grammaire*, 'that the uncertainty of the value of the signs of our ideas is inherent, not in the nature of the signs but in our intellectual faculties. It is impossible for the same sign to have exactly the same value for all those who employ it or even for the individual who employs it on different occasions.'[47] The conventions of a language are established by habit and it is only by habitually using it that one can hope to master its resources. Hence the importance for Tracy of the spoken language of the people and his insistence on the rôle it can play not only in the expression but also the formation of the most sophisticated and subtle ideas:

> ...according to the theory of the formation of ideas and of the influence of habit, even unusually gifted men have a great deal to lose when they study and write in a language which is not their natural language and which is not associated intimately and completely with their most deeply rooted habits. Although the truth of this last consideration is rarely acknowledged, it is of extreme importance, for it follows from this that those men who write as scholars and philosophers in the language in which they normally converse enjoy an incontestable advantage...[48]

One might add: not only scholars and philosophers. There is an obvious analogy between these arguments and Beyle's often repeated assertion that the poet should write in the language in which he speaks to his mistress and his rivals.

The same view of the importance of the vernacular is expressed by the now forgotten critic and poet Jean-Marie Clément in his *Lettres à M. de Voltaire*, which Beyle studied closely and admired, and which are a refutation, among other things, of Voltaire's belief in the possibility of a 'fixed' literary idiom which lends itself with perfect ease to translation into another language. The greatest writers, Clément argues, are often those who, like La Fontaine, are the most difficult of all to translate.[49] For Clément, as for Tracy, the use of the vernacular is a means of achieving 'precision'. No writer, he maintains, was ever more 'precise' than Montaigne, and Montaigne wrote at a time when the language of men of letters resembled closely that used in ordinary familiar conversation.[50]

Clément talks of the 'boldness' of the popular idiom and deplores the fact that the language used by the French upper classes and in works of literature has lost its former freedom and strength and become as a consequence 'sterile for poetry'.[51] Even the style of Racine, he argues, is closer to the popular idiom than that of the eighteenth century and in this respect has much in common with that of the Bible and Montaigne.[52] The 'boldness' and 'strength' of which Clément speaks are, needless to say, more than merely stylistic qualities. When Clément uses these terms one is reminded of what one of Beyle's other *maîtres à penser*, Thomas Hobbes, refers to as that quick ranging' of the mind 'from which proceed those grateful similes, metaphors and other tropes, by which both *poets* and *orators* have it in their power to make things both please and displease, and show well or ill to others, as they like themselves; or else in discerning suddenly dissimilitude in things that otherwise appear the same'.[53]

One could go on giving instances of how the philosophers and critics whom Beyle read as a young man may have helped to form his ideas of the nature of style; how also they may have helped him to understand the use of language of Shakespeare and La Fontaine. One thing, however, I hope, emerges from those instances I have already given: Beyle's education would not have *blinded* him to the ways in which a poet uses words. It would not have closed his mind, that is, to the use of language of those writers for whom words are the servant of the imagination, those, who, as Clément puts it, 'force their language... to express what they feel'[54] and for whom precision lies in the accuracy and vividness with which they convey perception and feeling rather than in the conformity of the words they use with conventional usage. The principles which underlie his criticism are on the whole simple and are confined deliberately, when he formulates them himself, to the maximum degree of generality. They resemble what is best in the thought of Helvétius and Tracy in the extent to which they allow for what is unpredictable in the expression of thought and feeling and in their freedom from anything at all resembling the deliberate conventionality of Voltaire. The principles that are implicit in Beyle's criticism, his conception of 'style', 'poetry', 'precision' and 'clarity', are implicit equally in the art of his novels. Sainte-Beuve recognised this when talking of their inadequacy. 'Beyle's failing as a novelist', he wrote in the essay from which I have already quoted, 'is that he came to this form of composition by way of criticism and by conforming to certain preconceived ideas.' While not agreeing in the least that this was a 'failing', I should like now to consider some of the other ways in which the development that Sainte-Beuve refers to took place.

The discovery of a 'natural' style

Léon Blum in his study of *Stendhal et le Beylisme* speaks of the precocity of the young Henri Beyle and of the speed with which he found himself as a writer. 'There is perhaps no other example of a formation so complete at the same age and involving so many aspects of the mind, of a self-awareness so lucid or of a personality so unique and carefully preserved.'[55] In saying this Blum is referring to Beyle's early letters and diaries and not to his unsuccessful attempts at drama or the alexandrines which he hammered out in order to train himself to write dramatic verse. If Beyle found himself so soon as a writer and took so long to find himself as an artist, it is partly because it took years for him to realise that what was true of writers such as Alfieri was also true of himself. It was impossible for him to write in a way which was lively, clear and dramatic unless he had the courage to 'be himself' and write in his own natural idiom.

What, however, do we mean when we talk about the 'natural idiom' of Beyle or, for that matter, anyone else? One answer is given in Tracy's *Grammaire*: it is the language which one commonly hears and speaks and which is 'associated intimately and completely' with one's most 'deeply rooted habits', the language in which one 'thinks immediately'.[56] This is no less true of the intellectual élite than of the people as a whole. For

the mass of the public reacts so powerfully on those who instruct it, by judging them, by offering them subjects of observation, by suggesting to them different points of view;...in short, it is so difficult to be to any great degree above the level of those with whom one lives and one is so strongly influenced by the state of enlightenment of one's country, that the very men who are made to surpass their compatriots have much to lose from anything that holds their compatriots back in a state inferior to that which they might have reached.[57]

To talk therefore of the natural idiom of any writer is to talk at the same time about the kind of audience he is addressing.

Beyle appears, as he grew older, to have to come to regard the latter assumption as axiomatic and it is partly for this reason that in later years when advocating a 'natural' style, he spoke several times of the intimate letter as one of the models that a writer should follow and which he himself preferred to any other. He tells us, for example, at the beginning of *Henry Brulard* that 'Since I seem to be good for nothing and not even able to write official letters to earn my living, I have had the fire lit and I am writing this without lying, I hope, and without deluding myself, for my own enjoyment as when writing to a friend. What will this friend's ideas be like in 1880? How different from my own?'[58] A year before, in a letter to Mme Jules Gaulthier, when criticising her attempts to write a romantic novel, he advised her to tell the story 'as if you were writing to me' and recommended as a model Marivaux's novel *La vie de Marianne*.[59]

Beyle's choice of the epistolary style as a model for the novelist appears to have been the consequence of many years of thought devoted to the whole problem of style. (The epistolary style, as Beyle understood it, is something quite different from the style of such epistolary novels as *La nouvelle Héloïse*.) It is obvious, and was obvious to Beyle, that the style of the intimate letter is only one of the virtually unlimited range of conventions to which the word 'natural' can be applied. The tone and idiom of a politician's speech, of verse written to a formal measure or of prose or verse recited from a stage can themselves be entirely appropriate to a given situation and 'be associated intimately and completely' with certain habits which the speaker and his audience share. It is possible to regard the style of Molière and even of Racine as natural in this way. Racine, according to the definition of Romanticism given in the *Racine et Shakspeare*, was in his own time himself a Romantic:

Romanticism is the art of presenting to a people the literary works which, given their habits and beliefs at the time, are capable of giving them the greatest possible pleasure.

Classicism, on the other hand, confronts them with the literature which gave the greatest possible pleasure to their great-grandparents...

I do not hesitate to affirm that Racine was a Romantic; he gave to the aristocrats of the court of Louis XIV a painting of the passions tempered by *the extreme dignity* which was then the fashion and which was such that a duke in 1670, even in the most tender effusions of paternal love, never failed to address his son as *Monsieur*.

This is why Pylade in *Andromaque* always addresses Oreste as *Seigneur*; and yet what greater friendship could there be between them!

The same dignity is nowhere to be found in the Greeks and it is because of this *dignity*, which chills us today, that Racine was a Romantic...[60]

One needs courage to be a Romantic for one has to *take chances*... It seems to me that the writer needs almost as much courage as the warrior; the one must no more think about the journalists than the other does about the hospital.[61]

The conventions to which the plays of the great seventeenth-century dramatists conform are at the same time literary and social. Moreover, they are not merely arbitrarily chosen and consciously held at the forefront of consciousness but resemble more the tacit assumptions on which intimate conversation depends.

For it to be possible for a dramatist to write for his audience in a natural-seeming way, it is necessary that there should exist already a certain understanding between them, an understanding such as that which there had been, so Beyle argued, in the time of Molière. Such an understanding, he came to believe in later life, was no longer possible and this was an inevitable consequence of the radical changes in French society brought about by the French Revolution. His own decision to become a novelist and to abandon his former ambition to be a dramatist was influenced, as he himself admits, by realising how far-reaching in their consequences these changes were. As he wrote in the title of an article of 1836 (intended originally as a preface to a new edition of the *Lettres* of the Président de Brosses), *La comédie est impossible*. The language used in the theatre, he argued here, was bound to be affected by the state of mind in which the new kind of audience came to the theatre:

> The Faubourg Saint-Germain [that is the old aristocracy] is afraid and has formed an alliance with the Church...As for the Third Estate, which is now so wealthy with its fine carriages and mansions in the Chaussée d'Antin, it is still accustomed to seeing courage only under a fine moustache. Unless one tells it at the top of one's voice: 'Listen, I am going to be witty', it fails to notice a single thing and it is capable of regarding a style which is simple as an insult to its dignity.
>
> Hence the impossibility of comedy in the present century.[62]

The boredom and enforced idleness of the courtiers of Louis XIV had at least, he argues, forced them to cultivate the art of conversation and had generally undermined their resistance to humour:

cette société avait été portée au même point de *détente pour le comique*, si j'ose m'exprimer ainsi...
(this society had been brought to the point at which its members were able *to feel at ease together and therefore laugh at the same things*, if I may put it this way)...[63]

Beyle's own contemporaries were far too preoccupied by class resentment, mutual rivalries and the preoccupations of business and politics, and literature had lost as a result 'the admirable effects of reciprocal sympathy in an extensive audience moved by the same emotion', as R. G. Collingwood has put it.[64] It could be objected perhaps that Beyle here lays too much emphasis on the part played by the courtiers of Versailles in the development of seventeenth-century taste, and underestimates the importance of the commercial and professional classes for whom Molière and Racine wrote most of their plays[65] and in which they themselves had been born. The general comparison he makes, however, between the theatre public of his own day and that of the *ancien régime* is, to say the very least, plausible, and whenever one thinks of the kind of entertainment provided in the best plays of each period, the comparison seems to be true. It helps us to explain, for example, why the wit of Musset's *Fantasio* or *Il faut qu'une porte soit ouverte ou fermée* is so different from that of the dramatist from whom one is often told he derives, the Marivaux of *La seconde surprise de l'amour* and *Le jeu de l'amour et du hasard*; why it is that Musset's characters seem to say: 'Listen, I am now being serious' and 'Now I am being witty.' The serious implication of what Marivaux offers as the lightest of entertainment is something that the audience is left to infer. Adultery, for example, is neither condemned nor condoned in his plays and both its comic and tragic possibilities as a theme are deliberately left unexploited.

The interest of *La comédie est impossible* does not, however, lie only in the truth – or likely truth – of the comparison Beyle makes between the theatre audiences of his own day and those of the eighteenth and seventeenth centuries. It lies also in the necessary relationship that he discerns between a way of writing and the kind of public the author addresses.[66] Beyle resembles Molière and the major writers of the seventeenth century in the importance he attaches to the social virtues, to literature seen as a social activity and to the possibilities of 'the art of pleasing'.

He is also free in this respect from the characteristically Romantic tendency to ignore or despise such considerations and to cultivate a non-conformity in keeping with a devotion to Nature with a capital N, with an intensive interest in the life of societies remote from one's own in space or time and with the dictates of artistic 'genius'. ('I am so tired of genius', the old-fashioned lady complains, in a play by Eugène Scribe.[67] 'I should so much like a little wit.')

Yet the paradox remains that in his own novels and in his conversation, from what we are told of it, Beyle was thought of by his own contemporaries as an eccentric, a blasphemer and a violator of most of the principles of good taste. The writer who had devoted so much thought to the ways of charming the public of his own day began to enjoy popularity more than half a century after he died. The paradox does not lie in his lack of success during his own lifetime. Beyle realised that any popular success he enjoyed would be in years to come, and his decision to write for a small number of unknown, isolated and sympathetic individuals – the 'Happy Few' to whom many of his books are dedicated – was a conscious decision made *en connaissance de cause*. 'I imagine that I may have a little success in 1860 or 1880', he wrote in his letter to Balzac two years before he died. The paradox lies rather in the simultaneous desire to win over an audience and play the rôle of public entertainer and his inability to do this except on his own terms. Beyle believed in the social virtues – or at least, in the degree of conformity necessary for strangers to communicate – but there is no evidence that he ever thought that they should take precedence over every other kind of virtue. He is never in his comments on *Le Misanthrope* an apologist for Philinte, the 'reasonable' conformist. In his *Racine et Shakspeare* furthermore, the seventeenth century's extreme preoccupation with the social virtues is something he positively deplores:

> All the subjects of Louis XIV prided themselves on imitating a certain model of elegance and good taste and Louis XIV was himself the god of this religion. There was *bitter laughter* when a man was seen to have made a mistake in his imitation of the model. The gaiety of the letters of Mme de Sévigné is nothing more in fact than this. In 1670 a man who allowed his imagination to run away with him would have been thought of not as amusing but mad.

Molière, a genius if ever there was one, was unfortunate enough to work for this society.

Aristophanes, on the other hand, undertook to entertain a society of amiable and happy-go-lucky people who sought their happiness *by every means*. Alcibiades, I have the impression, gave little thought to imitating anyone; he believed he was happy when he laughed and not when his pride was flattered by the thought that he had a great deal in common with someone like Lauzun, d'Antin, Villeroy or another of Louis XIV's favourite courtiers...[68]

Beyle's opinion of 'the contemporaries of Mme de Sévigné' is clearly very different in *La comédie est impossible*. Yet it is his judgment of this society, rather than the feelings and beliefs which had inspired the judgment, which have changed. At least, there is no glaring inconsistency between the views expressed in the above quotation and those that he develops here. 'The contemporaries of Mme de Sévigné', he writes, were not only able to 'laugh at the same things', and this whatever their social origin. They also 'shared a certain understanding of literary matters and in this respect had received the same education'.[69] The education they had received was one which gave them the immense advantage of not taking literature *too seriously*:

> True comedy, for our sins, is even less conceivable than before, now that we have political parties. We no longer think of literature as something to be taken lightly and enjoyed like a joke. It is now regarded with such esteem that the parties are longing to take it over; even the Government is meddling with it in the hope that we will return to the prudent moderate literature of the Empire.
>
> One could have hoped for something better from the descendants of the friends of Mme de Sévigné; but imagine what would happen if these gentlemen went to the theatre and saw for the first time, in a comedy which had just been written, the well-bred Dorante of *Le bourgeois gentilhomme*. They would think of it as an atrocious insult, an insult to be wiped out in blood.
>
> And it would be a waste of time for the poor dramatist to protest: 'But gentlemen, all I'm asking you is whether this character is true to life and whether or not you find him funny.'[70]

What Beyle had come to admire in the societies of the seventeenth and early eighteenth centuries was their freedom from the cares of personal ambition and, as a consequence of this, from the class hatreds of modern times. A man's career, in most classes of society, had been pre-determined at the time of his birth. There was little point in resenting the greater wealth or power of one's fellow-countrymen since there was little one could hope to change and little, consequently, for the powerful and wealthy to fear from those less fortunate than themselves. The upper classes of 1836 lived, by contrast, in constant fear of another Jacobin Terror. Personal ambition, the spirit of party and class resentment, Beyle argues, made it impossible for the theatre public to enjoy humour at its own expense.

Beyle's conclusions are optimistic. He believes that now that the 'atrocious abuses' of the old order have been swept away, French society will be the first to recover its former frankness and gaiety. The essay ends, however, with an appeal to the contemporary reader:

> Meanwhile, kind reader, as the angry waves grow calmer, try to hate as little as possible and try not to be a hypocrite. I can understand why a poor devil who is the fifth son of the weaver of my village prefers any job to that of tilling the soil. To lie all day long is certainly less painful. Not only that, the lies he tells don't react on his heart, don't corrode it as they corrode yours. What the rascal utters aren't really lies but only words that he doesn't understand: he doesn't realise that he is robbing the man to whom he is speaking and that he deserves his contempt; but you, kind reader, who have enjoyed Voltaire's poem and Courier's pamphlets, you who have three horses in your stable, how can you possibly agree to render your life dismal through foul hypocrisy?

It will only be when the reign of hatred and hypocrisy has come to an end that comedy will once again 'be possible'.

What is defined in *La comédie est impossible* are certain conditions on which a human community depends, one could almost say, for its existence as such. The community is one which Beyle sees as having existed among the French upper classes of the old régime and to whose return under a new dispensation he looks forward in years to come. No explicit reference is made to Beyle's own novels in the essay. Yet it describes also, I should like to suggest, the kind of reader for whom they are written.[71] Reading the essay can help us to understand the characteristic tone of the novels, the attitude to the reader, that is, which determines the nature of his style. It indicates the kind of audience with which he was able to 'be himself' and write in a 'natural'-

seeming way. It indicates too why Beyle should have attached so much importance to positive enjoyment as a criterion of literary value.

Le plus grand plaisir possible

Few of Beyle's readers can have failed to notice how often he talks of the enjoyment to be derived from literature, music and painting and it has even been objected that he talks about it far too much. Rémy de Gourmont, for example, maintained that it was this preoccupation with *le plaisir* which prevented him from being a serious literary critic:

There was no principle...to which Stendhal was more faithful than that of the greatest possible pleasure; it is also unfortunately the principle on which it is most difficult to found a literary doctrine which possesses the merits of good sense. Moreover, the idea of such a doctrine scarcely ever occurred to him; [in the *Racine et Shakspeare*] he merely sets out the purely personal reflections inspired by his impressions of the theatre.[72]

Stendhal has many more admirers today than when these remarks were written and much of his criticism which Gourmont could not have seen is now collected and in print. Yet the remarks which I have quoted have never, as far as I know, been challenged and few critics have commented on the fact that he usually tries to be clear about why and in what sense he is stressing enjoyment. We find this even when he is writing as a professional reviewer of work which has little interest for him and when he is explaining why it bores or repels him. Take, for instance, these comments in *The London Magazine* for February 1825 on *Monsieu le Préfet*, a political satire by the former prefect Baron Lamothe-Langon (I quote from the English translation of the time, the French original having been lost):

We cannot deny the author the merit of resemblance; but this resemblance is hideous. On reading *M. le Préfet* I experienced the disagreeable feeling of a profound but *impotent hatred*. Now impotent hatred destroys in an instant all literary pleasure. For this reason I suppose it is that a mixture of politics is in France fatal to a work of literature. If the author of this romance, which I beg of you to read, had had the least dramatic genius, he would have perceived the necessity of *softening* the abject servility of his characters.

Even in Byron's *Beppo* and *Don Juan*, which he warmly admired, Beyle was disturbed by what he saw as an implicit appeal to the reader's feelings of 'hatred and misery':

> Lord Byron's humour is bitter in *Childe Harold*; it is the anger of youth; it is scarcely more than ironical in *Beppo* and *Don Juan*. But this humour does not bear too close an examination; instead of gaiety and light-heartedness, hatred and misery lie beneath.[73]

One answer to Gourmont would be to say that the enjoyment Beyle sought in literature was, as it happens, of the deepest kind and that he was unusually aware of the temptations to bitterness and despair which can make the sympathetic reading of a novel or poem intolerable.

Both of these passages were written between 1823 and 1830, a period immediately following the emotional crisis described in the *Souvenirs d'égotisme*, after Beyle had left or rather wrenched himself away from Milan and the house of Mathilde Dembowski. The preoccupation which is common to these passages is one, however, which had been with him from late adolescence at least. It scarcely need be added that if these reflections are those of a literary critic, they are in no way exclusively literary. As so often in Beyle's criticism, the literary judgments are all the more telling for being at the same time those of a man reflecting on his own experience.

A proneness to feelings of hatred and misery is one of the most obvious characteristics of the young Henri Beyle and was to remain one of his most vivid memories of his childhood and early youth. 'At one time', he writes in *Henry Brulard*,

> when I used to hear of the innocent joys and follies of childhood or the happiness of early youth, which, one is told, is the only genuine happiness a man ever knows, my heart would contract. This is something I never experienced; and what is more, this period of my life was one of constant misery and hatred, of a constant and always impotent desire for vengeance. The reasons for my misery can be summed in a few words: I was never allowed to play with a child of my own age. And my relatives, bored by their social isolation, honoured me with their constant attention.[74]

Beyle's disposition does not seem to have changed after he had escaped from the claustrophobic atmosphere of his home in Grenoble. The one member of the family circle whom Beyle was later to remember with affection, his maternal grandfather Henri Gagnon, wrote to him when he was twenty-two and engaged in a business enterprise in Marseille: 'The contact you have had with one or two men has inspired in you a contempt and disrespect which are far too general. Normally one is pleased to come across honest men who can behave generously; but I feel that you, my dear boy, like nothing better than to discover an act of treachery or some other horror.'[75] The pleasure he derived from such discoveries was bound to be of an equivocal kind and he himself noted in his diary a few years later how much he was the victim of this habit. 'How is it', he asks, 'that I may not give a damn for a sum of twenty-five louis that I've lent and yet my heart is shaken with anger and I'm in a rage if someone tries to outwit me and get out of paying me back? And yet no one proves better than I do that the man who is in a rage is the first to be punished.'[76] One can only assume that it was because of the circumstances of his early life and the fine and easily exasperated sensibility, which was due as much to physiological as to other causes, that the temperament revealed in his writings resembles less that of his beloved Montesquieu than that of his younger contemporary, Flaubert. I say temperament, for Beyle's character and intelligence – what he made of his temperament – were clearly very different.

It is interesting to recall that to Rémy de Gourmont it was Flaubert who seemed the superior artist and whose art seemed the incarnation of a superior wisdom, much though he admired the intelligence he found in Beyle's writings as a whole. 'Stendhal', he writes, while 'more personal' is somehow 'less complete' than Flaubert. 'He gives little satisfaction which is not a satisfaction of the mind, whereas Flaubert delights both our intelligence and our sensibility for the plastic beauty of his style matches the spiritual beauty of his thought.'[77] It is also significant that the Flaubert he admired was the Flaubert of the later novels and for the reasons given in his essay entitled *Flaubert et la bêtise humaine*: '*Bouvard et Pécuchet* amuses us (and I am using the word in its deepest sense) as much as *Don Quixote* amused our ancestors and still amuses many of our contemporaries. It is perhaps the book of books, the book for the strong, for it contains much bitterness and the taste of nothingness which it leaves (*son goût de néant*) goes straight to the heart.'[78] The standards by which

Beyle is found wanting are presumably therefore those set by Flaubert's narrative of the comic adventures of his two indefatigable autodidacts engaged in a quest for knowledge which is doomed from the very outset. The vision of life which Gourmont offers as the most bracing and realistic is one which springs from a belief in the sheer futility of most if not all of human endeavour.[79]

It is true that both the vision and the belief correspond to a mood with which few people with good memories could honestly say they were unfamiliar. Yet as the expression of a consistently held or consistently tenable philosophy of life, *Bouvard et Pécuchet* doesn't exist, for all its magnificent slapstick humour and despite the wonderful plastic beauty of its style. If all endeavour is futile and all knowledge unattainable, how can we know even this and what is the point of making this clear with such meticulous and pondered art? It is this which may lead one to conclude that Gourmont's idea of 'strength' and 'bitterness' was a poor idea, an idea which he himself was incapable of taking with complete seriousness. Despite its truculence and the momentary conviction with which Gourmont, like Flaubert, is able to express it, it is something very different from the 'strong pessimism' which Nietzsche, Beyle's self-proclaimed 'posthumous son', looked for in Greek tragedy: 'A penchant of the mind for what is hard, terrible, evil, dubious in existence, arising from a plethora of health, plenitude of being...Could it be, perhaps, that the very feeling of superabundance created its own kind of suffering: a temerity of penetration, hankering for the enemy (the worth-while enemy) so as to prove its strength, to experience at last what it means to fear something?'[80]

To return to what Beyle himself was looking for when he spoke of the enjoyment which art can give and of the *'impotent hatred* which can destroy in an instant all literary pleasure', one can find no better illustration of what he meant or, at least, of what he was able to imagine, than the art of his own novels. It may be useful here to anticipate what should properly fall into the argument of a later chapter and consider for a moment the penultimate chapter of *Le rouge et le noir*, in which we are told of Julien Sorel's meditations as he waits for death in the condemned cell having been accused 'justly', he confesses, of an 'atrocious crime'. The chapter provides ample evidence of Beyle's ability to understand the feelings of misery and impotent hatred of which he so often speaks in other writers. Julien admits that he has been justly condemned, but asks himself whether the word justice can ever have any other than a conventional meaning:

'There is no such thing as *natural law*: the word is only an antiquated piece of humbug worthy of the advocate general who hunted me down the other day and whose ancestors were enriched by property confiscated by Louis XIV. There is only *law* when a man is prevented from doing something by fear of punishment. Before the *law* exists, there is nothing *natural* at all except the strength of the lion or the need of any cold or hungry creature. There is only *need* in fact...No, the men one honours are only scoundrels who have had the good fortune not to be caught in the act. The prosecutor whom society sets on to me was enriched by a crime...I have committed a murder and am justly condemned, but apart from this, a man like Valenod who found me guilty is a hundred times more harmful to society.'

'Despite his avarice then', Julien added sadly but without anger, 'my father is no worse than any of them. He has never loved me and now I have added the final touch to his displeasure by dishonouring him. To think of his only son condemned to a humiliating death! His fear of being without money, his exaggerated belief in human malevolence, which is really what we mean when we talk of avarice, shows him one prodigious source of consolation and security: a sum of three or four hundred louis which I shall be able to leave him. One Sunday after dinner he will show his gold to all those who envy him in Verrières. "At the price", his look will say, "which of you would not be delighted to have a son sent to the guillotine?"'

This passage has been taken by one of Beyle's most gifted critics, and one of the first in France to champion his reputation, as an expression of Beyle's philosophy of life and a striking instance of his own intelligence:

Julien's intelligence is of the first order; it is quite simply that of Stendhal himself: penetrating and tormented, lucid as an algebraic theorem and as biting and acid as a formal indictment.[81]

'Penetrating', 'tormented' and 'lucid' describe it well and it is true that Beyle never pretends that Valenod or Julien's father are any different from what Julien sees them as being. Nor does he ever appear to have thought of 'natural law' as anything other than the Hobbesian kind of which Julien speaks. Yet is this an example of 'intelligence'? Did Beyle himself think of it as such? If these facts and beliefs were to correspond to the *whole* of truth about human life, a thoughtful and generous mind would have either to turn his back on the truth or bring his life to an end in despair. The 'philosophy', Beyle goes on to say, to which Julien's life and circumstances have led him is not just pessimistic but suicidal:

This philosophy might have been true, but it was such as to make one long for death. Five long days went by in this way. He was polite and gentle towards Mathilde, whom he could see was tormented by the keenest jealousy. One evening he thought seriously of taking his own life. His spirits were oppressed by the profound unhappiness into which he had been thrown by the departure of Mme de Rênal. Nothing gave him pleasure, whether in the real world or the world of the imagination. The lack of exercise began to impair his health and to give him the weak overwrought character of a young German student. He lost that masculine self-respect which is able to dispel with a vigorous oath certain uncongenial thoughts by which the minds of the unhappy are assailed.

Julien's meditations bring home to us the full extent of what he has to endure as he waits for death in a damp cell visited every day by a woman he no longer loves. His mortification and despair are unendurable, though *how* unendurable we are made to understand by his efforts to overcome them or rather to understand their true cause and what it is he is deprived of and needs:

'To live in isolation! What torment!'
'I am becoming insane and unjust', thought Julien striking his brow. 'I am isolated in this cell; but I have not lived in *isolation* on this earth; the thought of duty has always given me strength. The duty which, rightly or wrongly, I have always forced myself to accept has been like the trunk of a solid tree against which I leaned during the storm; I wavered, I was shaken. After all, I was only a man...but I wasn't swept away.
It must be the damp air of this cell which makes me think of isolation.'

This consolation, though real (for Julien's self-imposed challenges have obviously been real as well) is less effective than the consolation which comes from realising what has given him most happiness, what it is of which he is now deprived and what it really is therefore that he now has to endure and suffer:

'And why curse hypocrisy and be still more hypocritical? I'm not feeling like this because of death or this cell but because Mme de Rênal isn't here. If I had to live for weeks on end hidden in the cellars of her house in Verrières in order to see her, would I complain?'

It is at this point that the mood changes and that we realise how in longing passionately to go on living, Julien has been released not only from despair and self-loathing but from the horror which the prospect of death had come to hold for him:

'So *I* am going to die at the age of twenty-three. Give me five more years to live with Mme de Rênal...

This is what makes me feel isolated and not the absence of a just, good, all-powerful God without malevolence or the thirst for vengeance.

Ah! if he existed...Alas, I would fall at his feet. "Death is what I have deserved", I would say, "but God in your greatness, goodness, indulgence, give me back the woman I love."'

By this time it was late at night. After an hour or two of peaceful sleep, Fouqué arrived.

Julien felt strong and resolute like a man who sees clearly into his own mind.

It is stating the obvious to say that the note on which the chapter and the novel end is not one of misery or hatred. Nor has it anything in common with the mood of *Bouvard et Pécuchet*. If the reader experiences when he finishes the novel a sense of enjoyment and invigoration, it is an enjoyment different from the grim 'amusement' which Gourmont derived from the latter novel. It has in fact far more in common with Nietzsche's 'strong pessimism'. The novelist and the reader follow the hero into an appalling trap in which he is unable to escape from brutally disconcerting truths and at the same time deprived of what he most wants and needs as a man. Julien is shaken to the point at which a self-respecting bracing of the nerves and a manly oath are no longer enough to keep away the horror and despair he has come to feel. Yet the point of the exercise for the novelist and the reader is not simply to enjoy the thrills of a nightmare vision. It is to think about the ways in which horror and despair might be confronted, tracked down and overcome in the one place in which they can be fought and on the only terms on which the fight is possible: namely in the imagination and with the weapons of the imagination. For a man whose intelligence and imagination were less quick and resilient than Julien's would probably have been incapable of the victory he wins over himself. This is something on the novelist's part – though not, of course, on Julien's – akin to Nietzsche's 'temerity of penetration, hankering for the enemy (the worth-while enemy)' and it is something alien to Flaubert's and Gourmont's would-be candid and defiant, though necessarily incomplete or insincere, surrender to horror and despair.

It is unlikely that Beyle's remarks on the kind of enjoyment which art and literature can offer will make much sense to the casual reader unless he appreciates how clear Beyle was in his own mind from an early age about the *usefulness* of art. However much he may have been bored and irritated by the moralising cant of his own contemporaries, he never in reaction took up the understandably extreme stance adopted by those who, later in the century, were to proclaim that art is by its very nature *useless*, existing in a world of its own, and that this is its principal justification. *Si la comédie est utile* is the characteristic title of an essay on Molière's *L'école des femmes* written in 1811 and in it the aim of comedy is described explicitly as 'showing up for the benefit of each society what is ridiculous in the bad habits which prevent them from achieving happiness'.[82] *Le bonheur*, the full uninhibited enjoyment of life is the end which, for Beyle, art must serve and the function of comedy as such is to laugh us out of whatever it is which holds us back from such enjoyment:

> It requires a certain strength of mind in a man for him to be able to understand what impedes or advances his happiness and not to have tears brought to his eyes by the thought of the extreme importance that this has for him, tears which can blur his vision. It often happens that when one is talking to a woman about what goes to make up her happiness, she begins by not understanding you and then, when she has, she will burst into tears simply because she has at last understood that she too could be unhappy. Thus you find that you have been unable to hold her attention; at first, she was unable to understand what you were saying and then, when she did, she was too overcome to be able to reason or judge.
>
> Moreover, in order to persuade the bourgeois from Auxerre whom I mentioned earlier that such and such a thing is contrary to his happiness, it would be necessary to present a *tableau* of the plight into which habits similar to his own have led the hero of one's comedy. This spectacle will certainly not delight his heart; he will not want

to come back to it and he will simply dismiss it from his mind like a bad memory.

I conclude then that this method will have to be left to the writers of sermons, if there are any who are good enough to carry it off with the necessary degree of conviction.

It remains then *to show up for the benefit of each society what is ridiculous in the bad habits which prevent them from achieving happiness.*

Arnolphe [in *L'école des femmes*] could have been happy. He is wealthy and he is certainly no fool. During his youth he has cuckolded many men and he has always laughed at all the absurdities he has come across. He is now forty-five years old but he still has plenty of sap. Five or six paths might have led him to happiness, but he stubbornly insists on carrying out his pet scheme of marrying and yet *never being deceived.*

Molière could, if he liked, have shown to the Arnolphes in real life all the miseries that the pursuit of this chimera are likely to entail. He could have shown us Arnolphe dishonoured or even an Arnolphe led to the scaffold or blowing out his brains.

What he did was to make Arnolphe ridiculous and to allow us only a glimpse of his unhappiness.

The same is true of Orgon [in *Tartuffe*] whom he shows as ridiculous and not unhappy.

Beyle is perhaps the most acute and penetrating critic of Molière who has ever written, though it is unfortunate for his own reputation that his best remarks were made in the notebooks in which he developed his ideas rather than in the *Racine et Shakspeare,* by which his work as a critic is principally known and in which we are often merely given the conclusions which he had reached by the age of forty. He is aware, as for example, Bergson seems not to be, in his own study of *Le rire,* of the *tact* which is an essential feature of Molière's humour and which normally prevents it from being of the merely satirical, crudely punitive kind to which all humour, if we are to believe Bergson, somehow conforms by its very nature. He is also a remarkably perceptive critic of Molière's failings as a comic dramatist, particularly in his notes written two years before *Si la comédie est utile,* on Molière's strange and uncharacteristic *Georges Dandin* – a play, incidentally, whose humour Bergson analyses as if it were of the same kind as the rest of Molière's dramatic *oeuvre.* Beyle notes how little the audience is left to learn, after the first few scenes, of Dandin's, the deceived husband's plight and how much the play is taken up with the prolonged spectacle of Dandin's ordeal. Dandin, the simple-minded but wealthy peasant, has married the daughter of a poor nobleman and is alternatively deceived by his wife and snubbed, patronised and reprimanded by his wife's doting snobbish parents. What, Beyle asks, could have led Dandin to contract such an impossible marriage? Vanity? Perhaps, but poor Dandin, when the play begins, has no vanity left:

> Molière, in short, for reasons best known to him and which I am unable to discuss, shows us:
> 1. Dandin when he is already repentant.
> 2. Dandin with no escape holes left (*les trous bouchés*). He thus deprives himself of a host of what might have been comic situations.[83]

Beyle, of course, might have added that often the audience, or at least part of the audience, does in fact go on laughing right through to the end of the play, though not presumably if it is looking at Dandin with any degree of fellow-feeling.

Beyle's observations on comedy and on the feelings of misery and hatred which can make any deep or sustained enjoyment of literature impossible are an obvious expression of the beliefs and outlook which he himself described as *Beylisme*, and to say this brings us back to the problems touched on earlier in the present study. Is it true to say that pleasure is always what men pursue, not only by choice but by definition in that whatever we desire is always, as far as we are concerned, desirable, irrespective of whether it may prove to be satisfying? Is pleasure the only possible measure of goodness or the good? The English reader will probably be familiar with the objections raised against both of these beliefs by G. E. Moore in the *Principia Ethica*, objections which perhaps deserve more serious attention than those of Beyle's own French contemporaries. Moore rejects both the 'naturalistic fallacy' which identifies the simple predicate 'good' with something different, such as happiness or whatever is regarded as 'desirable' (as in the system of Bentham and John Stuart Mill) and 'metaphysical ethics' which, similarly, assume that good actually means something else: namely, in the system of Kant for example, compatibility with ultimate realities and with obligations imposed on us by universal authority. It is impossible in a study of this length to do justice either to the beliefs which Moore regards as fallacious or to the objections he and others have raised against them. But it may be enough in this context to point out that Beyle was not himself a systematic thinker or rather did not have a system to offer – which is different from saying that his thought was lacking in coherence, depth or consistency – and that Moore's objections do not necessarily apply to anything that he actually wrote. It can be brought against him that his admiration for the thought of Locke, Helvétius, Bentham and Tracy was, on the whole, uncritical, or, at least, that what he says in their favour does not begin to answer the more serious kind of objection that has been brought against them. Yet he took from them what he needed and did not, at least in any of his writings which survive, place himself in a position where he needed to believe or pretend that 'good' or 'desirable' or any of its synonyms are merely different words meaning exactly the same thing. Nor, since Moore mentions this fallacy too,[84] did he identify pleasure and the objects of pleasure, or the experience that is anticipated or enjoyed and the enjoyable feelings which may be indistinguishable from but are only part of that experience.[85] This, however, is merely to defend Beyle's thought, as it evolved, against possible objections and there are more positive reasons for hoping that what he wrote about art and ethics may one day be recognised as of interest even to philosophers as such.

'Le beau idéal' in painting

'Beauty is merely the promise of happiness', Beyle wrote in his *History of Painting in Italy* of 1817. The definition is one which Nietzsche compares in chapter 6 of his *Genealogy of Morals* with Kant's argument that what is beautiful is what gives us 'disinterested pleasure':

Disinterested! Compare with this definition that other one, framed by a real spectator and artist, Stendhal...Here we find the very thing which Kant stresses exclusively in the aesthetic condition rejected and cancelled. Which is right, Kant or Stendhal? – When our aestheticians tirelessly rehearse, in support of Kant's view, that the spell of beauty enables us to view even *nude* females 'disinterestedly' we may be allowed to laugh a little at their expense. The experiences of artists in this delicate matter are rather more 'interesting'; certainly Pygmalion was not entirely devoid of aesthetic feeling. Let us honour

our aestheticians all the more for the innocence reflected in such arguments – Kant, for example, when he descants on the peculiar character of the sense of touch with the ingenuousness of a country parson...

I do not myself feel competent to judge whether Beyle's writings on art have received the recognition from writers on aesthetics they deserve. But I suspect that they have not and that once again his friend Mérimée's judgment of his competence in these matters is the one that has on the whole prevailed:

> He appreciates the great masters from a French outlook, that is from a literary point of view. He examines the paintings of the Italian school as if they were dramas. This is still the way we judge in France where we have neither the sentiment of form nor an innate taste for colour. To love and understand form and colour calls for a particular type of sensibility and prolonged practice...[86]

Another acquaintance, nevertheless, Eugène Delacroix, though on the whole he despised the amateurish opinions on painting of men of letters, copied out in his notebooks extracts from the *History of Painting in Italy* and in an article on Michelangelo,[87] described Beyle's description of the *Last Judgment* as among the most striking and poetic he knew. He also recommended warmly Beyle's chapter on Leonardo's *Last Supper*.[88]

My purpose here is not, however, to consider Beyle's past or possible future influence on others but the growth and nourishment of the sensibility and intelligence which are manifest in the art of his novels. Beyle's writings on the other creative arts have no immediately obvious relevance to his education as a novelist. And if we say that it has, this may sound as if we are agreeing with Mérimée that what he saw in the paintings by which he was moved and fascinated was not colour and form but only stories and poems. My own contention is that Nietzsche and Delacroix were right to attribute to Beyle a truly professional eye, that of what Nietzsche calls a 'real spectator and artist', and that this is apparent particularly in what he says of *technique*.

'No one loved Virgil more than Dante and nothing resembles the *Aeneid* less than the *Inferno*. Michelangelo was deeply struck by the art of antiquity and nothing is more opposed to it than what he created himself.'[89] It has been said that the highest tribute that one true artist can pay to another is to admire or even worship and then do otherwise. This could certainly be said of Beyle. In any case, if he learned from the technique of Correggio, it was not by including in his novels descriptions of heads or poses which would sound like detailed descriptions of one of Correggio's paintings. (There is only one detail specified, for example, in the remark in *La chartreuse de Parme* concerning Fabrice's 'Correggio-like physique':[90] he has 'a certain expression in his eyes of tender voluptuousness'. A novelist like Zola is far closer to painting in this sense and the description, for example, in *La curée* of carriages on a showery sunny day driving through the Bois de Boulougne reads like a sketch for an Impressionist painting.) Beyle's understanding of technique is apparent in what he says of it as a means to a particular end:

Everyone realises that when a woman is waiting to see her lover she will not wear the same hat as when she sees her confessor.

Each great painter has looked for those devices which would convey to the soul that *particular impression* which was for him the one main purpose of painting.

It would be absurd to ask the connoisseurs to point out the end which any painter seeks to achieve [*le but moral*]. But, to make up for this, they excel at distinguishing the hard abrupt strokes of a Bassano from the melting colours of Correggio. They have learned that Bassano can be recognised by the brilliance of his greens, that he can't draw feet and throughout his life repeated a dozen of the same familiar subjects; that Correggio goes in for graceful foreshortening effects, that his faces are never in the least severe or forbidding, while his eyes have a celestial voluptuousness and that his paintings look as if they are covered by six inches of crystal...

The draughtsmanship or the contours of the muscles, the shadows and the draperies, the imitation of light and of local colours have all a particular tonality in the *style* of each painter, that is if he has a *style*. In the work of the true artist, a tree will have one kind of green if it throws a shadow over the pool in which Leda is playing with the swan and another if robbers are taking advantage of the obscurity of the forest in order to cut a traveller's throat.[91]

Technique, style and convention are seen as appropriate also to the spirit of the age, in so far as this is determined by the state of existing knowledge and belief, the ways in which an individual or a community are in the habit of defending themselves and the existing political dispensation. *The History of Painting in Italy* has been described as the first of his Romantic manifestos and it is because of the closely argued development of the idea of the relativity of style and taste that it has an imoprtant place in the history of ideas. Taste and style are not, however, the only terms that Stendhal uses. The key term in the development of his main argument is *'le beau idéal'* or 'ideal beauty', as it has somewhat inadequately to be rendered in English, and Books 5 and 6 of the *History* are devoted to a comparison between ideal beauty in antiquity and today. The imitation of antiquity, with its veneration for athletic prowess and the visible virtues of the warrior or wise counsellor, is seen as inappropriate in an age when women are no longer the mere servants of their husbands and when elegance and amiability have taken precedence over every other human quality. As Beyle was to put it in his *Salon* of 1827: 'Beauty in each century is simply then *the expression of the qualities which are useful at the time...*'[92] He is saying to the contemporary painter, in other words, what he was to say also to the contemporary dramatist in the *Racine et Shakspeare*: it is absurd to imitate the art that satisfied the different needs of a different generation or epoch. Ideal beauty today is bound to take another form.

In the section on the *History of Painting in Italy* in his *Stendhal romancier*, M. Maurice Bardèche has suggested that what Stendhal is saying in effect is that, given the complexity of the character and social habits of modern man, painting and sculpture can no longer express them in either their real or their ideal forms[93] and that the *History* is addressed not so much to the contemporary painter as to the contemporary novelist. Certainly, no contemporary painter or sculptor is hailed as an evident genius comparable to Michelangelo or Leonardo, and among his older and younger contemporaries only Ingres, David and Delacroix seem momentarily to have fired his enthusiasm,[94] David, interestingly enough because of his rejection after 1780 of the *niais* style of Boucher and Fragonard and his bold return to the imitation of antiquity. The historical appropriateness of this 'revolution' in style is something that the present study has already touched on.[95]

M. Bardèche argues that the 'amiable man' of modern civilisation, as Beyle saw him in the memoirs of Bezenval or the Prince de Ligne, was *the* hero not only of modern times but for Beyle personally and without reservations – at least, M. Bardèche doesn't mention any. For Beyle he was also, we are told, an ideal representation of himself. It is this interpretation that we may find more difficult to accept, particularly when it leads M. Bardèche to analyse what he sees as profound contradictions in Beyle between the idealist and the realist painting his contemporaries as they really were and at the same time knowing that passion can transform a man utterly and give him 'a new goal in life, a new way of going after happiness which will make him forget any others and make him forget any habit he has formed'.[96] Beyle is certainly aware of how much the life within us can astonish us and make nonsense of our ideals and it is not he, surely, but M. Bardèche who has made the ideal of the modern amiable man seem somehow final and supreme. It is obviously an ideal to which the heroes of his novels conform on occasion only and they are capable when under pressure of acting with animal-like ferocity and decisiveness. In the *History of Painting* itself, moreover, the ideal is described, on the whole, neutrally, or rather with a half-serious, half-amused respect;[97]

> If ever we meet Socrates or Epictetus in the Elysian fields, we will tell them something that will shock them considerably: that a great character for us is not what makes the happiness of private life.
> Leonidas, who is so great when he traces the inscription: 'Traveller, go and say to Sparta', etc. could have been and I shall go further and say certainly was an insipid lover, husband and friend.[98]

The subject of Beyle's *History*, however, is painting in Italy during a period far closer to that of modern times and with far more obvious resemblances, particularly as far as Italy itself is concerned. And it is clear that Beyle is capable of seeing the great painters of the Renaissance and wrote as if his contemporaries might see them too as being, like Shakespeare, still very much alive. To write or paint in a way which satisfies modern needs by no means excludes an ability to respond to and learn from the art and literature of the past, and in the last chapter of the *History*, Beyle predicts that now that the age of mere elegant mockery is over – that is the age of Pope and Voltaire – men will learn to treat gay things with gaiety, serious things seriously and a great man as truly great. It is then that Michelangelo will come back into his own.

It is in the portrait of the lonely, embittered Abbé Pirard in

Le rouge et le noir, passionately austere and devout and yet helplessly drawn to the young Julien Sorel, and in the chapters describing Julien's own confrontation with the realities of death in the condemned cell that we may be reminded of what Beyle had written both on the overwhelming effect and the technique of Michelangelo's *Last Judgment* as he stood looking up at it in the Sistine Chapel noting down his immediate impressions.[99] After a detailed description of each of the figures he concludes:

> In Michelangelo, as in Dante, one's soul is chilled by the excess of seriousness. The absence of any rhetorical device adds considerably to this impression. We see the face of a man who has just seen something which has struck him with horror.
>
> Dante tries to arouse the interest of men whom he assumes to be unhappy. He does not, like the French poets, describe external objects. His one device is to excite sympathy for the emotions by which he is possessed. It is never the object he shows us but the impression it produces on his heart.
>
> Possessed by divine fury like that of a prophet in the Old Testament, the pride of Michelangelo rejects all sympathy. He is saying to mankind: 'Think of your own interest. Here is the God of Israel come to you in all his vengeance.'[100]

It is in the portraits of Stendhal's heroines and young men that we may be reminded of what he has written of Correggio. Yet between Michelangelo, Veronese and Correggio there is 'nothing in common'.[101] M. Bardèche talks of the contradictions in Beyle's aesthetic principles and practice as a novelist. I would suggest as an alternative to this view that the range and flexibility of imaginative response for which the novels are remarkable corresponds to that which we find in *The History of Painting in Italy*.

'Le beau idéal' in music

That Beyle borrowed directly in *The History of Painting*, and without acknowledgement, from a number of sources, principally Luigi Lanzi's *Storia pittoresca dell'Italia* of 1792 and Vasari's *Lives of the Painters*, is well known. So too is the fact that his first published work, the *Lives of Haydn, Mozart and Metastasio*, is, for the most part, a word-for-word translation from Giuseppe Carpani's *Letters on Haydn*. Beyle chose to describe himself as a 'dilettante' where music and art were concerned, and his outrageous plagiarism and preposterous choice of pseudonyms have discouraged those who look no further than a man's professed valuation of himself from taking either his art criticism or his music criticism seriously. Yet even Hector Berlioz, who, in many ways, reminds one almost uncannily of his fellow-Dauphinois – both passionately loved Shakespeare, reacted contemptuously against the academicism and provincialism of Paris and preferred to make utter fools of themselves rather than timidly following a prescribed model – even Berlioz regarded Beyle as an impostor. In chapter 35 of his *Memoirs* we are given a glimpse of the Consul from Civita Vecchia driving through a Roman carnival, 'a little man with a round stomach and a mischievous smile trying to look serious' and Berlioz adds in a footnote that this is 'M. Beile, or Beyle or Baile, who has written a *Life of Rossini* under the pseudonym of Stendhal and the most irritating stupidities on music for which he believed that he had some sort of feeling.'

As a music critic certainly, Beyle was less influential than in his *History of Painting in Italy* and none of his lives of the composers, not even the *Life of Rossini* of 1824, brought recognition to neglected masterpieces. The success of the latter volume was due almost certainly to that of Rossini himself and those composers who badly needed recognition in France – Beethoven notably and the young Berlioz – had little or nothing to thank him for. Berlioz's extreme irritation at Beyle could possibly be due to this latter circumstance more than any other, for despite Beyle's qualified admiration for Rossini,[102] he could easily be taken for one of the 'dilettanti' whose lionizing of Rossini in the 1820s prevented far better music from being heard and whom Berlioz dreamed of running through with a red-hot poker or blowing sky high by means of a well-placed mine during a performance of Rossini in the *Théâtre Italien*.[103]

Beyle's first-hand experience of music was more limited than we might imagine from reading his music criticism, and Professor Coe has pointed out, for example, that while warmly recommending *The Magic Flute* and insisting that it should be heard in the original version and not in the travesty of it performed in France, he had almost certainly never heard the original version himself.[104] Yet the experience of listening to Cimarosa and Mozart – above all perhaps the Mozart of *Le Nozze di Figaro* –

seems to have been among the happiest and most moving memories of his life and there is no reason to assume that he was not perfectly candid when he asked for his love of Mozart, Cimarosa and Shakespeare to be commemorated on his tomb. Rossini, however much Beyle may have enjoyed his music and however fascinating he may have found him as the perfect living example of the Italian *maestro*, formed by the most individualistic, least impartial and most attentive music lovers in the world, is repeatedly shown to be inferior to Mozart, both in the *Life of Rossini* and in the reviews of productions of his work that Beyle wrote during the 1820s for the *Journal de Paris*. And in the various tributes that he pays to Mozart, we can perhaps, as in what he has said of Michelangelo and Correggio, find the clue to certain effects of his novels.

Both in *Le rouge et le noir* and *La chartreuse de Parme*, Beyle apologises for interrupting the story with the details of political intrigue. His apology in both novels is couched in almost identical terms:

Politics...are a stone tied round the neck of literature which drown it in less than six months. Politics, amidst the interests of the imagination, are like a pistol shot in the middle of a concert. This noise is ear-rending without being energetic. It clashes with every other instrument...

(*Le rouge et le noir*, book 2, ch. 23)

Beyle might have written: 'in the middle of an opera'. As an epigraph to chapter 6 of book 1, in which Mme de Rênal and the youthful Julien Sorel begin unconsciously to fall in love with one another, we are given two lines from an aria by the passionate little Cherubino in *Le Nozze di Figaro*. The epigraph is plainly only a hint and one of the great, if obvious, lessons that Beyle learned from Mozart was that music is capable of saying far more than the written or spoken word:

One's first reflection on hearing *Figaro* is that the composer, dominated by his sensibility, has transformed into veritable passions the somewhat light predilections which in Beaumarchais occupy the amiable inhabitants of the Chateau d'Aguas-Frescas. Beaumarchais's Count Almaviva desires Suzanne and nothing more. He is far from feeling the passions which breathe in

     Vedrò mentr'io sospiro
     Felice un seno mio!

and in the duet

     Crudel! perchè finora?

...In the play, one feels that the attraction of the little page for Rosina could become more serious. But her state of mind, her sweet melancholy and her reflections on the share of happiness which destiny affords us; in other words, all the agitation which precedes the birth of great passions, are brought out infinitely more by Mozart than by the French dramatist. There are almost no words to express this state of mind and it is perhaps one which music can render far better than words.[105]

The deliberately prosaic style of the novels, the lack of declamation or of what Beyle called *emphase* are like a constant implicit acknowledgement of the limitations of prose as a medium. The lesson of Mozart in this respect was the same as that of the great Italian painters.

And yet, paradoxically, a novelist's prose can hint at and evoke what it is unable to present directly or explicitly, and this more successfully than prose or verse in the theatre where there is so much to impede the imagination and confine it to the visible realities of the stage. Perhaps the most interesting remark of all that Beyle makes concerning the nature of music in general is the one which also helps us to understand why he should have eventually chosen the novel as the only possible medium for what he had to convey:

Why is music so consoling to misery? Because, in an obscure fashion and one which in no way offends our amour-propre, it induces us to believe in tender pity. This art can change the sterile grief of the sufferer into the grief which is that of regret; it depicts men as being less hard, it brings tears to the eyes, it brings back the happiness of the past in a way that the sufferer might have thought impossible.

The main disadvantage of comedy is that the characters who make us laugh seem far too dry and lacking in emotion to sadden the more tender side of our nature. The spectacle of suffering would make us forget to think of our superiority to those at whom we laugh; this explains the charm for some people of a good comic opera and why it is superior to a good comedy: a good comic opera is the most astonishing combination of pleasures. Imagination and tenderness are engaged at the same time as the wildest laughter.[106]

As a footnote to this footnote in *The History of Painting in Italy*, Beyle gives as an instance of this kind of opera Cimarosa's *I nemici generosi*.

Music can make us believe in 'tender pity' without offending our amour-propre. And in *The Life of Rossini*, developing an idea of Richard Payne Knight's,[107] he reminds the reader of how sometimes the power of Mozart's music is such that 'the image it presents to the imagination is extremely indistinct and, as a result, one feels suddenly as if one had been invaded and inundated by melancholy'.[108] This is a development of the earlier idea that, unlike painting, music 'carries us away, we do not judge it', whereas 'pleasure in painting is always preceded by a judgment'.[109] Beyle no doubt stresses too much the melancholy of Mozart's music. He claims, rather surprisingly, that Mozart was only ever gay twice during his whole musical career: in *Così fan tutte* and when Leporello in *Don Giovanni* delivers his message to the Commendatore.[110] What he says, none the less, of the shared feelings and freedom from the inhibiting distractions of vanity of any public to whom Mozart and Cimarosa appeal is similar, in one respect at least, to what he was to write in *La comédie est impossible* of the seventeenth century public of men and women who were able 'to feel at ease together' and 'laugh at the same things.' The modern would-be dramatist, Beyle argued, could hope to find such an audience again among the isolated individuals for whom he would have to write novels. It would not, I think, be misrepresenting him to say that if Molière, in this respect, was among the formative influences on his own art as a novelist, so too were Mozart and Cimarosa. To say that this is evident from the novels themselves would, in any case, have been for Beyle among the highest compliments one could have paid him.

4

The chronicler and historian

Beyle and Napoleon

It is for a historian to assess the value of Beyle's contribution to our knowledge of the past. This book is concerned with the ways in which, rightly or wrongly, he came to think of 'his place in time, his own contemporaneity'[1] and of the thinking and exploration that, without his knowing it, was to lead to the writing of his three major novels.

Unfortunately, historians have not always taken him sufficiently seriously even to examine what he tells us of his own age[2] – at least until recently. The best work on Beyle as a chronicler of the France and Italy of his day is M. Fernand Rude's *Stendhal et le pensée sociale de son temps* and M. H. F. Imbert's *Les métamorphoses de la liberté*, both of which appeared in 1967. Thanks to these and to the articles by M. Lucien Jansse on Beyle as an economist and political scientist,[3] we now know more than earlier admirers about the opinions he held, in so far as we know more exactly how they resembled and differed from those of his own contemporaries. We may be less inclined as a consequence to congratulate him merely on having anticipated our own opinions and we are in a better position to judge the truth of his insights and the nature and interest of his idea of history.

It is still probably common, none the less, to assimilate Beyle to Tolstoy in this respect and to attribute to the former a scepticism with regard to historical truth as such similar to that which is expressed and exemplified in *War and Peace*. Professor Henri Marrou, for example, has described the affinity between them in the following terms:

...when it was the present, the past was like the present that we are living at this very moment, lacking cohesion, confused, multiform unintelligible, a dense network of causes and effects, a field of forces infinitely complex that the consciousness of man, whether he be actor or witness, is unable to grasp in its authentic reality (there is no privileged observation point, at least not on this earth). We have to go back here to the example which has been the classical one ever since...Stendhal's Waterloo in *La chartreuse de Parme*, or even better (for Napoleon himself, according to Tolstoy, is as lost as Prince Andrei or Pierre Bezuhov), the Austerlitz and Borodino of *War and Peace*.[4]

Professor Marrou describes graphically what may seem at times like the impossible conditions in which the historian seeks to understand the truth. But neither Beyle nor Tolstoy leave the problem there. And despite Beyle's influence on Tolstoy,[5] their approach to history, and specifically the history through which Beyle lived as a public servant under Napoleon, is as divergent as their whole philosophy of life.

This is most obviously the case if we compare the ways in which each looked on the dominant figure of the age, 'the greatest figure the world has seen since Caesar',[6] as Beyle put it, and whom Tolstoy tells us was as unimportant as all so-called dominant men. For Tolstoy, there is a law according to which 'men concerned to take common action combine in such relations that the more directly they participate in performing the action, the less they can command and the more numerous they are, while the less they take any direct part in the work itself the more they command and the fewer they are in number'.[7] And the folly of Napoleon lay in his failing to understand this law; unlike his Russian adversary Kutuzov, who recognised his own inability, as a general, to influence events in any decisive way or even to know what was happening while a battle was being waged.

For Beyle, the difficulties of understanding events while they are unfolding and of influencing them decisively are not insuperable, and genius lies in realising this more quickly than other men. He nowhere suggests, for example, in the famous example of his Waterloo in *La chartreuse*, that Napoleon or Wellington were as unaware of what was happening on the battlefield as a whole as his innocent novice in the art of war,

Fabrice. Take this account, moreover, of Bonaparte's Italian campaign written in the same year as *La chartreuse*:

The principle on which a commander-in-chief works is absolutely the same as that of the thieves who, on a street corner, ensure that they will be three against one and a hundred yards away from a patrol of ten men. What does the patrol matter if it will take three minutes for it to reach the hapless victim of the theft?

Every time Napoleon cut a wing of the enemy army, he merely put himself in the position of being two against one...

Any other general of the day would have thought himself lost in Napoleon's position [in July 1796 after the retreat of Masséna from the Adige]; he, however, saw that the enemy by dividing, gave him a chance to throw himself between the two wings of the Austrian army and to attack them separately.

But he had to make an immediate decision; and if one can't do this, one isn't a general.

It is obvious, incidentally, why it is so easy to write in a perfectly reasonable way about war and to indicate the decisions that should have been taken, with the wisdom of hindsight.

It was necessary to avoid at any price allowing Wurmser to join up his forces at Quasdanowich on the Mincio, for then he would have been irresistible. Napoleon had the courage to raise the siege of Mantua and abandon 140 pieces of heavy artillery in the trenches, the only heavy cannon the army possessed.

He had the courage to reason as follows and to believe in his own argument: 'If I'm beaten, what use will my siege equipment be to me anyway? I shall have to abandon it at once. If I succeed in beating the enemy, I shall go back to Mantua and find my cannon waiting for me...'[8]

And compare this with Tolstoy on the same campaign:

The incompetence of his colleagues, the weakness and inanity of his rivals, the frankness of his falsehoods and his brilliant and self-confident mediocrity raise him to the head of the army. The brilliant quality of the soldiers of the army sent to Italy, his opponents' reluctance to fight and his own childish insolence and conceit secure him military glory...[9]

Beyle may be charged with giving in to a naïve mystique of the great leader in his writings on Napoleon, 'the only man he respected', as he wrote in a note for his own epitaph in the year of the Emperor's death. Yet the alternative to such a mystique may easily be merely another form of irrationalism such as that which led Tolstoy to attribute all the events of Napoleon's career to something other than Napoleon's powers of judgment. It is true that there is much in Beyle's two attempted lives of Napoleon which is unconvincing, if only because of the adoring hearsay on which it seems based; though we should remember, when saying this, that it was not he himself who was responsible for publishing them as they stand.[10] We should perhaps remember too that, though he was anything but blind to Napoleon's many disastrous errors, he was also, as in his writings on literature, conscious of the timeliness or, in the Nietzschian sense, 'untimeliness' of the effect of any judgment he made on his immediate public in France.

The first attempted life of Napoleon was written, as he says in the opening words of the manuscript, 'in reply to a libel... launched by the outstanding talent of the century against a man who for four years has been a target for the vengeance of the mightiest powers on earth'. The defence of the exile in St Helena begun in Milan in 1817 has something of the noble eloquence of Mme de Staël to whose account of Napoleon (in the *Considérations sur la Révolution Française*) his own biography was to have been a reply. And it is in contrast with the tone of all Beyle's surviving comments on Napoleon during the Consulate and Empire. Under the Consulate, he had sympathised strongly with Bonaparte's political adversary General Moreau, and he claimed afterwards that he had taken part in the conspiracy for which Moreau was tried and exiled.[11] As a republican, he had deplored the crowning of the Emperor; 'religion come to sanctify tyranny and all this in the name of the happiness of men'[12] and though his comments on Napoleon are more loyal in the letters written after he had himself entered the Imperial service, he had sought employment under the first Bourbon restoration, welcomed the Restoration in his first published writings[13] and even spoken of Wellington as the 'liberator' of Portugal in his *Lives of Haydn, Mozart and Metastasio* in 1814.[14]

The conversion to a passionate Bonapartism seems to have been partly due to Beyle's horror at the reprisals following the Hundred Days, the treatment of his former fellow administrators who had remained at their posts and the barbaric execution of Marshal Ney. Also to a realisation that, even if Napoleon were no longer appreciated in France (where Beyle hoped his former treacherous subjects would be 'well vexed' by the Prussians billeted in their homes)[15] he was deeply respected and seen as a liberator in the enlightened circles of Italy and even of England itself. In the circle of Ludovico de Brême, a former chaplain to Napoleon, Beyle met and conversed with Silvio Pellico, Vincenzo Monti, John Cam Hobhouse and Byron during the latter's visit to Milan in 1816 and passed himself off as a former secretary to the Emperor and subsequently to Murat, during the retreat from Moscow, retailing anecdotes about what he had seen and heard in this capacity which Hobhouse eagerly noted down.[16] The extravagance of these fantasies suggests that Beyle may have regretted not being more fully and loyally identified with the Napoleonic epic while the epic was taking place; though his letters of the period, particularly those from Moscow and Smolensk for 4 October and 7 November 1812, are masterpieces of first hand *reportage*, historical documents in their own right and bear ample witness to how much he had seen. The heroes of his major novels, however, will all regret not having lived through the epic themselves, and in the case of Fabrice regret not knowing whether the fighting he joined in was the Battle of Waterloo or not; while Beyle himself saw the final overthrow of Napoleon as bringing an end to an age of immense opportunities. 'Everything that will happen in France from now on', he wrote in his diary during a trip to Venice in the July of 1815, 'will bear the epigraph "under the extinguisher"' and the words, as often at moments of emotional stress, are accompanied by a sardonically meticulous sketch.

How adequately though, we may ask, does Chateaubriand's account of the Bonapartism which became increasingly popular in France during the next thirty years describe that of Beyle himself:

> It is a matter of daily observation that the Frenchman's instinct is to strive after power; he cares not for liberty; equality is his idol. Now there is a hidden connection between equality and despotism. In both these respects, Napoleon had a pull over the hearts of the French, who have a military liking for power and are democratically fond of seeing everything levelled. When he mounted the throne, he took the people with him. A proletarian king, he humiliated kings and noblemen in his anti-rooms. He levelled the ranks not down but up...Another cause of Napoleon's popularity is the affliction of his latter days. After his death, as his sufferings on St. Helena

became better known, people's hearts began to soften; his tyranny was forgotten...His misfortunes have revived his name among us, his glory has fed on his wretchedness.

The miracles wrought by his arms have bewitched our youth, and have taught us to worship brute force. The most insolent ambition is spurred on by his unique career to aspire to the heights which he attained.[17]

A superficial reading of Beyle may leave us with the impression that his 'respect' for the Emperor amounted to no more than this, that it was indistinguishable, in other words, from that of Julien Sorel. Yet it is as a self-professed lover of liberty that he praises and condemns Napoleon. And there is no fundamental difference in this respect between the angry young republican walking back to his lodgings on the day of Napoleon's coronation to read Alfieri and the Bonapartist of later years. In the ringing dedication to Napoleon in the *History of Painting in Italy* published in 1817, Beyle claims that posterity will see his overthrow as a disastrous setback for *'les idées libérales'*, and in the eloquent Roman simplicity of the prose, the word *'libérales'* is given the full weight of its original connotations; while in the first attempted *Life of Napoleon* begun in the same year, he regrets that, none the less, he did not do more to create liberal institutions. Beyle's idea of the form such institutions might take seems, incidentally, to have varied little over the years. Two chambers, he argues in 1817, might have saved the Republic before Bonaparte seized power. And the Directory fell 'not because a Republic is impossible in France' but 'because there was no conservative Senate to maintain the equilibrium between a House of Commons and the Directory...' (chapter 17). It is this form of government that Beyle outlines in detail in his notes of 1810 on 'the constitution desired by the people in 1789' and his allegiance in later years if not to the governments, at least to the constitutions of the Restoration and the July monarchy is clearly due to the extent to which they both conform to this model.

Beyle's fascination with the form and effect of constitutional arrangements, of which his notebooks offer ample evidence, corresponds frequently to a lack of faith in any collective genius or will. The Republic, given the right institutions, might have been saved in France but, in terms almost identical with those of Chateaubriand, he blames not only Bonaparte but the French themselves for the tyranny he created after 1799:

...Bonaparte didn't want institutions to be rooted in public opinion. It was necessary, he considered, for an acutely intelligent people to hear constant solemn reminders of the need for *stability* and safeguards for the interests of *posterity* and to feel that nothing was stable but his power alone and nothing progressive but his authority. 'The French', he said round about this time, 'are indifferent to liberty: they neither understand nor love it; vanity is their sole passion and political equality, which gives to all the hope of arriving at any place in society one wishes, is the only political right they regard as worth having.'
Nothing truer has ever been said... (*Vie de Napoléon*, ch. 23)

Napoleon's dynastic ambitions, his Concordat with Rome, his encouragement of mediocrity and flattery and his inability to act as an efficient commander-in-chief while weighed down with the responsibilities of a head of state are consistently deplored in all that Beyle wrote on Napoleon over a period of thirty years. He reveres him, and in the manuscript of 1837 in which he identifies himself with the veterans of the Revolutionary wars, claims always to have revered him for his 'usefulness' to the nation at a particular moment in time,[18] for having in fact saved the Revolution and in doing so, saved humanity itself. Had it not been for the reorganisation of France after Bonaparte had become the virtual dictator of France,

...the conquering kings would have divided France among themselves. It would have been found prudent to destroy this source of Jacobinism. The Duke of Brunswick's manifesto would have been applied to the letter and all the noble writers who adorn the academies would have proclaimed the impossibility of liberty. Never since 1793 had the new ideas been in such danger. The civilisation of the world was on the point of being set back by several hundred years. The wretched Peruvian would still have groaned under the iron yoke of Spain and the conquering kings of Europe would have abandoned themselves to the delights of cruelty, as [after the fall of the Empire] in Naples... (*Vie de Napoléon*, ch. 16)

And after France had been saved from the fate of Poland, Bonaparte rendered to the rest of the world his most inestimable service:

For the last century, it has not been exactly good intentions that Europe has lacked but the energy necessary to shake the enormous mass of contracted habits. Any profound movement now can only be morally advantageous, that is conducive to the happiness of men...
(*Vie de Napoléon*, ch. 23)

The reorganisation of the former states of the Empire after Waterloo showed the beneficial effects of the shock produced by Napoleon and corresponded, he adds, to a more 'true equilibrium' than the habits and institutions of the old order.

Beyle is very different from Tolstoy in his belief in the influence that an individual can exert on a nation, different, that is, from the Tolstoy who wrote the epilogue to *War and Peace*. (The utterances and thoughts of Pierre Bezuhov in the same novel show that even Tolstoy felt the power of the Napoleonic charisma.) Beyle is closer in his account of Napoleon to D. H. Lawrence:

Peter the Great, Frederick the Great, and Napoleon... They established a *new* connection between mankind and the universe, and the result was a vast release of energy...[19]

though his interest in the actual mechanism of society is very un-Lawrencian and much closer to the spirit of the eighteenth-century enlightenment. One of Napoleon's greatest achievements, he believed, was his establishment of a rational code of law; while his analysis of the various kinds of liberty that existed under Napoleon is reminiscent of Montesquieu in its epigrammatically succinct and consciously paradoxical account of the ways in which institutions make themselves felt by the mass of ordinary citizens.[20] It is reminiscent also of the manner and arguments of Mme de Staël and Chateaubriand, to whose accounts of Napoleon his own were intended as a reply. It would be wrong certainly to say that he goes in for that 'naïve method of interpreting history merely as the story of great tyrants and great generals' against which Sir Karl Popper tells us Tolstoy rightly reacted.[21] Beyle's firm insistence on the *usefulness* of Napoleon is itself an evident refusal to surrender to any such cult of the personality. Yet there is more obviously to Napoleon for Beyle than any political argument could adequately explain. And in the *Mémoires sur Napoléon*, which was written a year before *La chartreuse de Parme*, far more wonder and joy are associated with the arrival of Bonaparte's army in

Italy than can be expressed in conventional historical terms. There is probably, in other words, more significance than critics and admirers of the lives of Napoleon have seen in the fact that Beyle never tried to publish them and that it is in the unsophisticated minds of the heroes of his novels that he was to make the Napoleonic legend appear most real and at the same time most clearly comprehensible.

Italy and the eruption of energy

I have argued in an earlier chapter that Beyle's conscious utilitarianism and his belief in the heroic follow from one another and that to understand one we must take into account the other. In his anti-Saint-Simonian pamphlet of 1825, he had claimed that the citizens most worthy of public esteem were those who 'risk a great deal in order to obtain what, rightly or wrongly, they believe to be useful to the public' and not those whose own pursuit of wealth is of only incidental benefit to society as a whole. The qualification, 'rightly or wrongly' is crucial to Beyle's argument about those who seek the public good, for though the public good is something real and desirable, there is no certain way of knowing what this is.

Beyle was the last person to denigrate the benefits of prosperity, but he seems to have regarded this always as one means only, and this one by no means indispensable, to the realisation of happiness. The good society, as he conceived it, was not merely one in which prosperity and the opportunities for social advancement would be universal; though, in the late 1830s in the *Mémoires sur Napoléon* and the *Mémoires d'un touriste*, he looks forward to a continuation of progress in this direction. It would be one which would encourage the greatest possible release of human 'energy', one of his most frequently used terms, though to understand what he meant by it, we have to read what he said about the society he most admired, that of Italy from the age of Dante to the end of the sixteenth century.

Despite his early republicanism and his fondness for Plutarch and Livy, Beyle did not become a classical historian or an active member of the Jacobin opposition to Napoleon, and the period of political disillusion followed by professional conformity as a civil servant after the crowning of Napoleon was the period in which he discovered the past of Italy and became increasingly absorbed in its way of life and its art. The pages of Alfieri with which he had 'rinsed out his mouth' on the day of Napoleon's coronation may have been from *Del Principe e delle lettere* in which he would have read that 'the fearful and sublime crimes' committed even in the depths of Italy's moral degradation, are a proof of the hot and ferocious spirits that abound within her more than anywhere else in Europe...'.[22] And in Sismondi's *History of the Italian Republics*, which he had bought in 1808, he would have read that 'political passions', such as those the republican spirit inspires, 'make more heroes than individual passions and though the connection may not be obvious, more artists, poets, scholars and seers...'.[23] A return visit to Milan in 1811, followed by a tour of the peninsula, had confirmed him in his lifelong attachment to Italy and much of his career as a writer from then on was to be spent describing and explaining the innate superiority of the Italian people as a whole.

This did not lie merely in the republican spirit. According to Professor Carlo Cordiè, 'the Renaissance with its tyrants and city states...represents for him an aesthetic ideal...'.[24] And in the introduction to the *History of painting in Italy*, written between 1811 and 1818, Beyle tells us how 'after three centuries of misfortune, and what misfortune – the most fearful, that which renders men vile – there is nowhere one hears pronounced as in Italy the words "*O Dio, com' è bello*"'. Beyle's 'aestheticism', if this is the right word, is certainly not the exclusive variety associated with the belief in art for art's sake. (And the word *bello* has a less restricted application than 'beautiful' or even '*beau*'.) It is rather a deep interest in life lived with a fulness of energy and a vulnerability and sensitiveness which are manifest *both* in art and in life. Freedom is essential to such energy and one of the merits of the *History of painting* is its reminder that liberty can exist without liberal institutions to protect it and that the latter can exist in a society in which the spirit of liberty itself is dead:

> Let me say to the modern princes, so proud of their virtues and who so despise the little tyrants of the middle ages: 'These virtues on which you pride yourselves are only private virtues. As a king, you are nothing. Whereas the tyrants of Italy had private vices and public virtues...

Florence, a republic without a constitution, but in which the horror of tyranny enflamed every heart, knew that stormy liberty which is the mother of great characters...It was constantly necessary to resort to arms against the nobles; but it is degradation and not danger which kills a people's spirit...[25]

(Introduction)

It is natural for Beyle to approach each of the painters in his history as a biographer, so much so that even his admirer Taine agreed with Mérimée that he was not sufficiently interested in painting in its own right. And the anecdotes which make up the biographies illustrate, among other things, the general truth that he will state twenty years later in *L'Abbesse de Castro*:

Melodrama has so often shown us the Italian brigands of the sixteenth century and so many people have spoken of them in ignorance, that we now have the most false ideas concerning them. In general, one can say that these brigands formed the *opposition* against the atrocious governments which, in Italy, succeeded the Republics of the middle ages. The new tyrant was usually the wealthiest citizen of the defunct Republic and in order to win over the people, he would adorn the city with magnificent churches and fine paintings. Such were the Polentini of Ravenna, the Manfredi of Faenza, the Riarios of Imola, the Bentivoglios of Bologna, the Viscontis of Milan and, the most bellicose and hypocritical of all, the Medici of Florence. Among the historians of these little states, none has dared to recount the poisonings and assassinations without number commanded by the fear which tormented these little tyrants; the grave historians were in their pay. Consider that each of these tyrants knew personally each of the republicans by whom he knew he was loathed, that several of these tyrants were assassinated and you will then understand the profound hatreds and eternal suspicions that gave so much intelligence and courage to the Italians of the sixteenth century and so much genius to their artists. You will see how these profound passions prevented the birth of the ridiculous prejudice that went by the name of *honour* in the days of Mme de Sévigné and which consists essentially in sacrificing one's life for the master to whom one is subject by birth or in order to impress a lady...In Italy, a man distinguished himself by merit *of every kind*, by wielding a sword or discovering ancient manuscripts: think of Petrarch, the idol of his age. A woman in the sixteenth century would love a scholar of Greek as much as, if not more than a man celebrated for his military prowess and valour. It was then that one saw passions and not the habit of *galanterie*. This is the great difference between Italy and France and why Italy saw the birth of the Raphaels, Giorgiones, Titians and Correggios, while France produced all those brave captains of the sixteenth century, so little known today and each one of whom killed such an impressive number of enemies... (ch. 1)

In his earlier writings on Italy, *Rome, Naples et Florence en 1817*, and his most serious attempt at a conventional guide book, the *Promenades dans Rome* of 1829, it is the miraculous survival of the old Italian spirit, despite centuries of oppression, he records; though painting

...is now dead and buried. Canova has burst through to the light by chance, by dint of the vegetative force with which the soul of man is endowed in this lovely climate: but like Alfieri, he's a monster; there is nothing else like him, nothing that even approaches him, and sculpture otherwise is as dead in Italy as the art of Correggio... Music alone remains alive, and in this beautiful country, the only other thing to do is to make love; the other pleasures of the soul encounter obstacles and constraints; in so far as one feels one is a citizen of the country, one will die poisoned by melancholy...
(*Rome, Naples et Florence en 1817*, 17.11.1816)

The implications of this comment are pursued in detail in each of the travel books, in *The life of Rossini* and, as far as 'love' is concerned, in the story of Fabrice del Dongo in *La chartreuse de Parme*. And it expresses Beyle's simultaneous reverence for the irrepressible Italian spirit and his conviction that Italy has become ungovernable except through a naked assertion of power. The rulers and statesmen of the Italy of his own day that he admires are autocrats like Napoleon, whom he pardons for having suppressed the Republic of Venice – a republic only in name and one which was especially mourned, as he points out, by English aristocrats[26] – or like the Austrian governors themselves whose rule of Lombardy he deplores while recognising the fairness with which they apply their laws, their success in restraining the fanaticism of the Church and their encouragement during the eighteenth century of the work of Beccaria and consequent services to the cause of Utilitarianism.[27] Rome itself also fascinated Beyle and in his travel books he devotes many pages to its ceremonies, to the history of Papal intrigues and to its primitive constitution, for which he sketches a number of reforms. He admired particularly 'the military talents and force of will' of Michelangelo's patron Julius II, and among his own contemporaries the administrative genius of the reforming minister Cardinal Consalvi; while in the letters he wrote as Consul in Civita Vecchia to the Minister of Foreign Affairs in Paris and which are among the best things he wrote about the Italy of his day, we learn of the 'active intelligent' Minister of Police in Rome, Mgr Ciachi, a former officer of dragoons, who is 'adored by his subordinates because the only harm he has done is that which is useful to himself...' (8.4.1835). In all these figures and especially the last, Beyle's reforming minister, Count Mosca della Rovere in *La chartreuse de Parme* is foreshadowed, together with the despotic rule he successfully wields. There is even perhaps an intended significance in the fact that Julius II and Mosca share the same family name.

Beyle's conviction that Italy since the sixteenth century has needed the strong enlightened rule of individuals, given the absence of what sociologists since Hegel have often referred to as 'civil society', consorts naturally with his frequent admiration for the anarchic and even criminal ways in which Italian energy is displayed. Beyle shared and was one of the first to express the common nineteenth-century interest in the psychology of crime, and *Promenades dans Rome* in particular is full of anecdotes concerning the use of poison in Italy and the refinements of cruelty invented by the country's many assassins. The *Promenades* contains also Beyle's eulogy of the common people of Rome, whose long history of submission to the caprice of the Popes and the consequent need to *'inventer et vouloir'* [28] have made them more courageous than the people of London or Paris. It is an animal freedom that Beyle is celebrating, however, under the name of energy, and he reminds us consequently of its atrocious as well as its more attractive forms. Between 1775 and 1800, for example, there were '18,000 assassinations in Rome, that is two a day'.

The atrociousness of Napoleon's laws, to employ the manner of speaking of Cardinal N...has done something to correct these bad habits. In Rome, it is the arrested assassin who is pitied and if the pious and retrograde government which has succeeded Cardinal Consalvi's is popular in any way, it is because it rarely employs capital punishment for any other crime than *carbonarismo*...[29]

Energy for Beyle, in general, has an equivocal value – necessarily, in so far as, by his own definition, it is liable to threaten the interests of any living man. It is a law unto itself, and in all its manifestations a terrifying or breathtakingly beautiful reminder that morally there is no other kind of law. This may account for its fascination for Beyle, for in innumerable ways, whatever energy may destroy, it merely confirms the reasonableness of the Beyliste point of view. Though it is worth remembering also that for Beyle who was a pioneer in the form of *Kulturgeschichte* that we find in his travel books and history of painting (Nietzsche's friend, Burckhardt in his *Civilisation of the Renaissance in Italy* was among those who were to pursue it more methodically) the strain of violence running through Italian history had something of the fascination of a new discovery.

To summarise all that Beyle ever wrote about energy is, however, an even more hopeless task than to indicate the broad outlines of his writings on Italy. The loose, deliberately unschematic and freely digressive form of the latter, which is that of a diary kept by an enthusiastic traveller, overflows with facts, in Beyle's own sense of the word: that is, particular insights and pointed anecdotes, almost any one of which throws light on some different aspect of the Italy as Beyle saw. The fascination with energy was to remain with him till he died. Even his early republicanism and veneration for the heroes of Plutarch, Corneille and Alfieri can easily be seen as a deep interest in one particular kind of energy; though, with the discovery of Shakespeare and of the Italian Renaissance, the growing dissatisfaction with Alfieri and, coinciding with this, the realisation that, with the advent of Napoleon, the early promise of the Revolution had gone, one might say that it was the diversity of forms that energy might assume that absorbed him rather than the single heroic model he had worshipped as a boy.

The true meaning of energy as Beyle uses the term can only be determined by reference to his deepest and most thoughtful writing, and this is to be found in his three major novels rather than in the works with which this chapter is concerned. The *History of Painting in Italy* was undertaken partly to cover the expenses of a further tour of Italy and partly in order to acquire something of the grace of a Correggio, to rid himself of the 'detestable dryness and precision' into which he was afraid of falling as a dramatist,[30] drama being still his chosen vocation, as it was to remain until he decided that the would-be dramatist in the nineteenth century would have to resort to the novel. There is no account in the books on Italy of the nature of energy and of its growth comparable in its logic and inwardness to that which is offered in *Le rouge et le noir*, germane though we may find such thoughts as the following from the *Promenades dans Rome*:

The other assassination took place near St Peter's in the Trastevere district; this is also a bad area, one is told, which makes it sublime for me. One finds *energy* here, that is, the quality most absent in the nineteenth century. Today, we have found the secret of being brave without either energy or character. No one knows how to *will what he desires*[31]; our education simply unteaches this most important subject of all. The English know how to will what they desire; but it is not without difficulty that in doing so they violate the whole spirit of modern civilisation; their life, as a result, is one constant effort... (27.1.1828)

The almost prophetic tentativeness of such remarks, which makes one see why Nietzsche said that it had taken 'two generations to catch up with him', is not that of systematic thought. Which is why Taine's eulogy of Beyle as a historian and chronicler seems always entirely inappropriate. It is Beyle, according to Taine,

...who has explained the most complicated of the internal mechanisms, pointed out to us the principal springs of behaviour and introduced into the study of the human heart the methods of science and the arts of calculation, analysis and deduction. It is he who has shown us the fundamental causes, by which I mean climate, nationality and temperament, and who has approached the study of human feeling as one has to, namely as a natural scientist...[32]

Among those whom Beyle influenced was the Breton aristocrat Gobineau, who, in *Les Pléiades*, his study of the *Renaissance* and his *Essai sur l'inégalité des races humaines*, set out to be systematic in the way Taine describes. The nearest Beyle himself comes to finding reasons in nature for the Italians being as they are is to refer occasionally to their 'beautiful climate'. He differs, in fact, from those who have tried to establish the causes of superior energy and intelligence and then to ensure their survival by maintaining the purity of races and castes, in his readiness to acknowledge energy and intelligence in all their forms and irrespective of their source: in his admiration, for example, both for the 'sublime' assassins of the Trastevere district and the firm measures of Cardinal Consalvi which succeeded in keeping the crime rate down. What makes his writings on Italy so unique, in other words, is the breadth and fearlessness of his sympathies, which presumably owe something to the circumstances of his life. Like Nietzsche, who followed him so eagerly in his study of energy, he was a childless bachelor, and his works on Italy are those of a traveller writing under an assumed name. It is difficult to believe that this has nothing to do with his exceptional ability to appreciate the justice and truth of rival claims.

Saying this leads one to conclude that there may be some justification after all for Professor Cordiè's saying that his love of Italy was 'aesthetic'. The vantage point from which Beyle looks down on society is a privileged one, in that it is so detached and adventurous. But this is not to say that it is one from which no practical lesson can be learned. Beyle's fears for the Europe of his time and our own were that as society became more prosperous and democratic, it would become more American too – more dominated, that is, by the spirit of mutual surveillance and mutual servility that he was to see after 1830 as the price of American popular democracy.[33] (The lawlessness and energy of the American expansion westward were something he did not predict.) And his allegiance to the democratic ideals of his boyhood and to the utilitarian principles of later years was to be qualified only by his fear lest society should lose that energy that he still finds among those who have to 'struggle with real needs'[34] and without which life can no longer be lived as an individual or collective destiny.

The chronicler of contemporary France

Beyle's account of the life of his own contemporaries in France is to be found principally in the articles he contributed to various English periodicals after his return from Milan in 1821 and which were to furnish his main source of income for a number of years, in the *Mémoires d'un touriste* and, most important of all, his own novels. The point of view from which he writes is that of a liberal of the period before 1830, an admirer of the liberal orators Benjamin Constant and General Foy, of the popular Bonapartist and democratic poet Béranger, and the pamphleteer Paul-Louis Courier. The society he describes is one dominated by the Jesuit conspiracy, by the new Puritanism introduced by Napoleon (who had made marriage respectable by insisting that women should never appear at court without their husbands), by the new literary and journalistic industry made possible by the relaxation of censorship under the Restoration, and by the mysticism and religiosity which had invaded philosophy, literature and the fashionable salons. Beyle's diagnosis of the ills of the Restoration is not in itself very unusual. Even Chateaubriand was afraid of the Jesuits,[35] Sainte Beuve and Balzac have left their own accounts of the new commercialism in literature;[36] while the contrast between the melancholy and earnestness of the nineteenth century and the life of pre-Revolutionary France has struck many other contemporary observers of the so-called *mal du siècle*. No other contemporary commentator that I know of, however, seems to have understood the relation between these phenomena so clearly; there is, surely, no better contemporary critic of the literature of the period; none writes with that combination of intellectual excitement, anger and amusement that makes even Beyle's lightest journalism unlike that of anyone else; and few were able to see France, as Beyle was, from the cosmopolitan point of view which enabled him to discuss, for example, the different kinds of freedom enjoyed by the English and French respectively, a subject which continues to baffle both nationalities.[37]

The gossip and the fecundity of ideas that make the articles in the English reviews so readable, even today, may owe something to Beyle's frequenting liberal salons, such as those of Mme d'Aubernon, where he would meet among others Victor Cousin, and on leaving which he had been known to say, 'Now my article's done!'.[38] And their frequent facetiousness may be due both to this and to the fact that they were written to order and with an immediate audience in mind: a foreign audience, in addressing which Beyle seems to have felt even more conscious than usual of the possible absurdity of his claims to be telling the truth. The variety of pseudonyms he chose for his articles and which seems to have enabled him to review at least one of his own books – with reservations, though warmly and with a sense of its true merits[39] – released him from the obligation to be an unfailingly honest reporter; and even when he is carried away by heartfelt enthusiasm or anger, much of his journalism is characterised by an evident reliance on hearsay and a high spirited simplification of the facts.

Beyle seems, moreover, to have flattered his English readers, at least to the extent of concealing from them his dislike of the English character, his disapproval of the Old Corruption of the English governing classes, his anger at the treatment of Napoleon after Waterloo, and his belief that Napoleon should have crossed the Channel and imposed on the country a constitution similar to that of the United States.[40] He was not, on the whole, one of those who utters the truth as they see it fearlessly to anyone who cares to hear. He feared, like Julien Sorel and often with justification, allowing his secret thoughts to be known, a tendency perhaps originating in the days when, as a ten-year-old Jacobin during the Terror and civil war, he lived in a family of political enemies. And this may account partly for the sunnily optimistic view of the future and his seeming faith in the wisdom of the July monarchy expressed in the *Mémoires d'un touriste* of 1837 and which come remarkably near to obsequiousness.

His private views of the new order established in 1830 seem very different, at least during the period before the *Mémoires d'un touriste* appeared. Despite his nomination, through the good offices of the liberal Count Molé as consul in Civita Vecchia, Beyle was one of those who first welcomed the Revolution of 1830 but were speedily disillusioned by its outcome. His novel *Lucien Leuwen* is his most extended and passionate expression of his dislike of the reign of 'this most crooked of kings', and was a book that he knew he could not possibly publish as long as he remained in the service of the crown. His private correspondence of 1831 expresses his indignant sympathy with the unjustly imprisoned Auguste Blanqui and his anger that his former school-friend Félix Faure, in his capacity as President of the Royal Court of Justice in Grenoble should be 'allowed to insult continuously for a whole fortnight all those who think and are twenty-five years old...' (1.2.1831).[41]

The social disturbances that marked the opening years of the July monarchy: the sacking of St Germain l'Auxerrois, the violent repression of popular demonstrations in the Rue Transnonain in Paris and the rising of the *canuts*, the silk workers of Lyon, demanding the right to collective bargaining[42] are often taken as marking the end of the alliance of interests between the liberal bourgeoisie and the urban proletariat, and the beginnings of what was to become in 1848 and 1871 open war between the two classes. M. Jean-Paul Sartre has spoken of 1831 as the year in which the bourgeoisie 'recognised itself for what it was...'[43] and began to live out the contradictions between its avowed beliefs and its actual behaviour as the governing class in society. And in his recent study of Flaubert, *L'idiot de la famille*, Sartre has portrayed Flaubert's father, the distinguished Rouennais surgeon, as one of those who chose to accept such a contradiction and Flaubert himself as one of its spiritual victims.[44]

The terror of the proletariat among the middle classes after the first rising of the *canuts* is expressed in a letter to Beyle by his friend Prosper Mérimée, whose relish of energy however ferocious when it is that of Corsicans and Spaniards, deserts him when it is that of his fellow citizens. After alleging that the rising was the result of the preaching of Saint-Simonian agitators, an allegation that Beyle was later publicly to deny,[45] Mérimée offers his friend the following advice: 'Please note that what happened in Lyon has happened in Bristol and Dresden too. Which proves that those who eat hard tack now want white bread and have just realised that nothing is easier. Believe me, you had better deposit a million or two in Turkey. It's the only country where a man who loves tranquility will be able to live from now on...' (1.12.1831). This note is conspicuously absent from Beyle's own private correspondence; the inhuman callousness of the upper classes after the defeat of the *canuts* is dwelled on at length in *Lucien Leuwen*,[46] and even in the *Mémoires d'un touriste* he will note how, whatever errors they committed in 1831 and again in 1834, the *canuts* of Lyon gave proof of 'superhuman courage'.[47]

His admiration for their courage does not prevent him from dwelling in the same work on the mean-spirited enviousness of both the *canuts* and their masters, and that 'unfortunate thirst for enjoyment and rapid fortune which is the folly of all young Frenchmen today', for which the rise of Napoleon created an unforgettable precedent, and to which, more than any actual misery, he attributes the silk workers' revolt:

> It is in vain that the voice of philosophy cries out to them: 'But all the odious abuses are now abolished in France; if the Almighty himself put a pen in your hand to correct such abuses, you would be at a loss; you wouldn't know what to write; there are no more radical reforms needed in France, no great upheavals *to hope for or fear*. France has been deceived by the glory of Napoleon and tormented by absurd desires. Instead of *inventing* its destiny, it wishes to *copy* it; it wants to see, starting once again in 1837, the century that began in 1792 with Carnot and Dumouriez...[48]

Like Beyle's new-found admiration when he visits Chambéry, for the Jesuits, whose fanatical devotion to their own order makes them the most exemplary of schoolteachers (as many liberal parents have discovered to their advantage),[49] these thoughts on Napoleon indicate a point of view very different from that of *Le rouge et le noir*, though how literally, or un-ironically, we ought to take such judgments is never clear. The *Mémoires d'un touriste* are ostensibly the work of an iron merchant travelling through the length and breadth of France on business as well as for his own amusement, and the assumed personality of the traveller gives Beyle a freedom to express views he may not actually have held; such as those on the 'wise government of a king who is also a superior man, who refuses to authorise the insolence of the rich towards the poor that one sees in England...'[50] or on the 'growing prosperity of France under the government of Louis Philippe', in expressing which he hopes that no one will think he is in the pay of the crown.[51]

Sincere or not, the *Mémoires d'un touriste* and their unfinished sequel, the *Voyage dans le midi de la France,* leave us with the most attractive impressions he was ever to form of the lives of ordinary Frenchmen and of the diversity and uniqueness of the French provinces; and despite his dislike of the landscape and people of the region of Fontainebleau and his yearning to thrash the wealthy bullying liberals he meets in the coach to Saint Malo, they convey what seems like an unsimulated pleasure after more than two years abroad at the general state of France. Henry James found him still the ideal companion half a century later, and in his *Little Tour of France*, recommended him to every traveller, comparing him in his digressiveness with Sterne;

though a more obvious comparison might have been with Sterne's admirer Diderot, to whom Beyle pays homage during a visit to Langres in the Haute-Marne:

> No doubt this writer is guilty of over-statement, but how superior he will seem in 1850 to most of the grandiloquent writers of the present day! His overstatements are not the result of poverty of ideas and the need to hide it! On the contrary, he is weighed down by all he is bursting to say...[52]

Beyle's devouring interest in the human scene and in the organisation of local trade and industry, his delight in painting and architecture (to which James does rather less than justice) and his many digressions on literature remind one of the Diderot of the *Salons* and the *Encyclopédie*, though without the obtrusive excitable self-consciousness which Beyle characterises in a deceptively laconic aside:

> Diderot's talent was lacking in one respect only. He never had the good fortune to pay court when he was twenty to a young woman of distinction, and the courage to appear in her salon. His habit of over-statement would have disappeared...

M. Lucien Jansse has paid tribute to Beyle's insight into the economic needs of France at the dawn of her industrial revolution,[53] his understanding of the dangers of inflated credit,[54] of the arguments for and against protectionism[55] and above all, of the real purchasing power of money,[56] of the physical well-being, for example, of the Italian weaver compared with his better-paid and more hard-working French counterpart. M. Rude has drawn attention to Beyle's remarkable receptiveness in the *Mémoires d'un touriste* to the new social ideas; though he perhaps exaggerates Beyle's admiration for Fourier and says nothing of what has come in our own century to seem like the truth of his forecast of the development of the spirit of Fourieresque 'association':[57]

> Fourier, living in solitude, or what amounts to the same thing, with disciples who never dared to raise an objection (in any case, he never answered objections) never saw that in each village, an active scoundrel with a glib tongue (a Robert Macaire) will put himself at the head of the association and pervert all its fine consequences. It is, none the less, true that the *competition* which still exists between one individual

and another will end up by being exercised only between one big company and another. This characteristic of the industry of the future is already apparent today....[58]

If Beyle is not a distracting or obtrusive presence in his own travelogue, nor is he obviously a neutral one. The clarity and depth of his impressions of France are the effect rather of that lifelong joy in discovering how others find happiness without which no one can be a novelist or even, one is tempted to add, a historian. His willingness to learn about different ways of being happy and of evolving one's way of life accordingly is apparent, for example, in his account of a bird-shooting expedition in the hills above Marseille, where the inhabitants wait for their prey in little cabins made with the branches of thorn trees:

It must be confessed that one derives the most enchanting pleasure from the lovely climate in these cabins of dead wood, that the sea breeze penetrates from every side. There reigns here an enchanting silence, a silence such that one can *hear one's soul*; one can enjoy here a total liberty; no care can penetrate this peaceful retreat. Even if one gave a Marseillais millions to go and live in Paris, I am sure he would miss his little 'post' and I must say I almost agree with him...[59]

By contrast, the wealthy liberals travelling to Saint Malo who 'drag his imagination in the mud', see liberty as 'the power to prevent one's neighbour doing what he likes' and, during the period of their enforced company, 'convert' Beyle himself to their way of thinking. The enjoyment of the diversity of human pleasures is a precarious one, as Beyle is the first to confess, and his own interest in his fellow men never purports to be that of a disembodied mind. Beyle is often intolerant. As in the polemic against Saint-Simon, moreover, he makes his own interests clear before judging society as a whole; and by adopting the rôle of a prosperous iron merchant, he confesses that these are the social and economic interests of a typical member of the middle bourgeoisie.

In the articles in the English reviews, for which a model is the *Correspondance littéraire* of Diderot's friend, the German born Grimm (and in which one of his most frequent pseudonyms is 'Grimm's grandson'), there is no such clearly defined point of view; though this may also be attributed to historical circumstances, to the unsuccessful attempt by powerful factions in the Church and the aristocracy to reverse history, which made a liberalism like Beyle's perhaps inevitably seem like the noble all-too-obvious enlightenment of all parties in opposition. The *Mémoires d'un touriste* and the *Voyage dans le midi de la France* are written from a more unequivocally committed standpoint and with a corresponding sobriety. The image that pervades them is that of a superb mountain torrent, in which the dramatic cascades are compared with the inevitable revolutions of the past and are now seen winding through a prosperous plain.[60] The truth of the comparison may be contested (though the second of the great social revolutions predicted by Marx has still not, at the time of writing, occurred). The value of the *Mémoires* as a document lies in the candour and completeness with which, if nothing else, they express the bourgeois point of view.

M. Sartre has no difficulty in pointing out the contradiction between the interests and commitments of writers like Vigny and Flaubert and their professed contempt for their own way of life and the social order on which it depended.[61] There is no such contradiction in Beyle's writings on France and the aristocratic pseudonym he insisted on retaining, to the amusement of his friends, is no more than a carnival disguise.

History and truth

'Take up history', he wrote to Pauline from his regiment in Italy when he was eighteen years old, 'but only that philosophical history which shows in all events the consequences of men's actions...'.[62] Plutarch was at this time one of the favourite authors of the young republican, and Roman history the reading he most enjoyed. He admired particularly the *Révolutions romaines* of the Abbé Vertot, which had enjoyed considerable currency throughout the eighteenth century, and his continuing interest in the subject and desire to keep up with the latest works on ancient history can be seen in many passages in the *Promenades dans Rome*.

It is perhaps Volney, however, who more than anyone else, helped to 'crystallise', in the sense defined in *De l'amour*, the relation for Beyle between 'history' and 'philosophy' and we should be grateful to Professor del Litto for having dwelled at length on the affinities between their ways of thinking of the past.[63] Beyle read Volney's *Voyage en Syrie et en Egypte* and his *Leçons d'histoire* during his period of service in Brunswick and may have learned in doing so that memory (which Tracy sees as the source of all our errors and the training of which is tantamount to the training of reason itself) is not merely a function of the individual mind. 'The more I have analysed the daily influence exerted on the actions and opinions of men by history', Volney writes, 'the more convinced I have become that it is one of the most fertile sources of men's prejudices and errors....'[64] Volney's plea for critical history, including the critical interrogation, if possible, even of first-hand reporters, may well have impressed Beyle at a time when he was in a position to judge the difference between official bulletins and what was happening in reality. 'Posterity', he writes in *La vie de Henry Brulard*, 'will never know the grossness and stupidity' of Napoleon's immediate underlings 'off the battlefield. And their prudence on it...or how I would laugh when reading in Vienna, Dresden, Berlin and Moscow the *Moniteur*, which no one in the army ever received, in case all the lies were seen and ridiculed...' (chapter 23). In Volney too, he would have found one of the principal models for his own method of writing the history of the present and the past, in the travel books on Italy and France. For Volney – and the view is now well established in France, where history and geography are thought of as the same academic subject – travel is not merely an interesting complement but one of the principal means to our understanding of the past.[65]

Few writers, none the less, have been less suited by nature and the influences of their early years for the career of an exact historian than Beyle, and his writings bear out his confession in *La vie de Henry Brulard* that 'the only memory' he can claim is of his own feelings. 'As for *facts*, I've never had any memory at all, which is, incidentally why the famous Georges Cuvier always beat me in the discussions he sometimes deigned to hold with me in his salon every Saturday from 1822 to 1830...' (chapter 11). The recounting of events in his lives of the composers and of Napoleon, in his travel books and his *History of Painting in Italy* is, sometimes avowedly, unreliable; while in his

THE CHRONICLER AND HISTORIAN

recollections of his meetings with Byron in Milan, which enjoyed considerable success in his own day and have been regarded as a reliable source by many biographers of Byron even in recent years, it is now clear that he invented almost all he retails.[66] Significantly perhaps, the pseudonym he used as a chronicler was the same that he used as a novelist, and the comic deception involved in its use is a virtual admission that, whether he appears to be writing fact or fiction, the distinction should not be too readily assumed.

Something akin to Volney's concern for truth in history is to be found, nonetheless, in all that Beyle writes of the past, however extravagant his own imagination and however inclined we may be to agree at times with Nietzsche that the Europe he discovered was very much 'his own'.[67] Beyle will sometimes express what seems like almost total scepticism as to the possibility of reaching the truth about the past,[68] and he recommends in his articles in the English reviews the German historian Niebuhr, whose sceptical approach to the best-known sources of Roman history was one of the common topics of conversation in the salons of the day.[69] It is, nonetheless, in the name of truth itself, even if in pursuing it one has to 'know how to be ignorant', that Beyle attacks those historians who are in the pay of a prince or a church or who, like Montesquieu himself, pay more attention to the history of laws than to that of their application.[70] The historians Beyle recommended with enthusiasm were those who, like General Philippe de Ségur, author of the *Histoire de Napoléon et de la Grande Armée en 1812*, were prepared to give the lie to official history; though the enthusiasm here may admittedly derive from the fact that he is writing for an English public:

This young officer has revealed things which, say the partisans of the *national honour*, ought never to have escaped the lips of a Frenchman. As a historian, he has ventured to tell the truth. He says there existed a secret agreement between Napoleon and his army. This army was mowed down by the cannon as rapidly as the English regiments which you send to Ava or the Cape are destroyed by the diseases of India or Africa. The French army submitted to this horrible lottery and in return, Napoleon promised his brave fellows, not only the advantage of pillage (that would have been a peccadillo) but licence to murder the citizens on whom they were billeted (the baker at Cassel in 1809, for instance), to murder the *maires des communes* in France; to pillage their own waggon-train (as in Spain in 1809), which pillage caused the defeat of the French army. M. de Ségur has committed a crime which the French army will never forgive – he has forced the attention of the French people on the military leprosy introduced into France by Napoleon...'[71]

He also recommended and was to edit and translate the unknown unofficial sixteenth-century chroniclers, like the author of the story of Vittoria Accoramboni, who prudently 'never judges a fact, never prepares it in any way' and whose 'sole preoccupation is to tell the truth...'.[72] Beyle would probably have agreed with Professor Marrou that good writing is not an incidental quality but indispensable to good history.[73] And it is the good writing which consists in boldness and simplicity of utterance which he valued in the *Life* of Benvenuto Cellini and the tales of the sixteenth century *novelliere* Bandello, both of whom, he believed, give us more of the actual history of the Italy of their day than any historian as such.[74]

How a work of fiction like Bandello's or the testimony of a Cellini, who Beyle admits is sometimes 'un peu Gascon', gives us a true picture of the life of their age, and how we can know this is so are not questions on which Beyle has left any extended thoughts; though in the articles in the English reviews written immediately before his own first novel, *Armance*, he frequently recommended even minor novels as an aid to the study of social history, and in Rome in 1834 in the margin of a book he was carrying, he sketched out the following tentative explanation:

I wrote biographies in my youth, which are a kind of history, lives of Mozart and Michelangelo. I regret it now. With the biggest just as much as with the smallest things, it seems to me impossible to get to what is true, at least to what is true in *some detail* [du moins un vrai *un peu détaillé*]. M. de Tracy once said to me: 'One can no longer reach the truth [atteindre au vrai] except in a novel...'[75]

The novelist's advantage over the historian lies in his freedom to speculate on what might happen and in the reality of the possibilities he imagines; in his devotion to the 'interests of the imagination', as Beyle calls them,[76] without which a historian cannot interpret his evidence and is therefore left with no evidence at all. To say this, however, is to give a very approximate idea of Beyle's meaning; and what is meant by the underlined 'un vrai *un peu détaillé*' is something we can almost certainly best decide by referring specifically to Beyle's own work. The remarks were scribbled in a copy of *Le rouge et le noir* and it is to this work, which Beyle describes as a 'chronicle of 1830' that any discussion of Beyle the historian must lead.

5

Le rouge et le noir

The problem of form

The jotting quoted at the end of the last chapter indicates one of the most important senses in which Beyle discovered he was a novelist. It was as a novelist only that he could be a historian. The claim is by no means inconsistent with the observation developed in his essay of 1835, *La comédie est impossible*, that the would-be dramatist of this phrase of history could only hope to write for individuals not too different from himself and not for the heterogeneous audience of the theatre. Nor obviously is it contradicted by another claim, made on several occasions in the 1820s, that 'all systems of philosophy are addressed to the young' and that many philosophers, such as Plato, Abelard and Victor Cousin, have in fact written *novels* for the young, in the guise of systems of philosophy.[1]

'The novel is a great discovery: far greater than Galileo's telescope or somebody else's wireless. The novel is the highest form of human expression so far attained....'[2] Beyle might have endorsed at least the first of these propositions, though he had no Dickens, Flaubert or Tolstoy to look back to and could not have said it, as Lawrence was able to, with a sense of this being overwhelmingly evident. The great creative work of the past, according to his own account, was that of Shakespeare, Dante, Michelangelo and Mozart. He never spoke in the same terms of Cervantes, Mme de Lafayette or Fielding, thoroughly though he enjoyed and admired the latter. Among his own contemporaries, he welcomed the fact that Mme de Flahaut-Souza showed a delicacy in the portrayal of human feelings lacking in the novels of Sir Walter Scott,[3] that Constant's *Adolphe*, despite its 'affectations', 'does say something, well or badly, which distinguishes it from most other modern books'[4] and that *Le Père Goriot* shows what the government of M. de Villèle is like, much as Scarron's *Roman comique* shows the real France of Colbert.[5] There was no living contemporary, however, on whom he was to model himself. In grasping the possibilities of thought and expression that novels, by their very nature reveal, Beyle was, even more than Lawrence, a discoverer and a pioneer. For the possibilities opened up by the novel as such, on which he seems to have begun to dwell during the 1820s (there is no dateable sudden inspiration) were possibilities that, as we know, he was to develop in practice. Had he not done so, it is perhaps worth adding, it is most likely that *War and Peace* would not have been written in the way that it was. For, though Tolstoy is unfortunately not on record as having said much specifically about the influence of Stendhal, he claimed that it was very considerable indeed.[6]

The relation in which Beyle stands to the great European novelists who succeeded him and of which he was conscious towards those whom he read is not one which encourages us to look in the work of the latter for a significant foreshadowing of the techniques or the sense of life which we find in *Le rouge et le noir*. For this reason a study of the education of the novelist that Beyle became will not be much concerned with novels as such. Beyle wrote little on the technique of the novel, far less than on that of the drama. The most extensive commentary that survives on the former are his notes on the manuscript of *Lucien Leuwen*, the one novel, he tells us, he wrote to a plan – and it is perhaps significant that he was unable to finish it. His most illuminating statement on the history of the novel is the short article which appeared in *Le National* on 19 February 1830, entitled 'Sir Walter Scott et *La Princesse de Clèves*.' (The argument is presented more succinctly than any summary of which I am capable):

Everyone knows the story told by Voltaire. He was instructing a young actress in tragic diction and she was reciting a very moving passage in a cold straightforward way. 'But you ought to act as if you are possessed by the Devil', cried Voltaire. 'Mademoiselle, what would you do if a cruel tyrant had taken away your lover?' 'I would find another one' was the reply.

I don't say that all creators of historical novels think as *reasonably* as this prudent young lady; but the most sensitive among them will not want to accuse me of slander if I say that it is infinitely less difficult to describe in a picturesque fashion the costume of a character than to say what he feels and to make him speak. Don't let's forget another advantage of the school of Sir Walter Scott; the description of a costume and of the posture of a character, however minor he may be, take up at least two pages. The movements of the soul, which first of all are so hard to detect and then so difficult to express, with precision and without exaggeration or timidity, will provide the material for barely a few lines. Open at random one of the volumes of *La Princesse de Clèves*, take any ten pages and then compare them to ten pages of *Ivanhoe* or *Quentin Durward*...

Every work of art is a *beautiful lie*; all those who have written know this well. There is nothing so ridiculous as the counsel given by members of the fashionable public: 'Imitate nature'. Confound it, I know we have to imitate nature; but to what extent? That is the whole question...Art then is only a beautiful lie but Sir Walter Scott has been too much a liar...[7]

The obvious antithesis to Beyle in this respect, as in so many others, is to be found in the theory and practice of his contemporary, Balzac, the Balzac who aspired to be the 'French Walter Scott'[8] and who commended Scott for having 'elevated the novel to the philosophical dignity of history'.[9]

Balzac's attitude to Scott varied more over the years and was less simple than these phrases taken in isolation might suggest, and there are indications that he had read and been impressed, if not moved to any fundamental reappraisal, by *Sir Walter Scott et la Princesse de Clèves*.[10] The novel, as he conceived it, as well as history itself, are, none the less, radically and (for the purposes of definition, conveniently) different from what they were for Beyle. And though both stress the importance of 'detail', it is obvious that for Beyle this was not something whose value lay in a merely external verisimilitude or in the accumulation that might eventually reveal the laws and configurations of society. Beyle never sought, in the way that Balzac did, 'to compete with the Registrar of deaths, marriages and births' (*'faire concurrence à l'état civil'*). There are no social laws that can be easily extrapolated from *Le rouge et le noir* and *La chartreuse de Parme*, certainly none as inclusive and predictable as those invoked in the introduction to *La comédie humaine*. Beyle's own sense of verisimilitude is indicated defiantly (to the point of exaggeration) in the review he wrote of his own novel and which he was hoping would be translated into Italian (it is reprinted conveniently as an appendix to the Garnier edition of *Le rouge et le noir*): 'M. de Stendhal, bored by all the talk of the middle ages, the Gothic arch and the costume of the fourteenth century, has had the audacity to recount an adventure which takes place in 1830 and to leave his readers in total ignorance of the style of costume worn by Mme de Rênal and by Mlle. de la Mole, his two heroines...'

Beyle came to the novel along paths very different from those of his younger contemporary (Balzac indignantly denies in his introduction to *The Human Comedy* that he himself is a 'sensualist', a 'materialist' or, in other words, an 'idéologue') and his early experiments in fiction have very little in common with those of the young Balzac in the best-selling *genres* of the day, the 'Gothic' novel and the historical novel à la *Waverley*. The term 'experiment' misrepresents, in fact, the intention of at least some of the earlier fiction by Beyle. 'I like *examples*, and not, like Montesquieu, Buffon and Rousseau, systems...' he wrote to Pauline (August 1804) and according to Henry James, it was 'this absorbing passion for example, anecdote and illustration that constituted Beyle's distinctive genius...'[11] Narrative, in other words, was for Beyle at first a way of thinking rather than of merely exercising or indulging the imagination, and one of his first completed *nouvelles* was appropriately included by his first posthumous editor as an appendix to *De l'amour*. *Ernestine* is the story of the only child of a wealthy landowner, brought up in the mountains of Dauphiné and passing through the 'seven stages' of the awakening of love and self-esteem when she is pursued ardently but discreetly by an unknown and at first mysterious neighbour, an eligible bachelor considerably older than herself; '...it is no more than thirty pages long', as George Eliot was to write in a review of *De l'amour*,[12] 'and at the expense of only half an hour's reading, we have the story of a naïve girlish passion, given with far more finish, that is, with more significant detail, than most of our writers can achieve by the elaboration of three volumes'. The significant detail and the fable-like (almost fairy-tale) simplicity of the story spring obviously from the clarity and completeness of Beyle's thoughts on the subject that meant so much to him, and *Ernestine* resembles, in this respect, his best and most mature fiction. Its relative lack of substance and reality is due only, as in a play by Marivaux, to the exclusion of almost any other interest than the dictates of passion and pride. It is easy to imagine that the real Ernestine may have been Mathilde Dembrowski and certainly, if this is true, it would account for the lack of contact or intimacy between herself and her eminently well suited admirer, whose love, though she is too proud to tell him, she returns. It would explain too the one serious weakness in the story: her unaccountably cruel behaviour towards her lover and herself in marrying another man.

Life as it presents itself to the man or woman with exceptional intelligence as well as strength and delicacy of character; that is the focal and developing preoccupation in most of Beyle's stories and novels, and in all those we think of as characteristic. And this perhaps more than anything else is what distinguishes him from Balzac both as a novelist and a historian. It is this too which accounts for the difficulties we see him at times only partially overcoming: technical difficulties in so far as his fiction could only succeed on any level in so far as they were solved, but also difficulties of belief; the difficulty especially of believing in a man or woman whose pursuit of happiness was worthy of interest (and the contemplation of which would afford the 'greatest possible pleasure') and yet whose demands on life were not impossible. Ernestine, in what we can only imagine as a fit of unaccountable perversity, turns down an ideal match; Vanina Vanini, in the story of that name, confesses unnecessarily to her *carbonaristo* lover that she has betrayed his comrades in order to save him for herself and loses him for ever, after he has almost throttled her in rage. The unnecessary confession of a crime inspired by passion leads at the end of *Mina de Wanghel* to a more decorous but no less final estrangement between lovers. Beyle seems incapable in all these stories of imagining either a happy ending or a good reason for the lack of one. All of them clearly are to this extent failures. And in noting this, one suspects that the difficulties he experienced in imagining a life worth living were due to a failure to succeed in what he wanted to achieve rather than to want of trying. A settled pessimism concerning the possibilities of such a life would presumably have led him to show it as being doomed from the very outset rather than thwarted at the end by nothing more than a perverse whim or a mere error of judgment. By contrast, in Balzac, since Charles Grandet and Eugène de Rastignac are already corrupt when we first meet them, or at least patently corruptible, the melancholy and bitter endings of *Eugénie Grandet* and *Le père Goriot* are in perfect harmony with what has gone before.

Armance has the weaknesses and faults of all Beyle's fiction before *Le rouge et le noir*. The crudity of the stratagem by which its hero is deceived into thinking that the bride he loves feels coldly towards him is so obvious as to require no comment. He 'finds' a letter forged by a scheming relative in his bride's handwriting addressed to a friend. His suicide by passion when on his way, ostensibly, to take part in the War of Greek Independence is a piece of conventional romanticism in the tradition of *Werther*, no less romantic or conventional for being at the same time 'ironical'. Yet it is a novel which goes a considerable way towards overcoming the difficulties I have in mind and hence one which anticipates in often impressive ways the achievement represented by *Le rouge et le noir*. For one thing, as in *Le rouge*, exceptional intelligence and unusual delicacy of character are not shown as inexplicable or undefinable virtues. They are, as far as possible, explained by circumstances and shown from the inside in terms of often painful experience rather than as a merely external and enviable impressiveness. Failure, moreover, to find a way of life compatible with the hero's ideal demands does not exclude – on the contrary, it ensues upon – a prolonged examination of what the age has to offer.

The circumstances which make the hero of *Armance*, the young only son of one of the oldest families in France, a man of *strictly* unusual character include the most notorious fact about the novel and the clue, it is often argued, to his enigmatic behaviour: Octave is sexually impotent. The novel appeared shortly after the scandal surrounding Henri de Latouche's *Olivier*, in which the same theme had been discreetly developed, and it is perhaps for this reason that Beyle found it unnecessary to refer to his hero's affliction explicitly. Not that the clue is indispensable or one that cannot be easily guessed at. Octave de Malibert's melancholy and mad impulsiveness, his horror of sexual attraction and his deep love and tenderness for his mother can be taken, in their context, as self-explanatory. Moreover, as a nobleman, he is condemned to impotence of another kind in a constitutional monarchy. He is wealthy and a future peer of the realm, but only on sufferance. The restitution of his future inheritance is due to the vote in the Assembly indemnifying former émigrés, a privilege of which he is reminded by a provincial deputy who congratulates him on the 'two million' he is going to 'vote him' ('these were the very words of this man...'). At the same time his intelligence is that of a well-read and enlightened former pupil of the Ecole Polytechnique, a reader of the Utilitarians and the Idéologues and hence a man fully aware of the absurdity of his position. Octave's physical impotence in this respect is merely one aspect of a general predicament.

It is in the presentation of the latter that Beyle writes as a novelist or rather as the kind of novelist we are to find in *Le rouge et le noir*. 'Detail' here is not an accretion of fictitious accidental facts but the close development of a real possibility. What difference does it make, Octave finds himself asking, after narrowly escaping from being crushed by a passing carriage, whether he goes on living or not? He has no doubt of his mother's love, but his father and his snobbish buffoon of an uncle love only the name he bears:

'I am bound to them by the smallest of obligations...'

The idea of a *duty* to perform, however, is 'like a flash of lightning' to Octave, a sudden illumination:

'Can I really say that it's of little importance if it's the only duty I have left? If I can't overcome the difficulties that chance confronts me with in my present position, what right have I to believe that I am so sure to conquer all the difficulties I may meet in the future? Here am I proud enough to believe that I'm equal to all the dangers and to every kind of harm of which a man can possibly be the victim, and yet when suffering actually presents itself to me, I ask it to go away and come back in some other form that will suit me better, in other words be only half as painful. And I thought I was so firm and resolute! I was merely being presumptuous...

Soon the disgust Octave felt for everything was less violent and he appeared to himself less wretched. His spirits, depressed and disorganised, as it were, by the absence for so long of any happiness, were reanimated and strengthened a little as his self-esteem returned. Thoughts of a different kind began to occur to him. The low oppressive ceiling of his room displeased him beyond endurance; he envied the magnificent drawing room of the Bonnivets' house. 'It's at least twenty feet high', he thought. 'It's a room in which I feel I can breathe...'

He begins to plan a room for himself which only he will ever enter and of which 'the tiny imperceptible key' will be carried always on his watch chain. A servant will dust it once a month but under his own surveillance in case he should guess his thoughts from his books or find what he has written 'in order to guide his soul during his moments of folly'. The room will be decorated with three seven-foot-tall mirrors:

'I have always loved mirrors. They make a sombre and magnificent ornament. How big are the tallest mirrors they make at Saint-Gobain?' And the man who for three quarters of an hour had just been thinking of ending his days climbed up on a chair to find the catalogue of prices. He spent an hour making an estimate of the costs of his own private drawing room. He felt that he was behaving like a child but this made him write with even greater rapidity and seriousness... (ch. 2)

Julien Sorel will, of course, think of 'duty' in terms reminiscent of these, though he will pass beyond the stage at which self-contemplation is not only a necessary precaution in a hostile world but a wholly absorbing pastime. He is far less than Octave a special case and *Le rouge et le noir*, correspondingly, tells us more about the world. For all the beauty and poignancy of the nearly successful love-affair between Octave and his bride, and for all the brilliance of its social comedy, Maurice Bardèche is surely right when he complains that 'those elements within *Armance* which make it resemble a case-history weigh heavily on the novel and reduce its general significance'. Octave's 'condemnation of the world' is, after all, that of 'someone who is ill'.[13] The malevolent trick which wrecks his marriage prevents either the reader or himself from knowing whether he might have been in any way cured through love.

In *Le rouge et le noir*, the difficulties to which the failures of the early fiction bear witness are overcome, most obviously in the last chapters of the novel, and we have the first of his three most complete, that is detailed and self-sufficient, accounts of life as he understood it. The self-sufficiency, even though *Le rouge* is a beautifully finished work of art, is not of the kind that presupposes little or no knowledge of the world. The ideal reader is someone who will be alive to the nuances of its social comedy.[14] Yet at the same time Beyle is at pains to prevent it from being comedy or satire at the expense of a merely *contemporary* world, another version of Lamothe-Langon's *M. le Préfet*. He cannot avoid making oblique references to the politics of the day and this may distract the modern reader. But the social world of *Le rouge et le noir* has its own laws and structure, like those of Manzoni's Lombardy in *I promessi sposi* or Shakespeare's in *Julius Caesar*. How much it corresponds to the actual society of the reign of Charles X is a question that the historian may want to ask. We don't have to answer it, however, or at least not with any professional exactitude, in order to understand and enjoy the novel.

The impression with which the novel leaves us of finish and completeness is also, however, the effect of a kind of romantic rhetoric; not the rhetoric which consists in declamation but the more difficult and less obvious kind which leaves the facts to speak shatteringly for themselves. The guillotine, of which Julien has received a premonition in the church at Verrières in the opening chapters of the novel, falls when his head is at 'its most poetic' and the last two paragraphs of the novel describe the reactions, both violent and very much in character, of the two well-bred ladies who have been his mistresses. The guillotine, which may owe some of its fascination to the fact that it has bathed in royal and noble blood and is the modern version of the sacrificial knife, falls with the same horrifying and yet satisfying thud as at the end of the fourth movement of the *Symphonie fantastique* of Berlioz. There is the same almost ritualistic appropriateness in Julien's shooting of his former mistress during mass as the bell is ringing for the consecration of the Host. *Le rouge et le noir* is a romantic thriller, one that can easily be read as blasphemous and seditious, and the sense of gratifying completeness with which it leaves us is partly that of a point made with an eloquent absence of explanation or apology: 'How could a man as intelligent, sensitive and courageous', the reader may find himself asking, 'a man, moreover, from the working classes, end his life in any other way in such a world?'

When we come to the unfinished *Lucien Leuwen*, which, despite the state of the manuscript, is a finer and deeper novel and in this sense if no other more 'complete', we may be able to look back to the romantic dénouement of *Le rouge* and see it as, potentially at least, a distraction. The public Julien, with his pistols and sensational trial and death, can distract us from the Julien whose inner life is so different from what it seems to others. We can find ourselves forgetting that he has not only committed his crime publicly but left his appeal till too late and gone out of his way to anger the Besançon jury. And we can easily miss the subtlety of the device by which Beyle suggests to us a form of ideal happiness by showing this as a possibility only; as the dream of a man looking back on his life and longing to go on living during his last days in a condemned cell. For in its own way too, like the earlier fiction, *Le rouge et le noir* leaves us in suspense and with many questions unresolved.

'Apprendre à vouloir'

The possibility of ideal happiness is of course that of 'living with Mme de Rênal', a possibility frustrated by the guillotine. Mme de Rênal is shown to us as more than worthy of Julien's yearning for her. The measure of the devotion of which she is capable is given by the fact that she believes quite sincerely that she is damned to eternal torment for loving him. Yet she remains human and not in herself ideal – and conceivably, in so far as a life shared with Julien *can* be imagined, a far too timorous and conscience-ridden companion for her adventurous free-thinking lover. The value of the life that Julien longs for is something quite distinct from what that life itself might have been, however blissful and profitable.

This, however, is different from saying that Mme de Rênal, as a person, is unimportant to Julien or Julien's creator or that she is *unworthy* of the ideal estimate made of her, like Proust's Odette de Crécy, or else conveniently held at a distance and, as a result of this alone, enigmatic and appealing, like Flaubert's Mme Arnoux in *L'Education Sentimentale*. Julien's dreams of happiness are nourished by real and undeluded memories. The ideal value she comes to represent is due to the peculiar circumstances of her life and Julien's and to the perspective in which she is now seen. Thinking of her as he does in prison gives Julien the greatest possible happiness.

In the last two chapters of the novel, the difficulties Beyle had wrestled with in his earlier fiction are overcome. For if Julien is an 'interesting' character it is because he is capable of knowing what he wants and hence what he values more than anything else. The question whether he will be fortunate enough to get what he wants, or would have been had a reprieve come through, could only be answered in a different novel. After Julien's meditations in the penultimate chapter, *Le rouge et le noir* can end with at least one point well made.

What does it mean to be capable of knowing what one wants? *Le rouge et le noir* is concerned with this question, and its usefulness and corresponding beauty are those of the answers it offers. We are told that this is a rare accomplishment, at least in the middle and upper classes, and we are shown many times that it is far from easy. This is the point of much of the comedy of the novel, such as that of Julien's ordeal during the first visit he pays in his life to a café:

But the young lady behind the counter had noticed the charming features of the young farmer or tradesman from the country, as he seemed to be, who, with his package under his arm, was standing three yards from the stove studying the fine white plaster bust of the king. She was tall and had the attractive figure of the young women of Franche-Comté; she was smartly attired and in such a way as to make the café seem all the more elegant; and she had already called out twice in a tiny voice intended to be heard only by Julien: 'Monsieur, Monsieur!'

He walked eagerly towards the counter and the pretty girl standing behind it as if he were marching on the enemy. And in the middle of this sudden manoeuvre he dropped his package on the floor.

What pity the schoolboys of Paris are going to feel for our young man from the provinces, those schoolboys who already at the age of fifteen know how to walk into a café with so distinguished an air. But these children who are so well trained at fifteen, by the time they are eighteen have *turned common*. The passionate timidity one meets in the provinces is sometimes overcome and when this happens it teaches a man to know what he wants and the will to get it ['*elle enseigne à vouloir*']. As he walked up to the beautiful girl who had deigned to address him, Julien thought: 'I must tell her the truth' and as he overcame his shyness, became all the more courageous.

'Madame, this is the first time in my life I've ever been in Besançon and I should like some bread and a cup of coffee, which I'll pay you for.' (book 1, ch. 24)

Julien is comic throughout much of the novel, with his would-be scoundrelly and often touchingly ineffectual show of hypocrisy, his habit of treating everyday life as a hazardous military operation and even during his fateful struggle to work up the courage to hold Mme de Rênal's hand. But he is comic above all in that he seems so unusual. The joke, as so often in Beyle, can become a joke at the expense of the more conventional reader. Not only does Julien go far in society, much further than almost anyone ever goes. He is shown to us as a 'superior being', even when his preoccupation with his own dignity has gone far beyond a joke. We see this during the first night he spends with Mme de Rênal:

But during the best moments [*les moments les plus doux*], the victim of a curious pride, he continued to aspire to the rôle of a man accustomed to conquering women: he took incredible pains to spoil what was most lovable in himself. Instead of noticing attentively the transports he aroused and the remorse which so clearly betrayed their depth and passion, he never once ceased to consider the idea of carrying out his *duty*. He dreaded a fearful remorse and an eternal humiliation if he forgot to follow the ideal model which he had set up for himself. In fact what made Julien a superior being was precisely that which prevented him enjoying the happiness which lay at his feet...

'Is there nothing more to happiness than this? Is this all that it means to be loved?' These were Julien's first thoughts on returning to his room. He felt all the astonishment and misgiving of someone who has just obtained something he has long desired and who still feels the habit of desire, finds that there is nothing left to desire and yet still has no memories. Like a soldier returning from an exercise, he was absorbed in going over every detail of his own behaviour. 'Have I failed in any way towards myself?' he thought, 'Have I played my rôle as I should?'

And what rôle? That of a man who is accustomed to shining in front of women. (book 1, ch. 15)

Beyle's attitude to his hero is far from simple hero-worship[15] and even if it may be true that in some ways Julien is a self-portrait, it is by no means an indulgent one. The novel shows us the cost as well as the immense advantage of learning to know what one wants. And it is not necessarily because they have failed to understand him that some readers have been shocked or horrified by the form that Julien's single-mindedness takes.

Julien is, of course, born into circumstances in which he can survive only by defending himself and if necessary without mercy, circumstances too in which his puny physique forces him to rely on ruse as his principal weapon, though the use of the more ungentlemanly forms of violence is also characteristic of his class. Beyle's interest in the trial of the poor seminarist Antoine Berthet, who was accused of shooting a former mistress, to whose children he had been engaged as a private tutor is well known. And in *Promenade dans Rome*, written only a year before *Le rouge et le noir*, he comments on and reproduces the newspaper account of a similar case judged by a court at Tarbes in the Pyrenees:

> While the upper classes of Parisian society seem to have lost the ability to feel anything with either force or constancy, passion is manifested with a frightening energy in the petty bourgeoisie among the young people who, like M. Laffargue, have received a good education but are obliged to work and struggle for the real necessities of living.
>
> Exempted by the need to work from the thousand tiny obligations imposed by polite society and by its ways of thinking and seeing... they still have the strength to know what they want and get it ['*ils conservent la force de vouloir*'] by the very fact that they feel strongly. All the great men of the future will probably come from the class to which M. de Laffargue belongs. Napoleon himself once combined the same circumstances: a good education, an ardent imagination and extreme poverty.
>
> Only the artist perhaps may benefit from wealthy parentage and hence freedom from charlatanism and the 'fatal temptation of title and crosses'.
>
> But if one is born rich and noble, how can one be exempt from elegance, delicacy, etc. and maintain that superabundance of energy which makes artists and renders men so ridiculous?
>
> I hope with all my heart that I may be completely wrong.[16]

The description, incidentally, that we are given of Julien in the first chapter of *Le rouge et le noir* reminds one of the portraits of the young Bonaparte, but he has one trait reminiscent of Laffargue himself, whose 'expression and fine-looking eyes, which are normally gentle, become sinister when he stares and his eyebrows meet'.[17]

Le rouge et le noir is a chronicle of 1830, as the title page indicates, a novel about the life of typical social groups in the France of Charles X.[18] Julien is himself typical to a considerable extent of his class and an anomaly only in that he lacks the physique which will enable him to work in his father's sawmill or survive in the brutal world of his brothers and other young men of his class. In the games played on Sundays and feast days, he had always been beaten, we are told in the opening chapters. Critics of the novel have tended very much to underestimate the extent to which Julien's temperament and even his intelligence can be explained by the circumstances in which he has grown. And they have underestimated accordingly the extent to which his career can be seen as *exemplary*: the story of Everyman when Everyman grows up in those circumstances rather than that of the rise and downfall of a romantic freak and an inexplicable genius. Even the extraordinary gifts to which Julien owes his initial rise in society are a reflection of what that particular society expects of the children of his class who seek to improve their lot and win the world's approval. His famous Bible-recitation show, for example, is an exhibition not only of cerebral vigour but of time spent in more worthy occupations than thinking or reading for oneself, and it is for this reason that it impresses not only children and servants but their masters who are men of the world:

Adolphe, the eldest child, had picked up the Bible.
'Open it anywhere', Julien went on. 'Tell me the first word in a verse and I shall recite the Holy Scripture by heart, the rule of conduct for all of us, until you tell me to stop.'
Adolphe opened the Bible, read out a word and Julien recited the entire page as easily as if he had been talking French. M. de Rênal looked at his wife with an air of triumph. The children, seeing their parents' astonishment, stared. Soon Mme de Rênal's chambermaid and the cook were to be seen near the open door. By then, Adolphe had opened the Bible in eight different places and Julien had recited with the same ease.
'Gracious heavens, listen to the pretty little priest!' cried the cook, who was a very devout young woman.
M. de Rênal's self-esteem was becoming perturbed by now and far from thinking about the tutor he had just engaged for his children,

he was busy hunting in his memory for one or two Latin phrases to quote. At last, he managed to recite some lines from Horace. Julien, however, who knew no other Latin than the Bible, replied with a frown that the Sacred Ministry which he was destined to enter prohibited him from reading an author so profane.

M. de Rênal quoted quite a fair number of verses that he claimed that Horace had written. He also explained to his children what Horace was. But his children, overcome with admiration, hardly paid any attention to what he said. They were staring at Julien...
(book 1, ch. 6.)

A repeat-performance at the house of M. de Rênal's rival, the governor of the local workhouse, brings him invitations to dinner from the head of the gendarmerie, the tax inspector and a number of 'wealthy liberals' who talk even of voting for a scholarship for Julien to be paid out of communal funds. The dining room echoes with this 'imprudent idea', while Julien, after making his farewells, escapes with 'agile' steps into the night. (Later, with the benign scholarly Bishop of Besançon, he will find that he can unbend and discuss not only Horace but Virgil, Cicero and the subversive Tacitus.)

The pious parrot-learning and the show of saintliness are all part of Julien's strategy to survive. As M. Sartre would put it, it is his way of 'being in the world'. Julien has chosen 'the uniform of his century' and particularly of a period in which the Church was seeking to extend its domination throughout the whole of society. Under Napoleon, he believes that he would have risen from obscurity by being killed in battle or made a general at thirty. Under the Restoration it is necessary to compete with the Jesuits on their own terms. His own studied duplicity has its counterpart in the spying and intrigue of which we hear so much in the novel and which lends it its (characteristically Stendhalian) conspiratorial atmosphere. He is part of this world in so far as he has adapted himself to it, so much so that the local Jesuits think of him as *récupérable* and intrigue to save him from the guillotine. And for all his inner pride, he is able to sympathise readily with the shameless servility of his companions in the Besançon seminary:

Not to smile with respect at the mere mention of the Prefect's name is deemed imprudent by the peasants of Franche-Comté and imprudence is soon punished if you are poor by your having no bread

to eat...the fathers of many of his comrades had often known what it is to come back to one's cottage on a winter's evening and find no bread, chestnuts or even potatoes. 'Why should it seem strange then', thought Julien, 'if a happy man, as far as they're concerned, is first and foremost, someone who's eaten a good dinner?'
(book 1, ch. 26)

Yet he remains distinct from the other seminarists. He tries diligently to imitate them and finds that there is even a devout-seeming way of eating a boiled egg. But as a hypocrite he is a conspicuous amateur whom they instinctively persecute until his air of superiority, that is his failure to subordinate himself utterly to his rôle, is justified in their eyes by his promotion to the post of *répétiteur* and the gift of a slain boar sent by a friend and proof seemingly of powerful connections in the world.

Julien *is* unusual, unusual in being completely unhypocritical towards himself about the rôle he is playing, though this again is something that his creator explains, or rather enables those readers whose lives are very different to think of not only as a psychological phenomenon but as an experience that could be shared. Deprived in early life of a mother, and brought up brutally in a small provincial town by a man whom we may suspect is not his natural father, one of his few friends as a boy is the old army surgeon who bequeaths him the only books he owns and fills his imagination with stories of the Grande Armée. The surgeon dies and Julien is left alone in a world which his imagination has taught him to see in military terms. And it is impossible for him to believe in his rôle as a future priest as anything but a necessary ruse in a world in which he is despised and oppressed and in which there are only dead heroes to turn to as guides.

He is superstitious though a secret atheist, and, prophetically as it happens, sees portents in the light falling like drops of blood through the red stained glass of the church in Verrières. He owns a miniature portrait of Napoleon which he treats like a secret talisman and he is terrified of allowing his feelings for the Emperor to be known, not only because this would be indeed imprudent but lest it should be seen by others that this is the god he adores. The superstition and the terrible discipline that Julien imposes constantly on himself are those of a lonely man in a dangerous world. They are those of any man who finds that, over long periods of time, he can rely only on his own nerve and presence of mind. The novel is sometimes comic, of course, in that his fears on occasions, like those of Catherine Morland at Northanger Abbey, are groundless.

It is Julien's response even to those challenges he has merely imagined which makes him, however, a 'superior being', this and the discipline he exercises to prove his nerve. It is a truly stupendous feat for the timid suspicious Julien to seize Mme de Rênal's hand, when they are sitting in the garden on a hot summer night, overjoyed though she is as well as dismayed by the liberty. And the record Beyle gives of Julien's thoughts and feelings up to this moment are a sign of the importance he himself attaches to moments of this kind.[19] For it is here that we are shown the reasons for Julien's eventual ability to know what he wants and values in the world. The idea of seizing Mme de Rênal's hand has occurred to Julien the previous evening when it has brushed accidentally against his own:

The hand quickly withdrew; but it occurred to Julien that it was his *duty* to see that it would not be drawn back when he touched it. The idea of a duty to be carried out and a feeling of ridiculousness or rather inferiority to be undergone if he should fail, immediately deprived him of all pleasure.
(book 1, ch. 8.)

He vows the following evening that if he has not taken her hand by the time the strokes of ten have ceased chiming he will walk upstairs and blow out his brains. His voice trembles as he chats to Mme de Rênal and her companion. So does that of Mme de Rênal who wonders what is wrong with him, though he fails to notice this. 'The fearful conflict between duty and timidity was so powerful that he was unable to notice anything outside himself.' At last the hand is grasped on the last stroke of ten, Mme de Rênal tries to pull it away and then surrenders it. Julien's soul is 'inundated with happiness' not because he loves her but because a 'frightful torment' has now ended (book 1, ch. 9). Love for Mme de Rênal is something he will experience later.

Beyle gives us nothing but Julien's thoughts and feelings, 'the movements of his soul', to use a phrase from 'Sir Walter Scott et la Princesse de Clèves'. (As the clock strikes ten, each stroke 'echoes in his heart' and causes 'something like a physical movement'.) He leaves the reader to draw his own conclusions from these essential data, or to use his own word, 'details', and among these conclusions it may occur to us that it is by no means a coincidence that duty should present itself to Julien in this particular form. As Julien's previous and subsequent feelings towards Mme de Rênal reveal, this is more than a Gidean 'acte gratuit'.

'Duty' is none the less the word Julien uses to describe this and his other self-imposed challenges and the irony and, for the reader, humour of the word lies in the fact that this is not duty in any ordinary sense of the word, though the obligation imposed on himself is as strict as if he were carrying out a mission on the battlefield. The idea of a duty to be performed *occurs* to Julien unexpectedly. (We are reminded of the often forgotten truism that all decisions, however long premeditated, are in their origins spontaneous and without conscious motivation. We may decide to do something long before we do it, but we never decide to decide to do it.) It occurs to him as an absolute obligation, an unevadable test of his will. Passing the test gives Julien freedom because of the *sense* of freedom he has now acquired from his previous weaknesses and fears. The next day he oversleeps, is scolded by M. de Rênal and retorts with confident uncontrollable anger that he can easily find another post in Verrières if M. de Rênal is dissatisfied. The confrontation ends with his winning a series of running victories including a rise in his wages and permission to absent himself for the rest of the day, and part of this he spends on a tall rock exulting in the beauty of an immense landscape on a glorious summer afternoon.

Julien, to put with crude explicitness what Beyle conveys by more poetic means, is at one with nature here in the mountains inasmuch as he is at one now with his own nature. Tall beech trees, beneath which there is a 'delicious freshness', reach almost as high as the rock on which he stands and, rooted in the mountains, they prefigure the tree of which Julien speaks during his last days alive when he is recalling what duty has always meant to him:

'I am isolated in this cell; but I have not lived in *isolation* on this earth; the thought of duty has always given me strength. The duty which, rightly or wrongly, I have always forced myself to accept has been like the trunk of a solid tree against which I leaned during the storm; I wavered, I was shaken. After all, I was only a man...but I wasn't swept away.' (book 2, ch. 44)

Significantly, it is near this spot in the mountains that Julien will ask to be buried.

Julien's duty has been of his own choosing but, as the word itself suggests, it has the effect on him of an external obligation. It is something of which he has been acutely conscious and yet it has its origins beyond the conscious self.[20] The life and intelligent purpose to which Julien remains faithful and to which he clings for support are his own and yet, literally, not his alone. Paradoxically, the more utterly dependent he has made himself on his own resources, the more strength he has derived from this other source. A similar paradox occurs in the history of religious experience and it is significant that he is befriended by the two priests in the novel whose Christian faith is most exacting and sincere, even though both of them doubt the sincerity of his own professed vocation. It is significant too that just before these thoughts on duty, Julien should have longed consciously for the consolation of genuine belief:

He was troubled by all his memories of the Bible that he knew by heart...'But how, when as many as *three are gathered together*, can one believe in the great name of GOD, after the fearful way it has been abused by our priests...'

It is significant, finally, that immediately afterwards he should realise what it is that he really wants, what it is of which he is now deprived and what, despite this, gives his life its value:

'So I shall die at the age of twenty-three. Give me five years more to live with Mme. de Rênal...'

Julien, we are told in the scene in the Besançon café, has the 'passionate timidity' of the young provincial which, when it is overcome, *'enseigne à vouloir'*. The phrase cannot be translated directly into English. 'It teaches one to will' is an inadequate rendering, as is also 'It teaches one to desire.' The novel shows us the relation between these two meanings and gives meaning itself to the words 'commonness' and 'vulgarity'; the commonness and vulgarity that can ensue upon failure to conform to one's own standards and satisfaction if one has conformed to the wishes of the powerful or the numerous or at least what one imagines these wishes to be. The Parisian schoolboys who may laugh at Julien's way of ordering a coffee for the first time 'turn common' by the time they are eighteen. Julien, by contrast, though he dreads doing what he believes he ought to, dreads even more surrendering to his own fear. In this he is the most exacting judge of his own behaviour, and the confidence he acquires in carrying out his self-imposed challenges makes it that much easier for him to do what he thinks right. In Julien, in other words, we are shown a man in whom the common distracting tension between duty and inclination is overcome and who is capable of the single-mindedness which is also wholehearted desire.

'Scènes probantes' and the historical revelation

We are also shown a man who is capable of learning from experience and his own mistakes. 'Every novel by Stendhal', M. Bardèche has written, 'is the story of an education'[21] and this is certainly true of *Le rouge et le noir*. This is one of the main differences between Stendhal's novel and a novel whose ostensible subject may remind us of it, Flaubert's *Education sentimentale*. One of the most striking impressions of all given by Flaubert's novel and one of its most impressive ironies is that it isn't really the story of an education at all. By the end of the story, as Flaubert himself makes it clear, the hero, Frédéric Moreau has learned nothing. An epigraph to *Le rouge et le noir* might have been: 'Ask and it shall be given you; seek and ye shall find; knock and it shall be opened unto you...' (Matthew VII, 7). For it is because Julien knocks and seeks that he goes into the world and because he goes in that he and hence the reader himself are able to learn from his experience. Throughout his life, by contrast, Frédéric evades confrontation and towards the end of his life can only attribute its uneventfulness to ill-fortune including the fact that he was born at the wrong time. This, as much as anything else, accounts for George Sand's criticism of the lack of *drama* in the novel.[22] Frédéric is in love with the beautiful Mme Arnoux, who is neglected and wronged by her affable brute of a husband; with what is clearly her own grateful assent he spends hours with her alone in her house in Auteuil; yet the dread of intimacy and responsibility (presumably) paralyses his will; his *liaisons* are all with women who mean less to him and the relationship with Mme Arnoux comes to nothing. In the same way, despite his ambition, he fails to take advantage of his many opportunities. He is discouraged by the world of politics as rapidly as by the world of business and he reaches old age as a much travelled but completely undistinguished gentleman of means. The principal result of this infirmity is that we are told remarkably little about the world of politics, the world of business or even Mme Arnoux. We are told a great deal about what they seem like to Frédéric – Flaubert, in contrast to Stendhal, deals painstakingly in external appearances – but the realism of the novel lies in what they seem like to a man who is lacking in curiosity and whose contact with the world is so slight as to seem accidental. Flaubert's intention, in fact, in writing his story of an education was wholly different from Beyle's.[23]

Julien's resolute ambition and his determination not to be sat upon are of the kind that bring out the best and the worst in those he meets and it is in this sense that *Le rouge et le noir* is more 'dramatic' than *L'éducation sentimentale*, not only, that is, more vivid and engaging but psychologically and morally more revealing. It is this too which bears out Beyle's own claim that *Le rouge et le noir* is a 'chronicle of 1830' and, as such, a study of *mœurs*.[24] The good looking, high principled and unsuccessfully domineering mayor of Verrières; his devout, retiring aristocratic wife; his rival, M. Valenod, the affable, mercilessly opportunistic governor of the local workhouse; the Besançon seminarists and their passionately devout director; the clever, powerful Marquis de la Mole and his brilliant, rebellious daughter; all, as a result of their encounter or rather collision with Julien reveal themselves for what they are and leave us to draw our own conclusions about the true nature of their class and background. The revelation of character corresponds to what Beyle in his *Racine et Shakspeare* calls 'des scènes *probantes*', that is 'scenes which *give proof* of the characters or the passions of the personages who take part in them.'[25] The revelation is not only something from which the reader can learn, it is also part of Julien's education. He learns, for example, that Mme de Rênal, the Marquis de la Mole and his daughter Mathilde are not the contemptuous snobs he had thought they were. Nor are the members of their class, at least not always and by no means necessarily. As he loses his dread of being treated 'like a servant' and comes to recognise in Mme de Rênal the deepest devotion of which a woman with her beliefs and in her position is capable and, in the Marquis de la Mole, genuine respect and cordiality, he forgets his former distrust of the world. Interestingly too, he forgets his former cult of Napoleon. He acquires ease and openness of manner and is only at moments of unusual strain – for example, when Mathilde invites him to her room and he suspects that this may be a plot to have him killed on his way through the window – 'an unhappy man at war with the whole of society' (book 2, ch. 13).

This last description of Julien has often, I find, been quoted out of context and taken to refer to something both constant and predictable in his character. Yet there are few novelists who have remained more faithful to the ways in which not only mood but the entire corresponding code of behaviour and philosophy of life can change from one moment to the next. The development of Julien's character is so erratic that many readers will protest that they are unaware that it develops at all. Yet take the account we are given of Julien's *ambition* when we first meet him:

For Julien, to make one's fortune meant first getting out of Verrières; he abhorred his native town. Everything in it he saw chilled his imagination.
Since his early childhood, he had known moments of exaltation when he would dream rapturously of the day when he would be presented to the beautiful ladies of the town of Paris and attract their attention by some daring exploit. Why should he not be loved by one of them, as Bonaparte had been by the brilliant Mme de Beauharnais in the days when he was still poor?
(book 1, ch. 5)

and compare this with what we are told after the attempt on Mme de Rênal's life when this dream has been realised in every particular:

Julien felt unworthy of so much devotion; to tell the truth, he was tired of heroism. He would have responded gladly to an unassuming, naïve and almost timid tenderness, but Mathilde's proud soul needed constantly a public and a sense of what *others* might think.[26]
(book 2, ch. 39)

To take a young man setting out on his career is Beyle's principal method in all his major novels of showing what a society has to offer to those whose courage, capacity for enjoyment and intelligence are unimpaired. The intensity and yet haziness of his dreams of the future are necessary to the process of growth and discovery and, as in the case of Julien, the realisation of a dream can itself be the cause of disenchantment and lead the dreamer to know better what he really wants.

The very form that Julien's ambition takes, moreover, is a sign of his conditioning. He is not born into the conspiratorial world of the Restoration in innocence, innocent or unrepentant though he may feel in the privacy of his own heart. The adoration of Napoleon, whom, unlike Beyle, he fails to distinguish from Bonaparte, is adoration for a ruler who built a new dynasty on the ruins of the old and who chose ostlers' and innkeepers' sons to play the roles of princes and kings. Julien is no Jacobin, despite his tears of sympathy for the inmates of the work-house who are forbidden to sing when their master, M. Valenod, is entertaining guests to dinner and despite his revolutionary fervour in the salons of the Marquis de la Mole when the exiled eccentric Count Altamira is confiding in him as if he were a fellow-radical. Their conversation is overheard, rather too obviously, by Mathilde de la Mole whom he later submits to a deliberately provocative tirade on the virtues of ruthlessness in any reformer of mankind, so that she reverently thinks of him as 'another Danton'. Yet this Danton can act with pride in his efficiency and in the trust placed in him as the secret emissary of the Marquis de la Mode and a group of fellow conspirators who are prepared to seek foreign aid to maintain the power and privileges of the throne, the Church and the ancient nobility of France. Even his speech to the Besançon jury, in which he tells them that they are 'outraged bourgeois' judging him not for his ostensible crime but for having dared to rise in society, is provoked by the triumphant expression in the eyes of its president, M. Valenod. And his speech is directed not against class distinctions as such but against those who would deny a man's right to move into the class he prefers.

Beyle was not himself a socialist by any means, despite some recent attempts to pass him off as one, or at least a *socialiste avant la lettre*.[27] And Julien has certainly nothing in common with the hero of the Communard Jules Vallès's semi-autobiographical trilogy, *L'enfant, Le bachelier* and *L'insurgé*. Julien's political attitudes are more irresponsible and inconsistent than those of Vallès or his hero and in this sense far more commonplace. Yet a Marxist may find interest in the fact that the realisation of Julien's early dreams turns out to be an empty victory. He may also find historical significance in the fact that this is not even really a victory. Julien has striven to overcome his weaknesses and prove equal to any challenge to his self-esteem. But his rise in society has been due entirely to patronage, and to patronage he has not even sought. He has proved to be an excellent choice as personal secretary to the great Marquis de la Mole and once introduced into the noble household, his success in society has been due to his ease and liveliness, which are those of a man with no pretensions to being anything other than he is and with the good sense to behave accordingly.[28] His elevation to the title of Chevalier de la Vernaye is due to the most formidable social asset he will ever possess: the fact that he is a plebeian and that Mathilde de la Mole is prepared to acknowledge him as the father of her child. The normally adroit, imperturbable and courtly Marquis de la Mole goes almost out of his mind with grief and rage. No greater or more final and effective blow to his pride and interests can be conceived. Even Julien is at first mortified by what he has done to his benefactor and offers to lay down his own life if this will be of any assistance. And it is true that fifty years before, he *might* have been disposed of – or at least Julien and Mathilde put away, Julien permanently. But in Restoration France the old nobility, with its mystique of caste, is without defences, history is on the side of the Julien Sorels, and Julien has immense advantages of which he is not even aware. 'My novel is finished', he tells himself in a mood of dazed wonderment when he receives, in addition to his title, a commission in the Hussars, 'and the credit is mine alone' (book 2, ch. 34). Both the events that have led up to this moment and the sequel show that he is deluded, however, on each of these scores.

The mind of the assassin and the language of the author

The by now irresistible-seeming course of Julien's career is checked dramatically by the letter of denunciation which Mme de Rênal sends to the Marquis de la Mole, a letter written, as it turns out later, under the dictation of her confessor and in reply to a request from the Marquis for information concerning the man who is to marry his only daughter:

'Poor and avid for gain, it is with the aid of the most consummate hypocrisy and by the seduction of a weak and wretched woman that this man has sought to make for himself a place and become something in society. It is part of my painful duty to add that I am compelled to believe that M. Julien Sorel has no religious principles. In conscience, I am constrained to think that one of his ways of succeeding in a household is to seek to seduce the woman who enjoys the principal credit in that house...'
(book 2, ch. 35)

The Marquis decides to prohibit the marriage and offers Julien 10,000 francs a year if he will agree to live outside France and preferably in America. The setback to Julien's fortunes is unmistakable though by no means permanent. Many possibilities of action remain open to him. Yet he voluntarily ends his career by travelling to Verrières and shooting Mme de Rênal in a crowded church during Mass. And after this, despite the sympathy with which he is regarded during his imprisonment and trial by the public, by Mathilde and even by Mme de Rênal, he deliberately attacks the integrity of the jury at the moment when they are about to consider their verdict.

Has Beyle spoilt what might otherwise have been a good novel by making his hero forget his former astuteness and ambition and behave like the desperate Antoine Berthet, who, when he shot and killed Mme Michoud de la Tour, his former mistress, also publicly in church, had so much less to lose than Julien? Critics of the novel have disagreed over this for many years, and in so far as they feel that Julien's act is consistent with what we have been shown of him in the novel, they have offered various explanations of his behaviour. The most convincing of these that I have read, convincing in that it is the most scrupulously related to the text itself, is the one given by Mme Henriette Bibas in her article on *Le double dénouement et la morale du 'Rouge'* in *La revue d'histoire littéraire de la France* for January 1949. Mme Bibas points out that the most shocking and wounding phrase in the letter written by Mme de Rênal is the one in which we are told that Julien is 'poor and avid for gain' and has used seduction as a way 'to make for himself a place and become something in society'. It is an accusation all the more intolerable to Julien in that there is so much seemingly to justify it. ('I could have forgiven everything', the Marquis himself writes in a letter to Mathilde 'except the plan to seduce you because you are rich.') We laugh off usually only those accusations which are not only untrue but utterly implausible. Julien may have wanted to 'be presented to the beautiful ladies of Paris and attract their attention by some daring exploit' but he has always despised cupidity. '"I cannot blame M. de la Mole"', he tells Mathilde, '"he is just and prudent. What father would want to give away his beloved daughter to such a man?"' He leaves at once for Verrières and there demonstrates, in the only possible way in the circumstances, that, when weighed against honour, social success and riches mean absolutely nothing to him.

This is how Mathilde de la Mole sees his gesture. At last, here is a man who is going to be condemned to death, 'the one distinction which cannot be bought'. '"What you call your crime"', Mathilde tells him '"...is only noble vengeance which shows me what a proud heart beats in your breast."' The novel, however, as Mme Bibas reminds us, brings out the depth and complexity of Julien's motivation. It also confronts us with an apparent contradiction in the fact that Julien repents bitterly of his crime and only, moreover, when he knows that the person for whose principal benefit it was performed is alive, with nothing worse than a broken shoulder, and fully aware of what he has done.

Mme Bibas very rightly points out how much the Faguets, Blums, Thibaudets and Prévosts, who have argued over the motivation of Julien's crime, have ignored Stendhal's text and spoken of Julien as if he were not a fictitious personage every one of whose characteristics is given us by the author but a real person concerning whose real state of mind no one can make more than reasonable guesses. Yet, when discussing the sequel to the crime, Mme Bibas herself falls into the same error – an error, of course, which it is very difficult to avoid – and in doing so, she reiterates the views of Sainte-Beuve and almost every other critic since him that Beyle was 'naturally deaf and blind to poetry':[29]

If so many readers fail to respond to this great theme of the descent into the self, this can only be blamed on the language. There is no doubt that Stendhal's language remains constantly unequal to the emotion that he wishes to communicate. Nor is there any doubt that this is eminently suited to poetry. He will fall back unhesitatingly on expressions like 'no word can describe...'

How is it, one naturally asks, that if 'the emotion that Stendhal wishes to communicate' is eminently suited to poetry and if this is something we can know, he *fails* to communicate it? Perhaps if Mme Bibas had followed the text of the last chapters of the novel with the same scrupulousness as those concerned with Julien's crime, she would not have wanted to reduce them to the level of significance of Tracy's *Traité de la volonté*, a work which may have helped Beyle to write the novel but which he certainly didn't need in the way that Bunyan needed the New Testament, to quote Mme Bibas's own analogy.

Beyle's debt to Tracy was very real, and especially to the *introspective* Tracy of the *Logique* who had taught himself to distinguish between the real and apparent precision of language and in doing so realise our utter dependence, in all that we think or say, on memory, our 'most deeply rooted habits' and on the language of those among whom we live. And, as I have argued in an earlier chapter, this must have influenced the way in which Beyle simultaneously thought and wrote. By contrast, the *Traité de la volonté* is highly speculative writing, involving much deduction from a few original premisses and very little observation. It is an example of the kind of reasoning which both Beyle and Tracy, at his best, thought that we should try to avoid[30] and it may be for this reason that, unlike *Le rouge et le noir*, it is now read by scholars alone.

The kind of attention we find ourselves paying to the prose of *Le rouge et le noir* is obviously very different from that which is demanded by Tracy's more speculative writing. Consider only the music of the prose and, to take a single instance, the meaning that is conveyed (either unmistakeably or not at all) by the note we hear in Julien's voice and in Beyle's:

Julien entra dans l'église neuve de Verrières. Toutes les fenêtres hautes de l'édifice étaient voilées avec des rideaux cramoisis. Julien se trouva à quelques pas derrière le banc de Mme de Rênal. Il lui sembla qu'elle priait avec ferveur. La vue de cette femme qui l'avait tant

aimé fit trembler le bras de Julien d'une telle façon, qu'il ne put d'abord exécuter son dessein. Je ne le puis, se disait-il à lui-même; physiquement, je ne le puis...
  (book 2, ch. 35)
[Julien entered the new church in Verrières. All the tall windows of the edifice were hung with crimson curtains. Julien found himself a few feet behind Mme de Rênal's pew. It seemed to him that she was praying with fervour. The sight of a woman who had loved him so dearly made Julien's arm tremble in such a way that at first he was unable to carry out his plan. 'I can't do it', he said to himself. 'Physically, I can't do it...']

The sense of unbearable strain that is conveyed at this point has no possible substitute in an *idea* of strain. Beyle is not presenting ideas in fictitious form. Nor is he making the book more interesting by refusing to explain what is happening and leaving this as a puzzle for his cleverer readers to work out. One of the necessary clues to Julien's behaviour is given when the news reaches him that Mme de Rênal is alive. The tension gives way to joy, wonder and a sense of overwhelming humility:

Dans ce moment suprême, il était croyant. Qu'importent les hypocrisies des prêtres? peuvent-elles ôter quelquechose à la vérité et à la sublimité de l'idée de Dieu?
  Seulement alors, Julien commença à se repentir du crime commis. Par une coïncidence qui lui évita le désespoir, en cet instant seulement venait de cesser l'état d'irritation physique et de demi-folie où il était plongé depuis son départ de Paris...
  (book 2, ch. 36)
[During that supreme moment, he was a true believer. Why care about the hypocrisies of the priests? Is there anything they can take away from the truth and sublimity of the idea of God?
  Only then did Julien begin to repent of the crime he had committed. Through a coincidence which saved him from despair, it was at that moment only that the state of physical irritation and semi-madness ended, in which he had been plunged since his departure from Paris...]

The 'semi-madness', as Mme Bibas points out, is one of the clues to Julien's behaviour that critics tend to overlook. And when it has been noted, it is perfectly easy to say what is happening to him, in that one can readily think of other cases in which men have gone mad from a blow to their pride, 'over-reacted' and then repented with a correspondingly full heart. Yet this is not really an *explanation*: we know that such reactions follow one another commonly but not that they follow inevitably. Moreover, Beyle does not try to explain them. Hence perhaps the difficulties that so many readers have in following the text. The text reminds us of what is unaccountable in such an experience, commonplace though it may be.

We are given no explanation either of why it should be that Julien repents of his crime not as soon as he has committed it (as far as he knows, successfully) but only when he knows that Mme de Rênal is alive and well. M. Georges Blin has described Julien's feelings at this moment in terms of Sartrean psychology and in particular Sartre's study in *L'être et le néant* of those cases in which we know suddenly that someone else knows what we are doing so that its whole significance *for us* is transformed.[31] But this is not an explanation either, and for Sartre himself such experiences are among the given facts of consciousness and not susceptible to further analysis. That such experiences are not only unaccountable but commonplace is something of which Sartre wishes to remind us and he does so with solemn amusement at his readers' possible baser instincts by taking as one of his main examples a peeping Tom aware suddenly that he is himself the object of interested observation. The comic situation, as so often in Sartre, depends for its effect on its sleazy familiarity. By contrast, Beyle reminds us of what is unique in Julien's experience and hence more obviously beyond comprehension. For Julien, learning that Mme de Rênal is alive is literally learning of a miracle.

The prose in which such an experience is conveyed is not the poetic prose or *style noble* that Beyle detested because of its obscurity.[32] But we have to respond to it as we respond to genuine poetry if we are not going to reduce it in our minds to banality or incoherence. We have to read it, that is to say, with the sense of living through a real situation and with the full and undistracted response to detail which for Beyle constituted the poetic experience.[33] It is unfortunate that Mme Bibas should refer only to the *boutade* in his letter to Balzac about reading the *Code Civil* every day as a model of style and not to the passage in the same letter in which he tells him of the one rule he understands: '*to be clear*. If I am not clear, *my whole world is annihilated.*'[34]

The usefulness of prose of this kind is that it can give us, if not explanations of why men behave in certain ways, at least the clearest possible sense of all that their behaviour and experience imply. The undistracted imagination of the author and reader is, of course, an advantage they have over the desperate protagonist and also the economy of the novel which enables author and reader to see crucial moments in the protagonist's experience with the simultaneous wisdom of hindsight and foresight. But these are advantages any novelist enjoys. Beyle's exploitation of the possibilities of the novel can be seen in what he conveys to us of these crucial moments themselves: the dominant physical sensation, for example, the 'physical irritation' which ends suddenly, together with the state of 'semi-madness' and which makes the madness itself an experience that can be understood in the sense at least of being more easily shared in imagination; the sense of how much life itself – one's own life or another person's – matters. Standing behind her in the church, Julien is unable to fire at Mme de Rênal until her head is 'almost hidden in the folds of her shawl'. Afterwards, he is indifferent to what has happened to her and what will happen to himself, as he lies in gaol. It is the knowledge that she is alive that startles him into awareness of who and what she is.

The chapter leading to the final collapse of Julien's morale and, following this, to the self-interrogation which leaves him ready to face both life and death depend in the same way on our ability to conceive a whole outlook, involving far more than the immediate focus of consciousness. *Le rouge et le noir* is a wonderfully constructed novel and to say this is to point not only to the striking dramatic effects which, like superb rhetoric, speak for themselves but to the way in which circumstances combine to produce something analogous to the conditions of a controlled experiment. In the prison cell, Julien is visited continually by those who have known him in the past: Mathilde whose efforts to turn him into a public hero are like those of an actress in a play that bores him, Fouqué, the semi-literate timber merchant who loves money but loves Julien even more, and his father, the justice of whose reproaches he can now no longer deny. 'The trouble with prison is that one cannot close one's door', he jokes unhappily. One of the first visitors is the priest who has taught him Latin and whom we have seen in the third chapter of the novel with 'eyes in which, despite his advanced age, the sacred fire is shining which tells of pleasure at carrying out a fine deed which is also a little dangerous'.

The features which had once been so animated and which had expressed with such energy the most noble feelings were now sunk in apathy. Someone who must have been a peasant soon called to fetch the old man. 'We mustn't tire him', he said to Julien, who realised that he was the nephew. This apparition left Julien in the depths of a misery too cruel for tears. He saw nothing that was not sad and unconsoling; he felt as if his heart were frozen in his breast.

This was the cruellest instant which he had had to endure since his crime. He had just seen death and in all its ugliness. All the illusions he had ever entertained of greatness of soul and of generosity were scattered like a cloud before the tempest.

If life (his own and Mme de Rênal's) had seemed a matter of indifference to him before, so too obviously had death; whereas now:

There was no longer anything rough and grandiose about him, no more Roman virtue; death seemed more formidable than he had ever imagined [*à une plus grande hauteur*] and something far less easy...
(book 2, ch. 37)

Two kinds of heroism

This is not the place in which to argue at any length a claim I should like to throw out in passing, but it is relevant to my general thesis concerning the education of Stendhal the novelist and his immediate relation to his predecessors, a relation which is a matter not of passive inheritance but of the living continuity which T. S. Eliot sought to define in his essay on 'Tradition and the individual talent' and one might say even more, an evolution of awareness. I believe that there is much in Shakespeare that Beyle was unable to surpass and his veneration for Shakespeare is an acknowledgement of the fact. There is nothing, for instance, in Beyle corresponding to what is appealed to in us or rather wrenched out of us by Macduff's cry, 'He has no children.' Yet the comparison with Shakespeare does not always force us to conclude that Beyle's was the inferior intelligence and imagination. The best known speech in *Hamlet*, for instance, though it suffers now from its excessive familiarity, suffers also as a meditation on the actual choice between 'To be and not to be...' when we read it after the last nine chapters of *Le rouge et le noir*. Despite the nightmare focus on 'a bare bodkin' and the swift sequel of events, including the encounter between Ophelia and the distracted prince, we are carried along too thrillingly to register the shock of an actual thought about death of the kind we have after the visit to Julien of the Abbé Chélan. We may be reminded, if we make the comparison, of Beyle's misgivings soon after he first read Shakespeare concerning the facility of Shakespearean rhetoric:

Shakespeare's characters have perhaps a fault which is very brilliant but none the less a fault: they are too eloquent.
Eloquent with the poetic eloquence which speaks to the soul while exercising the mind as little as possible, as was necessary with an uncouth people. Eloquence is a falsity of passion. Well no, if you assume that the character has a natural talent for it...[35]

and we may feel that Beyle's prose in passages such as those I have quoted has some of the characteristics not only of genuine but also of great poetry.

Beyle knew *Hamlet* well, both in French and English, and at the age of twenty saw Talma play the rôle in the version by Ducis. But the Shakespearean tragedy to which he alludes directly in the final chapters of *Le rouge et le noir* is the one which seems always to have fascinated him most. In his letter to Mathilde written after his arrest and before he knows Mme de Rênal is alive, he orders her to take a false name for a year and never once to mention his name, far less his crime, even to his child. 'From this time forth I never will speak word', he writes to her in English, remembering Iago. An earlier chapter of this study touched on the question of Beyle's deep lifelong interest in the heroic, and in the violent noble passions of Othello in particular. Julien, like Othello, commits a *crime passionnel* and afterwards bitterly regrets it, though why this should be and what it means is something we are shown in more 'detail' than by Shakespeare. Beyle's sense of the heroic came to be far closer, as he acknowledged, to that of Shakespeare than to Corneille or Alfieri. It was, none the less, very much his own and involved distinctions between different kinds of heroism with which Shakespeare was not apparently concerned.

Julien's self-imposed challenges take a form dictated by his boyhood reading of the *Memorial of St. Helena* and the Bulletins of the *Grande Armée*. The duty he forces himself to perform is always a 'heroic' duty. Like Octave de Malibert, he broods vigilantly on his own resilience and temerity, though, far more than Octave, he is able to enjoy the freedom to know and do what he wants to. Julien's very distinction, in fact, that which saves him from the 'commonness' of the young schoolboys of Paris who merely imitate a distinguished model *lies* in this freedom; a freedom he achieves, of course, with enormous difficulty and, presumably, if he were to live, would have to fight for again. But knowing what he wants and values at the moment when he dies allows him to go to the guillotine 'without affectation'.

After reading *Cinna* in 1811, Beyle and his friend Louis Crozet had noted that 'in what we have seen of the play, we do not acquire an intimate knowledge of the characters. Basing our judgment merely on what they say, we are able to form three or four totally distinct impressions of their character...'.[36] And a few years earlier, he had noted in his diary that 'there is no sensibility *without detail*. Their failure to remember this is one of the principal failings of French dramatists...Shakespeare is much closer to the kind of tragedy I have in mind but shall probably never write' (12.12.1804). (See page 55 above.) Beyle is far closer, obviously, in *Le rouge et le noir* to Shakespeare than to Corneille. And the Shakespearean freedom and precision of his writing would have been impossible were it not for something akin to Shakespeare's freedom of spirit and lack of servility (as expressed by Falstaff and Thersites, it is often a deep cynicism) with regard to any model of behaviour, however sublime. Julien himself grows 'tired of heroism', though it is clear at the point at which this occurs that he is tired specifically of the form of heroism that he is being required to conform to by Mathilde de la Mole:

Mathilde's plans included not merely the sacrifice of her reputation; she cared little if the whole of society learned of the condition she was in. To throw herself on her knees in front of the king's carriage as it galloped past and to draw his attention to beg for mercy for Julien, at the risk of being crushed a thousand times to death, was one of the least of the dreams pursued by her exalted and courageous imagination. Thanks to her friends who were employed at court, she was sure to be admitted to the private enclosures of the park at Saint-Cloud.

Julien found himself on the whole unworthy of so much devotion on her part; to tell the truth, he was tired of heroism. He would have responded gladly to a simple, naïve and almost shy tenderness, whereas the proud soul of Mathilde needed constantly a public and a sense of what *others* might think.

Amidst all her anguish and all her fears for the life of her lover, with whom she wanted to die, she had a secret need to astonish the public by the excess of her love and the sublimity of all that she undertook on his behalf...
(book 2, ch. 39)

The distinction between Mathilde's idea of heroism and Julien's is crucial to our understanding of the novel and, of course, more than the novel alone, and it is a distinction for which I know of no precedent in Shakespeare or elsewhere. Mathilde, by her own standards, is wholly equal to the rôle she imagines for herself as the mistress of a free man. Beyle invites us to share the dreams of her courageous and touchingly schoolgirlish imagination, all the more touching for being more than just dreams. ('Thanks to her friends employed at court, etc.' is both her own and the author's assurance that she is perfectly capable of putting her plans into effect.) Yet there is a profound contradiction in Mathilde which 'the idea of a public and a sense of what *others* might think' and its antithetical juxtaposition with 'the proud soul of Mathilde' makes clear and for which we have been prepared ever since her first appearance in the novel. The italicised 'others' (which clearly mystifies the author of the Penguin translation) refers us back to her thoughts after they first meet:

'Is it my fault if the young men at court are such devoted partisans of all that is *fitting* and go pale at the idea of the least adventure which happens to be a little strange? A little journey to Greece or Africa is for them the height of audacity and even then, they can only march in a troop. As soon as they are alone, they are afraid not of the Bedouin's lance but of ridicule and this fear drives them mad.

My little Julien, on the other hand, likes only to act on his own. Never in this privileged being, is there the least idea of relying on others for support or help. He despises the others and that's why I don't despise *him*...'

(book 2, ch. 12)

It also refers us forward to Julien's exasperated cry to her and to his friend Fouqué who tell him how public opinion is being mobilised on his behalf:

'Leave me my ideal existence. All your fussing, all your details about the real world grate on my nerves and would pull me out of heaven. One dies as best one can; I only want to think about dying in my own way. What do the *others* matter to me? My relations with the *others* are about to be cut short abruptly. For heaven's sake, stop talking to me about all those people; it's quite enough to have to see my judge and my lawyer...'

(book 2, ch. 40)

Mathilde's intelligence and spirit (she is very much her father's daughter) lead her, like the Marquis de la Mole himself, to see the absurd dependence of her class on public tolerance[37] and hence on established form. She wears mourning once a year to honour an ancestor who had been executed for breaking the law and sees in the plebeian Julien the self-reliance which, far more than pedigree, make the true aristocrat. Yet flouting the opinion of others, as she does by her displays of cruel wit at her suitors' expense and by her unabashed acknowledgment that she is to be the mother of Julien's child, she paradoxically depends upon it. The audience, whether it is shocked or admiring, is necessary to her, and this is what Julien cannot stand. The contradiction is symptomatic of a deeper flaw in Mathilde's nature, of a profound inability to know what she wants. Beyle summarises it in his own review of *Le rouge et le noir* and in doing so reminds us of one of the best-known of the categories defined in *De l'amour*. Why, he asks, does the brilliant noble Mathilde fall for her father's secretary?

Because it so happens that, out of sheer pride, Julien has behaved in the way necessary to goad the vanity of Mlle de la Mole. Two or three times, with every intention of doing so and not in the least in order to play with her, he has been on the point of *throwing her over completely*. This is all one need do today in order to win the love of a Parisian lady...This depiction of love in Paris is absolutely new. We have the impression that no other book has touched on it. It makes a fine contrast with the simple, genuine and *unselfregarding* love of Mme de Rênal. It's the *love of the head* [*l'amour de tête*] as opposed to the love of the heart.

However, the intelligence of the novelist, as opposed to the self-advertising reviewer, is seen in his rejection of such facile categories and in his compassionate presentation of the inner life of this (in many ways) unpleasant girl. Mathilde, after she has invited Julien to her room for the first time in the middle of the night, is almost overcome with horror at her own foolishness:

As she listened to him, Mathilde was shocked by his air of triumph. 'So now he's my master', she thought. She was already feeling remorse. Her reason was horrified by the astonishing act of folly she had committed. If she had been able to, she would have annihilated both herself and Julien. During the moments in which, by an effort of will, she succeeded in overcoming her remorse, she suffered agonies of timidity and shame. She had never anticipated for an instant her present horrible state.

'Still, I must say something to him', she thought to herself. 'That is the custom. One is supposed to talk to one's lover...'

In spite of the fearful violence she was doing herself, she was in perfect command of every word she spoke.

No reproach, no regret occurred to spoil a night which seemed to Julien less happy than singular. What a difference between this and his last stay of twenty-four hours in Verrières. 'These fine Parisian manners are capable of spoiling everything, even love', he thought to himself in his extreme injustice...

(book 2, ch. 16)

Mathilde's brave loneliness of spirit is part of her appeal. On another occasion, despite her customary haughtiness, she can be described without incongruity as 'like a poor girl living on the fifth floor of a tenement' (book 2, ch. 42). After their first assignation, however, her overwhelming attractiveness for Julien has a more obvious cause: after the dry tense nightmare horror of her night with Julien, she recoils from him utterly. Julien's pride is, of course, mortified and he becomes obsessed with the desire to reassert his rights, obsessed, that is, with longing for the love and submission of a woman he regards as a 'monster of pride'. He succeeds by simulating an indifference even greater than her own, but meanwhile becomes a 'maniac'. Mathilde 'absorbs every other thought'. He 'sees her everywhere in the future'. 'Everywhere in this future he saw lack of success. This young man whom we first saw so proud and full of presumption in Verrières had fallen into an excess of ridiculous modesty' (book 2, ch. 24). His own vacillations when Mathilde finds she is pregnant, his absurdly considerate offer to the Marquis of his own life as a convenient sacrifice and his state of dazed self-contemplation when a commission is bought for him, he becomes a chevalier and marriage with Mathilde seems imminent, can all be seen as symptomatic of a state of extreme distraction and an (uncharacteristic) inability, akin to Mathilde's, to know what he wants. It is significant, of course, that it should be when he is in this state of mind that he reads Mme de Rênal's letter of denunciation and travels to Verrières to end her life and his own.

Mathilde, with her desire to relive the middle ages, her contempt for the social virtues and her constant need for an audience, has three at least of the characteristics of early nineteenth-century Romanticism. She is formidably intelligent and alive but her feeling for the sublime and the heroic is, in the last analysis, self-frustrating and parasitic on what she scorns. In the salons of the aristocracy 'Mathilde was often bored', we are told. 'It is possible that she would have been bored anywhere' (book 2, ch. 11). Yet there is a great deal more to Mathilde than to her poor Norwegian counterpart Hedda Gabler or to Madame Bovary, whose true capabilities neither she nor the reader has the chance to find out. Her gestures of defiance and her sense of what is wrong with an age in which the young leaders of society are the slaves of the conventions to which they owe their position (this anticipates Beyle's warning after 1830 against the imminent Americanisation of society) cannot be dismissed with contempt, and it is for this reason, presumably, that she is made, for all her faults, to seem so impressive and sympathetic, a suitable partner for Julien in many ways, despite their eventual profound differences. She has the makings of an actress in the grand manner, yet she is portrayed by an author who could be carried away by grand gestures and spectacles.[38] In *Le rouge et le noir*, moreover, ceremonies, and specifically ecclesiastical ceremonies, are described with gusto and appreciation of the fact that they bring life to a dreary age. Julien admires, as Beyle himself seems to, though with a great deal more amusement than Julien, the aristocratic young Bishop of Agde whom Julien catches unawares in front of a mirror practising benedictions and trying to look old; while the celebrations at the shrine of the martyred Saint Clément are described with admiring delight as well as a tingling sense of their sheer absurdity. It is the Marquis de la Mole who has financed the ceremonies, and the enjoyment with which every detail is dwelt on reads like appreciation not only of a wonderful show but of the fact that the Marquis is playing politics with panache and masterful efficiency. Beyle writes as a member of the liberal opposition but with a characteristic *Beyliste* (in English here, sportsmanlike) relish of the cool acumen of the traditional enemy:

> There was a *Te Deum*, billowing clouds of incense, an infinite number of discharges of musketry and artillery; the peasants were drunk with happiness and piety. A day like this undoes the work of a hundred issues of the Jacobin press...

Julien himself is so carried away that he would have 'fought for the Inquisition and in perfect good faith' (book 1, ch. 18).

M. H.-F. Imbert has drawn attention to the parallel between the ceremonies at the shrine of Saint Clément and those that accompany Julien's funeral on the last pages of the novel when Mathilde, like her father, distributes largesse to the peasants.[39] What M. Imbert does not bring out is that there is an essential difference, none the less, between the shrine of an improbable Roman saint and the graveside of Julien Sorel. Beyle does not tell us what we ought to think of Mathilde, but the facts speak eloquently for themselves when she stage-manages Julien's funeral and, with a characteristic effort of will, forces herself to imitate Marguerite de Navarre kissing the severed head of her lover before the appalled eyes of the unassuming Fouqué and at the funeral trying to bury the head herself. The word 'vulgarity' is not used to describe either the ceremonies at the graveside or the expensive embellishments she chooses for Julien's tomb on the mountainside where he had asked to be left and forgotten. Yet the associations for Julien of the mountainside and his inability when he dies to take an interest in either Mathilde or her brand of heroism make explicit condemnation unnecessary:

> Through Mathilde's cares, this wild grotto was adorned with marble sculptured at great expense in Italy.

The marble monument, like so much of nineteenth-century art, is out of place. The Romanticism which is so powerful an element in the novel's appeal has by now been shown as insensitive to more lasting human needs and desires.

6

Lucien Leuwen and autobiography

Souvenirs d'égotisme

Beyle's dissatisfaction with *Le rouge et le noir* after its publication in 1830 is expressed in numerous jottings in the margin of a copy that was found after his death in his library in the consulate of Civita Vecchia[1] and in the manuscripts of other novels and stories. The style seemed to him too 'abrupt' and 'dry', the 'tone' of the novel insufficiently 'familiar'. 'How familiar ought the tone of a novel to be? Doesn't the extreme familiarity of Scott and Fielding predispose one to follow them in their moments of enthusiasm?' And then, the decisive question indicating how different the next novel was to be: 'Isn't the tone of *Le rouge* too Roman?'

Even more than to *Le rouge*, these objections can be made to the two short stories that appeared in the *Revue de Paris* for May and June 1830, *Le coffre et le revenant* and *Le philtre*, and that may have been inspired by a first brief visit to Spain the previous year. These and *Le juif*, written during hours of boredom after his appointment as consul to Trieste are of minor interest in any case, though they anticipate the narrative manner of much of *La chartreuse de Parme* and *Les chroniques italiennes* and indicate what after *Les promenades dans Rome*, was to become a growing fascination with the psychology of human cruelty. His dislodgement from Trieste at the behest of the Austrian government and his removal to Civita Vecchia coincide with a period when he wrote little, but from the summer of 1832 until four years later, he was to become increasingly absorbed in and was to write prolifically on subjects deriving from his own experience and obviously close to his heart. And he was to leave unfinished the manuscripts of *Lucien Leuwen* and the two volumes of memoirs, *Souvenirs d'égotisme* and *La vie de Henry Brulard*.

One can only guess the reasons that led him to plunge into the record of his own recent past, abandon it, take up what was to become his longest and most penetrating work of fiction and then go back in *La vie de Henry Brulard* to salvage what remained alive in his memory of his childhood and youth. But the same tensions calling for release seem common to all three works and the same preoccupation is made explicit in all three manuscripts concerning the crucial differences between fiction and fact.

I have tried to show already that it would be wrong to conclude from Beyle's thoughts on history that he ever despaired of man's ability to understand the past, clear though he became in his own mind that most historians were really novelists in disguise and that the novel was definitely his own vocation. Presumably he would have agreed that 'where the historian really differs from the poet is in his describing what has happened, while the other describes the kind of thing that might have happened',[2] even if, like Aristotle, he considered the knowledge the poets (and novelists) can give us as potentially more true and important than that of historians. Our sense of what might have happened, however, depends on what *has* happened, at least to us personally. And Beyle was deeply imbued with the beliefs of Locke, Condillac, Helvétius, Tracy and Richard Payne Knight that there is nothing in our experience of the world or in our wildest fancies concerning it that has not come to us originally through our five senses. As a critic, he preferred those poets whose imagination was nourished by their contact with the world:

I am perfectly aware that a poet is permitted to be ignorant of the realities of life. I will go further, it is necessary to his success as a poet that he should be so. If a man of honour and sensibility like M. de Lamartine knew as much about mankind as a Sir Robert Walpole or a Villèle, his imagination, his sensibility, would become arid. This I have always thought the sense of the reply made to Hamlet by the ghost of his father.

If Lord Byron had not enjoyed the advantage of being born an Englishman; if he had not been compelled by his pride, as a peer, to take at least a tinge of the prevailing good sense of his country; if he had not associated with Douglas Kinnaird, the Hobhouses and others,

well versed in the real state of interests and parties; if he had not seen a little of the world *as it goes*, which he could not avoid doing in his quality of Member of the Literary Committee of Covent Garden, never would he have written *Don Juan* – never, in my opinion, would his genius have risen above the level of that of M. de Lamartine.
(*London Magazine*, July 1825)

As Alain was to point out in 1935, he never 'echoes the commonplace that one now hears everywhere that we can never really know other people'.[3] And it is unlikely that he would have endorsed Marcel Proust's belief that for a writer, there is only one 'true life' and that is 'the life of his novels'[4] or that he would have relished the quasi-solipsism that is so powerful an element in *A la recherche du temps perdu* and defended in *Le temps retrouvé*.

Souvenirs d'égotisme and *La vie de Henry Brulard* are unmistakably autobiography, and *Lucien Leuwen* a novel. The distinction is crucial and the fear of turning the one into the other admitted repeatedly in the margins of the latter and the text of the memoirs themselves. It seems necessary to insist on the distinction, even at the risk of doing so pedantically, because scholars and critics are constantly denying that it exists. We cannot, of course, check more than a few episodes in the latter for their actual veracity, and we know that on occasions Beyle suffered from what the French politely call mythomania.[5] But the difference between illusion and reality is itself one of Beyle's main preoccupations in the autobiographies and in *Henry Brulard* in particular. Both are concerned with the nature of memory and with what makes it at the same time precarious and indispensable, a way of remaining alive. In *Henry Brulard* he tells us that in making his inventory of what remains of his past, he is seeking to know what he is and has been; and his conception on what, in any other context, would seem like wholly unimportant details suggests that the autobiography is serving a need far deeper than what is normally meant by self-knowledge. In *Souvenirs d'égotisme* he is writing about a more recent past and the fear that the past may be irretrievable is less pressing; though the same preoccupation with the exact truth is expressed and the same fear of the 'egotism' which is, presumably, referred to in the title,[6] the endless 'I's and me's' to which he sees an antidote only in a 'perfect sincerity'.

As it happens, the fears are much exaggerated – certainly if one compares this one with most other autobiographies; and the title, if it is intended to be apologetic, misleading. *Souvenirs d'égotisme* is a record of the period following his departure from Milan and his life in Paris and London after he had broken finally with Mathilde Dembowski. And it can be enjoyed, if nothing else, for the vivid and economical, since utterly candid portraits of other people: Lafayette, Destutt de Tracy, Mérimée, Charles de Rémusat and other influential figures of the day, as well as the shy lady-like London prostitutes in whose suburban villa off the Westminster Road Beyle and two of his French companions spent much of their time during a visit to England in the autumn following his departure from Milan.

This last, if one likes to think so, reprehensible episode has the virtue at least of bringing to life an often forgotten corner of the London of Blake and Dickens. It is recounted with a simple affectionate appreciativeness and it records Beyle's first awakening from the grief ensuing upon the break with Mathilde Dembowski. It is Mathilde herself who is conspicuously absent from the memoirs and for that matter from Beyle's writings as a whole; absent, that is, as an identifiable voice and personality with recognisable virtues and faults, and it is perhaps significant that in one of the few physical descriptions he has left of her, she is compared with the type of 'Lombardian' (and notoriously enigmatic) beauty to be found in the paintings of Leonardo da Vinci.[7] It is she who inspired, as the marginal notes testify, the portrait in *Lucien Leuwen* of Mme de Chasteller, though even here she is a woman of mainly unrevealed possibilities who enjoys solitude and virtuous seclusion and betrays her fascination with Lucien most freely when she is watching him go by beneath her window.

The real Mathilde may well have resembled what we are allowed to imagine of Mme de Chasteller. She was as wholeheartedly devoted to the seemingly lost cause of Italian freedom after 1815 as Mme de Chasteller to that of the traditional monarchy. She was proudly sensitive and, as Beyle tells us in the *Souvenirs*, easily wounded by the imputation of loose and dishonourable behaviour, and all the more so as she was publicly separated from her husband. Hence probably her shrinking from Beyle's indiscreet and unintentionally comic advances when disguised ineffectually by a pair of green spectacles he pursued her to Volterra, where she was visiting her sons' college. Yet the unguarded affection of which she was capable, as well as the pride and spirit, can be seen if one reads the letters to her 'stimabile amico' Ugo Foscolo, for whom she expresses a devotion almost certainly more warm and intense than anything she felt for the importunate Beyle.[8] 'When will you come back?', Mathilde asks the latter in the first chapter of *Souvenirs d'égotisme.* '"Never, I hope." After which, there was an hour of beating about the bush and useless words of which one alone might have changed my life, though not for long, for this angelic soul hidden in so beautiful a body departed from this life in 1825.'

The memory of Mathilde seems to dominate both *Souvenirs d'égotisme* and the first half of *Lucien Leuwen*. In the second half, attention is turned abruptly to the hero's father and the relations between father and son are explored before the novel is abandoned and Beyle takes up the story of his childhood and family circle in *La vie de Henry Brulard*. The need to write during this period seems to be one that takes him through the memories of his most formative relations with others. A psychoanalyst may find this significant and may note that Beyle had adored his mother with a fierce sensual passion before she died when he was seven years old. And he may wish to account for Beyle's worship of a woman whom he could never love physically by showing this to be a re-enactment of the bitterly thwarted passions of the child. This may be a helpful and revealing exercise but it would be overlooking an essential part of the case if one were to regard the value for Beyle of his experience as merely private and symptomatic.[9] Mathilde's influence in the memoirs can be seen as that of a woman who brought him grief and deprivation – which are at the same time a sense of what might have been supreme happiness and hence, paradoxically, an astounding awareness of being alive.

Landscapes have always been like a *bow* drawn across my soul and especially the aspects of which no one ever speaks (the line of rocks as one approaches Arbois – I think it is – along the main highway coming from Dôle, was for me an evident and sensible image of the soul of Mathilde...)
(*La vie de Henry Brulard*, ch. 2)

As Beyle admits, such an experience is, in one sense, *strictly private*, but there may be many readers who, for this very reason, will be able to understand immediately what he means.

The differences between the memoirs and the novels are crucial, but in both we find the same disconcerting potency of detail, in other words the same confidence in an overwhelming impression which is characteristic of poetry. Prose which is so intensely alive is almost bound to be fragmentary, and in the memoirs it lapses frequently into wandering reminiscence and often mere gossip. The outstanding passages in the *Souvenirs d'égotisme* themselves include the accounts of the journey from Milan in the first chapter, the visit to London in chapter 6 and, perhaps most remarkable of all, in chapter 3, of the sexual fiasco he experienced during a first attempt to console himself for the break with Mathilde. All these episodes are related with a simple wonder at the unexpected things that may happen to anyone, in other words a total lack of egotism. In so far, moreover, as Mathilde played a part in Beyle's life not unlike that of Laura de Noves in Petrarch's, they more than justify comparison with some of the better known expressions in verse of that kind of love and tribute.

The difference between Beyle's autobiography and his novels is not that the former is, in any obvious way, more prosaic. Nor is it, as so often is claimed, that in the latter the imaginary hero succeeds where Beyle himself had hopelessly failed in real life. M. Victor Brombert may be right when he says that the story of Lucien and Mme de Chasteller is the story of Beyle and Mathilde told in a form soothing to the former's vanity.[10] Lucien still, partly through his own foolishness, fails to reassure or conquer Mme de Chasteller, and if day-dreaming vanity had been Beyle's only creative impulse, Lucien would have been happier, more perfect and certainly far less interesting than he is. The most obvious difference between the memoirs and *Lucien Leuwen* is that the latter is sustained by many more interests and takes in a far wider panorama of contemporary life. For all his memories, presumably, of Mme de Chasteller, Beyle is literally, as a novelist, carried out of himself, and though he may be unable to forget his former state of mind, he relives it with an exploratory zest and a concentration of his mental powers which is unequalled in his writing before or afterwards.

Lucien Leuwen, part one

The inspiration for *Lucien Leuwen* and the outline of the story seem to have occurred to Beyle in much the same way as those of his other novels. Like the newspaper account of the trial of Antoine Berthet and the manuscript relating the adventures of Alessandro Farnese, the draft of a novel by a friend seems to have provided the branch, to adopt a metaphor from *De l'amour*, round which a whole novel was to 'crystallise'. Having an idea and developing it straight away on paper seem to have been for Beyle always much the same thing, and having the freedom to do so one of the advantages of the life of a self-professed 'dilettante'. He had been only for a few years – and even then not completely – dependent on writing for a livelihood and he was in the habit of thinking pen in hand. The novel, entitled *Le lieutenant*, is the subject of two letters from Civita Vecchia of May and November 1834, in which Beyle recommends the authoress, Mme Jules Gaulthier, for instance, to

...efface in each chapter at least fifty superlatives. Never write: 'the burning passion of Olivier for Hélène.'
 The poor novelist has to try and make the reader believe in the *burning passion* but he must never name it: to do that is slightly immodest and indecent [*cela est contre la pudeur*]...
Don't make your characters too rich and let your hero commit some little blunder at times, because we heroes do make blunders. We run; the dull man hardly ever even walks; and even then it's with a stick; that's why he never falls...

Why not call the novel, Beyle suggested as well, *Leuwen or the student expelled from the Ecole Polytechnique*? How much else he was to add to or borrow from the novel we don't know, since the manuscript has been lost. But realising what could be made of such a story and with many hours of solitude to fill, he began immediately to sketch out and then write the novel that was to occupy him for more than a year.

That it was never finished may be due to his realising, by the time he reached the end of the second part, that it could only be published after his retirement or death. 'As long as I serve the Budget, [i.e. the government] I shan't be able to print it, for what the Budget detests most of all is that one should give oneself the air of having ideas.'[11] The ideas, moreover, and the portrayal of Louis Philippe's ministers (based on a good deal of embarrassing inside information) could easily be thought of as seditious, despite his assurances in the second sketch for a preface that he would rather have to pay court to the Minister of the Interior than to his grocer, that he is by no means a whole-hearted democrat and that he would be in despair if he had to live in New York. By the time he gave up the novel, he had well and truly unburdened himself of his contempt for the government of this 'most crooked of kings', as he called him in private. (The *memoires d'un touriste* written two years later for publication are, of course, far more discreet.) He had also left in the margins of the manuscript the most valuable guide we possess to his method of composition, in the form of notes for his *own* guidance in rewriting the text. Not surprisingly, among these is the admission that he had deliberately made the manuscript of *Lucien Leuwen* too long, unlike that of *Le rouge et le noir*. Hence, 'among other faults' in the latter 'the abrupt phraseology and the absence of those little expressions which help the imagination of the benevolent reader to picture to himself what is happening'.[12] 'I want the style and any indecencies corrected', he wrote in the notes for a will,[13] 'but leave all the extravagances.'

The uninhibited portrayal of the social and political worlds that Beyle knew more intimately than any other, and the general copiousness of detail contribute towards making *Lucien Leuwen* the most profound and penetrating of his novels, despite its unfinished state and a lapse at the end of the first part into absurd contrivance. One can make too much of the fact that the novel would have benefited in parts from revision and lacks the third volume Beyle had originally planned. The manuscripts end with the death of M. Leuwen *père* and the winding up of his affairs by Lucien, who then sets off via Switzerland to take up a post as secretary to a French embassy. Within its context, this is an eloquent dénouement to and comment on what has gone before, and there is no reason why the novel should not have ended there; though Beyle himself seems to have had other ideas, and among them possibly the conventional one that a novel should end in a death or a marriage. Beyle's plans for and comments on the novel, however, for all the acuteness of the latter, are by the nature of things completely different from the intention revealed in his art. (Paul Valéry, in his clever, confusing and much too often quoted preface to the novel refuses to see that they are different.)[14] And I should like to suggest that it is in the very nature of his art that the novel should have been left unfinished. A solution to the issues it raises, and a happy or a tragic ending, would have been almost certainly a falsification both of the issues themselves and the spirit in which they are brought home to the reader.

What that spirit is can be best pointed out by saying what is, in any case, obvious. Much of *Lucien Leuwen* asks to be read as high-spirited social comedy, and this is apparent from the very first page. Lucien has been expelled from the Ecole Polytechnique for taking part in the demonstrations that accompanied the funeral of the republican General Lamarque and which may have seen the first appearance in Paris of the red flag.[15] Before deciding to make the army his career, he lives at home in luxury with his mother and father, the celebrated banker and wit, who pays the debts and pulls the leg of his only child mercilessly:

'A son is a creditor provided by nature...Do you know what we'd put on your marble tomb in the Père Lachaise if ever we had the misfortune to lose you? *"Siste viator!* Here lies Lucien Leuwen, a republican, who for two years waged an incessant war against cigars and his new pairs of boots."'

At the moment when our story begins, this enemy of cigars hardly thought any longer about the republic, which is taking far too long to appear...
    (ch. 1)

The opening chapters of the novel have something of the effect of the overture and first act of a comic opera and this is not merely because of the brilliant dialogue and swift sequence of events but the boisterousness of the comedy, which leaves us wondering from the outset how far Lucien is irredeemably naïf and Quixotic. The principal themes of the novel are briefly stated, as it were, and the wind knocked straight away out of any illusions that the hero or reader may share about easy paths to glory or self-respect. Lucien is ribbed also by his energetic and candidly opportunistic cousin Ernest Dévelroy, a contributor to the leading literary reviews and a candidate for election to the Academy of Moral Sciences (today he would be a candidate for a university chair) who cheerfully recommends him at least to appear more grave:

'To look at you, one would say you're a child and, what is worse, a contented child. You're beginning to be taken at your own valuation, I warn you, and in spite of your father's millions, you don't count anywhere; there's nothing solid about you, you're just a nice schoolboy. At twenty, that's almost ridiculous and worst of all, you spend hours attending to your appearance and this is known...'
    (ch. 1)

The banker and the man of letters have come to terms with their age (though Ernest temporarily miscalculates by accompanying an influential academician to the waters at Vichy, where the old gentleman dies on his hands; having 'lost four months', Ernest vows that next time he will attach himself to one who is younger.) Lucien has not. An age in which glory means being a millionaire or elected to the Academy of Moral Sciences is not one in which he would have chosen to live; though the comedy of the first two chapters lies partly in the good humoured, merciless and very Parisian way in which he is assured that in being so unworldly, he is merely a fool. What right has he not to care for worldly success or, after he has obtained his commission in the lancers, to feel disgust on his first meeting with Colonel Filloteau at the vile and calculating unction of the man who, to his dismay, is now to be his superior? Doesn't he feel ashamed, Ernest asks him, that he can't even pay for his own cigars? '"Vile or not, M. Filloteau is a thousand times your superior. He has been active and you have not...He's probably supporting some old peasant who's his father and your father's supporting you..."' Lucien can only reply in despair:

'I can see you'll be elected to the Institute at the next vacancy and I'm just a fool, I know it. You're right a hundred times over, I'm sure, but I really deserve pity as well. I can't stand the thought of the gate I must go through. There's too much dung lying underneath it...'
    (ch. 2)

His hopes that he will be able to silence Ernest and his father and step round or over the dung are to survive many intolerable humiliations and many hours of boredom and disillusion. And the fact that they stay alive may explain why the reader is left in a state of constant suspense throughout the novel and why the comedy of the opening chapters is sustained with such power, variety of mood and inwardness.

The most sympathetic and helpful account of the comedy I know is the one given by Maurice Bardèche in his chapters on the novel and on Beyle's marginal notes to the manuscript in *Stendhal, romancier*. M. Bardèche brings to the novel the eye of a historian who knows the period well and of a committed politician who is able to enjoy many of Beyle's bitterer ironies, and he provides what can be valuable for the reader who is not French: an account of how many of the social types whom Lucien encounters are still alive in France today or at least were alive in 1947, when the book first appeared – a great deal, of course, has changed in France since then. I find, none the less, that M. Bardèche tends to underestimate as literature the comedy he enjoys and admires, for according to his account, this is a matter of wonderful separate portraits *à la Célimène*, a kind of 'magic lantern show' throughout the first half of the novel giving us the identifiable features, and nothing more, of the officers and genteel inhabitants of Nancy, where Lucien spends the whole of his short military career. As M. Bardèche points out, almost none of the characters thus portrayed influence his destiny or are heard of or seen again when he returns to Paris; though M. Bardèche concludes too rapidly, I think, that the inhabitants of Nancy are therefore merely 'amusing', with 'no more life or weight than the comic characters of Walter Scott' and that Lucien remains a mere witness of their absurdities. The admirer of Tolstoy will not, it is true, find anything in Beyle's Nancy comparable to the crowded, varied and yet always individually focused portraits of the society of Moscow and St Petersburg in *Anna Karenina* and *War and Peace* and one of the obvious reasons for the greater range in Tolstoy is that we are not merely being shown, as in *Lucien Leuwen*, the experience of one onlooker and protagonist. Yet Beyle is more like Tolstoy, surely, in the way he brings a whole society to life than he is like his contemporary, Balzac to whom, as a social historian, he is still commonly judged inferior. Compare, for instance, Beyle's Nancy with the world of the *Curé de Tours* or the Angoulême of the first half of *Illusions perdues*. It may occur to the reader that M. Bardèche's description of Beyle's social comedy applies, if anything, more aptly to the last two works and we may be reminded, if we re-read them, that it was Balzac who, of the two, was the greater admirer of Scott. A crucial difference between the minor characters of Beyle and Balzac lies in the point of view from which they are seen, a point of view which, in Beyle, is not merely, or principally, that of the omniscient novelist. Among the 'amusing characters', as M. Bardèche calls them, in *Lucien Leuwen* is Colonel Malher de Saint-Mégrin, who has his officers watched carefully and who forbids Lucien to visit the local reading room, his usually unsmiling brother lieutenants and his protector and 'uncle' the vile Colonel Filloteau. They do not, it is true, decisively affect his destiny. But they serve a dramatic – in the Beyliste sense; that is, a psychologically revealing – function. His determination to go through with a military career having once embarked on it, and despite these vexations, is the first sign we have that his cousin Ernest may have under-rated him. The horrors of a provincial garrison are no less real for being the horrors of seemingly endless hours spent in rented lodgings and darkened streets or, for a change, gambling and drinking in the company of officers who have no objection to seeing him provoked into a duel, wounded and then, fainting from loss of blood, left to make his way back to his rooms alone. The 'life and weight' of the members of the garrison corresponds to the degree to which Lucien himself is unavoidably aware of them. After the duel, he makes a joke 'which must have been a bad one, as it was not understood' (ch. 7) and the narrator's rueful irony reads like that of Lucien; the narrative manner, here as elsewhere, presupposes an identity of views between the narrator, the reader and the hero himself. The question touched on but not pursued by M. Bardèche is what makes any depiction of *mores* in a society remote from our own worthy of more than accidental or expert interest, what makes us, the readers, whose imagination alone has the requisite recreative powers, find more 'life and weight' in some characters than others. Novels, particularly very original ones, differ completely in this respect. My suggestion for an answer in the case of *Lucien Leuwen* is that the interest for us of Nancy and its inhabitants is due more than anything else to what Lucien expects of them and to the kind of man that Lucien is: in other words, that it is the very unusual light in which ordinary people are seen and scrutinised that makes their portraits so life-like and memorable. This is perhaps what Beyle had in mind when, after a year's work on the novel, he wrote:

...each sentence tells a story, so to speak, if I compare them with those of M. de Balzac's *Médecin de campagne* or M. Sue's *Koatven*. Now the first thing one asks of a novel is that it should do this, amuse us by what it narrates and, so that it can amuse readers endowed with sense, portray characters who exist in nature.

Like Beyle himself, we may feel like protesting: 'Confound it, I know we have to imitate nature; but to what extent? That is the whole question',[16] but he goes on to suggest an answer in the same note:

In general, *idealise*, as Raphael *idealises* in a portrait in order to make it more life-like. But idealise in order to approach the perfectly beautiful in the figure of the heroine only. Excuse: the reader will have only seen the woman he has loved through idealising eyes...[17]

This note can be interpreted in many different ways, but one of them at least is consistent with the notion that imaginative fellow-feeling with Lucien is necessary to our realising of what he sees; furthermore, this may be a matter of our recalling what is private and incommunicable in our experience, as well as what it has in common with that of other men. In what is both communicated and incommunicable, for example, in the allusion to the idealising eyes of the reader, we may be reminded of those particular aspects of landscape of which 'no one ever speaks'.[18]

Many critics tell us, nonetheless, that *Lucien Leuwen* is an attempt – and some, including M. Bardèche himself, find that it is an unsuccessful one – to write a novel in the manner of Balzac. He had, it is true, thought of dividing it according to the Balzacian categories of *Scènes de la vie de province, Scènes de la vie parisienne*, and so on. But he also left instructions that if any other writer were to correct the style and cut out the repetitions after his death, it should *not* be Balzac.[19] And, as the note I have just quoted suggests, style for Beyle was anything but a separate or secondary consideration. Far from being an imitation of Balzac, as Mr Michael Wood has recently argued,[20] and a departure from the kind of thing he was good at, namely the manner of *Le rouge et le noir*, *Lucien Leuwen* can be seen as a development out of Beyle's earlier work and evidence of what he had learned in writing it. In *Lucien Leuwen*, for example, it seems clear that Beyle needed a hero as *unformed* as Julien Sorel and whose capacity for enjoyment, courage and intelligence were as unimpaired and unfathomable in order to answer the question: what does this particular world and its civilisation have to offer such a man and what potentialities for living, can be realised within them? The most obvious difference between the two novels is that in Lucien Beyle has chosen a hero as privileged as Julien Sorel is deprived, and who lacks the ferocious energy and mental powers that Julien needs to overcome his disadvantages. It is true that Lucien has to brace and assert himself many times, and that he learns the value of self-imposed obligations, including a military punctiliousness in carrying out some very hard work and several missions of which he disapproves. But the obligations are chosen *faute de mieux* – constantly, he will compare his various duties ruefully with those he would have had to carry out on the battlefield – and meeting them does not give him the immense satisfactions which Julien can enjoy and which count for so much in the total effect of *Le rouge et le noir*. In other words, Lucien is less self-preoccupied, less mistrustful of himself and the world and, as a result, Beyle is far more free to present his hero's career as a chronicle of his time.

Why Nancy, however? It would be absurd to attribute the interest of a series of portraits and interiors merely to the intelligence of the eye through which they were seen. There are many possible valid answers to the question and one is that, not only in the garrison but in certain of the homes of local inhabitants he enters, we are shown the common experience of enforced company and the consequent need for sensitiveness and skill on the part of those who are free to escape, without which life for the virtual prisoners can be rendered intolerable. In the household of Mme de Serpierre, for example, with her six plain unmarried daughters, Lucien finds himself in a world which is by no means remote from that of the novels of Jane Austen[21] and his own (and his author's) evident understanding of and respect for it are shown by the fact that though the eldest daughter, Théolinde, is clearly in love with him and she and her sisters enjoy happy excursions in his company, he is able to avoid behaving in a way of which either Colonel Brandon or Mr Knightley would have disapproved. The Serpierres are loyal to the exiled Charles X and live in semi-poverty. Hence the usefulness for the daughters' excursions of Lucien's large private carriage. M. de Serpierre has his old military uniforms turned into coats and trousers he can wear around the house. The town, moreover, serves as a refuge and a capital for others like him. It keeps alive as far as possible the allegiances and the social order of the past and in this sense is provincial in a way that no English town has been since the seventeenth century. (Its way of life is still perpetuated as M. Bardèche points out, in certain quarters of the cathedral towns of Vendée and Anjou.) And it stands in contrast and opposition to the Paris of the July monarchy that has overthrown for the last time the principle of hereditary monarchy and, at least in theory, hereditary privilege and power.

This, in any case, is what it represents in the novel. Beyle himself had never actually visited Nancy, and there is no evidence that he tried to inform himself, while writing it or beforehand, of the actual politics of the town. Nancy offers – and this is perhaps the principal reason for his devoting so much attention to it – an obvious alternative to the democratic ideals and way of life to which Lucien has felt until now half-committed; though characteristic of the way in which the novel works is the fact that Lucien enters the legitimist circles of the town, not on principle or out of a kind of sociological curiosity but from weariness with the company of his fellow-officers and in search of amusing or even ordinarily pleasant company. It is in a mood of high-spirited exasperation, after his duel, that he buys his *carte d'entrée* into the circles he wishes to enter in the form of a sumptuously bound missal, attends benediction in the exclusively aristocratic Chapelle des Pénitents and willingly exposes himself to the series of invitations which follows. He has already, before this, repudiated in the officers' mess the unnecessarily damaging charge that he is a 'republican' and he has been condemned as a 'renegade' in a note from his conspiratorially silent republican fellow-officers. Though what principles is he betraying anyway? It is easier for him to say what he doesn't believe than what he is prepared to die for. He comes to realise this during one of the evenings he spends with his friend, the mathematician Gauthier, the utterly honest and wholly committed editor of the local republican newspaper.[22] In the course of an earnest lecture from

Gauthier on 'America, democracy, prefects chosen by law from among the elected representatives of each department' and other arguments 'that can be found in print anywhere', Lucien finds that despite his 'profound esteem' for his friend, he has difficulty in keeping himself awake.

'Can I really call myself a republican after this? This shows me that I'm not made to live in a republic; for me it would be the tyrannical rule of all the mediocrities and I'm incapable of calmly tolerating even the most estimable of mediocrities. I need a prime minister who's an amusing scoundrel, like Walpole or M. de Talleyrand.'

At that moment, Gauthier ended his discourse with the words: 'But we have no Americans in France.'

'Take any shopkeeper in Rouen or Lyon who's avaricious and without imagination and you'll soon have an American', Lucien replied.

'Ah! you really grieve me', cried Gauthier rising sadly to his feet and leaving, as the hour after midnight struck.

'Grenadier, you grieve me...'

Lucien sang when he was gone [a song from a vaudeville in the Théâtre de Variétés] 'And yet, I esteem you with all my heart.'

(ch. 8)

Lucien, like Beyle, is no doubt unjust to Americans. But, a century later, his inability to share the Utopian view of America can scarcely seem like incorrigible naïvety.

In the emphatic retort to Gauthier, however, there is a force that comes not from mature reflection on politics and not only from a mounting revulsion against his friend's sincere addiction to numbers and equations, but from an instinct which, without attempting to define or name it, Beyle makes us recognise as profoundly corrective and springing from an undeniable need. The vexations and above all disappointments of his life until now can be easily imagined as contributing to his outburst to Gauthier and to the balefulness with which he tells himself that he'd prefer the rule of an 'amusing scoundrel'. And his instinctive reaction leads him to cultivate the acquaintance of Gauthier's principal political rival in Nancy, Dr Du Poirier, an 'amusing scoundrel' *par excellence* and Lucien's guide into the aristocratic society of the town. Du Poirier is a type of politician and intriguer who is to reappear as Rassi of the *Chartreuse de Parme* and Dr Sansfin of *Lamiel*, and he is 'as crooked as Gauthier is honest'. Lucien's astonished admiration for the histrionic unction, patently false plebeian self-abasement and dialectical brilliance of this self-appointed organiser of the legitimist and aristocratic cause is the uncensurious delight one is able to feel in an exuberantly and perfectly incorrigible rogue. Able to feel, that is, in certain circumstances such as those in which Lucien finds himself at this moment. This is not life to which he might normally have been drawn and the description of Du Poirier's remarkable features, which are compared successively to those of a boar, a hyena and a fox, conveys Lucien's astonished wonder during their first encounter at the sheer and unaccountable otherness of the life in this childless, landless advocate of a return to – of all things – the pre-Revolutionary laws of primogeniture.[23] Lucien suspects immediately, and correctly, that he is a natural traitor – a fox, not a boar – and M. Bardèche argues that after his election to the Chamber of Deputies, he becomes a type of the modern French deputy. Du Poirier is also – a typically Beyliste detail, calling for no further explanation – a man who, despite his tireless scheming, lives in perpetual terror of retaliation.

The usefulness to Lucien of Du Poirier is not merely that he offers much needed entertainment – the need prompting him to cultivate his acquaintance is less desperate, in other words, than that which leads a Prince Hal to consort with a Falstaff; it is above all, and in a way that suits Du Poirier as well, that Lucien can be shown off as a convert to the cause of throne and altar, in front of people whom he is far more happy to know. Both commoners, Lucien and Du Poirier, simulate piety in order to deceive the noble inhabitants of Nancy – they make a good pair to this extent – but in order to gain very different kinds of advantage. Mme de Commercy, for example, noting Lucien's glances at her beautiful English garden, modelled on that of Louis XVIII's house during his exile at Hartwell, begs him to come and walk round it when he wishes and 'without calling to see the old proprietor'.

After this invitation made with cordial simplicity, Lucien was no longer in a mood to mock; he felt as if he were returning to life. It was several months now since he had last seen polite company...
    (ch. 10)

This sensation is one that neither Gauthier nor Du Poirier have been able to give him, and that he experiences again when M. de Serpierre, seeing a look of horror on Lucien's face and correctly interpreting it, explains that, though a lieutenant at Colmar in 1822, he had been absent at the time of one of the more shameful crimes of the régime to which he owes his allegiance, the ambush prepared by his fellow-officers for Colonel Caron, and his subsequent execution. The reply 'sanctifies his entire household' in Lucien's eyes and he is unable any longer to mock inwardly at the sour-tempered Mme de Serpierre and her red-headed daughters, tall as grenadiers. The scruples and generosity of Mme de Commercy and M. de Serpierre outweigh for Lucien the injustice and absurdity of the social order they represent.

Yet Lucien does not commit himself to a belief in inherited privilege as a guarantee against barbarism, as his presence in the salons seems to imply, any more than in the past he had seen any positive hope in the prospect of its final elimination. And the novel fails to offer any such final or simple answer to the question: what makes civilisation possible? The local aristocracy is prone, like any other, to the accidents as well as the advantages of birth and includes the vindictive Roller brothers, impoverished ex-officers embittered by their poverty, and the prosperous Marquis de Sanréal, whose yelping voice repeats at full pitch the word *'voleur'* (thief), whenever Louis Philippe is mentioned. 'The noble ladies of Nancy' never tire of the joke, and Lucien is soon 'shocked by the eternal repetition and the eternal gaiety' (ch. 11). Lucien could never, in any case, have hoped to find in the legitimist circles of Nancy company by which he would never have been offended or bored; and if this had been the only point for the novelist of his taking this particular social plunge, his surprise at finding himself in such shallow water would have been merely farcical and surprising to himself alone. The attraction of the world he enters is far deeper: specifically, it is that of Mme de Chasteller, who, as he rides beneath her windows, has twice seen him thrown and on one occasion with unconcealed amusement. Attending benediction at the Chapelle des Pénitents is the first step in a progress that is to lead him to this beautiful retiring young widow who is a willing semi-prisoner in her father's house and the most sought-after match among the noble young bloods of Nancy.

Mme de Chasteller occupies the centre of Nancy, in a manner verging on the symbolic. Her father's Gothic house with the huge white wall, from which her green-shuttered window looks out, is like other buildings in the novels of Beyle in that it is obviously something more than a piece of incidental décor. Newly decorated, it stands in contrast to the lugubrious buildings surrounding it and to the peeling walls of the other houses of Nancy between which flow rivulets of slate-coloured mud, into one of which Lucien falls. Lucien is drawn to the house at first by its appearance, then by pique at having looked foolish to the occupant of the window with the green shutters, and finally by curiosity at the many stories that circulate concerning this wealthy widow of a general, whose father has no wish to see her fortune bestowed on another husband, and this former mistress, according to certain rumours, of the colonel whose lodgings Lucien has inherited.[24] Soon he falls into the habit of spending hours at night strolling beneath Mme de Chasteller's windows, and she, without his knowing, for as long as he is there, watches the glow of his cigar in the darkness below. The setting and Lucien's nocturnal vigils, together with his increasingly deep respect for Mme de Chasteller, suggest a form of courtly romance. And certainly in so far as Mme de Chasteller represents an extreme form of the aristocratic spirit, the hint of mediaeval overtones is not irrelevant. Nor is it more than a hint.[25]

Mme de Chasteller, as we discover, is more truly an aristocrat and more profoundly in revolt against her age – in that she has no desire even to shock those she cannot respect – than Mathilde de la Mole, whose conscious re-enactment of mediaeval dramas is a form of nineteenth-century romanticism. She is unlike Mathilde also in that even her profound indignation at the Jacobins who have sought 'to shake the throne of the Bourbons' never 'troubles her heart for more than an instant'. Before she meets Lucien, her devotion to the cause of the exiled monarchy is the main object of her thoughts, and since other considerations fail to disturb her, she enjoys an 'imperturbable gaiety'. The tears she sheds are tears of pity at the spectacle, for example, of the sun-tanned flesh under the tattered dress of an old pauper in the street. In this respect, one might say that she is more like Mme de Rênal, to whom the language of love, until she meets

Julien, evokes the embraces of her husband and the advances of M. Valenod. Mme de Chasteller too has been profoundly unaffected, both by her marriage and her early bereavement. 'Her most marked characteristic', we are told, 'was a profound nonchalance. Beneath an air of complete seriousness, rendered more imposing by her beauty, her character was happy and even gay. Her greatest pleasure lay in her thoughts and dreams. One would have thought she paid no attention to the little things going on around her: but, on the contrary, not one escaped her; she could see very well what was happening and it was these trivial occurrences which nourished the reverie that others assumed was mere aloofness...' (ch. 15). One might say that she is an aristocrat in the sense that she knowingly does what she wants, like the very different but, in this one respect very similar Mme d'Hocquincourt, her future rival as far as Lucien is concerned, who is good-naturedly promiscuous, indifferent to her reputation and, with her admirably philosophical lover of the moment, very like the courtiers who, presumably, helped to set the tone in pre-Revolutionary Versailles.

The attractions of Mme de Chasteller, as contrasted with Mme d'Hocquincourt, are obvious, if only in so far as they constitute a poignant challenge to Lucien's pride. Pride too is what makes the most profoundly disturbing demands on the normally serene nature of Mme de Chasteller herself. As a model for Mme Jules Gaulthier to follow, Beyle has recommended *La vie de Marianne*. And in the circumstances which bring Mme de Chasteller and Lucien into conscious and compromising intimacy, we can follow, as in a novel or play by Marivaux, the kind of predictable, yet for the lovers themselves wholly unpredictable, chain-reaction of pride, humiliation, reassurance and gratitude that are entertaining only for those who are uninvolved.

If pride counts for a great deal in their relationship, as well as mutual attraction, it would be wrong, nonetheless, to argue as if their relationship could be explained in such conveniently simple terms. If it could, much of the first part of the novel would be merely an all too predictable *marivaudage*, reminiscent, that is, of the worst of Marivaux. Even as it is, the contest of wills between them goes on, I find, just a little too long and can weary those readers who ask in what direction, if any, not only the lovers are moving but also the novelist and the readers themselves. Certainly, anyone looking for an ending along the lines of Musset's *Il faut qu'une porte soit ouverte ou fermée*:

Le comte.... You, my mistress? No, my wife.
La marquise. Ah! Well, if you'd said that when you came in, there'd have been no need to argue...

is bound to feel cheated when he comes to the end of Part one. And it is the absence of any such dénouement that I had in mind when I said that a tragic or happy ending to the novel would have been almost certainly a betrayal of Beyle's inspiration and art. Marriage itself, as it happens, hardly occurs to the two lovers, even during the calm periods of unchaperoned truce they eventually spend together and of which the all too happy Lucien fails to take advantage in order to consolidate or advance his position. And the modern reader will certainly regret that Beyle doesn't tell us what sacrifices and obligations marriage would have entailed between the daughter of a wealthy nobleman and the son of a plebeian millionaire in the 1830s. Yet marriage itself would not have disposed of the problem posed by the story; for this is once again, rethought in an entirely new situation, the problem implicit in the novels and tales: namely, how can any happiness we pursue or simply know that we lack be anything other than a perpetual possibility? And how can even a semblance of satisfaction be achieved without our denying what we genuinely desire? Beyle does not resolve the problem by recommending to mankind in general the divine dissatisfaction which ensures ultimate salvation for Goethe's Faust. Like the greatest of the French Petrarchan poets, he believes that the realisation of desire can take place, miraculously, in the real world:

> Car en *mon corps*: mon Ame, tu revins,
> Sentant ses mains, mains celestement blanches,
> Avec leurs bras mortellement divins
> L'un coronner mon col, l'aultre mes hanches.
> (Maurice Scève, *Délie*, 367)

[For in *my body*, you came back my soul, feeling her hands, hands celestially white, with their arms mortally divine, one crown my neck, the other my hips.]

It is with the man or woman capable of experiencing the miraculous, that is, unable to forget or deny what he genuinely desires, that the novels of Beyle are concerned. And one might say that it is in this sense that Julien Sorel, Mme de Chasteller or Lucien Leuwen are, in their widely differing ways, humanly representative and at the same time exceptional.[26] Lucien and Mme de Chasteller are well matched – during their long conversations, they can agree easily on a *political* truce; they both agree to sacrifice to their friendship their former republican and legitimist sympathies – and because of their obvious suitability and the length at and detail in which the story of their turbulent, idyllic and unrelentingly chaste relationship unfolds, we may find that Beyle comes closer than in any novel to imagining how the ideal possibilities of mutual love might come to be fulfilled in reality.

The failure of the relationship is partly the fault of Lucien, who is alternatively first tactless and importunate in his advances and then unnecessarily submissive and respectful; though the clumsiness and frequent miseries of his courtship and his total lack of worldliness in these matters are, Beyle tells us, commensurate with the genuineness of his feelings:

> Given the present state of good sense and somewhat elderly wisdom that characterises our nation in matters of the mind and spirit, I agree that we shall have to make an effort in order to understand the fearful struggles to which Lucien was the prey and not to laugh at them...
> (ch. 29)

His troubles are made worse by memories of the jibes of his cousin Ernest, who has told him that in his dealings with women, as in every other respect, Lucien is incapable of what Ernest calls 'success'. Yet the humiliations alternate with moments when both partners find that they can meet in pride, joy and peace of mind. After an exchange of letters, for example, ending in an imperious note from Mme de Chasteller indicating that the correspondence must promptly cease, they meet accidentally at the Serpierres' before there has been time for the note to be delivered. Mme de Chasteller feels that she has behaved both honourably and decisively in writing as she has and allows herself the pleasure of a last encounter with Lucien. They join Mme de Serpierre's daughters in an excursion to the cabaret in the woods outside Nancy which has already been the scene of some of the happiest and most carefree moments in the novel and afterwards, walking back to their carriages, Mme de Chasteller on Lucien's arm, find themselves more gladly and irrevocably involved than before.

Le chasseur vert, as the cabaret is called, is one of the titles Beyle had thought of giving the novel; and if it is the setting for some of the most idyllic moments in Beyle's fiction as a whole, it is all the more so for being wholly conceivable in reality. It has perhaps a modern equivalent in the *guinguettes* where on a summer afternoon and evening, friends and strangers dine, drink or dance together on the banks of the Garonne, the Loire and the Marne. Compare the beautiful wistful *unreality* of the Arcadian setting of *Le grand Meaulnes* or of Verlaine's evocations of an enchanted world, which were to haunt the end of the nineteenth century and inspire some of its most exquisite music. I described the opening of *Lucien Leuwen* as an 'overture' and the metaphor will perhaps not seem wholly pretentious when one thinks of the function served by music in Beyle's novel as well. There are many occasions when we may be reminded that his sense of comedy had been formed not only by Molière (as in the portrait of the Tartuffe-like Du Poirier) but by Mozart and Cimarosa.[27]

A number of episodes in the second half of the novel take place in M. Leuwen's box at the Opéra, while at the *Chasseur vert*, a German wind band, handsomely tipped by Lucien, plays extracts from *Don Giovanni* and *Figaro*. The plain enthusiastic Serpierre sisters, the troubled Mme de Chasteller and the lovesick Lucien forget themselves in their chaperoned, uncompromising and hence uninhibited freedom as they sit or dance beneath the trees. The music follows them as they walk back to their carriages and the reader may find that every detail of the episode, including whatever he likes to remember of Mozart, adds to his sense of what it is like to be Lucien and of the calm, deep and yet matter-of-fact reality of the scene. Only Tolstoy, among the authors I know, allows us to enter into the spirit of a festivity or a holiday as freely and unwistfully as Beyle in *Lucien Leuwen* – in the excursions and masquerades of the Rostov children in *War and Peace*, for example. And it is strange, while one is on the subject, why Jane Austen should so often associate such occasions with a menacing thundery atmosphere, wounded susceptibilities and the release of deadly instincts, as in the trip to Box Hill in *Emma* or to Sotherton in *Mansfield Park*. *Lucien Leuwen*, however, reminds us not only of the moments when, as in Jane Austen, we are thrown violently back onto ourselves but of those too when we are released from ourselves and leap forward, as it were, into a new and welcome sense of what we are and of our relation to others. Lucien's relationship with Mme de Chasteller 'comes to nothing' in one respect only: the memories of moments such as these give him an awareness, in the second half of the novel, that he would presumably have lacked otherwise, both of what he wants and emphatically doesn't want in any foreseeable future; and this is particularly evident in his dealings with the very different and distinctly *bourgeoise* Mme Grandet. Even the thought of Mme de Chasteller's supposed infidelity cannot alter or spoil the memories. The memories, in other words, are the form through which Mme de Chasteller exerts the purifying and strengthening influence that, in the few expressions that have survived of courtly or Platonic love that are an honest account of experience and not just specious flattery, can be seen as emanating from the object of adoration with a power greater than that of the lover's will.

One answer to the question to which I have claimed that Beyle repeatedly seeks an answer as a novelist (though it is not explicitly stated) seems to be that the realisation of the greatest conceivable happiness is, possibly by its very nature, a matter of astonished wonder at the unforeseen. Which does not mean that such happiness cannot be sought or even that it is possible *not* to seek it, with more or less success and corresponding assurance. Lucien's failure with Mme de Chasteller is a partial failure only, a failure to regain what he loses after their last meeting and to transform their relationship into what would presumably have had to be something else: marriage, for example, whatever that would have entailed. But Beyle also fails himself to see beyond the moment of perfect understanding between the two, and to pursue the story of the relationship to the point at which it would have been crucially affected by and itself affected Lucien's pursuit of a career compatible with his desire for a sense of purpose and the demands of his self-esteem. One can only imagine that if in Mme de Chasteller Beyle was showing us Mathilde Dembowski as he remembered her, and if the novel was a way of trying to satisfy in imagination the irrepressible hopes and curiosity thwarted by the failure of his own love affair, then, as a novelist, Beyle paid the price of owing so much to Mathilde for his sense of the possibilities of life; he could not imagine a life shared with her other than he had known or could at least persuade himself, recalling his happiest moments with her, that he had known in reality. 'You are only a *naturalist*', he told himself in a margin of the manuscript. 'You don't *choose* your models, but you always take as a model for *love* [in English in the manuscript] Métilde and Dominique...' [one of Beyle's own favourite names for himself.] Whatever the explanation, Mme de Chasteller, except when we are introduced directly into the privacy of her thoughts, is too shadowy a figure, her longing for calm and retirement is too much a simple *donnée* to be taken on trust, and the reader may find that she resembles too closely the Princesse de Clèves, another young widow tempted by a very eligible bachelor, in the novel Beyle had recommended four years earlier as a more worthy model for a modern novelist than the fashionable works of Sir Walter Scott. She resembles, that is, the Princess in her shrinking from anything that will disturb her 'repose' after the death of her mother and the Prince. In a way uncharacteristic of his practice as a whole, Beyle fails to give us as many essential details as the authoress of *La Princesse de Clèves* does concerning the childhood, upbringing and marriage of his heroine; to this extent she is less real and more enigmatic than her seventeenth-century predecessor. The first part of *Lucien Leuwen*, furthermore, ends ludicrously as the result of an improbable diabolical plot reminiscent of the one that brings about the dénouement of *Armance*. Beyle is unable to hit on a device as effective as that used in *Le rouge et le noir* for leaving the questions raised by the novel in effective abeyance, and resorts to comic melodrama. The Roller brothers and the Marquis de Sanréal vow that the plebeian outsider who has stolen the heart of the noblest lady in the town will have as many duels to fight as he now has enemies; and they are only dissuaded from executing this plan of semi-legal assassination by Dr Du Poirier, who knows how to outwit both the would-be assassins and their victim. Taking advantage of an attack of nerves, he confines Mme de Chasteller to her bed and then arranges for Lucien to be present when a howling blood-stained babe is brought out of her bedchamber by a servant he has bribed. Lucien asks for no explanations: this is clearly, he tells himself, the child of a rival and Mme de Chasteller is not as 'chaste' as he had foolishly thought. He returns to Paris without even asking for leave of absence and finds himself once again in the genial ironic presence of his father who, as usual, is interested to know what his son intends to do.

Lucien Leuwen, part two

In the first part of *Lucien Leuwen*, we are taken into a world of the past, alive still in the present but in conscious opposition to it and offering those who belong to that world the security of an inherited and an unearned superiority. After Lucien's return to Paris, we come back to what, even to the twentieth-century reader, and to a Frenchman in particular may seem like the modern world. Some of the political intrigues are extraordinarily reminiscent of what went on, notoriously, under the successive governments of the Third and Fourth Republics, though there is a more profound sense – of which I shall say more later – in which *Lucien Leuwen* is a comedy of our times, for it turns on a dilemma peculiar to an age which believes in the necessity of progress. The failure to resolve it can have grimly farcical consequences both in public and private life.

To say that the second part of the novel is a political comedy is to make a fairly obvious remark. It is less easy to find adequate terms to describe the kind of comedy it is and the point of view it presupposes. One difficulty is that almost no one in the novel is ever what he seems. Dissimulation and the playing of assumed rôles are as tireless and time-consuming an activity as in Shakespearean comedy, and for no one more than Lucien's father, who dominates the second part of the novel like an omnipotent, though more human and fallible Prospero.[28] Lucien could, if he chose, work, without any need for dissimulation, in his father's bank, but also with no purpose; he doesn't love money, the 'metal' itself, enough to pursue the career seriously. His father proposes instead that he accept the post of *maître des requêtes* in the Ministry of the Interior and with it responsibility for the correspondence of the minister himself, for whom M. Leuwen acts as a stockbroker using confidential information received on the ministerial telegraph. Only

'Think about this: how much do you feel that you have the strength to be a rogue, that is, to assist in the execution of some minor skulduggery, for there's been no question of shedding blood for the last four years...'

'Merely of stealing money', interrupted Lucien.

'*From the poor unfortunate people!*' M. Leuwen interrupted him in turn and affecting an air of contrition. 'Or rather, using it a little differently from the way the people would have used it otherwise', he added in the same tone of voice. 'But then, the people are really a little stupid and their deputies not quite as intelligent as they should be and more than a little concerned with their own interests...'

'So what do you want me to become?' asked Lucien with an air of ingenuousness.

'A rogue', replied his father. 'I mean a politician, a Martignac, I won't go so far as to say a Talleyrand. At your age and in your newspapers, that is what is known as being a rogue. In ten years time, you will realise that Colbert, Sully, Cardinal Richelieu, in fact anyone who has been a genuine politician, that is someone who has been able to *direct and control other men*, has raised himself at least to the level of roguery that I wish to see in you. Don't go and behave like N..., who was appointed secretary general of police and then, after a fortnight, resigned because he found the job too dirty.'

(ch. 38)

Resigning too is a matter of playing a rôle; a virtuous one, but ineffectual. M. Leuwen approves of those who find that there are limits to the skulduggery to which a man may go and mentions as an example the murder of a political prisoner a few years earlier by the police, on the pretext that he had sought to elude arrest, an incident that had helped to precipitate N...'s resignation and for refusing to condone which a prefect called C... was dismissed. The prefect, M. Leuwen's esteemed friend, had not been enough of a rogue; the secretary general was not ready to be a rogue at all. Does this mean that his decision was any less harmful in its consequences? As in *La chartreuse de Parme*, we discover as soon as we enter the Paris of the second half of *Lucien Leuwen* that appearances in politics are deceptive, whether or not they are deliberately assumed.

Beyle's irony about professions of virtue on the part of politicians has led many commentators to conclude that the novel was written in the mood of disillusionment and exasperation into which Beyle often and easily relapsed, and which he would sometimes express after the age of fifty by the letters S.F.C.D.T., *se foutre complètement de tout*; in other words, not give a damn for anything. This may be partly true, but it fails to take into account how volatile his temperament was and the tonic restorative effect on him of 'blackening a page', as he put it. The conversation from which I have just quoted is pursued with eager seriousness, all the more so in that both Lucien and his father have definite standards of behaviour, standards, moreover, which Beyle presents without any of the amusement or contempt with which Flaubert invites us to contemplate practically all of the political discussions in *L'éducation sentimentale*. M. Leuwen is serious in his preference that cruelty and injustice should be prevented as far as possible, and judges the government of the day accordingly; serious too in his probity about money. His fortune is based on the reputation of his banking house for honest dealing, and the independence, esteem and power he enjoys are a guarantee that his ethic is a practical one. He enjoys an immense advantage over the Minister of the Interior because it is the minister who is acting improperly (and knows it) in using state secrets to his private advantage on the stock exchange; though the King of France, we are told, does the same. M. Leuwen is merely, having received the information, acting as any other stockbroker would. The virtue he practises is its own reward and we may not be surprised to learn from a chance remark of Lucien's that his father is a personal friend of Jeremy Bentham. In politics, we are told, he looks forward to the day when justice, probity and prosperity will prevail in every sector of public life, but knows that it would be foolish to behave or expect his contemporaries to behave as if that day had arrived. This does not make him an enthusiastic partisan of the 'July monarchy'.

He had dined once or twice with the king shortly after the July revolt. It then had another name and Leuwen, whom it was difficult to deceive, had been one of the first to discern the hatred inspired by so pernicious an example. He had then seen clearly written in the august eyes: 'I am going to frighten the property holders and persuade them to believe that there is a war taking place between those who have something and those who have not.'

In order not to seem as stupid as the country deputies invited with him, Leuwen had made a few not too obvious jokes at the expense of this idea that nobody would express directly.

He feared for a short while that the small shopkeepers of Paris would find themselves compromised by being made to shed blood. He found the idea in bad taste, and without hesitation resigned the post of battalion commander in the National Guard to which he had been appointed with the support of the shopkeepers to whom he would lend, with a certain generosity, a few thousand franc notes from time to time and which they would even occasionally pay back later. He had also stopped accepting invitations to dinner from ministers, on the pretext that he found them boring.

The Comte de Beausobre, Minister of Foreign Affairs, would say to him, however, 'A man like you...' and pursue him with invitations. But Leuwen had resisted such adroit eloquence...
(ch. 60)

As a young man, we are told, he had fought in one or two campaigns in the Revolutionary wars and the name of the French Republic is now like that of 'a mistress one has loved and who since then has misbehaved.' 'Meanwhile', he believes, 'her hour has not yet struck.'

By the end of the novel, in fact well before then, Lucien has come to resemble his father in all these respects, and there is no question of his revolting against his father's standards. The standards are impressive, particularly from a hedonistic and utilitarian point of view, M. Leuwen is himself impressive because in observing them he is so exuberantly and with so much vitality to spare his own master, despite his small frame, delicate health and fear of exposure to cold, humidity and boring conversation. It is their inadequacy when observed with no regard to other standards that the novel finally reveals. And that M. Leuwen should have nothing better to which to devote his remarkable mental energies may explain why he seems throughout the novel, as Beyle puts it, 'a little mad'. To say that his standards are shown as inadequate, is not to say that, as far as Beyle is concerned, they are basically misconceived. And I find nothing in the novel or elsewhere to suggest that they are seen from any other standpoint than that of a middle-class liberal, 'a moderate supporter of the constitution of 1830', as Beyle puts it in one of his prefaces, contemptuous certainly of the king and the ministers who had betrayed the hopes of the July Revolution, but seeing no necessity for revolutionary social or economic changes to eliminate mere temporary abuses, and looking forward to eventual fulfilment of the promise of that dawn in which, for Beyle as for Wordsworth, it was 'bliss to be alive'.

The confidence and buoyancy of the comedy are due to the effective presence throughout the novel of these positive implied beliefs. Yet they do not provide a simple code of conduct in the present and they are necessarily (and even hearteningly) imprecise as far as the more distant future is concerned. Even M. Leuwen, for instance, is never deluded by the ardent tragic hopes which Conrad's Gould in *Nostromo* invests in the automatically humanising benefits, as Gould imagines them, of capitalist enterprise; or by the semi-religious Saint-Simonian cult of productivity against which Beyle had protested in his pamphlet of 1825. One of M. Leuwen's fears for his son is that he too might be taken for an ardent Saint-Simonian because of the deep gloom in which he has been plunged since leaving Mme de Chasteller, though it is obvious that this is not all that M. Leuwen fears in the spectacle of his son's real unhappiness; M. Leuwen's own dissembling with Lucien and his insistence that Lucien too should conceal *his* true feelings are evidence of how little mutual confidence there is between them, though they have so much in common and though Lucien has never so far questioned M. Leuwen's authority. M. Leuwen, we realise as the novel unfolds, cannot afford not to dissemble. Even his immense fortune, it turns out after his death, is based to an alarming degree on credit and on the personal confidence that he has been able to inspire. And Lucien, in winding up his father's affairs, has difficulty in saving his name and business from the scandal of bankruptcy.

It is obvious that M. Leuwen carries duplicity to an extreme, but then he is an unusually successful business man who, from any moral viewpoint, has earned the right to be known as the 'Talleyrand of the Stock Exchange'. And his success has not blinded him to the even greater need for duplicity on the part of many ordinary men who have been less successful and on whose confidence in himself his fortune is founded. We are never given to understand that he deludes himself that he has any other than a legal right to his fortune or that the morality he practises is anything other than a conventional one and a matter of personal convenience. Nor, of course, does his creator, who, in this respect, remains faithful to the precepts of Helvétius. In reading the novel we are never, as a consequence, made to feel that a natural order is being violated and, however menacing or despicable the behaviour of a number of the characters, never left with the sense of evil or sacrilege that are evoked in the presentation of the same society in *L'éducation sentimentale* or *Le père Goriot* and *La maison Nucingen*. For the same reason, presumably, Beyle shows no sign in the novel or his other writings of having shared the traumatic horror that Sartre has attributed to the bourgeoisie in general in 1831 (see page 117 above), during 'the moment of truth', as Sartre puts it, 'when the bourgeoisie for the first time knew itself for what it was'[29] – no longer the enlightened and successful representatives of general humanity but a class threatened in its very being by a lower order with an alien culture and morality. M. Sartre quotes as an example of this state of mind the article, which caused a sensation at the time, by Saint-Marc Girardin on 'the new barbarians'.[30] There is no evidence that Beyle shared either the mood or the opinions of the young journalist and he was more probably struck by the author's appeal to Christian charity in urging that the conditions of the alleged barbarians should be raised as soon as possible to those of the civilised middle classes. 'The function of this Saint-Marc Girardin', he wrote in a note to *Lucien Leuwen*, 'is to render somnolent the passions of the young who are alarming the power that subsidises *Le journal des débats*.' And he declares that he is too lazy to imitate his style.[31]

The violent suppression of the 'Republican' demonstrations in the Rue Transnonain in Paris and the second rising of the *canuts* of Lyon, followed by the bombardment of the city by the forces of the crown and the killing, wounding and imprisonment of hundreds of workers, are referred to several times in the novel, and without attributing to Lucien or his father the sense of frightened class-solidarity to which Sartre refers and which Beyle's younger contemporaries, Balzac and Mérimée, had both expressed in their different ways.[32] We are repeatedly shown the reactions of the upholders of the new established order, but it goes without saying that these are not those of the novelist himself. One has only to think of Colonel Filloteau, who disgusts Lucien after their first meeting by trying to impress him with his talk of 'loyalty to the king' and the need 'to repress the seditious'; of Mme Grandet, whom Lucien is unable to forgive for her disapproval of a public subscription for imprisoned *canuts* in transit to Paris in open carriages, many of them sick and wounded and without blankets or coats in the depth of winter; of Colonel Malher de Saint-Mégrin who tells his officers, loudly enough to be heard by his troops, to have no pity for the wretched weavers who have dared to form themselves into a trades union and that there are crosses to be won when they occupy the offending weavers' town; and of the absurd young prefect of Nancy, M. Fléron riding beside the troops with an enormous sabre:

The dull murmur of the lancers' talk turned into shouts of laughter from which the prefect endeavoured to escape by forcing his horse into a gallop. The laughter redoubled, like the cries of 'Look, he's going to fall off. No he's not. Yes he is.'

But the sub-prefect soon was avenged; hardly were the lancers obliged to make their way through the narrow dirty streets of N... when they were jeered at by the wives and children of the workmen stationed in the windows of the poor houses and by the workmen themselves, who from time to time appeared at the corners of the narrowest alleys. The shops could be heard rapidly closing their shutters everywhere.

At last the regiment emerged into the main shopping thoroughfare of the town; all the shops and stores were closed, there was not a head to be seen at any of the windows and a death-like silence reigned. They came to a long irregular square adorned by five or six stunted mulberry trees and divided along its entire length by a filthy gutter bearing all the sewage of the town; the water was blue because the gutter was also used as a drain for a number of dying factories.

The washing hung out to dry at the windows was horrifying in its wretchedness, tattered condition and dirtiness. The windows of the houses were dirty and small and a number of them, instead of glass, were covered with oiled paper on which handwriting could be seen. Everywhere was a vivid image of poverty which gripped one's heart, though not the hearts of those who were hoping to win a cross by distributing sabre blows among the inhabitants of this poor little town.

The colonel lined his regiment along the gutter as if they were on the battlefield. There the unfortunate lancers, overcome by thirst and fatigue, spent seven hours exposed to the burning August sun without food or drink. As we have mentioned, when the regiment arrived all the shops had closed and the estaminets most quickly of all.

'They've got us where they want us', one lancer said loudly.
'We look a right lot of fools', replied another.
'Keep your f...g observations to yourself', yelped some lieutenant or other who was a political moderate.[33]
Lucien noticed that all the officers with self-respect maintained a deep silence and a very serious air. 'So this is the enemy we have to fight', he reflected...
   (ch. 27)

Lucien's own reaction is not one of solidarity with the workers or one that tempts him to go in for zealous intervention on their behalf. It is rather one of compassionate and self-respecting chivalry. It is dishonourable, as he later explains, to 'cut down workers with one's sabre and become 'a hero of the rue Transnonain.' 'You can forgive the soldier who sees a Russian defending an enemy battery in the inhabitants of the home he is told to attack; but could you forgive me, an officer, who understands what is happening?' (ch. 49). These bitter reflections occur after he has himself been mobbed by an indignant crowd who have recognised him as an agent of the Ministry of the Interior, pelted him with mud, nearly thrown him into a river and told him that the mud on his face is the image of his character. It is an occasion on which Lucien might have been expected to behave in the way that M. Sartre sees as characteristic of his class during this phase of history. His reaction, however, is that of a proud individual. He is ready to brave the mob in order to find and fight the man who has jeered at the mud on his face, and he is thrown into the deepest humiliation afterwards at the thought that the insult is in many ways deserved and the mission he is engaged on is indeed dirty.

I have so far been speaking of Lucien and his creator as virtually indistinguishable, so far as what they most value is concerned, and the reader may agree that on the many occasions when he is invited by the novelist to feel contempt for Lucien, the invitation is a trap for the literal-minded and the very opposite of what it seems. He may agree too that he never feels that he is being entertained to an irony at Lucien's expense as unsparing and as indicative of incorrigible inadequacies as Balzac's at the expense of Eugène de Rastignac or Flaubert's at the expense of Frédéric Moreau. I would suggest that this is because Beyle neither knows, nor writes as if he knew, what a wisdom superior to Lucien's would entail. The story of Lucien is exploratory, in other words, in a way that those of Rastignac and Frédéric Moreau are not; it lacks the inevitability that in Balzac's novels is repeatedly made explicit and in *L'éducation sentimentale* is the constant point of Flaubert's ironic rhetoric; and it is perhaps for this reason that it takes place in an atmosphere less confined and oppressively picturesque than that in which lovers of Balzac or Flaubert feel at home and others, like myself, find claustrophobic. Beyle, of course, was a liberal with eighteenth-century Jacobin nostalgias, and a self-professed Utilitarian unable to abandon hope of progress towards a better world, whatever this would mean; and in this he differed from his two younger contemporaries. And the hope – certainly not sustained by a belief in the *inevitability* of progress; it is difficult to imagine that he would ever have been able to accept the metaphysical presuppositions of Marxism, as witness his somewhat scornful indifference to German historicism in general,[34] is apparent in the acute seriousness with which he dwells throughout the novel on the problem of what this young representative of the governing class is to make of his life and career. The problem is not only that of doing but of discovering what will be for the best, and Lucien's lack of positive political conviction, his inability to believe in Gauthier's egalitarianism, or in any natural right of his or any other class to privilege and power renders the problem not less but more pressing and acute. Throughout the novel and to a degree which is often maddening and bewildering to Lucien, his pride and honour are constantly at stake.

Lucien's first opportunity to take an active part in affairs of state, and to do so in a way consistent with honour, comes when the Minister of the Interior entrusts him with the task of silencing Kortis, the *agent provocateur* shot by a sentry whom he has tried to disarm in an all too successful attempt to test the sentry's loyalty, and now dying of his wound in a Paris hospital and the object of scandalous disclosures in the press. The episode, based on a number of exact details (including the name of the *agent provocateur*) of an incident that occurred in Lyon while the novel was being written, is a typical drama of the age of uncensored journalism, and Lucien's mission is the thankless one that many idealistic young men have had to shoulder, as the only alternative to resigning their posts: that of saving the reputation of the government he serves, at the risk of sacrificing his own. As at the time of the *affaire des fuites* in the 1950s, when the leaking of state secrets was divulged at such a time as to cause the utmost embarrassment to the allegedly responsible Prime Minister,[35] the scandal in *Lucien Leuwen* is complicated by the existence of more than one police force working independently. The branch of the police responsible directly to the king, and by which Kortis is paid, has tried to suppress the scandal by having Kortis silenced with an overdose of opium, but the outraged surgeon whom they have attempted to bribe has responded by knocking the police emissary down and making a scene throughout the entire hospital. It is this situation that the Ministry of the Interior, in the person of Lucien, has now to prevent from deteriorating further.

Lucien's handling of the ghastly affair turns out to be as successful as it possibly could be, not only as far as he is concerned but from the very different point of view of his anxious minister. Kortis dies in loyal and willing silence, the doctors in the hospital are placated, and no further crimes are broached or committed. The episode includes some of Beyle's most powerful and sustained dramatic writing: the unobtrusively symbolic description, for example, of the dark foul-smelling hospital ward into which affairs of state have led both Lucien and the dying man, who lies awake in the darkness while two male nurses sleep in their chairs with their feet stretched out on a lavatory seat.

Lucien looked at his watch. 'To think that in an hour, I shall be at the Opera', he thought...
    (chapter 45)

It brings home to us, moreover, how much matters of immense moment can turn on the tact, firmness and sense of timing of those whose job it is to persuade other men to follow their lead in dangerous situations. (Unlike the modern conventional liberal, Beyle had the utmost respect for the military virtues.) Lucien wins the confidence of the surgeons by assembling them and entreating them to ensure that the patient receives no treatment other than that which they agree together that he needs. And he reassures the dying man by speaking to him as a fellow-soldier, assuring him of his protection and pressing into his hand an advance on a pension for his wife ('The hand was burning; Lucien felt ill as he touched it'). Though it is a typical stroke on the part of the novelist that the suspicions of the dying man should be allayed finally when he realises that Lucien is the son of 'the rich banker Leuwen who keeps Mlle Des Brins of the Opera' and that if the son of such a man is involved in this affair, it is not because he is in need of money and is ready, as Kortis has been, to do almost anything to earn it. The confidence Lucien has been able to inspire has been due not only to his genuine comradely regard for Kortis and his determination that he should not be murdered in his bed, but to a reasonable calculation by both of the parties to the agreement that Kortis will hold his tongue. Lucien, to his surprise, feels happy as he brings the affair to a conclusion. '"I am sailing close to the public's contempt and to death", he repeated to himself a number of times, "but at least I've known how to steer my boat."'

The assurance Lucien acquires, however, is short-lived and though the episode has shown how it may be possible to make the best of a bad job in the world as it is, the sequel leaves us with no excuse for assuming that he has found a way of guaranteeing for the future a sense of his own usefulness compatible with his self-respect. 'Being a rogue', as his father puts it, and thus keeping out an even greater scoundrel may be more generally useful and personally satisfying than merely wishing that politicians and policemen were better men. But it is a gambler's choice. M. Leuwen has persuaded Lucien to embark on a game which is one both of skill and chance. How much of a rogue can one afford to be by one's own standards, so far as these can be distinguished from those of the public at large? It is by trial and error, and therefore often too late, that one finds out; which is what happens to Lucien on his next important mission: to ensure the election of the government's candidates to the Assembly at Champignier in the Cher and at Caen. Pamphlets written for this purpose fall off his coach as it passes in front of a Republican café, and Lucien and his companion are pelted with mud, some of which finds its way into Lucien's mouth. He escapes with the help of the local gendarmes, whose own amusement is plain, and he is then plunged into the most atrocious mortification he has known in the course of his recorded career.

Any anthology of French prose should include, among other extracts from Beyle's writing, the account in chapter 49 of the sequel, in which Lucien pours out his bitterness to his companion and friend (the impassive former Polytechnician, Coffe, whom he has rescued from a debtor's jail) and in which Lucien is then watched writhing 'like St Lawrence on his grill'. Technically, it is superior to those passages in *Armance* and *Le rouge et le noir* in which we are allowed into the privacy of the hero's thoughts, and it is as if Beyle had found yet another way of improving on what, twenty-five years earlier, he had seen as a weakness of the monologues in Corneille's *Cinna*.[36] The heroine of *Cinna*, he had written then, talks to herself with all the 'clarity and eloquence of a woman addressing a stranger'. Octave de Malibert and Julien Sorel may also strike us as unnaturally eloquent in their moments of solitude[37] and this may be why even the portrayal of Julien has seemed to certain readers like a series of notes for a novel, rather than an evocation of what can be taken without further thought as a living presence. It may also be why Beyle himself found that the tone of *Le rouge et le noir*, when he read it again, was insufficiently 'familiar' and 'too Roman'. The disadvantage of the clarity and eloquence of Corneille's poetry, he had written in 1811, is that they do not allow 'an *intimate knowledge* of the characters'. And intimate knowledge, he could have added, is not always the same as the awareness one has or believes that one has of one's true state and feelings. Hence the importance in this chapter of his friend's unpitying eye as he watches Lucien's silent anguish and reflects on his presumptuousness and endless talk as a student and on the suffering which he has brought on himself since then, when he could be enjoying his health, youth and riches:

'But I have to admit, and it's a *capital point in his favour*, that he said nothing I could possibly object to when he took a fancy to the idea of getting me out of prison...yes, and in order to turn me into an executioner's apprentice...The executioner himself is more worthy of esteem...It's out of sheer childishness and as a result of their usual stupidity that men can't stomach the thought of him. He is fulfilling a duty, a necessary duty...indispensable...Whereas, we! we who are on our way to every honour of which society disposes, we are on our way to commit a turpitude as well, a *harmful* turpitude. The common people, who are so often mistaken, as it happens are completely right this time. In this sumptuous English coach, they have found two scoundrels...and called them by that name. Well spoken', he laughed. 'Notice carefully, the crowd didn't say: "You, Leuwen are a scoundrel," but "You are *both* scoundrels!"'

And Coffe pondered this word for himself. At that instant, Lucien sighed aloud.

'There is he suffering from his own absurdity: he thinks he can enjoy the benefits of his office and the delicate susceptibility of the man of honour as well. How stupid can one be! If you're going to wear an embroidered coat, my friend, you'll need a thick skin, I can tell you...'

(ch. 49)

The contrast between Lucien's view of himself and that of his pitiless friend may leave many readers feeling more free to form their own impressions of his state of mind than if only the hero's own thoughts had been given, as in some of the principal monologues of *Le rouge et le noir*. And Coffe's own thoughts and example oblige us to ask what indeed Lucien thinks he is up to, playing a game he despises and weeping with anger and shame when his own contempt for it is expressed by others? Coffe is a mathematician, but, unlike Gauthier a misanthropic one, and he would gladly retire to a small property in the south of France if he could afford to do so. Why should Lucien then, with all his wealth, pursue success of a kind he despises in a world he so obviously loathes? As a rational man, Coffe fails to see the necessity.

For their different reasons, Lucien and Coffe continue on their mission with what might be described as zeal if it were inspired by devotion to the cause they serve; and their collaboration with the prefects of Champagnier and Caen is an extended study of administrative *moeurs* of a kind which the Consul of Civita Vecchia and former high-ranking member of the Imperial civil service was particularly well qualified to write. According to a note in the margin, Lucien's quarrels with the stubborn, vain and politically inept man of letters who has been appointed prefect of Caen is a reminiscence of the scenes in which Beyle had himself taken part during his mission in 1814 to assist in organising the defences of his native Grenoble. And he is able to show, as very few other novelists have been able or ready to, how every official decision, however impersonal it may seem, is the expression either of an all-too-human childishness or simple adult good sense. If some readers find the scenes in Caen lacking in credibility, it may be because they are unable to credit how often power is wielded by childish men. The mission to Caen fails because of the prefect's refusal to countenance Lucien's scheme to have a legitimist elected rather than the government candidate, who has no chance on his own of defeating the much-feared representative of the republican cause. The republican, a man with a reputation for integrity, sense and an unsparing tongue, wins the election, despite the battle of wits in which Lucien, Coffe and a retired general in government service engage against an adversary whom all three admire. And the strength, confidence and consequent generosity of the republican supporters become apparent when the General registers his own vote.

'Well, the time has come', said the General with evident emotion. He put on his uniform and left the observation room with deep emotion to register his vote. The crowd opened to allow him to walk the hundred yards to the door of the booth. The general went in and just as he approached the electoral officers, he was applauded by all the Republicans who were there.

'He's not a dull rogue, like the prefect', a voice was heard saying. 'He's only got his pension and salary and he's got a family to keep...'
(ch. 54)

Lucien is rewarded on his return to Paris for his part in the riot in which he was pelted with mud. As Mr Michael Wood puts it, 'the only decoration he receives is for a wound to his pride'. But his outrageous acting on his own initiative, together with the speed and efficiency with which he has begun to conduct his official affairs in Paris, have brought him into evident disfavour. An administrator himself, Beyle knows how the notorious inefficiency of bureaucracy can be the result of a constant evasion of responsibility by those who know that their promotion will be jeopardized far more by a single mistake than by the lack over the years of any success. Lucien's father decides to intervene in his career once again; having, on a caprice, had himself elected to the Assembly, he plots how to bring down the government of Lucien's ungrateful minister. He creates a party united merely by the common interests of its members: hungry and simple-minded deputies, new to Paris, whom M. Leuwen invites to dinner and treats as personal friends and who, at his instigation, vote as a single man, even on the most absurd motions. The government is repeatedly within a few votes of defeat, and the instability of successive administrations in the 1830s, as under the Third and Fourth Republics, is simultaneously parodied and explained. M. Leuwen's own speeches, which are his normal caustic conversation pursued from the tribune of the Assembly, become newspaper sensations. The king, unknown to his own ministers, anxiously consults him, and M. Leuwen finds himself close to becoming the most powerful public figure in France.

It is at this point that much which has been until now enigmatic in the novel suddenly becomes clear, as M. Leuwen confesses that, having acquired the power to influence the destiny of others, he is at a loss to find any purpose in his own. The confession is made during a conversation between himself, his wife, whom he adores, and Lucien:

'There is another disadvantage in my becoming a minister: I would be ruined. We are feeling more than ever the loss of my partner, poor Van Peters. We've been *caught out* by two bankruptcies in Amsterdam simply because I haven't been to Holland since we lost him. It's because of this accursed Assembly and this accursed Lucien, who is the principal cause of all our troubles. First of all, because he has robbed me of one half of your heart and secondly, because he ought to know the price of money and take charge of my bank for me. Have you ever heard of a man born rich who had no thought of doubling his fortune? He deserves to be poor. I was amused by his adventures at Caen. And if it hadn't been for the idiotic way his Minister received him when he came back, I would never have thought of making a *position* for myself in the Assembly. Now I've taken a fancy to this fashionable plaything. And I shall have a great deal more to do with the fall of the present government, if ever it does come down, than I ever had with its formation.

But there's one terrible objection to all this: *what can I take for myself*? If I take nothing substantial, the government I shall have helped to form will laugh at me in two months time and I shall be in a *ridiculous position*. Suppose I am appointed to the Treasury, the income will mean nothing to me and it will be too small an advantage, given my present position in the Assembly. If I make Lucien a prefect, whether he likes it or not, I shall provide whichever of my friends becomes Minister of the Interior with the means of throwing me into the mud by dismissing him from his post, which he is bound to after three months...

Mme Leuwen, who has 'the severe morality appropriate to a new despotism' of Napoleon's Empire, makes what, to almost any reader, may seem an obvious suggestion:

'Wouldn't it be nice just to do some good and take nothing?' asked Mme Leuwen.

'Our public would never believe it. M. de Lafayette played that rôle for forty years and was always on the point of being ridiculous. The French are too gangrened to understand such things. For three quarters of the inhabitants of Paris, M. de Lafayette would have been an admirable man if he had stolen four millions. If I refused a ministry and built up my business by spending a hundred thousand a year, at the same time investing in land, in order to show that I'm not ruining myself, people would think I was even more of a genius than they do already and I would maintain my superiority over the semi-crooks who are going to fight for a ministry...'

(M. Leuwen, as a banker and speculator on the stock exchange, understands the value of public confidence and the public mistrust of a man whose motive in seeking power is not obvious. Why is it, after all, that in so many societies the public tolerates not only the wealth but the ostentation of dictators and demagogues? M. Leuwen's answer tells us something about the nature of what we choose to call 'corruption' and the word 'gangrened' slips too easily off his tongue to suggest that he is himself censorious. We may be reminded here of the dying Kortis's calculating trust in Lucien when he hears that he is the 'son of the rich banker Leuwen, who keeps Mlle Des Brins of the Opera' and of the Republican crowd in Caen applauding the old general who has sold himself to the government because he has, after all, 'a family to keep'.) M. Leuwen turns to his son laughing:

'If you don't solve this problem for me: *what can I take for myself*? I shall look on you as a man with no imagination and I shall have nothing else to do but tell people I'm ill and go off to Italy for three months, so that they can form a new government without my help. I shall be forgotten when I return but at least I shan't be ridiculous...'
(ch. 60)

The responsibility then is his. Lucien is being asked to find a justification for his father's wealth and power.

Why, Coffe has wondered, should Lucien go to such immense

pains to put himself in a humiliating position which he could so easily afford to leave to others? The reason has been becoming increasingly obvious as Lucien's Parisian career proceeds and as he has come to realise how much his self-esteem and his desire to prove worthy of his advantages have been partly a desire to pay off a debt of his gratitude to his father, a debt, furthermore, of which his father's good natured jokes and advice have been a constant reminder. The burden of gratitude is so heavy as to outweigh other feelings:

'When I think of how much I owe my father! I am the motive for practically all he does; it's true that he wishes to conduct my life in his own way. But instead of ordering, he persuades me. I shall have to watch myself carefully.'

He had to confess to himself something of which he was profoundly and secretly ashamed. He had no tender feelings for his father at all. The thought of this tormented him and, during his 'black' days, caused him almost more bitterness and pain that having been, as he put it, 'betrayed by Mme de Chasteller'...
 (ch. 60)

M. Victor Brombert alone among critics of the novel I have read, seems to have been struck by the crucial importance of M. Leuwen's subtle domination of his son,[38] though even M. Brombert, I think, underestimates its significance; for his account of the novel tells us nothing of the ways in which the family drama turns on the wider political issues raised in the novel and nothing of the general human relevance of both, which makes *Lucien Leuwen* in its way a moral allegory. M. Leuwen's arranging of his son's affairs, his refusal to allow him a quarter of an hour's solitude between his work at the Ministry and his attendance at the Opera and his insistence that Lucien should go through all the throes, publicly at least, of a grand passion are not only obstacles to Lucien's search for an 'identity'; though they are certainly this and M. Brombert describes the process well. Lucien also has the task of enjoying the benefits of his father's life-long endeavours and skill:

'He is like all fathers, which I hadn't realised till now. With infinitely more wit and sentiment than any other, he none the less wishes to make me happy *according to his own ideas*...'
 (ch. 65)

The reasons for Beyle's choosing to make Lucien an only child and hence the sole beneficiary of paternal solicitude become clear when we reflect how common ('like all fathers') and perhaps inescapable the dilemmas of both M. Leuwen and Lucien are. As in Racine's *Britannicus*, the fact that there are no other children brings to a focus the dangerous mutual dependence of two generations and we are shown how the conduct of life for both can be determined both by the parent's ambition for the child and by the forms that gratitude and honour correspondingly assume:

> C'est le sincere aveu que je voulois vous faire.
> Voilà tous mes forfaits. En voicy le salaire.
> Du fruit de tant de soins à peine jouïssant,
> En avez-vous six mois paru reconnaissant,
> Que lassé d'un respect, qui vous gênoit peut-estre,
> Vous avez affecté de ne me plus connoistre...
> (acte IV, scène ii)

[This is the sincere confession I have been meaning to make to you. These are all my crimes. This is my reward. You have hardly begun to enjoy the fruit of all my cares on your behalf and you have shown your gratitude for a mere six months and now you're weary of the respect you owe me, and which probably embarrassed you anyway, and you have pretended that you no longer recognise me...]

M. Leuwen's parental solicitude may be less terrifying than that of Agrippine, but it is scarcely more conducive to complacency. Few of us become millionaires or Roman empresses and not all of us have children. But we care for the future and do all we can to create a world fit for future generations, or at least we encourage one another to think of this as the justification for our lives and what is meant by 'responsibility'. How, other than by not caring at all, as the prematurely aged Coffe seems able to, or by postponing any concern for the future by acquiring more wealth and power, as Lucien could if he were to work in his father's bank (and how even then?) can we avoid that simultaneous assumption and evasion of responsibility to which M. Leuwen confesses in the end? Beyle does not tell us, though he makes it clear that the magnitude of the problem is proportionate to the power and opportunities that the older generation has made available to the young. And he leaves us with the reminder that the child too is responsible for his destiny and not necessarily incapacitated by his elders – though he may be badly led astray – from finding the road to happiness. The novel ends with Lucien acting more responsibly than his father had in his final years, more responsibly moreover by his father's standards and, by an ironical reversal of rôles, with a readiness to sacrifice his own inherited fortune to save his father's posthumous reputation. The freedom he acquires in paying back what he has always thought of as a debt of honour is felt in the elation of the journey through Switzerland on his way to begin his diplomatic career.

Lucien Leuwen and the critic

Anyone who knows the novel at all will realise how little of what is memorable in it an account as short as my own can describe and how many different and no doubt better arguments could be put forward for regarding it as an important novel. I have said, for instance, nothing of M. Leuwen's fear that his son should be taken for a Saint-Simonian or of the irony of this being at a time when, under the editorship of Bazard and Enfantin, the *Producteur* was taking a more obviously socialist line than during Saint-Simon's own lifetime and inveighing particularly against the scandal of inherited wealth. And I have only referred in passing to the comedy of Lucien's affair with the ambitious Diana-like Mme Grandet, anxiously stage-managed by Lucien's father. The revelation that even Mme Grandet's passion for him has been roused, not as Lucien at first believes, by his own attractions but by the promise of a ministry for her husband leads to Lucien's final recognition of how much he has been 'serving the passions of another' and is a further blow to his fortunately resilient pride. I have no wish to suggest that these episodes are inferior to others to which I have referred at greater length, though they are obviously of minor interest compared with those which concern Lucien's relationship with his father or Mme de Chasteller. The same can be said of his portraits of the would-be overbearing Minister of the Interior, perpetually obliged to remind himself that France is now a Parliamentary democracy and of the Minister's beautiful pathetic wife, Lucien's flirtation with whom is so much better observed than the very similar relationship in *Une position sociale*. The latter novel, fortunately left unfinished in 1833, gives us, incidentally, in the principal character what Beyle himself in a note calls an 'idealised' self-portrait. It takes place in the French Embassy in Rome where the hero tries to seduce the wife of the ambassador, and Beyle thought at one stage of adapting it to form the third part of *Lucien Leuwen*. Having written the first two parts, however, he may probably have realised that it would require a great deal more than adaptation and that even the idealised self-portrait was a poor vehicle for the pursuit of interests such as those he had already brought to life in creating Lucien.

I have said that there are many reasons for regarding *Lucien Leuwen* as an important novel and this is obviously true of any important work of art; the greater the art, the more often and unexpectedly one is likely to find it relevant. It is equally obvious that any account of its importance is, by its nature, restricted and likely to restrict the significance of the work in the minds of those who cling to this one single interpretation, unless they are able at the same time to see its inadequacy as a description or definition of the art. My own argument follows on from and is intended as a qualification of two different interpretations of *Lucien Leuwen* that have been put forward in the past. And one of these is that the novel is interesting (like all Beyle's novels) because it contains a self-portrait and the personal reminiscences, transformed into a fictitious setting, of an uniquely interesting and complex man. The most persuasive version of this argument I know is M. Victor Brombert's in *Stendhal et le voie oblique*. I have no wish to contradict it and no special information that gives me the right to do so, but I have tried to show how much more there is both to Lucien's adventures and to the mind of his creator than is suggested by this view when it is taken on its own, and I have tried to draw attention to what I see as Beyle's concern with the human as well as Lucien's and his own condition.[39] In saying this, I am probably revealing my inability to share the view which tells us that though there is much literature can teach us about the laws of history and men's response to *particular* conditions, there is no human condition as such and it is a sentimental delusion to speak as if there were. One of the most influential advocates of this view had been George Lukács and it is against his interpretation of *Lucien Leuwen* that I have also found myself arguing here. For Lukács, Beyle is a romantic because he is 'unable to accept the fact that the heroic period of the *bourgeoisie* has ended and that the "antediluvian colossi" – to use a Marxian phrase, have 'perished for ever'. Beyle's optimistic forecast of what the bourgeois society of the year 1880 would be like 'was a pure illusion, but because it was an historically legitimate, basically progressive illusion, it could become the source of his literary fertility...'[40] This account of Beyle's allegiances and nostalgias is obviously apt, though whether the hopes he placed in the future were an illusion is more debatable. By 1880, in spite of the atrocities accompanying the suppression of the Paris Commune, the franchise had been extended, trades unions were recognised and a repetition of the suppression of the *canuts* in the 1830s an impossibility. By the time of the Second World War, partly as a result of the legislation of the government of Léon Blum (as it happens, one of Beyle's most enthusiastic commentators), the condition and education of the poorer peasantry and working classes were almost certainly superior to what they had been when Beyle wrote *Lucien Leuwen*. I say this not because I am convinced that Lukács is wrong but because it is by no means obvious that he is right, or that Beyle's hopes for the future were misconceived.[41] The hopes, moreover, as expressed by either M. Leuwen or Beyle, are never more than hopes and, unlike Lukács, Beyle was under no self-imposed obligation to think of ultimate progress as inevitable. Beyle's disillusion with his age is accordingly less intolerably at variance with his ideas of what the world ought to be like than Lukács claims. What Beyle is showing us, Lukács writes, in the destinies of Julien, Lucien and Fabrice del Dongo, is 'the vileness, the squalid loathesomeness of the whole epoch – an epoch in which there is no longer room for the great, noble-minded descendants of the heroic phase of *bourgeois* history, the age of the Revolution and Napoleon. All Stendhal heroes save their mental and moral integrity from the taint of their time by escaping from life. Stendhal deliberately represents the death of Julien Sorel on the scaffold as a form of suicide and Fabrice and Lucien withdraw from life in a similar way, if less dramatically and with less pathos...'[42] Lucien, of course, doesn't 'withdraw from life... and though Lukács's saying he does is unimportant in itself, it is in keeping with a widely held view of Beyle's writings as a whole and one which, as I have argued in talking of *Le rouge et le noir*, superficially his art invites. Lukács fails or chooses not to remember how much Lucien, like Julien, experiences welcome surprises as well as unwelcome ones in his dealings with his contemporaries of every class, and how sensitively Beyle's prose registers not only the immense changes of mood but also of the hero's whole *character* and outlook on life as an immediate result of these surprises. He overlooks, in other words, what other critics, who are either far more settled in their outlook or who have bad memories, refer to as Beyle's hopeless inconsistency. (Take, as an example of this inconsistency, the superb account in chapter 3 of Lucien's arrival in Nancy.) It is unfortunately common for critics to write of Beyle either as if he were inconsistent to the point of buffoonery or as if the freedom with which he can convey disgust at his contemporaries were like a final defiant slamming of the door on them followed by contemptuous contemplation from a superior vantage point of all except those who share the same disgust, suffer intolerably and long to escape as well.[43] This is not the reaction of the sympathetically portrayed General Fari as he makes his way through the crowd to register his vote in the election he has helped unsuccessfully to rig. Nor is it that of the crowd itself, which is able to forgive him for selling himself since it knows that he needs the money. It *is* the attitude of Flaubert, and the point of his irony throughout much of *L'éducation sentimentale*, and it is expressed with painful directness on one of the few occasions when he drops his rhetorical irony and recalls the horrors of 1848:

...and in spite of the victory [of the forces of law and order], equality (as if to chastise its defenders and deride its enemies) was made triumphantly manifest, an equality of stupid brutes, a common level of sanguinary turpitudes; for the fanaticism of self-interest was balanced against the delirium of need, the aristocracy gave vent to all the fury of the lowest scum...Public reason was shaken as after one of the great natural catastrophes. And intelligent men became imbeciles for the rest of their lives...

(part 3, ch. 1)

It is also the attitude of Balzac, as Lukács himself admiringly describes it, in *La maison Nucingen*. (M. Bardèche as well in his chapter on *Lucien Leuwen*. The right-wing M. Bardèche and Lukács make the same comparison and draw the same conclusions.) And because Balzac, as a conservative catholic, was even more contemptuous of his age than Beyle, it makes him for Lukács the greater realist of the two. Lukács praises the portrayal of M. Leuwen père, for example, 'the embodiment of a superior spirit and superior culture...' and a 'very lifelike transposition of the pre-revolutionary traits of the Enlightenment into the world of the July monarchy. But however delicately portrayed and lifelike the figure is, Leuwen is an exception among capitalists and hence greatly inferior to Nucingen as a type...' What Balzac shows in *Le père Goriot* and *La maison Nucingen* 'is how the rise of capitalism to the undisputed domination of society carries the human and moral degradation and debasement of men into the innermost depths of their hearts'.[44]

A comparison of the biographies of the principal Parisian bankers from 1810 to 1835 may well show that Nucingen was in fact the prototype of them all; though among the exceptions in this case would be not only Leuwen but the politician and banker Laffitte, whom commentators have seen as a model in some respects for the portrait of Leuwen himself. Though, even if in our ignorance, we may have to concede that Nucingen may have been the typical capitalist of his time (and we have only Lukács's word for it), M. Leuwen has a representativeness that makes him a more ominous as well as a more sympathetic figure than Balzac's monster, and this whether or not we know anything about the France of the 1830s and whether we think of him as a successful man of the world, as a politician or as being 'like all fathers'.

La vie de Henry Brulard

Well Moore, what are you thinking about now?
I've been thinking about memory, because of what Russell says in the *Outline of Philosophy*.
What is it that you're thinking of particularly?
Well, the whole problem of memory hadn't struck me before. You see, I want to say that you have an immediate knowledge of some things you remember.
Yes, and does Russell deny that?
Yes, he denies that. He says that memory is entirely a matter of inductive consideration from the fact that you remember. He says that it's merely a matter of probability, and he makes what I consider is the fundamental mistake of supposing that when we say that a

person remembers so-and-so, we are talking merely of his present state, do you see, and not also saying that the thing did happen...
(From a broadcast conversation between G. E. Moore and G. A. Paul, 15 May 1957.)

Beyle's own father is a dominating presence in *La vie de Henry Brulard*, though, like Mathilde Dembowski in *Souvenirs d'égotisme*, largely an invisible one, as far as the reader is concerned. Practically all we are told of the relations between father and son is that they failed to understand one another. Most of Beyle's recollections of his childhood and youth after the death of his mother are consequently a record of years of loneliness in the enforced company of the family circle, which because of his father's royalist and religious allegiances, lived in near isolation in the fortunately peaceful and law-abiding Grenoble of the 1790s, untouched by Civil War or Terror. Beyle left home at the age of sixteen a few days before the 18 Brumaire:

What I am going to say is not very pleasant. When the exact time for my departure arrived, my father received my farewells in the municipal gardens beneath the windows facing the Rue Montorge.
   He was crying a little. The only impression his tears made on me was that I found them very ugly to behold. If the reader feels horrified by my reaction, will he design to remember the hundreds of compulsory walks I was forced to take *for my own pleasure*? It was this hypocrisy that irritated me most and which has led me since to execrate this particular vice...
   (ch. 35)

There are few similarities between Chérubin Beyle and the fictitious François Leuwen and the astonishing feat of imagination that went into the creation of the latter shows, among other things, how much Beyle had learned of what fathers are capable of after he had himself left home. Yet neither Lucien nor Beyle are able to feel 'tenderness' for their fathers; both adore their mothers who, none the less, are never shown as seeking to influence their lives; and both have fathers who in their very different ways are far more mercenary than their sons and who seek to make them happy 'according to their own ideas'. The bleak northern valley of the Alps in which Grenoble stands and the even more cheerless Paris that Beyle discovered when he first left home (and in which the absence of mountains made him physically ill) are the background to *La vie de Henry Brulard* and Grenoble is associated with his father who was to become its deputy mayor under the Restoration. His mother's family was originally from Provence and, he liked to think, descended from an Italian who had sought refuge in France after committing a crime of passion. *Henry Brulard* ends with Beyle crossing the St Bernard pass to join his regiment in Italy in the June of 1800 and with the discovery of the southern slopes of the Alps, the Lombard plain and his beloved Milan. The same journey is described briefly in the last chapter of *Lucien Leuwen*; like the young Beyle, Lucien is overjoyed to find himself passing through the country of St Preux and Julie Wolmar in *La nouvelle Héloïse*.

In *Henry Brulard* there is an unmistakeable desire on Beyle's part to pay posthumous justice to the father against whom he had rebelled as a child and railed as a young man in Paris for depriving him for long periods of his personal allowance. And the desire is apparent in the plainness with which the facts of the relationship are stated and in the absence of any self-exoneration on the part of the adult for his hostility as a child. We are given only the reasons he had as a child for this hostility: the fact, for example, that he was never allowed to play with other children of his own age. And the reader is repeatedly told that he may well be shocked to learn of the depth of his animosities. Beyle emulates, in other words, as in all his autobiographical writings, the freedom from either self-exoneration or self-condemnation, or as he puts it himself, the simple 'truthfulness' of the *Life* of Benvenuto Cellini; though without Cellini's very real egotism, the egotism that makes him not only the most but almost the only interesting personality in his book. Chérubin Beyle is described briefly but unforgettably: an 'arch-Dauphinois' constantly preoccupied with the buying and selling of land, 'excessively wrinkled and ugly, awkward and silent in the company of women and yet needing them', a quality which enabled him to 'understand *La nouvelle Héloïse* and Rousseau's other writings of which he would talk with adoration while cursing him for his impiety, for the death of my mother had thrown him into the extremes of the most absurd devoutness...' (ch. 7). The last trait is in revealing contradiction with what we have been told of his acquisitiveness and incapacity for 'noble folly' and we may not be surprised that as deputy mayor of Grenoble, he ruined himself in the legitimist cause.

We are given *only* the salient facts of the relationship between Beyle and his father in *Henry Brulard*. There is no imaginative exploration of the kind we have in *Lucien Leuwen* of all that such a relationship might involve and determine and it is as if the writing of the novel had left Beyle more sure of his own feelings in the matter and with the moral detachment of a man who has done his utmost to know the truth about others as well as himself. But the author's truthfulness in *Henry Brulard* cannot simply be taken on trust. Beyle himself confesses to his poor memory for facts and dates as opposed to feelings, and Stendhalian scholars such as Arbelet, Chuquet and Henri Martineau have devoted much research to checking the most innocent details of Beyle's autobiographical narrative.[45] The first performance that Beyle ever heard of an opera by Cimarosa seems to have taken place, for example, not at Ivrea, as he tells us, but at Novara (though he may well be right in telling us that one of the actresses had a front tooth missing) and it is highly improbable that he read Shakespeare 'continually from 1796 to 1799'.

However, the worst that scholars have discovered of Beyle's inaccuracies suggest that his memory was not so much poor as erratic and, as M. Ernest Abravanel has recently argued, on the evidence that we have, often astonishingly good;[46] particularly Beyle's visual memory. I have therefore followed the usual practice in the preceding chapters of relying on the testimony of the memoirs in my own account of Beyle's childhood and youth; though I would not have done this if I had been concerned with strict chronology, as Beyle's memory for dates was obviously wild. And I find myself agreeing with M. Abravanel that 'Henry Brulard' is a portrait of the child Beyle was, rather than of the ageing author forty years later recreating the child in his own image.[47]

In intention at least, G. E. Moore, in the dialogue I have quoted as an epigraph, sees the 'immediate knowledge' of the past implied by the word 'memory' as a necessary presupposition, Russell's attempted refutation of which is untenable even in its own terms. The desire to achieve and be sure of having achieved such knowledge is something of which Beyle constantly tells his readers and is apparent in the gladness with which he will seize on remembered details with no possible interest for anyone other than himself, unless incidentally, as an example of how memory is bound to operate if it operates at all:

> But the reader, if ever there is some one to read these puerilities, will soon realise that all my attempts to say *why*, all my explanations may be errors. I have only some very clear images, all my explanations are those that occur to me, as I write this, forty-five years later...
> (ch. 5)
> I can still see myself in the Municipal Library listening to my grandfather in the main hall which is full of people and to me seems immense. But why all these people? On what occasion? The image won't tell me. It is only an image...
> (ch. 5)
> I see myself going on an errand for my father to Allier's bookshop in the Place Saint-André with fifty francs to buy Fourcroy's manual of chemistry which gave him his passion for agriculture. I understand very well how this taste developed. He could only walk freely in his property at Claix.
> But then, wasn't all this caused by his love affair with Aunt Séraphie, if ever there was an affair? I can't see the actual shape of events [*la physionomie des choses*]. My only memory is that of the child...
> (ch. 17)

Professor Francesco Orlando has pointed out the contrast between this purported knowledge of the past and that of Rousseau in the *Confessions* and Chateaubriand in *Les mémoires d'outre-tombe*,[48] in both of which the evenly eloquent narration and the omniscient eye of the narrator are made possible by a freedom from any over-riding concern with the *difficulties* of reliving the past. And Professor Orlando compares Rousseau's minor confession, as far as he is himself concerned, that

> ...if I happen to have employed some incidental ornament, I have done so only to fill a void occasioned by some failure of memory on my part...[49]

with Beyle's

> The great difficulty of writing these memoirs is that of having and writing only those recollections that are those of the period I have succeeded in gripping hold of by the hair...
> (ch. 10)

To the names of Chateaubriand and Rousseau, Professor Orlando could, I think, have added that of Marcel Proust, and one of the reasons for recommending *Henry Brulard* to almost any reader and not merely those who wish to know about Beyle's childhood is that it offers an alternative to what many have come to think of as the truth and finality of Proust's thoughts on what a genuine reliving of the past is like, and to the instances of it he offers in his novel. Admirers of Proust tend at times, I think, to forget that *A la recherche du temps perdu is* a novel, not only when we are learning of the adventures of Swann, Charlus and Albertine but in the passages in which the revelation of an unsought memory gives him sudden access to the past. The famous instance of the madeleine dipped in a cup of tea and awakening the sudden poignant realisation that this has happened before, whatever *this* may be, derives no doubt from Proust's experience, but not the beautifully written sequel which plunges us into the world of the novel with something resembling total recall (*Pléiade* edition, vol. 1, p. 47). Proust has described his wrestling with the elusive memory before this revelation[50] and, significantly, in the following terms:

Grave uncertainty whenever the mind feels that it is being overtaken by itself; when it, the seeker, is at the same time the obscure country in which it must search and in which all its baggage and equipment are useless. Seek? Not only seek: create as well. It is confronted by what is not yet what it alone can make real and then bring into its own light...
(*Pléiade*, vol. 1, p. 45)

Later, when he revisits the little town of his childhood, we learn how different it is from what he had remembered of it earlier (vol. 3, pp. 691–3). And this prepares us for the meditation in which Proust defines that realm which is neither past nor present but 'outside time' and which is that of 'beauty', 'art' and 'reality' itself. 'The true paradises', Proust tells us in a mood of paradoxically exultant reassurance, 'are the paradises that one has lost' (vol. 3, pp. 869–75).[51]

To 'create' in Proust's sense of the word is for Beyle, a distraction, though a tempting one:

No doubt I am enjoying immensely writing as I have been for an hour and seeking to depict *just as they were* my sensations at the time

of the arrival of Mlle Kubly, [the actress]. But who the devil will have the time and energy to sink to the bottom of all this, to read this excessive quantity of 'I's and 'me's'? Even I find that it *stinks*. This is the main disadvantage of this kind of book and, moreover, I'm unable to add a little savour by spreading on to it the sauce of charlatanism. And dare I add, as Rousseau does in his *Confessions*...
  (ch. 25)

and he does not abandon, as the narrator of Proust's novel seems able to, his 'search' for the past as it was. Hence, presumably, his continual precautions against common tricks of memory such as the following:

I was very adventurous and consequently had two accidents which my grandfather would relate with terror and regret. Near the rock by the Porte de France, I stuck a pointed stick into a mule which had had the impudence to plant its hoofs into my chest and knock me down. 'A little more and he'd have been killed', my grandfather would say.

I have an impression of the event but probably it isn't a direct memory, only a memory of the image I formed of it long ago when I was first told about what had happened...
  (ch. 5)

The philosophical work which had influenced Beyle's ideas of the nature of memory more probably than any other is Tracy's *Eléments d'idéologie*, in which the accuracy of memory is seen as the only possible guarantee against errors of judgment, even in logic, as Tracy defines it.[52] And Beyle's journal and letters to his sister Pauline are full of exhortations to remember the past in order to judge correctly in the present. In *Henry Brulard*, memory is referred to, particularly in the opening chapters, as a means to self-knowledge. 'What have I been?' and 'What am I?' are clearly for Beyle two ways of asking the same question. Yet 'what eye can see itself?' (ch. 1). The questions which Beyle feels at a loss to answer are: 'Was my character a melancholy one?' 'Was I a man of wit and intelligence?' 'Did I have a talent for anything?' Self-knowledge as a means to self-perfection is in any case an ambition he had abandoned years before.[53] Hence his inability to reply to Alberthe de Rubempré's accusation, as he saw it, that Julien Sorel was a self-portrait.[54] *La vie de Henry Brulard* is therefore not a moral evaluation nor a psychological analysis of the author; that is an exercise for the reader to perform. The self that Beyle knows or believes he can know is known only in so far as he is able to relive what he has seen, heard and desired in the past. On a number of occasions, he will tell us that he is the same now as when he was a child. And the fact of memory presupposes that identity of awareness, that 'immediate knowledge', as Moore puts it, 'of some things you remember'.

There are no doubt ontological and epistemological implications of these assumptions that it would be fascinating to pursue. Beyle himself does not pursue them, though he takes us some of the way towards their discovery and with a care and intensity of purpose that arise from his characteristic need to be 'clear. If I am not clear, *my whole world* is annihilated.' *Henry Brulard* might have been a longer and more profound work than it is. But on 26 March 1836, he received the news of his leave of absence from Civita Vecchia, which was to last more than two years and enable him to settle in Paris and travel throughout France. His pleasure and excitement were too keen for him to continue. The manuscript of *Henry Brulard* ends in disjointed notes. And having evoked the joys of arriving in Italy, he himself a few weeks later took the boat to Marseille.

7
La chartreuse de Parme

Le rose et le vert and *Les chroniques italiennes*

Beyle's leave of absence from the early summer of 1836 until the August of 1839 was to be the last period of intense activity before the first of the serious heart attacks and the onset of the crippling gout that were to affect him during the last years of his life. During his absence from Civita Vecchia he travelled through France, Savoy, Switzerland and northern Spain and wrote continuously, in the way he most enjoyed, in the bedchambers of unfamiliar inns, sometimes after ordering up a bottle of champagne, or in an 'attic' in Paris off the Boulevard des Capucines, where in seven weeks during the winter of 1838, he was to dictate the whole of *La chartreuse de Parme*. The period was also one in which he wrote and published the *Mémoires d'un touriste*, tried again unsuccessfully to complete a life of Napoleon, began to publish his *Chroniques italiennes* in *La revue des deux mondes* and completed nine chapters of one of the best of his unfinished novels, a new version of *Mina de Vanghel*.

Like *Mina de Vanghel*, *Le rose et le vert* is the story of a wealthy heiress from Königsberg who travels to France in search of civilisation, and a lover or husband who will neither bore nor disgust her like her suitors at home. It is Beyle's version of the international theme which Henry James was to explore in *The Portrait of a Lady* and other stories; and Mina has in common with James's American heroines candour and independence as well as a willingness to admire and be carried away by whatever she may find in her promised land which make her the most exacting as well as intrepid of judges. It is not Beyle's first attempt to show his contemporaries how they seem through foreign eyes: there is the American visitor, for instance, in the dialogue on *France in 1821*[1] and the incorrigible German scholar in chapter 48 of *Lucien Leuwen*, holding forth on the origins of the mass in defiance both of French piety and French irony, both of which he counters with well-documented facts. But it is Beyle's most serious and sustained attempt to write in a way which, if it anticipates James, has a distant precedent as well in Montesquieu's *Lettres persanes*. And it was also an opportunity to write about a country in which he had lived as a public administrator for several years, in which he had fallen both happily and unhappily in love and some of whose ways of setting out on 'the hunt for happiness' he had always admired, particularly in so far as the Germans, like the Italians, were free from the French dread of social ridicule.

None the less, the story moves slowly, all the more so in that Mina is almost at once disappointed, after what she has been led to expect from the plays of Marivaux, by what she finds in post-Revolutionary France: the very ungallant talk among business-men and aspiring academicians who are afraid to utter a personal opinion, the amusement, such as it is, afforded by the intrigues of a Jesuit who tries to convert her, and the self-doubts of the decent young aristocrat, who is a less profoundly disturbed (and potentially more interesting) version of the hero of *Armance*. Much of the dialogue too is, for Beyle, uncharacteristically sententious: an opportunity to comment explicitly on *mores* rather than bringing them immediately to life. Yet if the novel moves slowly, it is by comparison chiefly with Beyle's other fiction and its weight is partly that of thought and reflection on two social worlds he had known at first hand. It is this, in fact, which makes it seem like the beginnings of a far more rewarding work than the superficially more gripping *Chroniques italiennes*.

The first of the stories usually collected under this title is *Vanina Vanini* of 1829, a work entirely of Beyle's own invention. *Vittoria Accoramboni, Les Cenci* and *La duchesse de Palliano* are taken directly from his collection of Italian manuscripts, now in the Bibliothèque Nationale, and are remarkable chiefly for their fidelity to the original sixteenth-century texts; to say which is to comment on the sensitiveness of his prose and the unobtrusiveness of his own personality. He lacks, for instance, the cultivated simplicity and terseness of his friend Mérimée, which, for the modern reader, far from putting him *en rapport* with the primitive passions of his Spanish or Corsican heroes, merely gives to his stories their now overwhelmingly obvious nineteenth-century literary flavour. These three more or less direct translations are noteworthy also for the reflections which precede them and in particular those in *Les Cenci* on Don Juan, which form an admirable rider to chapter 59 of *De l'amour*. The character of Don Juan, Beyle argues, is a product of Christian civilisation, as can be seen in the case of the incestuous Francesco Cenci, who sought to assert his individuality by flouting the common Christian morality of his day. Beyle adds almost nothing otherwise to his original sources and it is only in *l'Abbesse de Castro* and the stories he planned for a second series, to be published in *La revue des deux mondes*, that he uses the Italian manuscripts as a point of departure for a story of his own; also, of course, in *La chartreuse de Parme*, though the connection here between the novel and the seventeenth-century text from which it derives is as tenuous as between *Le rouge et le noir* and the story of Antoine Berthet.[2]

L'Abbesse de Castro was Beyle's opportunity to show what he could make, as an imaginative novelist, of the authentic chroniclers of an age he admired; that it is even less superficially gripping than the stories he had merely translated and edited suggests that his understanding of sixteenth-century Italy may have been less real and imaginative than he would have liked to believe. The world of *La chartreuse de Parme*, in which he had taken a chronicle of the sixteenth century and placed it in a nineteenth-century setting, is obviously one in which he was more at home, and *L'Abbesse de Castro* is a failure if one compares it with either *La chartreuse* itself or Manzoni's *I promessi sposi*, which has the same violent lawless setting as the former and similar dramatic contrasts between Christian virtue and ferocious lust and cruelty. It is true, of course, that the innocence of Manzoni's lovers, the saintly heroism of Don Cristoforo and the barbarity of the Innominato are so obvious as to make the book eminently suitable as a school classic. When I told an Italian lady once how much I admired it, she told me that she found its morality 'too tidy'. Yet it is the depth of Manzoni's veneration for a

Don Cristoforo and of his feeling for the moral and civil law – it is not only in his technique as a historical novelist that he resembles Walter Scott – that makes this seventeenth-century 'chronicle' read like a moral allegory and hence an account of Manzoni's own world.[3] In *L'Abbesse de Castro*, the agnostic Beyle has no such deep sympathetic involvement with either the peace-loving Jules Branciforte, forced into the life of a brigand and mercenary, or with the woman he loves, Hélène de Campireali, 'the long degeneration of whose soul' after their enforced separation the novel describes. There are many effectively sinister touches: the glimpses we are given, for instance, of Hélène's clandestine lover, the local bishop, after she has been made Abbess:

Since their first rendez-vous in November, he had continued to visit the convent more or less regularly every week. A slight air of triumph and silliness about him on these occasions was noticed by all who saw him and this gave him the privilege of outraging the proud character of the young Abbess. On Easter Monday, as on a number of other days, she treated him as if he were the most abject of men and addressed him in a way that the poorest labourer employed by the convent would never have borne. In spite of which, a few days later, she conveyed a sign to him that brought him without fail to the chapel door. She had sent for him to tell him she was pregnant. On hearing which, according to the report of their trial, the handsome young bishop became pale with horror and altogether *stupid with fear*...
(ch. 6)

Effects such as these belie, however, the author's claim in the opening pages to be showing us customs 'marvellously suited to the creation of men worthy of that name' and that 'produced the Raphaels, Giorgiones, Titians, Correggios'. Not surprisingly, Augustin-Thierry, in his book on the Princess Belgiojoso, who kept the embalmed corpse of her lover and secretary in a cupboard in her villa, regrets that Stendhal had not lived to hear the tale and feels sure that in a novel like *L'Abbesse de Castro*, he would have succeeded somehow in fitting it in.[4] The novel seems to fall, in fact, between the heroic drama Beyle seems to have wanted to write and the morbidity that was to be expressed uninhibitedly in the fiction of writers like Gautier and Poe.

La chartreuse de Parme presents us with an Italy very different from that which is exalted at the beginning of *L'Abbesse de Castro*:

During the middle ages, the republican citizens of Lombardy had given proof of a bravery equal to that of the French and had earned the distinction of seeing their city rased to the ground by the Emperors of Germany. Since becoming *faithful subjects*, their principal concern had been the printing of sonnets on little handkerchiefs of rose coloured taffeta whenever the marriage took place of a girl belonging to some rich or noble family. Two or three years after this great event in her life, the same girl would choose a *cavaliere servente* and sometimes the name of the *sigisbeo* chosen by the husband's family occupied an honourable place in the marriage contract. It was a far cry from these effeminate customs to the profound emotions aroused by the unexpected arrival of the French army. Soon there came into being new and passionate ways. An entire people realised, on the 15th of May 1796 that everything it had respected till then was supremely ridiculous and sometimes odious...

The natural voluptuousness of the countries of the south had once reigned in the courts of the Visconti and Sforze, those famous dukes of Milan. But since 1635, when the Spaniards had taken possession of the Milanese and assumed the character of proud, taciturn and suspicious masters living in constant fear of revolt, gaiety had fled. The people had learned to imitate its masters and were far more concerned to avenge the least insult with a dagger than to enjoy the present moment...
(ch. 1)

After the fall of Napoleon, the effeminate ways return, together with the morbid vanity which is the enemy of voluptuous gaiety, and the novel shows us what it is like to live in such a society when one has known and acquired the habits of a different way of life.

Fabrice and Clélia

'...and in this beautiful country, the only thing to do is to make love; the other pleasures of the soul encounter obstacles and constraints; in so far as one feels a citizen of the country, one will die poisoned by melancholy.'
Rome, Naples et Florence en 1817 (17.11.1816)

Beyle's attitude to the way of life which his principal characters are compelled to lead has often, I believe, been misunderstood, and the fault may well lie with his first publisher, Ambroise

Dupont, who miscalculated what would go into two volumes, objected to providing an absurdly short third volume and, as Beyle put it, 'sabred' and 'strangled' the end of his manuscript, making him compress into a few pages what presumably was a far more detailed and circumstantial version of the novel we now possess.[5] We can only guess what the original ending was like, though we know that Beyle thought of expanding it even further. But we can assume from the title of the novel that it included the events leading to Fabrice del Dongo's retirement from the world and that it was at least as obviously a tragic ending as the disconcertingly abrupt ending we know.

It will probably be generally agreed, however, that the overall effect of *La chartreuse* is not tragic; even though its dominating personality, Gina Sanseverina, suffers agonies of yearning for her nephew and both shame and despair at the thought that he can never be hers; even too though she, Fabrice and Clélia Conti die heart-broken at the end. Beyle told Balzac that he was exaggerating the merits of the novel by comparing Gina with Racine's Phèdre and it is true that we never enter into Gina's consciousness with the same horrifying completeness of immersion with which we enter that of Racine's heroine. The novel distracts us constantly with its swiftly unfolding intrigue and its varying degrees of seriousness and high spirited farce. Even the melancholy which underlies so much of the novel has a full-bodied energy of the kind a musician might convey by deep sustained chords on unmuted strings. Critics are fond of describing it as 'operatic'. And if the ending is tragic, it is tragic in the sense in which D. H. Lawrence uses the word in a letter from Lake Garda in October 1912:

I hate England and its hopelessness. I hate Bennett's resignation. Tragedy ought really to be a great kick at misery. But *Anna of the Five Towns* seems like an acceptance – so does all the modern stuff since Flaubert...

Lawrence himself was disappointed by a second reading of *La chartreuse* in 1928, as he mentioned casually years later when writing to his friend Aldous Huxley:

Am reading again *Chartreuse de Parme* – so good historically, socially and all that – but emotionally rather empty and trashy...

We cannot be sure what it was in the novel he disliked so much, though it is more than likely that the grand passion of Fabrice del Dongo for Clélia Conti, which brings the novel to an end was what stayed in his mind when he laid it down and that what Lawrence found 'trashy and empty' is what many readers like the late Henri Martineau have deeply enjoyed and admired:

It is the expression of a dream of tenderness which the author only ever fulfilled in his imagination and of which the most poignant note is heard in the very last pages of the novel in Clélia's appeal to her lover: *'Entre ici ami de mon cœur...'* ['Come to me here, beloved of my heart'].[6]

The idyll of Fabrice and Clélia is certainly presented sympathetically, and as a highly amusing and at the same time almost miraculous-seeming triumph of life over adversity. Fabrice, when he is led into prison in the Citadel of Parma, has every reason to think that he will suffer all the horrors of solitary confinement but as the result of a chance encounter with Clélia at the entrance, knowing that she will be near him, goes to the window of his cell and admires the view of the plain of Lombardy and the distant Alps in the afternoon sun. Seeing Clélia from his cell feeding her caged birds on the terrace of her own lofty apartment, hearing her sing and devising a means of signalling to her, give him happiness and a sense of purpose he has never known until now. The two of them, in spite of the obstacles separating them, live in a world of their own high above the city below; and, after escaping from prison, Fabrice returns voluntarily to his cell, pining away when Clélia marries and finding relief only in the heart-rending eloquence of sermons which draw crowds and which move Clélia herself to become his mistress.

The appeal of the story of Fabrice and Clélia is that of an almost dream-like abandonment to love as the one supreme emotion claiming precedence over every other. Enhanced and deepened by the absence of any obvious designs on the reader's sympathy ('I don't wish by artificial means to fascinate the reader's soul', he told Balzac), it is the appeal of *All for love, or the world well lost* or *If you were the only girl in the world and I were the only boy*. And it is this most obviously that runs counter to the spirit and letter of what Lawrence has written of love: his dislike of the relationship which leaves the man in a state of helpless child-like dependence on the woman, of 'love' in this sense and, for that matter, of any 'supreme emotion'.[7] What Lawrence may have overlooked is that, for all the sympathy and fellow-feeling with which the story of Fabrice is told, it has a catastrophic ending, the ending 'strangled' by Dupont and briefly sketched in the one surviving version of the novel. The 'dream of tenderness' which, Henri Martineau seems to imply, is all the more beautiful for being only a dream, leads to an unpleasant awakening. Clélia bears Fabrice a son and Fabrice wishes him to be brought up as his own. The child's legal father, the Marquis Crescenzi, is kidnapped with the complicity of the police and during his enforced absence, little Sandrino removed to his new secret home. On his return, Crescenzi is told that the child has died, but Sandrino's simulated absence and enforced confinement impair his health in reality. He dies soon afterwards and Clélia, convinced that this is divine retribution, follows him to the grave, while her lover retires from the world. The catastrophe is complete and if its pathos and absurdity are not overwhelmingly manifest, this can only be because it is related so abruptly and with such apparent nonchalance. 'I wrote *La chartreuse* with the death of Sandrino constantly in mind', Beyle wrote afterwards, 'an event I had found acutely touching in real life. M. Dupont has left me no space in which to present it.'[8]

The absurdity and pathos of the ending of *La chartreuse*, even in the version we possess, however, should be apparent if we take the trouble to weigh the full implications of the last few pages. It is foreshadowed, moreover, by what we are told at the very beginning of the novel, of northern Italy before the arrival of the French and of the way of life to which it returns after their final departure. And it is scarcely inconsistent with the kind of comedy for which the novel is justly famed: that of an almost wholly farcical social order in which, even more than in *Lucien Leuwen*, appearances are maintained only to impress and deceive, in which the Prince of Parma can dictate anonymous letters to his own Prime Minister alleging the faithlessness of the latter's mistress, the Prime Minister himself help his rival to escape from prison and the rival, Fabrice, live like an Italian version of Byron's Don Juan, while remaining a high-ranking, highly esteemed and sincerely devout priest of the Church. What tempers the comedy, gives it its weight and edge and prevents it becoming wholly farcical – makes it utterly different, that is, from other comic studies in decadence such as those of a Firbank or a Roger Peyrefitte – is the grim realism on the part of the author and at least one of the actors in the drama itself, which is at the same time a strong antipathy to a great deal of what such a way of life involves and an awareness of its human consequences. Its most obvious victims are the political prisoners in the Citadel of Parma, who subscribe to a *Te Deum* in thanks for the recovery of their principal gaoler who has been seemingly poisoned, and who even compose sonnets in his honour:

> May he who blames them be led by his destiny to spend a single year in a cell three feet tall with eight ounces of bread a day and *fasting* every Friday...
> (ch. 21)

Their chief persecutor is the minister Rassi, of whom the Prime Minister Mosca writes, with unindulgent amusement, when the people of Parma rise in revolt:

> They are intent on hanging him; they would be doing him a great wrong; he deserves to be drawn and quartered...
> (ch. 23)

Fabrice and Clélia are among the most privileged members of this society – Fabrice can stand and move around in his cell – but their tragedy is yet another consequence of its absurd values and the arrangements it tolerates, in so far as they are its children and have been trained to conform to its ways.

The early education of the aristocratic Fabrice, as of all Beyle's major figures, is of crucial relevance to what he becomes, and despite the rapidity of the narration, the essential features of his upbringing are dwelled on and emphasised at very adequate length. He is brought up, we learn, for a time under the influence of the French court in Milan at which his aunt Gina is one of the most brilliant personalities. And we are shown from the outset that the French rule in Italy, for all the 'enlightenment' it brings or rather seems to promise, does little to discourage the aristocratic spirit or the serene unquestioning acceptance of privilege on which a vigorous aristocracy depends:

> Fabrice spent his earliest years in the family castle at Grianta where he exchanged many blows with his fists among the peasant boys of the village and where he learned nothing, not even how to read.

Later, he was sent to school with the Jesuits in Milan where his father, the Marquis, insisted that he learn Latin not by reading ancient authors, who are always talking of republics, but in a magnificent tome illustrated by more than a hundred engravings, a masterpiece of the artists of the seventeenth century: the Latin genealogy of the Valserras, Marquesses of Dongo, published in 1650 by Fabrice del Dongo, Archbishop of Parma. As the fortunes of the Valserras had been, above all, military, the engravings depicted a great many battles, in all of which could be seen some hero bearing this name and dealing mighty blows with his sword. The book gave Fabrice a great deal of pleasure...

When Fabrice had made his first communion, the Countess, his aunt, obtained permission from his father to fetch him occasionally from college. She found him a singular, intelligent, very serious little boy, but attractive-looking and not altogether out of place in the salon of a fashionable lady; ignorant as one could wish, moreover, and hardly capable of writing a word. The countess, whose enthusiastic nature expressed itself in all that she did, promised her protection to the principal of the college if her nephew Fabrice had made astonishing progress by the end of the year and won lots of prizes to prove it; and to help him earn them, she would send for him every Saturday evening and often return him to his teachers only on the Wednesday or Thursday. The Jesuits, although lovingly cherished by the Prince Viceroy, had been banished from Italy by the laws of the kingdom, and the superior of the college, who was an astute man, was fully alive to the advantages to be gained by his relations with a lady all-powerful at court. He took care not to complain of Fabrice's absence from his lessons and the latter, now more ignorant than ever, at the end of the year obtained five first prizes...
  (ch. 1)

His father in alarm has him brought back to Grianta, where he runs wild once again and is sent to school with the village priest, an astrologer who seems more like a venerable Pagan magus than a priest of the Church, and from whom he derives that belief in prophecies and miracles which had been deliberately revived by the Italian church, so Beyle tells us elsewhere,[9] in its reaction against the Enlightenment and the rational spirit of Jansenism. The early influences are decisive and the contradictions of the mature Fabrice dwelled on explicitly on a number of occasions later on in the story: his love, for example, of French newspapers with their advanced ideas, which he will go to pains to obtain, though

The taste for liberty, the fashion and cult of *the happiness of the greatest number* with which the 19th century has become infatuated, seemed to him nothing more than a *heresy* which will disappear like others, but after destroying many souls...
    (ch. 7)

and above all, his incapacity, even when he is at his most sincerely penitent, for anything resembling self-criticism:

This is one of the most remarkable features of the religion he owed to the teachings of the Jesuits in Milan. This religion *weakens one's courage and resolve to think of unaccustomed things*, and forbids above all *self-interrogation*, as the most enormous of sins; for it is a step towards Protestantism...
    (ch. 12)

Yet Beyle is more than a moralist or social historian. What is bound to disconcert any reader who hopes to find in *La chartreuse* an opportunity to indulge simple feelings of approval or condemnation is the positive attractiveness in so many respects of a boy who has been brought up in such an appalling way and the constant reminder, though it is usually only implied, that this is the only life Fabrice knows and that any beauty or significance in the world as he understands it is due to the beliefs he has been brought up to hold. Do our own beliefs, we may find ourselves asking, give us more satisfaction and joy?

    Thus, without lacking intelligence, Fabrice was unable to see that his semi-belief in portents was for him a religion, a profound impression received during his emergence into life. To think of this belief was to feel, was happiness. And yet he persisted in his endeavours to see how it might be shown to be a proven science like geometry, for instance. He sought ardently to recall all those instances in which a portent he had observed had, surely, been followed by the event, either happy or unhappy, the portent had seemed to foretell; and, as he searched in his memory, his soul was overwhelmed with respect and with something like tender awe. He would have experienced an invincible repugnance for anyone who denied the truth of these portents and especially if this person had indulged in irony...
    (ch. 8)

Fabrice's superstition, like Julien Sorel's, is presented all the more sympathetically in that, whether through a coincidence or not it is left for us to decide, the premonitions they experience are all fulfilled.

Beyle's own irony at the expense of Fabrice is without malice. It is expressed, moreover, in a way that suggests that it is, in any case, irrelevant to the story of his life, as when he explains to Gina his decision to join Napoleon after seeing an eagle flying northward at the moment that he hears of the return from Elba. The novelist tells us that he is amused by Fabrice's solemn effusions and in doing so, he reminds us, as so often throughout the novel, of the sheer *otherness* of Fabrice, the immeasurable distance separating his life and beliefs from those of his worldly French creator. It is Fabrice's life as he himself lives it on which the focus of our attention constantly falls rather than the novelist's judgment of what is right or wrong with it; which is perhaps why readers have so often failed to notice that Beyle *is* judging this life, explicitly even, and without envy or sentimentality; for however deep and fine, it is a life of aspiration mainly and of promises tragically unfulfilled. This is the essential point, as I see it, of the Waterloo episode, which now has a recognised classical status as an account of the reality as opposed to the official historian's view of war. It is this, no doubt, but it is an indispensable part of the story of Fabrice's life as well and of the kind of man he becomes and is capable of becoming and not, as it may seem at first, a brilliant *tour de force* worked into the novel in the freely romantic way in which Berlioz, for example, worked the Rákóczy March into the *Damnation of Faust*. It has that kind of impact and we may read it also as 'picaresque' comedy, especially at the outset when Fabrice gallops into what he hopes is action, his head filled with scenes from the *Gerusalemme Liberata*. Yet 'picaresque' is not really the word. Nor is it comedy at the expense of an incorrigible simpleton. As an aspiring soldier, Fabrice turns out to be the most apt as well as the most willing of pupils. And it is the veterans he encounters who notice this: the motherly camp-follower, whose name we never learn, with her travelling canteen and the resourceful Corporal Aubry: both the most genuine of warriors, as it happens, in so far as they treat a battle as part of a day's work and a defeat as a natural disaster to be coped with accordingly; though Fabrice never realises that these ordinary folk are the true heroes of Waterloo, any more than he is able to tell whether this is a battle or not.

The stark vividness of every detail of the battle, that of the dirty feet and blood-soaked trousers of the first corpse he encounters or of the flying twigs and branches of a line of willow trees scythed by a cannon-ball, is the vividness of all that Fabrice experiences. Nowhere in the novel is the reader's impression of what it is like to be Fabrice more intimate and real; and nowhere are we so aware of what he might have become if Napoleon had won, if the course of history had been different and if he had been able to lead the life of a soldier in the Imperial Army for which his 'fanatical' education at the hands of the Jesuits, his childhood reading of the family genealogy and his Tom Sawyer-like rôle in the escapades of the Grianta peasant boys have prepared him as well as any military academy. To his aunt, he seems suddenly a man after Waterloo, though his baptism of fire and initiation into manhood have been a military débâcle and the downfall of Napoleon's empire and the only wound he has sustained a blow from the sabre of a retreating French hussar. It is true that his devotion to the Emperor has been very much that of a young Italian aristocrat. ('He wanted to give us a country and he loved my uncle', he tells Gina before leaving to join Napoleon.) But it is the only political dispensation in which he will ever be able to believe whole-heartedly. His political mentors when he returns to Italy will be his aunt and her lover Count Mosca, and conformity to the prevailing social order, he will be told, neither more nor less reasonable than to the rules of whist.

The principality of Parma in which Fabrice lives as an adult is a satellite of the Austrian Empire and owes its existence to the Congress of Vienna and the determination of the rulers of Europe, after twenty-five years of living with the sanguinary consequences of French egalitarian and nationalistic ideas, to restore the no doubt absurd institutions of the past. Fabrice is not accustomed, because of his Jesuit education, to criticise the prevailing order or criticise himself and realise to what extent his immense privileges depend upon it; and it is for this reason, presumably, that he becomes so serenely and engagingly indifferent to the world in which he lives. He enjoys, like his creator, digging up Etruscan remains, and his affairs with women, whom he has the courage and refinement never to deceive himself that he loves. But there is a painful void at the centre of his life, a profound aimlessness which leaves him the most amiable and least solemn of men and a man given, more than others, to distraction and dreams (which the people of Parma will later take for saintliness) but not by any means the most contented. Perhaps this is why one is left with the impression that the story of his life takes place in an almost uninhabited Italian landscape on a glorious, though slightly melancholy afternoon. Fabrice does not analyse his predicament in terms of what M. Sartre would call his *situation*, the connections, that is, between his own personal history and that of his fellow men in the Europe of his day. He is aware only, as he tells himself repeatedly, of his inability to love, to love even his aunt Gina in the way he realises, with some alarm, that she loves him. His deep sense of inadequacy and his indifference to the rôle he should be playing in society as a future Archbishop of the Church, are evident in the recklessness of the escapades in which he tries to fall in love and (according to Beyle's letter to Balzac, at the same time make it clear to Gina that he cannot love her), in which he kills a jealous travelling actor who assaults him and is thrown into prison to await trial for murder.

The uncharacteristic care that Beyle takes to describe the citadel of Parma, in which Fabrice becomes the most willing of prisoners, has been often noted and is obviously more than a piece of external verisimilitude in the manner of Scott and Balzac. (M. Robbe-Grillet is able to intrigue us in a superficially similar way when he reminds us that the known significant world may be for certain individuals that which is measured by the dimensions and shape of a single room; though, unlike Beyle, he is usually content with an impression of sinister suggestiveness and leaves us to imagine for ourselves what could have so badly damaged the mind whose experiences we share, that it can live with such unearthly fixity in its immediate surroundings, whatever these may be.) To Fabrice, for reasons which have become eminently clear, the prison is more real than anywhere in the world outside, and he comes to enjoy it as if it were his home, for he finds in Clélia what he had always craved, a woman he can love and who can give his life the purpose and meaning it lacks. His love excludes the world and is all the more compelling for his previous indifference to the world. And it is his absurd scheme years later, after their child is born, to take the child out of the world and bring him up in secrecy that precipitates the catastrophe which brings the novel to its close.

The education of Clélia, who is an accomplice in what she sees as their crime, is as crucial as that of Fabrice to an understanding of the tragedy that overtakes them. And though it is sketched far more briefly, its nature is no less clear. One obvious *donnée* is that her mother is dead and that her most agonising and vital decisions are made in solitude, like those of the unknowingly heroic Princesse de Clèves after the death of Mme de Chartres; and they are made with the same alternating terror and resolution. Clélia is also, despite her father's professed liberalism, the product of an Italian Catholic upbringing; though, thrown on supernatural guidance for lack of any human being to whom she can turn, she practises her religion with an earnestness far greater than her Church usually requires. Hence, presumably, her determined efforts to respect her father, who is so patently unworthy of either respect or trust, and the solemnity of her vows to the Virgin. After betraying her father, as she imagines, in aiding Fabrice to escape from prison, she vows never to see him again. And when she eventually becomes his mistress, their assignations take place in a darkened room,

for we have to confess what will seem strange anywhere north of the Alps, namely, that, despite her faults, she had remained perfectly faithful to her vow...
(ch. 28)

She is indeed admirably sincere according to her lights, but the lights, unfortunately, are somewhat dim.

Fabrice and Clélia should have married. Their suitability for each other is never in doubt. And there is no other visible road to fulfilment and continuing happiness open to either of them. It should have been possible for Clélia to see the folly of her father's wish that she should marry the opulent foolish Crescenzi, and for herself and Fabrice to take their places in the world as husband and wife and bring up their child accordingly. As it is, they meet furtively, out of the light of day and they are borne along, as they see it, by the supernatural forces to which Clélia attributes little Sandrino's death. And they fail utterly to understand the nature and extent of their own responsibility. A more frivolous couple, a man and woman less capable of whole-hearted commitment and desire and more skilled in the arts of conventional hypocrisy would have been more contentedly irresponsible, would have accepted the need for a *mariage de convenance* and afterwards met in either discreet or open adultery, for they live in a society in which both are tolerated. Before the arrival of the French, the bride's lover, as we have been reminded on the opening page of the novel, had been known to be named in the marriage contract. And it is something like the life of a typical *cavaliere servente* that Gina proposes to Fabrice after his return from Waterloo:

'Can you see yourself on the *Corso* of Florence or Naples,' said the Duchess, 'with your thoroughbred English horses! And in the evening, a carriage and an elegant apartment', etc. She dwelled at length on the delights of this vulgar species of happiness, that she could see Fabrice rejecting with disdain. 'He's a hero', she thought...
(ch. 6)

The hero-worship is characteristic of Gina, and on this occasion undeserved, for the priesthood, for which he settles, means little more to him than the life of a wealthy man about town.

The marriage code and sexual *mores* of the Italian aristocracy of the 1820s is the subject of an article which appeared in *The London Magazine* for October 1826 and which, for many years, has been attributed to Beyle himself;[10] though it seems far more likely that it was written by another friend and passionate admirer of Mathilde Dembowski in Milan, the poet Foscolo. Whoever the author was, its relevance to the story of Fabrice and Clélia is evident. A young Italian girl of good family, we are told,

...knows full well that the man she loves can never be hers, unless by some extraordinary accident, which she wishes but never dares to hope for. Yet she loves on – and the more noble is her blood, the more ardently does she persist in her attachment. But every passion which is not nourished by some hope either leads to madness or the grave, or yields to time and reason. She resigns herself, at length, to a marriage with a man chosen by her tyrants and revenges herself by refusing him any share in her heart. Marriage, instead of surrounding her, as it does here, with increased *surveillance* and more conventional restraints and decorums, invests her with complete liberty; so that, with greater facility and innocence she can converse with her first love and see him whenever she pleases. Some few, out of a feeling of self-respect or of religion, rather than go to the altar with perjury on their lips, choose the melancholy lot of dying alone...

She may, of course, though Clélia does not, openly choose a *cavaliere servente*:

A true *cavaliere servente* is a constant guest at his mistress's house; he acts as her steward and superintends her household; he always stands behind her while she sits at the pianoforte, and punctually turns over the leaves of her music-book; he sits by her and assists her in her embroidery, or any other work; he never goes out without her; or if ever he does walk out alone, it is to take out her lap-dog for exercise...

The enforced innocence of the unmarried Italian girl and the widespread toleration of her adultery after marriage are, of course, a well-known social phenomenon of the nineteenth century, however much or little the code of behaviour may have corresponded to what happened in reality. Henry James's Duchess in *The Awkward Age* stoutly defends the arrangement in its initial phase and is shown as answerable for its consequences. The author of the article in *The London Magazine* sees its cause in the custom of discouraging all but the eldest son and one daughter of an aristocratic house from marrying (for obvious social and economic reasons) and in the far from disinterested co-operation of the convents and the Church, many of whose leading prelates were recruited, like Fabrice, from among the younger sons of the aristocracy and led the lives of pleasure-seeking men of the world. And he praises Napoleon for having curbed the Church's influence and, through the Code Civil, having ensured the equal distribution among all the children of the parents' property and wealth. He concludes by seeing the political ineptitude of the Italian upper classes and their subjection to those who have divided their country, as a direct consequence of their marriage customs:

Thus, in a country, in which nature has, perhaps, endowed her daughters more liberally than in any other, with the treasures of the mind and heart calculated to render them the mothers of free citizens and the nurses of patriots, bad government and consequent bad usages have rendered them so degenerate, that their domestic life corrupts every germ of virtue in their children. We wish that we may be false prophets; but until such an abominable system of marriage is wholly extirpated, it appears to us that the aristocracy, and the great landowners of the country, will always be contemptible to themselves and others; inert and unfit for any attempt to liberate their country; that their lives will be spent in intriguing, their minds stupefied by idleness and their souls corrupted by sensuality.

The sombre peroration makes it seem more likely that this is a translation from the Italian of the author of *I sepolcri* and *Jacopo Ortis* than from the French of Beyle.[11] But there is nothing in *La chartreuse* to indicate a fundamentally contrasting view. The tragedy of Fabrice and Clélia is that of a man and woman brought up in such a world, who are unable to adapt themselves to its arrangements and who have the misfortune to be neither 'contemptible' nor 'corrupt'.

Mosca and Gina

Lawrence was wrong, surely, to say that '*La chartreuse* is so good historically, socially and all that – but emotionally rather empty and trashy'. Beyle never describes social and historical conditions better than when he is showing their effects on individual lives; for much the same reason, I find that I disagree with those critics who have said that Beyle's concern with the individual is fundamentally anti-social, or, as Mr Irving Howe puts it, that of a 'profoundly unpolitical man'.

Mr Howe's chapter on Beyle in his book on *Politics and the Novel* contains some of the most helpful comments I have read on *La chartreuse* and the point of view it presupposes. Much more can be said than he has space for about the paradoxes of political life in Parma, the ambiguous rôle, for example, of the official opposition ('God alone knows what kind of liberals', as Mosca puts it) who are tolerated and used by the authoritarian prince.[12] But Mr Howe points out 'the seriousness beneath the stillness' of *La chartreuse* and reminds us that even if the point of view of the author cannot be pinned down in conventional terms, it is obvious that Beyle was acutely intelligent about politics. He also provides the best reasons I have come across for thinking of *La chartreuse* as 'Machiavellian' and explains the terms by referring us not only to the Machiavelli of *The Prince* but the more idealistic and 'republican' *Discourses on Livy*.

What Mr Howe means, presumably, when he describes Beyle as a 'profoundly unpolitical man' is a man who was incapable of the servility of mind any political allegiance is likely to require. But this profound indifference is made, as the argument proceeds, to sound like indifference of a more commonplace kind: namely, a belief that politics is one thing; if one succeeds, it is a means to personal survival (Mr Howe's chapter is entitled 'The politics of survival') and the personal life something to be considered apart. Mr Howe is not the only critic of *La chartreuse* to assume that both Beyle and his heroes are 'unpolitical' in this way. 'The Happy Few' to whom the novel is dedicated, according to this view, compromise with society and observe its rules, while leading a life which excludes any other thought or care for the world outside.[13] If this is really true of the novel, Beyle would presumably have sympathised not only with the fierce outburst of Lawrence's Birkin in *Women in Love* against the tyranny of egalitarianism: 'I want every man to have his share in the world's goods, so that I am rid of his importunity', but also with Gerald Crich, on the same occasion (in chapter 5) when he argues that 'society' is a 'mechanism' and that every man is fit for his own little bit of a task – let him do that and then please himself'.

'...Between me and a woman, the social question does not enter. It is my own affair.'

'A ten pound note on it', said Birkin.

'You don't mean that a woman is a social being?' asked Ursula of Gerald.

'She is both', said Gerald. 'She is a social being, as far as society is concerned. But for her own private self, she is a free agent, it is her own affair what she does.'

'But won't it be rather difficult to arrange the two halves?' asked Ursula.

'Oh no', replied Gerald. 'They arrange themselves naturally – we see it now, everywhere.'

'Don't you laugh so pleasantly till you're out of the wood', said Birkin.

Gerald knitted his brows in momentary irritation.

'Was I laughing?' he said.

If *La chartreuse* can be seen to have been written in the belief expressed by Gerald Crich, then this may be yet another explanation of why Lawrence disliked it.

It is true that we are never shown in *La chartreuse* or even, for that matter, in *Women in Love*, how the common human dilemma which Birkin sees might be successfully resolved. But this is not to say that the problem is never posed or the dangers of ignoring it never contemplated. In fact, if there is any profound affinity between Beyle and Lawrence as novelists, it lies, I would suggest, in their refusal to treat the novel as anything other than a provocation to thought, one that however helpful and absorbing the process may be, leaves the responsibility for solving the problems it raises with the reader himself, rather than relieving him of it temporarily by inviting him to dream of enviable and successful lives. In saying this, I seem to disagree with Mr Howe, particularly when he is telling us how Mosca 'triumphs' over circumstances and his own nature:

When Mosca fails, it is precisely because he lives too closely by his own precepts, by his inured political habits. It is he who on behalf of Ernesto IV omits the phrase 'unjust proceedings' from the paper Sanseverina dictates to him, and it is this omission that allows Ernesto IV to throw Fabrizio into jail. Sanseverina rightly describes Mosca's behaviour as that of a 'miserable fawning...courtier'; she jabs him at his weakest point – the weakest point of all professional politicians and parliamentarians – when she says, 'He always imagines that to resign is the greatest sacrifice a Prime Minister can make.' On the other hand, Mosca's triumph, that is, his transcendence of his public self, comes when he breaks from the machiavellian system and allows his passion for Gina to imperil his career and perhaps his life. It is then that he becomes a truly magnificent figure, a man capable of every precaution, yet discarding all, a man for whom love is the means of recovering Fortune. In moving away from the Machiavelli of *The Prince*, Mosca approaches the other Machiavelli, the one who wrote that Fortune favours the young and impetuous: 'like a woman, she is a lover of the young because they are less respectful, more ferocious and with greater audacity command her.'

Mosca, it is true, is 'young' (at heart) and 'impetuous', even when we first meet him and he impresses Gina by his simple humanity and seeming 'shame' at 'the gravity and importance of his position'. Both the human warmth and vulnerability and the over-confident simplicity with which he regards his rôle in the world become apparent during one of their first meetings:

As the only other occupant of the opera box was the lady of strong liberal views to whom it belonged, the conversation continued with

the same frankness as before. When questioned, he spoke of his life in Parma. 'In Spain, under General Saint-Cyr, I allowed myself to be shot at in order to win the Legion of Honour and a little glory at the same time. Now I dress like a character in a comedy in order to set up a house and earn a few thousand francs. Once I'd started playing this game of chess and as I was shocked by the insolence of my superiors, I decided I would like one of the leading posts in the state. I succeeded, but my happiest days are still those I spend occasionally in Milan; here, I feel, the heart of your Army of Italy beats on...'
(ch. 6)

His simplicity is studied. The ever wakeful self-observation which makes him a master of ruse and diplomacy – the name Mosca is a hononym for 'a fly' while his illustrious family name means literally 'of the oak tree' – is apparent in the comic yet moving, almost elegiac scene in which we are shown him falling and watching himself fall in love:

Towards six o'clock, he mounted and rode to the *Corso*, where he had some hope that he might find Mme de Piatranera; not seeing her, he remembered that the doors of the Scala opened at eight; he entered and found less than ten people in the immense auditorium. He felt slightly ashamed of being there. 'Can it be', he thought 'that at forty-five, I am committing follies that would make a second lieutenant blush?' He fled and tried to spend the time strolling through the delightful streets around the Opera House occupied by cafés which, at this hour of the day, are bursting to capacity. In front of each of them, inquisitive crowds sit on chairs in the middle of the road eating ices and commenting on the passers-by. The count happened to be an unusual passer-by; so he had the pleasure of being recognised and accosted...He returned to the Opera House and decided that it would be a good idea to hire a box high up in the third tier, from which he could look down, without being observed by anyone, on the second tier boxes in one of which he was hoping that the Countess would eventually appear. Sure of not being seen, he abandoned himself to his folly. 'What is old age, anyway?' he thought. 'Merely not being able to enjoy oneself as I am now, behaving in an absurdly childlike way...'

He rose to go down to the box in which he could see the countess; but suddenly, he felt almost as if he didn't want to call on her, after all. 'But this is wonderful', he exclaimed and paused half way down the staircase. 'I'm feeling shy! I haven't felt shy for twenty-five years.'

He entered the box almost forcing himself to do so; and then, like an intelligent man of the world, took advantage of what had happened to him; he made no attempt to appear at ease or to show off his wit by plunging into some amusing story; he had the courage to be shy, he employed his wits in allowing his shyness to be apparent and yet not ridiculous. 'If she takes it the wrong way, I'm lost for ever', he thought...
 (ch. 6)

He is ready to give up his position as minister in order to live with Gina in Naples or Florence:

...this is at least what he succeeded in making the woman he loved believe. In all his letters he beseeched her with ever increasing passion and recklessness to grant him a second meeting in Milan and to this the Countess agreed. 'If I were to swear to you that I am madly in love with you', she said to him one day, 'I would be lying; I would be only too happy to love at more than thirty as I once did at twenty-two! But I have seen too many things fall that I had thought eternal! I feel for you the most tender affection, I place in you an infinite trust and of all men you are the one I prefer.' The Countess believed herself to be perfectly sincere in uttering these words and yet her declaration included a little lie towards the end. Perhaps if Fabrice had wished to, he would have taken precedence over everyone else in her heart...
 (ch. 6)

If the love of Fabrice for Clélia excludes any other care in the world, this is never the case with Mosca and Gina. For Mosca, the passion and recklessness are a glorious reprieve from advancing age. He enjoys falling in love as if he were a young lieutenant once more, gives himself excellent reasons for being 'mad' and relives the experience so authentically as to forget that young lieutenants are liable to fall in love with the sheer novelty of their own feelings.

The test of Gina's 'infinite trust' in Mosca and of his actual devotion to her comes unexpectedly – it is the unexpectedness that makes it a test – in the episode in chapter 14 to which Mr Howe refers. It is one of the supreme instances in the whole of Beyle's fiction of *'scènes probantes'* of the kind he admired in Molière, that is 'scenes which prove the character or the passions of those who take part in them...'[14] and it testifies to the seriousness of his ambition to be a dramatist, even if it is impossible to imagine it rewritten for the stage. For much of the dramatic effect depends on the actors' unspoken thoughts as they watch one another and on our sense of the virtually uncontrollable situation they create, by which they are borne along as if on a swift current and which makes the timing of every word they utter and expression they assume as decisive and revealing as the words they use. Mr Howe says nothing of the drama and thus overlooks the possibility that the responsibility for the disastrous upshot of their encounter may well be not merely Mosca's alone. Gina does not even consult him before defying protocol, confronting Prince Ernest Ranuce in his palace and delivering her ultimatum that she will leave the city and the court (of which it is well understood that she is the most distinguished ornament) unless an unconditional pardon for her nephew is signed. She is carried away by her furious protective instinct and but for Mosca's attempted diplomacy in drawing up the pardon and omitting the crucial phase on which she had insisted: 'this unjust procedure will have no sequel in the future...', would have triumphed over the easily disconcerted Prince's calculations. He is tired and 'would have signed anything'. Only the fact that she has ignored Mosca – he has to support himself by holding on to the back of a chair when he realises this – is not lost on the Prince:

'What must we do?' said the Prince to Count Mosca, not very sure what he was saying and carried away by his habit of consulting the Count in everything.

'I really haven't the least idea, your most serene Highness', replied the Count with the air of a man heaving his very last sigh. He could hardly pronounce the words and the tone of his voice gave the Prince the first consolation his wounded pride had received in the course of the entire audience; this minor satisfaction inspired him with the thought of a little speech he might make that would soothe his pride even further.

'Well then', he said. 'I appear to be the most reasonable of the three and I am perfectly willing to overlook my position in the world. I am going to talk *as a friend* and', he added with a charming smile of condescension reminiscent of the happy days of Louis XIV, *'like a friend talking to friends*. Mme la Duchesse, what must we do to make you forget a decision which may have been somewhat ill-judged and hasty?'

'I honestly cannot say', replied the Duchess with a heavy sigh. 'I honestly cannot say, I loathe Parma so deeply.' There was no epigramatic intention in these words. It was the voice of sincerity itself that spoke.

The Count turned away with a sudden impulsive movement; his courtier's soul was scandalised; then he turned on the Prince an imploring gaze. With much dignity and calm, the Prince allowed a moment to elapse; then said, addressing the Count, 'I see that your charming friend is no longer herself. The reason is perfectly simple. She *adores* her nephew...'
(ch. 14)

The Prince, profiting from the temporary advantage he enjoys over his humiliated Prime Minister, outwits them both. The bold unhesitating devotion to Gina's interests which, we are told, would have won the day – he needed merely to write the words that Gina dictated – is something of which he now proves incapable. Yet it is as if no trust had ever existed between them. Gina's face registers the utmost contempt for him, though there is no indication that she either knows or cares what her feelings are or how they will be understood.[15] The unhesitating devotion of which he proves incapable is a devotion for which she does not even ask. Mosca has this justification, though he has courage and intelligence enough to know that there are no excuses for a failure of this kind. When the consequences of his omission are known and Fabrice is arrested, he assumes the full responsibility and Gina does not hesitate either to condemn him for what both agree to describe as his 'courtier's instinct':

I shan't reproach you for having left out the words 'unjust procedure' from the letter you wrote out for him to sign; it was a courtier's instinct that gripped you by the throat; without even realising it you preferred the interests of your master to those of the woman you loved. You have placed your actions at my disposal, my dear Count, and for a long time now, but it is beyond your capacity to change your nature; you have great talents as a minister but you have the instinct of the trade as well [*vous avez aussi l'instinct du métier*]...
(ch. 16)

Mosca's desperate attempts to redeem himself in her eyes, and thus in his own, first by writing out his resignation and sending it to her to read – she tears it up and sends him back the pieces – and then by leading an armed guard to cover Fabrice's escape from prison are ineffectual. It is as a statesman only that he is able to live down his humiliation and this time, significantly, without needing to profess that utter devotion to her which both of them had thought of as evidence of his freedom of soul.

The revolt of the people of Parma is the occasion to which Mosca rises with the *brio* and decisiveness he has lacked in the conduct of Gina's affairs, as it bursts with a violent and exhilarating release of pent-up energy and feeling over the little Principality. Mosca enjoys himself hugely, relieving the arch-conservative commander of the royal guard of his rank when the latter talks in front of his troops of negotiating with the rebels, leading a battalion to defend the Prince's statue and relating the news in letters to Gina in which, despite 'the most lugubrious terms', the 'liveliest joy' breaks through. Mosca is faithful to the Prince and Princess but servile neither to the old nor the new potential masters of the state; unlike the general of the guard who basely flatters the people as once he flattered the Prince. And it is this that makes Gina decide that 'all things considered', she will 'have to marry him after all' (chapter 23). Yet the reconciliation is based on a more realistic understanding of the extent of their mutual devotion than the liaison to which they had agreed when they first met. There is no question of their going off to Naples or Florence together, and eventually they even live apart, Gina outside the frontiers of the state and Mosca seeing her when he can absent himself from his ministerial responsibilities. Gina, moreover, lives only for a short time after the death of Fabrice, whom she still adores, and Mosca is left alone, according to the last words of the novel, 'immensely rich' in a Parma in which the prisons are empty and the son of Prince Ernest Ranuce IV is adored by his subjects, who compare his rule to that of the Grand Dukes of Tuscany.

The equivocal-seeming conclusion to the novel and the nature of Mosca's rule as Prime Minister have understandably intrigued almost every critic of *La chartreuse*. Mr Martin Turnell, for example, finds the concluding sentence 'characteristically ambiguous':

The prisons are empty either because Ernest V is really a benevolent despot or because all the liberals are dead or in exile or because liberalism itself has died out. The Grand Dukes of Tuscany, to whom the Prince of Parma is compared, were notorious despots. It follows from this that his people worshipped him either because they really like despotism or because they had become so downtrodden that they were not aware of it. The only other alternative is that Stendhal is pulling our leg and that his people secretly detested Ernest V...[16]

I'm not quite sure what Mr Turnell means by 'notorious despots', but there are good reasons for thinking that the public personality of Mosca was based to some extent on that of Vittorio Fossombroni, the mathematician and prime minister of Tuscany, to whom Beyle attributed the relatively enlightened rule of that admittedly despotic state.[17] And I see no reason to think that Beyle regards the emptiness of the prisons of Parma as anything other than evidence of good government; though it is perhaps the most serious weakness of the novel that we have to make so many guesses about the régime which Mosca presumably helps to fashion and in any case agrees to serve, and hence about the kind of man he is in the exercise of what, despite his protestations to the contrary, remains his most absorbing passion; for Mosca forgets when he compares the rules of politics with chess, that both politics and chess can become lifelong addictions.

We are given, it is true, some idea of the kind of politics in which Mosca believes, though very little, apart from what we are told in the final sentence, of their practical and human consequences. One has the impression, for example, that having served in the armies of Napoleon, he wishes to bring about within the state of Parma something resembling the Napoleonic order, with institutions founded on the rule of law and guaranteed liberties allowing for dynastic continuity and the possibility even of peaceful evolution towards more democratic forms of government in years to come. Another precedent for such a régime is to be found in the Austrian states of Lombardy, the 'reasonableness' of whose administration is mentioned more than once in the opening chapters.[18] It is not the Austrians, for example, but their fanatical Milanese supporters who assassinate the Napoleonic minister Prina with their umbrellas and afterwards, in a so-called duel, dispose of Gina's first husband, Count Pietranera; the 'good hearted' Austrian General Bubna, we are told, 'a man of intelligence and feeling seemed altogether ashamed of the assassination of Prina' (chapter 2). It is perhaps for this reason that Balzac thought of Mosca as a fictitious portrait of Metternich (which Beyle denied, adding that he hadn't seen Metternich since 1810, at Saint-Cloud, when he carried a bracelet of the hair of the beautiful Caroline Murat). Mosca rules Parma like an arbitrary tyrant when he first assumes office, and shocks Fabrice by telling him how he has thought of ensuring that the authors of the abominable anonymous letters he has received would be not only tried but sentenced by his 'good judges'; though his retort to Fabrice's protest suggests that in a state like Parma, there is no other way to rule:

> 'I would rather have seen them condemned by magistrates judging according to their consciences', replied Fabrice, with a naïveté which in a court like Parma seemed comic.
> 'Since you travel so much for your instruction, perhaps you will give me the names of some of the magistrates you have in mind. I'll write to them before I go to bed...'
>   (ch. 10)

It is significant that when Fabrice himself has to be tried and found innocent of the murder of the travelling actor, he ensures that judgment will be passed by the twelve judges whose integrity and learning are least in doubt, explaining to Gina that if he is not tried with the 'utmost solemnity', the name of the man he has killed will be an embarrassment to him for the rest of his ecclesiastical career. Characteristically, he is concerned with the practical advantages of proper procedure and his political principles are frankly opportunistic. He is a hedonist rather than a utilitarian:

> The Count had no virtue; one may even say that what the liberals call virtue (i.e. seeking the happiness of the greatest number) struck him as fraudulent; he believed that he was under an obligation to seek the happiness of Count Mosca della Rovere...
>   (ch. 16)

But the pursuit of his own happiness induces him to seek power in a way compatible with his own needs and temperament and hence to avoid, among other things, being responsible in any way for the execution of helpless prisoners. He has had to do this once already, in his career as an officer in Spain, and the memory, he tells Gina, still returns to torment him, 'particularly in the evenings'. And in this he differs from his rival for office, the humble plebeian Rassi, for whom reassurance lies in being insulted and even thrashed by the Prince and who has ensured his royal master's dependence upon him by having two liberals executed in the Prince's name. The vicious circle of official terror, reprisal and the fear of reprisal which Rassi has deliberately set in motion, in order to make himself indispensable, is one that Mosca promptly ends. This does not prevent him ordering the troops to fire on the crowd which tries to overturn the Prince's statue. And on this occasion, Mosca has no remorse. But the statue is worth preserving. Its bullet holes serve as a warning to the Prince's heir that this is what comes of hanging Jacobins. ('And if he says this, I will tell him you must either hang ten thousand or none at all.') While to the people, it is the symbol of triumphant order:

But for me Parma would have been a republic for a month with the poet Ferrante Palla as dictator...
    (ch. 23)

Mosca has no objection on principle to republics, though he believes that it will take 'a hundred years for a republic' in Italy 'not to be an absurdity' and it is obviously preferable for a republic to last longer than 'two months'. He has the utmost admiration also for the revolutionary poet, Ferrante Palla, but cannot think of him as the ideal head of state.

It is Mosca's apparently reasonable as well as energetic behaviour in suppressing the revolt that epitomises more than anything else he does the kind of man he is (and in saying this, I disagree with Mr Howe) as well as the equivocal blessings of his kind of rule. Nothing in the novel suggests that he is wrong in thinking that victory for the insurgents would have been a disaster for Parma and for the insurgents themselves within a very short time:

The troops would have fraternised with the people, there would have been three days of murder and assassination (for it will take a hundred years in this country for a republic not to be an absurdity), then a fortnight of pillage, until two or three regiments provided by some foreign power were sent in to impose order...
    (ch. 23)

Yet the insurrection, however impractical, affects us as a revolt not only against institutions and rules but – what makes it seem so just and natural – against the intolerable boredom and constraint they have imposed. Even the court is normally plunged in boredom; which is why Gina with her grace and vitality has become indispensable to it. And it is significant that it should be her 'gold' that is distributed to the insurgents (even if this was not her intention) and the most devoted of her lovers who in carrying out her orders to assassinate the Prince unleashes the movement to overthrow the state.

The uncalculating devotion to Gina of Ferrante Palla has its counterpart in the untiringly self-watchful astuteness that gives Mosca, as Gina puts it, both the 'talents' of a prime minister and 'the instinct of the trade'; Mosca's candid egoism has its counterpart in Palla's total dedication to the happiness of the greatest number; and Mosca's readiness to make a fortune in the service of an ungrateful Prince its counterpart in Palla's proud integrity with regard to money: as a 'tribune of the people', he keeps a strict account of the riches Gina bestows on him in order to wreak her vengeance on the Prince. The fact that neither Palla nor Palla's ideals can hope to prevail in a state like Parma is one of the most melancholy realities on which the story turns. The valour and energy of the Lombardians of the middle ages, of which we are reminded in the opening pages, has gone *alla macchia* and is now to be found only among the brigands in the woods. It is in the forest surrounding her palace on the River Po in which Gina loves to wander and in which Mosca has told her to beware of brigands that Palla first darts out to confront her, looking like the survivor of some natural disaster or like the disguised Edgar in *King Lear*:

The stranger had the time to approach her and throw himself at her feet. He was young and very handsome but atrociously dressed; his clothes had rents in them a foot long; but his eyes blazed with all the fire of an ardent soul.

'I have been condemned to death. I am the doctor Ferrante Palla. I am dying of hunger and so are my five children...'
    (ch. 21)

For Balzac, Palla was the most sublime and beautiful figure in the book, whom he preferred even to his own Michel Chrestien in *Illusions perdues*, and he described him as 'sincere, mistaken, full of talent but unaware of the fatal consequences of his doctrine'.[19] Beyle is far less solemn about him and about the kind of danger he represents – his republic wouldn't last – and shows him as a beautiful but sublimely comic figure, even in the deadly quasi-professional efficiency with which, in the excess of his adoration for Gina, he has the Prince poisoned in the course of a royal bird-shooting expedition on Palla's own ground in the marshes by the Po. If the comedy is not exactly uproarious, it is because Palla is wholly serious, in fact alarmingly so and especially when he is at his most extravagant; and because he is a living reproach in the innocence of his heart and his profound energy to those who regard him as a madman or a 'great poet'. After the abortive revolution, he disappears once more – presumably back into the woods and marshes – and peace and order return to the state. The poignancy of what he represents is not the poignancy of pathos – for he is fierce and proud – but of the life that is banished from Mosca's Parma.

Ferrante Palla's rôle in the novel is clearly symbolic; for example, though he himself is condemned to death, his poems circulate and are universally admired, and it is difficult not to see this as typifying the part played by *romanticismo* in Metternich's Italy. It is, in fact, both a weakness of *La chartreuse* and the source of much of its imaginative appeal that so much of what happens in Parma should be indicated by such indirect means rather than by the detailed evocation of everyday life as in the more Tolstoyan *Lucien Leuwen*. Beyle had, in other words, already written much better 'historically, socially and all that...' Commentators, understandably, dwell on the novel's symbolism;[20] Croce readily forgave Beyle for giving us not the true historical Italy of the 1820s but the 'Italy of his dream';[21] and Professor J. D. Hubert, who draws our attention to the importance of play-acting in the novel – both the dissimulation to which even Clélia resorts and acting in the literal sense: the charades that Gina organises to cheer a dreary court – goes so far as to describe the overall effect of the novel as a 'devaluation of the real'.[22] If it is difficult not to think of Palla as having a significance that transcends his immediate rôle, the same is true of Gina, and increasingly so as the novel proceeds and as we see her not as she appears to herself but as an awe-inspiring and even sinister figure. One thinks of her light step and affected nonchalance as she comes to deliver her ultimatum to the Prince, the look that terrifies her servant as she orders the signal to be given for the Prince's assassination, and her self-possession as she persuades the

Prince's heir to burn the documents that could incriminate her and then flees from his burning palace with the most relevant of the documents wrapped in her shawl.

Gina associates herself with the best and the worst in the Italy of *La chartreuse* and those critics who think of her only at her most admirable, splashing water over the powdered hair of her elder nephew, the solemn Ascagnio, or persuading the Prince that it would be a kindness occasionally to address a few charming words to his wife, speak of her at times as if she were somehow above the intrigues which, together with amateur theatricals, form the main pastime of the court. Yet she is the life and soul of both activities, merciless even to the man she loves more than any other creature in the world:

> 'Is it in my interest to let Conti be dishonoured? Definitely not. If he is, the wedding of his daughter and that nice dull Marquis Crescenzi will be impossible...' The Duchess believed she no longer loved Fabrice, but still passionately desired that Clélia should marry the Marquis; she had a vague hope that if she did, the preoccupation weighing on Fabrice would disappear...
> (ch. 25)

And nothing makes her more representative of the Italy of her day than the fact that she is worshipped simultaneously – and with an unquestioning adoration that many readers of the novel seem to find it incumbent on themselves to share – by the leader of revolution in Parma and the authoritarian minister who puts the revolution down.

Beyle's apology for his characters in the preface to the novel clearly refers to Gina more than to anyone else:

> I confess that I have been bold enough to leave my characters as they were, with all their natural imperfections; but none the less, I declare for all to hear that I condemn many of their actions and in the most moral terms. What use would it be to give them the high moral standards of the French, who love money more than anything else and never commit sins out of hatred or love?...

Gina's blind yearning for Fabrice is what turns her in the end into an accomplished criminal and politician, a figure more reminiscent of Racine's Agrippine in *Britannicus* than of the Phèdre with whom Balzac compared her. It is also the source of her repeated protestations, despite her youthful looks and energy, that she is an ageing woman, unable to love as she once loved at twenty-two, of the smiling resignation with which she grasps what she sees as the few pleasures fate and time have in store for her and of her self-consoling angry pride, after Mosca has unintentionally betrayed them, when she tells herself that she and Fabrice belong to a class of beings apart and that even the soul of Mosca is 'vulgar' compared with theirs, a declaration that the novel almost persuades us as being literally true.

Gina lacks self-knowledge: understandably, in so far as any approach to an admission of the true state of her feelings is an acknowledgment of how little right she has to expect anything from Fabrice in return; though she is predisposed to blindness of this kind as well. The astonishing confidence, impulsiveness and on one occasion at least, overwhelming rightness of her instinct are those of a nature unaccustomed to self-questioning. She is a del Dongo and as such regards it as perfectly right and proper to take little Fabrice away from his lessons and offer her protection to his Jesuit masters on condition that he be given a number of first prizes; while she owes to her serene assurance of the rightness of her instinct and the innocence of her desires the grace and daring by which her many lovers are drawn. It would be a very humourless and dull-spirited reader of the novel who wanted Gina to be fundamentally different, for all her crimes: even though she is one of the most powerful personalities in an oppressive state and even though she has to bear much of the blame for the catastrophe that overtakes Fabrice. And to say this is to touch on the question of that extraordinary moral ambivalence which makes *La chartreuse de Parme* unlike any other novel and which Henry James has described better than any other critic I know:

His notion was that *passion*, the power to surrender oneself sincerely and consistently to the feeling of the hour, was the finest thing in the world, and it seemed to him that he had discovered a mine of it in the old Italian character...It is easy to perceive that this doctrine held itself quite irresponsible to our old moralistic canons, for *naïveté* of sentiment in any direction, combined with great energy, was considered absolutely its own justification. In the *Chartreuse de Parme*, where everyone is grossly immoral, and the heroine is a kind of monster, there is so little attempt to offer any other, that through the magnificently sustained pauses of the narrative we feel at last the influence of the writer's cynicism, regard it as amiable, and enjoy serenely his clear vision of the mechanism of character, unclouded by the mists of prejudice. Among writers called immoral there is no doubt that he best deserves the charge; the others, beside him, are spotlessly innocent.[23]

One of the great merits of James's criticism, though Ezra Pound thought otherwise (when talking of French literature, according to Pound, he tries to 'square all things to the ethical standards of a Salem mid-week Unitarian prayer meeting...') is that he tells us whenever there is a difference between his own notions of decent responsible behaviour and those of an author or his characters. He did not habitually read novels or poems as an escape from reality and would not therefore have been discountenanced if placed in the situation imagined by Yeats in 'The Scholars'. Those twentieth-century critics who talk less severely about Gina, Mosca and Fabrice don't always do so because they would approve of their behaviour in actual life and I am not convinced that it is by being less stern than James that one becomes a better critic of what Beyle had to say. Beyle's own preface and many of his passing comments on the action of the novel are addressed to the consciously moral public of his day; with the most unflattering sarcasm and yet with an acknowledgment – in the preface it is earnest and insistent – that he too judges his characters by standards very different from the characters' own.

The irony and amusement with which the story is told are characteristic of Beyle, but the difficulty of understanding their effect on us is greater than in either *Lucien Leuwen* or *Le rouge et le noir*. For one thing, there is no character in *La chartreuse*, not even Mosca, who appears to be invested by the author with the same hopes as Lucien or Julien Sorel or who is shown as being as capable of assuming the responsibility for his own destiny. M. Bardèche's claim that 'every novel of Stendhal is the story of an education' is far more obviously true of the two earlier novels, for much of the amusement that the principal characters can give, even to readers whose standards are very different from their own, lies in their shameless and perfect incorrigibility.

One of the clues to an understanding of the unsettling effect of opening the novel and being thrown into such a world is to be found, I believe, in the first chapter, where we are told of the arrival of the French in 1796. Bonaparte's army is not an army of moral reformers. (It is the propaganda of the priests in Milan which has portrayed them with a guillotine carried in front of every regiment.) And it is not the laws and institutions of the French but their infectious gaiety and youthfulness on which the story dwells. In the villages, we are told, the soldiers learn the Italian dances, the steps of their own *contredanses* being too difficult for the local inhabitants, and in doing so they encourage the Italians to become themselves again, for gaiety such as this has been long forgotten. The tumultuous joy of the opening pages is inspired by personal memories. 'I felt too keen a pleasure, I admit', Beyle wrote to Balzac, 'in talking of these happy times of my youth...' and some readers may feel that it is all too good to be true and that it is too much an expression of merely personal nostalgia. Yet it is the immense promise of these happy times that the novelist evokes, and the mood of

> Bliss was it in that dawn to be alive,
> But to be young was very heaven...

and if the enlightenment the French bring with them appears so brilliant as to escape all definition ('...the statues of Charles V and Philip II were overturned and the people suddenly found themselves flooded with light...') it is partly because the promise is not kept and because Italy returns to its old institutions and ways. (Palla's revolt will fail to overturn the royal statue and Gina's attempts to flood the streets of Parma will cause merely a few puddles, as if it had rained, while the defiant illumination of her own palace, when Fabrice escapes from prison, is on private property on the frontiers of Parma and Lombardy.) It is in any case in the nature of the French enlightenment as Beyle himself understood and believed in it – and of course not merely Beyle alone; the chapter helps us to understand the appeal to popular and nationalistic instincts of the French example – that it should liberate the oppressed peoples of Europe by helping them to liberate themselves. How they should do that, how, to use one of Beyle's favourite expressions, they should find their own 'path to happiness' is their own affair, and however intolerable the thought of the mistakes they make, their tragedy will lie in their depriving themselves of happiness as they themselves understand it. This is one of the points, as I see it, of

Beyle's many jokes at the expense of his French readers of the 1830s, who are so different from the young Frenchmen of 1796. And it is this 'Beyliste' attitude – in Beyle's own sense of the term – which enables us to contemplate the protracted catastrophes which overtake the main characters without censoriousness or resignation. Beyle's own dissatisfaction with Italy as it is in *La chartreuse* is a tribute to what Italy is capable of becoming again. It is a novel about men and women of wonderful spirit and courage and though so much of it shows us the thwarting of energies, it is not like *L'Abbesse de Castro* a study of 'the long degeneration' of souls.

Lamiel and *Suora Scolastica*

If *La chartreuse de Parme* is concerned with a way of life and an ethical code radically different from those of the public to which it is addressed, the same appears to have been true of *Lamiel*, the novel on which Beyle was working at the time of his death. Lamiel, the heroine, is a foundling brought up by a village beadle, and belongs, like Adrien Laffargue to the class of those who have to 'struggle with real needs'[24] and who alone in France are endowed with 'energy'. Astonished and then bored by the lack of energy and the weakness of character of two aristocratic lovers, she was to have fallen in love with a professional criminal, modelled partly on Lacenaire, whose sinister reputation in his own time has been revived in our own by Marcel Carné's film *Les enfants du paradis*. And according to one plan for the novel, she was to have set fire to the law courts in which he had been condemned to death and to have been found afterwards dead among the ruins.

The sensational ending, however, is only a sketch, and the substance of the novel, which can be read with sustained enjoyment for two or three hours, consists of two versions, which until recently have always been presented as one.[25] The first of these, written out in Civita Vecchia in 1839, includes her adventures with her two disappointing lovers; the second, which was dictated shortly afterwards, gives us only the story of Lamiel's childhood and youth among the leading personalities of her Norman village. And a comparison between the two shows that Beyle was working hard to produce an easy and highly finished narrative: he takes care in the second version, for instance, to make the narrator a character in his own right and a plausible observer of the provincial *mores* he describes; it also suggests that he may have had difficulty in making his Lamiel sufficiently sympathetic and appealing to seem plausible and interesting to himself and his reader. It is the brutal shock to her affectionate nature that we are shown, for instance, in the second version, when her foster parents tell her of her material obligations to them and not merely, as in the first version, her naturally aristocratic aversion to the vulgarity of a reminder of this kind.[26]

'The interest of the novel will become evident when Lamiel experiences actual love', Beyle wrote at the end of the first draft and her criminal lover was to have performed the miracle. Meanwhile, it is because she can feel no love for any man, doesn't know what she wants and is intelligent enough to know she doesn't know, that the novel creates its own suspense and unfolds with the natural precipitate energy of Beyle's comedy at its most outrageous. Lamiel, as Jean Prévost has suggested,[27] is reminiscent of Mathilde de la Mole and of the two Minas of *Mina de Wanghel* and *Le rose et le vert* in her innocence, her intense curiosity and her cruelty towards men who are unwise enough to seek to influence or dominate her in any way; and the most enjoyable scenes in either version are those in which she torments the good-hearted young local priest, who, to his horror, has fallen in love with her and the young Duke whose habitually divided allegiances (he wants to take part in the July Revolution in Paris and his mother insists on his staying at home) and deep self-misgivings make it so easy for Lamiel to throw him off balance; though he has a youthful resilience which Lamiel also enjoys. He is a devoted horseman and when they meet on a rainy day in a half-flooded wood, Lamiel sees that he is thinking more of Greyhound, his drenched thoroughbred than of himself or of her:

'...You've no blanket. He may catch cold. Why don't you take your coat off and put it on his back? Instead of talking to me, you should walk Greyhound round the wood for a while.'

The Duke couldn't reply, he was so worried for his horse and it was so obvious to him that Lamiel was right.

'That isn't all: now something worse is going to happen to you. Happiness is about to fall into your arms.'

'What do you mean?' said the Duke in great alarm.

'I'm going to run away with you and we're going to live together in the same apartment in Rouen,...the same apartment, you understand.'

The Duke stood motionless and frozen with astonishment; Lamiel laughed in his face and then went on:

'As being in love with a peasant girl may dishonour you, I'm seeing if I can kill this so called love of yours with my own hands; or if you'd rather I put it that way, I want to make you agree that your heart isn't strong enough to *feel any love*!'

He looked so funny that Lamiel said to him for the second time since they had first met:

'Now take me in your arms and do it passionately, but don't knock my cotton bonnet off.'

It should be explained perhaps that there is nothing more hideous and absurd than the Phrygian shaped cotton bonnets worn by the young women of Caen and Bayeux.

'You're right', said the Duke laughing.

He took off her bonnet, put his own hunter's cap on her head and embraced her with an impulsive passion which, for Lamiel, had all the charm of the unforeseen. The sarcasm vanished from her lovely eyes...[28]

To say that the comedy here is characteristically Stendhalian is to point to the qualities that make it read like a process of swift developing thought and discovery, to the qualities, in other words, that make it unlike anything by Balzac.[29] The Duc de Myossens, like the hero of *Armance* and the young aristocrat in *Le rose et le vert*, is a student of L'Ecole Polytechnique and a type of young Frenchman whom we always see torn between his natural aristocratic instincts and his sense of the overwhelming reasonableness of the new social enlightenment.[30] But it is Beyle's sympathetic interest in the type that leads him to imagine him responding to the challenge of a Lamiel and revealing new possibilities of character within himself; we last see the Duke after she has run away from him, peering from his saddle into every coach he passes on the road she tricks him into thinking she has taken. Another type by which Beyle was obviously intrigued is that represented by the hunchback Dr Sansfin, a clever physician and an amusing and unprincipled opportunist, like Dr Du Poirier in *Lucien Leuwen*. Sansfin occupies a dominant rôle in Beyle's second version of the novel and various sketches for episodes in which he was to appear (and which read a little like a modern *Roman de Renart*) are to be found among the manuscripts on which Beyle was working during the very last weeks of his life. Sansfin has an alarmingly candid and brutal version of the philosophy of Helvétius to offer, and a reason for his importance may be that he is Lamiel's spiritual mentor during the most impressionable years of her life. Beyle may well have felt that the reasons for her eventual lack of almost any moral scruple and her readiness to become the accomplice of Lacenaire needed the kind of explanation Sansfin's influence provides. His own flamboyant and almost exclusive concern with the interests of his own vanity – he is a marksman and shoots his own dog in the village street when it fails to obey him – has a natural explanation, like Richard III's, in his deformity; though it is the plausibility of his cynicism and what Lamiel sees as the 'granite-like' unshakeable quality of his arguments that Beyle may have wanted to test by imagining them put into practice by an intelligent girl setting out on a journey of discovery in the world.

Nothing in *Lamiel* or in the other story on which he was working at the same time suggests that when he died he was not in full possession of his powers as a novelist, despite the severe illnesses of his last two years. *Suora Scolastica*, though unfinished, is by far the best, or at least the most promising of the *Chroniques italiennes* which are primarily of Beyle's own invention and was begun, if we go by a letter written to the Comtesse de Tascher in March 1839, in an attempt to improve on *L'abbesse de Castro*. Like *L'Abbesse* itself and another of the later chronicles, *Trop de faveur tue*, it is a story of the intrigues of a convent and of the long desperate sieges laid to it by lovers ready to lay down their lives. It is also – in the version on which Beyle was working on the morning of his death – an evocation of the life of an eighteenth-century Neapolitan court, that of the young Don Carlos, son of Philip V of Spain, who, 'though educated by priests and in all the rigours of etiquette, was not, as it happened, an unintelligent man'. The magnificence and geniality of the life over which Don Carlos presides, despite the jealousies by which it is later to be poisoned, contrast with what we are shown of northern Italian society in *La chartreuse de Parme*, while in the preface to the story, we are introduced to an Italy in which politics, though clandestine, are an absorbing universal concern:

> In Naples, no one ever talks, even a little clearly, about politics. This is the reason: a Neapolitan family consisting, for example, of three sons, a daughter and the mother and father, will belong to three different parties, which in Naples go by the name of *conspiracies*. The daughter belongs to her lover's party; each of the sons belongs to a different conspiracy; the father and mother sigh for the days of the court which reigned over them when they were twenty years old. As a result of this isolation of each individual, no one ever talks about politics seriously. At the least assertion with an incisive ring and which does not sound commonplace, you will see two or three faces turn pale...

Lamiel and *Suora Scolastica* testify to Beyle's ability to renew radically his sense of human possibilities. It is pointless to speculate on what he would have written had he lived, but it seems unlikely that he would have tried to repeat in any way his previous achievements as a chronicler and novelist. The work which he tried to re-write was work with which he was *dissatisfied*, like *La chartreuse de Parme* itself, for which he planned a new version, encouraged partly by Balzac's enthusiastic review in *La revue Parisienne*. There is nothing to suggest that when he died he had acquired that satisfaction with his achievements that would have led him to merely imitate himself, in other words, no longer to be himself and to become instead what he fortunately never became, a consciously respectable man of letters.

8
Some conclusions

The sense of something uncompleted in Beyle's finest work is conveyed by Tolstoy in a letter to his wife of November 1883:

> I read it [*Le rouge et le noir*] some forty years ago, but remembered nothing save my relations to the author: sympathy with his boldness and a feeling of kinship – yet an unsatisfied feeling. And strangely enough I feel the same now, but with a clear consciousness of why and wherefore...[1]

It is significant perhaps that he should have been able to understand his 'unsatisfied feelings' after forty years and after he himself had written *War and Peace* and *Anna Karenina*; it is significant too that he should have continued to regard the influence of Stendhal on his work as greater than that of anyone else.[2]

If Tolstoy's thought and writing is in many ways a development and deepening of what he had found in Beyle, this is not necessarily because he was the more intelligent man – the comparison can easily become impertinent and we are concerned, in any case, if we dwell on these questions at all with something more than individual intelligence; it has something to do as well with the immeasurable advantages he enjoyed, as a sophisticated European, a combatant officer, an aristocrat, a landowner and a husband and father, in having intimate knowledge of so much more of life than Beyle was ever able to experience at first hand. It is not only the experience and growth of the individual consciousness that Tolstoy is able to give us or the moments that test and reveal what we are, but what takes shape in the course of everyday life and in particular the life of a home and family to which all generations can know they belong. This is the most obvious difference between Fabrice del Dongo and Nikolay Rostov in *War and Peace*, who on the field of battle have so much in common. It is because of historical circumstances that Fabrice is unable to follow the destiny for which he is prepared as a child, unable, for example, to live as a dedicated soldier like Nikolay and then as a devoted husband and father enjoying his responsibilities to the full; and it is on the tragic consequences of his fate that Beyle dwells, leaving his potentialities for living pointedly unfulfilled.

It is easy enough, in other words, to say in what ways Tolstoy offers a much wider range of experience than Beyle and why his principal figures are given more opportunities to discover their individual destinies. It is far less easy to account for the greater depth of Tolstoy, the depth that is apparent in the text locally, and, since he never formulates a critique of Beyle, to justify one's belief that he is speaking truthfully of his 'clear consciousness after forty years of the 'why and wherefore' of his dissatisfaction with *Le rouge et le noir*. All I can say is that I know of no one in France who gives the impression of having spoken of Beyle's limitations with Tolstoy's (unassuming) authority. Certainly not Sainte-Beuve. Nor even the André Gide whom Arnold Bennett hailed as 'the Stendhal of our time, but, thank God, better educated and more sensitive...'.[3] Gide is probably the most gifted and entertaining of the many novelists in France who have been influenced by Beyle and the gift can be seen in the reflective wit and the highly personal idiom which never, as in the later novels of Giono, for instance, lapses into virtual pastiche.[4] His Lafcadio in *Les caves du Vatican* cultivates hypocrisy and freedom from his own weaknesses like Julien Sorel, punishes himself for his lapses and in a scene reminiscent of Julien's self-imposed challenges, persuades himself that he has an obligation to push a fellow passenger out of a fast-moving train; while Bernard, in *Les faux monnayeurs*, is shown poignantly at the moment of his entry into the adult world, baffled by what he is to make of his inner freedom, while struggling to maintain it at the same time. Yet neither novel is completely realistic or serious, and Gide's intelligence and artistic gift lie in his not pretending for a moment that they are. The parody of conventional romance in the coincidence by which Lafcadio unknowingly chooses as his victim his own relation by marriage, and the comic ramifications of the crime distract both Lafcadio and the reader from pursuing its moral and psychological implications; while in *Les faux monnayeurs*, Bernard is left by Gide at an early stage in his struggle and the novel becomes increasingly a parody of itself and an eloquent admission, through the characterisation of the novelist within the novel, of his own lack of creative power and inhuman curiosity. It is an inhuman impulse too which dictates the particular form of Lafcadio's self-imposed challenge, when contrasted with Julien's suddenly wanting to hold Mme de Rênal's hand, and it is possibly for this reason that Gide did not attempt to show it as a crucial moment in the development into fuller humanity of a representative fellow-being.

Gide's recorded considerations of Beyle's work are far more copious than Tolstoy's, though his account of Beyle's limitations is not the most convincing evidence that he was 'thank God, better educated and more sensitive'. I mention them because they illustrate the extraordinary range of the appeal of Beyle's writings and also how rare it is to find a man who is more educated in that he is able to recognise and account for Beyle's limitations as a novelist. Beyle was obviously in advance of his time in many ways, but 'catching up with him', as Nietzsche puts it, involves more than the passage of time. Gide's preface to *Armance* of 1925 is a personal tribute of the best possible kind, in that it can remind those readers who are not all that interested in the torments and joys of the hero why these can seem of crucial significance to someone else. The dissociation between love and sexual desire in Octave de Malibert, Gide maintains, brings home to us the easily forgotten likelihood that the sexually impotent may, by the very fact of their impotence, be capable of the 'most fervent and tender love'. It is fairly obvious that Gide had a special interest in the novel, which served to illustrate his defence of homosexual love, in *Corydon* published the year before, as conducive, among other things, to a better understanding between men and women. It is clear too that, though what Gide is saying is in many ways true of *Armance*, it is not the whole truth; for the novel gives us the swift development of Octave's feelings and is virtually unfinished. We never know what Octave might have become.

It is in the preface to *Lamiel* of 1947 that we find Gide's most eloquent account of what he sees as Beyle's limitations, and here he talks of

> ...certain strata of the soul, into which Stendhal doesn't even seek to penetrate because he had no knowledge of them, those profound strata in which the religious feelings have their place that Stendhal dismissed so lightly; where the great Goethean *Schaudern* (for which I find no proper equivalent in our language) hold their sway over and grow in our minds, the region of trances and enchantments. It may be that these mysterious regions exist only in the imagination of men and are only constructions and substructions of the mind; but they matter none the less, and without them, the human being is utterly impoverished...

The preface has the merit of expressing a fundamental misgiving that is shared by many other readers of Beyle, and it is perhaps the judgment least susceptible to confirmation or refutation by reference to any text. I should like, none the less, to invite those readers who share Gide's feelings of dissatisfaction, as he expresses them here, to re-read the chapters in *Le rouge et le noir* giving us Julien's thoughts and experiences in the prison cell[5] and Fabrice's reflections on the beliefs he has derived from the Abbé Blanès in chapter 8 of *La chartreuse de Parme*. Gide, like many of Beyle's most intelligent readers, like Mme Henriette Bibas, for instance,[6] may well have been misled by Beyle's impatience with mere religiosity and his determination, whatever strata of the soul he had in mind, to write with boldness and in an honest language.

The most influential French thinker of our time, M. Jean-Paul Sartre, has made no attempt that I know of to assess Beyle's achievement as a whole or the quality of his intelligence, and though his occasional allusions to him are friendly, has never brought the intense scrutiny to his mind and work that we find in his writings on Baudelaire, Genet and Flaubert. Beyle is, if anything, conspicuous so far by his absence from Sartre's critical writings and in particular from Sartre's massive work on Flaubert, *L'idiot de la famille*, since much of it is devoted to an analysis of the self-delusions of Flaubert's older contemporaries and peers, torn between hatred of the Philistinism of their class and fear of the rising proletariat and seeking a false solution in the cultivation of art as a refuge from the horrors of contemporary society. One may be glad that M. Sartre does not try to pretend that Beyle also fits into the psychological and historical patterns he has traced, though the probability that he does not is one of the principal reasons for doubting whether the patterns correspond to any historical necessity. The incompleteness of M. Sartre's admirably documented picture of the age is apparent particularly when one reads of the influence of Condillac, Helvétius, Tracy and Bentham on men of the generation of Flaubert's own father, which happens to be that of Beyle himself. Sartre gives us only the most repellent and implausible aspects of their combined influence: the mechanistic interpretation of living phenomena and the encouragement they offer to self-love,[7] to which they no doubt lend themselves. But if this were the entire truth, we would have to assume that Beyle, in so far as he was very different from Flaubert's father (whom Sartre portrays as a French Gradgrind) either failed to understand them or, despite his assertions to the contrary, never really underwent their influence at all.

This has often been claimed, or, as an alternative, that it didn't matter with what philosophy Beyle began; what mattered was what he made of it as a creative artist.[8] My purpose in writing this study has been partly to argue against this view and to suggest that the astonishing intelligence of his art was a consequence of many years of self-training in which reflection on the basic tenets of the thinkers whom M. Sartre castigates played a crucial part. Beyle's allusions to Bentham may be sometimes deliberately provocative, an invocation of the name of a *chef de file*, as when he tells us that 'Jeremy Bentham helps us to understand the sense of beauty in antiquity a hundred times better than Plato and all his imitators...',[9] the *boutade* possibly being directed against the author of *Du vrai, du beau et du bien*, the apostle of disinterestedness both in art and in life and possibly the first person to talk of 'art for art's sake', the fashionable young philosopher Victor Cousin. And Beyle's professed Utilitarianism seems to owe more to Helvétius than to Bentham and even then to little of which Helvétius himself was the originator. ('In all ages of philosophy', Mill reminds his readers in his essay on Bentham, 'one of its schools has been Utilitarian – not only from the time of Epicurus but long before...') while Beyle's insistent defence of Helvétius is in part a response to the denigration from which he suffered in France, and not only in France, throughout most of Beyle's lifetime. The whole of the moral philosophy inspired by Kant, according to Nietzsche, was an attack upon Helvétius, 'the most maligned of all good moralists and all good men...'[10] and though Nietzsche himself speaks far less highly of Bentham than Beyle or even Mill, he too acknowledges their common master:

> Consider, for instance, those indefatigable, inevitable English utilitarians, so heavy and respectable who tread up and down (a Homeric comparison would express it better) over the footsteps of Bentham, who in turn treads up and down over those of the respectable Helvétius...[11]

Nietzsche too reminds us that Utilitarianism has a longer history than the name of the modern school, he accuses the English Utilitarians of seeking not the happiness of the greatest number but the happiness of England (the organisation of the colonisation of New Zealand by the Utilitarian Edward Gibbon Wakefield might be taken as illustrating the point) and of being, despite the Utilitarian cloak, essentially puritanical, that is the antithesis of *'Ein Moralist'*:

> For the moralist is a thinker who considers morality as dubious, hypothetical, in other words a problem. And is it not immoral to think of morality as problematic?[12]

The supreme modern example of the questioning moralist for Nietzsche was, of course, Beyle himself.

Beyle's questioning of the economic orthodoxies of his day – Say's theory of markets, for example, and Saint-Simon's cult of productivity (the early versions, that is to say, of the modern subordination of all interests to those of economic growth)[13] is pursued from the point of view of a man who avowedly wishes the happiness of the greatest number, everything, as he makes clear, depending on what we mean by happiness; while in *Lucien Leuwen*, the delusions inherent in the creation of wealth for others to enjoy and in making others happy 'in one's own way' are made to emerge from his presentation of M. Leuwen père, the financial genius and personal friend of Bentham. In Beyle, perhaps more than in any other thinkers of the school with which he identified himself, the pleasure principle and the general theory of utility take a critical and interrogative as well as an affirmative form: what is happiness? what do men really want? being, as he told Balzac, the questions he habitually asks. In Paris, as a young man, he studied, he tells us,[14] together with Adam Smith, Say and Shakespeare, Montaigne. And as in Montaigne, the interrogative cast of mind proves to be incompatible with systematic thought – that is, thought which seeks to demonstrate its consistency by defending itself against all possible objections – and to demand, far more than in most other men, enlightenment from particular instances. It is the scepticism which is dissatisfied with vague generalities or general propositions that ask to be taken on trust that led Beyle to evolve his own highly idiosyncratic idiom and to become a novelist; and in doing so he showed that readiness to rely on what is felt and perceived which is fundamental to the utilitarian method. 'It is the introduction into the philosophy of human conduct, of this method of detail', Mill tells us in his essay on Bentham, 'of this practice of never reasoning about wholes till they have been resolved into parts, nor about abstractions till they have been translated into realities – that constitutes the originality of Bentham in philosophy, and makes him the great reformer of the moral and political branch of it.' The inhuman abstractness, none the less, of Bentham's systematisation of the pleasure principle (which Mill goes on to demonstrate) may remind us that Bentham's ostensible concern with 'realities' by no means corresponded always with his actual 'practice'. I have suggested earlier that a similar contrast between practice and avowed method can be found in Tracy's *Traité de la volonté*, especially when contrasted with *Le rouge et le noir*.[15] Beyle learned certainly from Tracy, as he learned from Helvétius and to a lesser extent Bentham. But in learning, I should like to conclude by suggesting, he expressed the beliefs he shared with them more consistently than they had themselves, at the cost of neglect throughout his lifetime and by becoming the first of the great modern novelists. We see this whether we consider the form that the basic principles of utilitarianism take in his writings or his simultaneous reliance on and questioning of experience. It is for this reason, presumably that he should today prove so much more readable, on any level of seriousness, than the thinkers whose influence he underwent. And it may be for this reason too that he counts for so much in the formation of Nietzsche and Tolstoy, who belong to the age succeeding that of Beyle and have had a by no means negligible influence on our own.

Notes

NOTES TO CHAPTER ONE

1. F. Nietzsche, *Untimely Considerations*, book 1, ch. 2.
2. *La vie de Henry Brulard*, ch. 1 in *Oeuvres intimes* (Paris, Gallimard, 1955), p. 41.
3. *Correspondance*, 16.10.1840.
4. F. Nietzsche, *Beyond Good and Evil*, VIII, p. 254.
5. A. Lamartine, *Cours familier de littérature* (Paris, 1864), vol. 17, entretien 102.
6. J. Prévost, *La création chez Stendhal* (Paris, 1951), p. 29.
7. *Pensées* (Paris, 1931), vol. 1, p. 123.
8. See Picavet, *Les idéologues* (Paris, 1891), p. 585.
9. *Henri Brulard*, ch. 2, p. 53.
10. *Ibid.*, ch. 40, p. 375.
11. J. Prévost, *La création chez Stendhal*, p. 23.
12. H. James, *Literary Reviews and Essays*, ed. Mordell (New York, 1957), p. 157.
13. T. S. Eliot, 'Tradition and the Individual Talent' in *Selected Essays* (London, 1932), p. 14.
14. See A. Latreille, 'Le catéchisme impérial de 1806', *Annales de l'Université de Lyon*, 3e série, 1935. Dr A. P. Kerr has drawn my attention to this paper.
15. Chateaubriand, *Le génie du christianisme*, part 1, book 1, ch. 1.
16. C. Morazé, *La France bourgeoise* (Paris, 1947), ch. 3, p. 82.
17. *Ibid.*, p. 85.
18. Gérard de Nerval, *Quintus Aucler*, ch. 1, in *Les Illuminés*.
19. A thorough examination of Vigny's lifelong concern for public order and the maintenance of the established creed, despite his own religious scepticism, is to be found in M. Henri Guillemin's excellent *M. de Vigny, homme d'ordre et poète* (Paris, 1955).
20. Preface to *Mémoires sur Napoléon*.
21. *Courrier Anglais* (Paris, Le Divan, 1935), vol. 1, p. 330. *Paris Monthly Review*, June 1822.
22. F. Nietzsche, *Ecce homo*, II, 3.
23. In the essay on Balzac in *Portraits contemporains*.
24. C. A. Sainte-Beuve, *Causeries du lundi*, vol. 9 (Paris, 1856), pp. 264–5.
25. A. de Tocqueville, *L'ancien régime* (Paris, 1952), vol. 1, pp. 175–6.
26. *Ibid.*, vol. 1, pp. 207–8.

27 Reprinted in Charles de Rémusat, *Passé et présent* (Paris, 1859).
28 *Oeuvres intimes*, ch. 9, p. 119.
29 *Ibid.*, ch. 10, p. 127.
30 *Ibid.*, ch. 15, p. 172.
31 See the essay on Milton in *Etudes critiques sur la littérature contemporaine*.
32 See Emile Durkheim, *L'évolution pédagogique en France* (Paris, 1969), ch. 10.
33 See V. del Litto, *La vie intellectuelle de Stendhal* (Paris, 1959), pp. 12–15.
34 Beyle is alluding, presumably, to his *Vie de Mozart* (1815) and the chapter on Michelangelo in his *Histoire de la peinture en Italie* (1817).
35 *Mélanges de littérature* (Paris, 1933), vol. 3, p. 417.
36 L. Blum, *Stendhal et le Beylisme* (Paris, 1947), p. 7.
37 *Ibid.*, p. 9.
38 *Correspondance*, 19.2.1831.
39 *Ibid.*, 8.8.1804.
40 *Ibid.*, 29.8.1804.
41 Beyle's conduct towards his sister is one of the least attractive episodes in his life. For many years after leaving Grenoble he wrote to her the long persistent letters in which he tried to form her mind and character and transform her into another Mme Roland, the ideal embodiment, for Beyle, of enlightened femininity. Her marriage with François Périer-Lagrange was, as Beyle had advised, a marriage of reason rather than love and not, as it turned out, a happy one. (See 'Sur Pauline Beyle. Documents inédits présentés par V. del Litto' in *Stendhal Club*, no. 24, 15 July 1964.) After her husband's death, childless and in reduced circumstances, she joined her brother in Milan. He had many times in the past suggested that they might one day live together with a few friends and form an ideal community. (See, for instance, *Correspondance*, 22.8.1805.) Beyle describes in *Souvenirs d'égotisme* the outcome of her journey to Milan: 'I was severely punished for having advised a sister of mine to come to Milan, in 1816 I think it was. Mme. Périer attached herself to me like a barnacle, making me responsible for her destiny, virtually for the rest of her life. Mme Périer possessed all the virtues and considerable sense and amiability. I was obliged to quarrel with her in order to rid myself of a barnacle tediously clinging to my keel and who, for good or ill, placed on me the future responsibility for her happiness. It was a horrible business.' (*Oeuvres intimes*, p. 1,483.)
42 C. A. Sainte-Beuve, *Causeries du lundi*, vol. 9, p. 254.
43 *Oeuvres intimes*, pp. 38–9.

NOTES TO CHAPTER TWO

1 *La vie de Henry Brulard*, chapter 3 in *Oeuvres intimes* (Paris, Gallimand, 1955), p. 57.
2 *Racine et Shakspeare* (Paris, Le Divan, 1928), p. 35.
3 *Pensées* (Paris, Le Divan, 1931), vol. 2, p. 60.
4 *Mélanges de littérature* (Paris, Le Divan, 1933), vol. 3, p. 105.
5 See the article by Lucien Jansse in *Stendhal Club*, 36, 15 July 1967, 'Stendhal et la constitution anglaise.'

6 In this respect, his criticisms are similar to those made by Helvétius to Montesquieu himself. See *Oeuvres complètes d'Helvétius* (éd.) Didot, vol. 14, p. 61.
7 See V. del Litto, *La vie intellectuelle de Stendhal* (Paris, 1959), pp. 67–70.
8 'If Mme de Staël hadn't wished to be more passionate than nature and her early education have made her, she would have written masterpieces. She has tried to adopt something other than her natural style, she has written works full of excellent thoughts which are the fruit of a *reflective character* and which show nothing of a *tender* character. And as she has tried to display tenderness, she has fallen into mere gibberish.' Letter to Pauline Beyle, 20.8.1805.
9 Montesquieu, *L'esprit des lois*, part 3, book 14, ch. 2.
10 Stendhal, *De l'amour*, ch. 2.
11 Rousseau, book 5 (p. 448 in the Garnier edition, Paris, 1957).
12 *La vie de Henry Brulard*, ch. 44, p. 407.
13 *Ibid.*, ch. 46, p. 421.
14 See, for example, the letter to Pauline of 29 October 1804.
15 *Mélanges de littérature* (Paris, Le Divan, 1933), pp. 95–6.
16 See *Emile*, the seventh paragraph of *La profession de foi du Vicaire Savoyand*.
17 *Ibid.*, pp. 114–15.
18 *Correspondance*, 2.10.1812.
19 See, for example, Chateaubriand, *Le génie du christianisme*, part 3, ch. 2 and Mme de Staël, *De la littérature*, part 1, ch. 6.
20 *Pensées*, vol. 1, p. 119.
21 *Mémoires d'un touriste* (Paris, le Divan, 1837), vol. 3, p. 38.
22 In a note to *Lettres de la Montagne* quoted by Guy Besse in his very useful preface to Helvétius's *De l'esprit* (Paris, Editions sociales, 1959).
23 *Courrier anglais* (Paris, 1935), vol. 2, p. 166.
24 *Mélanges intimes* (Paris, Le Divan, 1936), vol. 2, pp. 166–7.
25 Cf. the epilogue to *L'histoire de la peinture en Italie*: 'A great genius mistrusts his discoveries... In a matter in which his happiness is so much at stake, he thinks of all the objections to them he can. Thus a man of genius can only make a certain number of discoveries. It is rare for him to have the courage to take his discoveries as an unassailable point of departure. Consider Descartes, who abandoned a sublime method and, after the second step only, began to reason like a monk...'
26 See the article on Kant in *Courrier anglais*, vol. 1, pp. 327–31.
27 *Correspondance*, 24.1.1806.
28 See Otto Gierke, *Natural Law and the Theory of Society*, translated by Ernest Barker (Boston, 1957), p. 97. The whole of this, I am told, still classical study – extracted from *Das deutsche Genossenschaftsrecht* – is relevant to the crucial issue of natural law and its social and metaphysical implications. See particularly ch. 2 for its bearing on the Enlightenment.
29 *Correspondance*, 8.2.1803.
30 *Courrier anglais*, vol. 1, pp. 301–4.
31 *Loc. cit.*
32 Helvétius, *De l'esprit*, discourse 2, ch. 5.
33 *La vie de Henry Brulard*, ch. 37, pp. 353–4.
34 Robert M. Adams: *Stendhal, notes on a novelist* (London, 1959), p. 184.
35 In Book I, part 4, section 6.

36 *Courrier Anglais*, vol. 3, p. 412 (*New Monthly Magazine*, September 1828).
37 See p. 16 above.
38 G. Cabanis, *Oeuvres complètes* (Paris, 1956), vol. 2, p. 348.
39 See A. Girard, *Le journal intime* (Paris, 1963). M. Girard's thesis is that the intimate journals of Benjamin Constant, Maine de Biran, Stendhal and other contemporaries mark a totally new departure in the recording of personal experience.
40 *Oeuvres intimes*, p. 962.
41 Stendhal's ideas of human perfectibility and of the nature of the known and knowable self came increasingly in fact to resemble those of D. H. Lawrence in the two versions of his essay on Benjamin Franklin in the *Spirit of Place* and *Studies in Classic American Literature*. Both these versions, together with the sketch for an essay on the influence of Rousseau, 'The Good Man' published in the first volume of *Phoenix*, provide an excellent foil against which Stendhal's own writings on the same themes stand out in peculiarly clear relief. The contrast, of course, between Lawrence and Stendhal is as illuminating as the resemblances.
42 See the letter to Alberthe de Rubempré quoted on p. 23, above.
43 In K. Marx, *The German Ideology*, vol. 1, 3 (pp. 447–54 in the Lawrence and Wishart edition, London, 1965).
44 In K. Marx, *The Holy Family* (Moscow, 1956), pp. 168–77.
45 Mme de Staël, *De la littérature*, part 1, ch. 6.
46 Preface to *De la religion* quoted by Beyle in the *Courrier Anglais*, vol. 4, p. 29. Beyle describes this passage as worthy of any commonplace fanatical preacher.
47 Victor Cousin, *Cours d'histoire de la philosophie morale au dix-huitième siècle* (Paris, 1839), lesson 4, p. 166.
48 *Correspondance*, 16.10.1840.
49 F. R. Leavis, *The Great Tradition* (London, 1948), p. 191.
50 *Pensées*, vol. 2, p. 294.
51 Utilitarianism, it is true, is often presented ironically in the novels themselves. Count Mosca in *La chartreuse* regards 'the greatest happiness of the greatest number' theory as a naïve absurdity, while the solemn Utilitarianism of the conspiratorial Liberal, Count Altamira in *Le rouge et le noir*, makes him something of a Pangloss or a Don Quixote. Beyle's own readiness to quote and stand by Utilitarian and specifically Benthamite principles seems on the whole, none the less, to characterise his writings from 1810 onwards after his discovery of the *Treatise of Civil and Penal Legislation*. In a letter to Mareste (24.10.1818) he describes Bentham as 'Montesquieu perfected' comparing Bentham again with Montesquieu to the former's advantage in *Mémoires d'un Touriste* (vol. III, p. 318 of the 1929 edition), in *De l'amour* he quotes Bentham several times on the nature of asceticism and in an essay of 1829, *Philosophie transcendentale* (see *Mélanges de littérature*, vol. II) he makes what is virtually a Utilitarian and Benthamite profession of faith.
52 George Santayana, *Five Essays* (Cambridge, 1934), p. 21.
53 In a letter to Stendhal of 22 December 1825 their mutual friend Victor Jacquemont told Stendhal that although Tracy had admired *Rome, Naples et Florence*, he had never believed 'and still doesn't believe that you've written this book *seriously*'. Henri Martineau points out in his preface to his 1957

edition of *De l'amour* that Tracy was personally, for one thing, unable to believe in any form of what is usually called Platonic love.
54 *De l'amour*, ch. 24.
55 Most obviously at the beginning of ch. 3.
56 Adams, *Stendhal, notes on a novelist*, p. 55.
57 See the unsigned article by George Eliot on *De l'amour* and other recently published or republished works in *The Westminster Review*, 65 (April 1856) included in volume 7 of George Eliot's letters (London, 1955).
58 See *The Second Sex* (London, 1953), pp. 247 and 652.
59 *De l'amour*, ch. 55.
60 L. Jansse, 'Stendhal et l'économie politique' in *Stendhal Club*, 28, 15 juillet 1965.
61 In an article in *The New Monthly Magazine* for February 1827 (see *Courrier Anglais*, vol. 3, pp. 287–98), Beyle resumes for his English readers Dupin's statistical survey for the whole of France showing the relative numbers of those in various regions attending schools and institutes of learning.
62 In his essays on *Saint-Simonian economic doctrine* to be found in *The Era of Tyrannies* (London, 1967).
63 How it is that Beyle did not apparently read Sismondi's *Nouveaux principes d'économie politique* of 1819 is by no means clear. He knew Sismondi's work, on the whole, very well and particularly his *Littérature du midi de l'Europe* and *Histoire des républiques italiennes*. As an economist, Sismondi, like Beyle, foresaw the saturation of markets and his critique of the theory of markets strongly influenced Robert Owen, whom he met in 1818, Proudhon and the early Marx. See the essay on Sismondi in Halévy's *Era of Tyrannies*. For Beyle's views on Fourier see *Mémoires d'un touriste* (1929), vol. II, p. 22 and vol. 3, p. 279. Also *Stendhal et la pensée sociale de son temps* (Paris, 1967), pp. 238–42.
64 Notice that Beyle says 'a sacrifice of interest to some noble end' ('*sacrifice* de l'intérêt à quelque noble but') and not 'sacrifice of *all* personal interest'. I mention this because one recent critic, Miss Margaret Tillett in *Stendhal, the Background to his Novels* (London, 1971) sees in this phrase a contradiction of 'his Helvetian principle' that 'self-sacrifice is simply a form of self-interest' (p. 96). The confusion and self-contradiction of which Miss Tillett complains stem perhaps from her use of the English phrase 'self-interest' of which there is no equivalent in Beyle's own French.
65 Beyle claims in *La vie de Henry Brulard* (*Oeuvres intimes*, p. 177) that, as a lieutenant of dragoons, at the Battle of Castel-Franco in January 1801 he took part in a head-on charge against the Austrian artillery. He also mentions an attestation written to confirm this by General Michaud to whom he served as aide-de-camp. Paul Arbelet in *La jeunesse de Stendhal* (Paris, 1914, 2 vols.) and Henri Martineau in *Le calendrier de Stendhal* (Paris, 1950) both give interesting arguments for believing that Beyle was lying ill at the time in Milan and that Michaud's certificate was one in which he perjured himself as a favour to Beyle.

NOTES TO CHAPTER THREE

1 See Martin Turnell's reviews of my edition of Stendhal's *Selected Journalism* in *The Spectator* for 26 July 1959 and in *The Twentieth Century* for October 1959.

NOTES TO PAGES 53–65

2 Mme de Chasteller finds Lucien Leuwen, when they first meet and he is tongue-tied, a mere 'hero out of Ariosto'. *Lucien Leuwen*, ch. 17.
3 *Pensées*, vol. 1, p. 30.
4 *Pensées*, vol. 1, p. 95.
5 See Helvétius, *De l'esprit*, discourse 2, ch. 16 and discourse 4, ch. 2.
6 *Oeuvres intimes*, ch. 7, p. 94.
7 *Correspondance*, 8.8.1804.
8 *Oeuvres intimes*, p. 1,174 (27.9.1811).
9 *Ibid.*, p. 563.
10 See V. del Litto, *La vie intellectuelle de Stendhal*, pp. 503–63 for a detailed account of Beyle's comments on and borrowings from *The Edinburgh Review*.
11 *Rome, Naples et Florence en 1817*, entry for 11 May 1817.
12 *Pensées*, vol. 1, p. 158.
13 *Mélanges de littérature*, vol. 3, pp. 81–3.
14 *Ibid.*, p. 86.
15 *Ibid.*, p. 87.
16 *Rome, Naples et Florence, en 1817*, entry for 11 May 1817.
17 *Oeuvres intimes*, pp. 620–1.
18 *Ibid.*, p. 614.
19 See *D'un nouveau complot contre les industriels* quoted on page 51.
20 *Molière, Shakespeare, la comédie et le rire* (Paris, 1930), p. 208. This is in Crozet's handwriting.
21 *Ibid.*, pp. 208–9 (in Beyle's handwriting).
22 *La vie de Rossini*, ch. 18.
23 C. A. Sainte-Beuve, *Causeries du lundi*, vol. 9, p. 254.
24 Georges Blin, *Stendhal et les problèmes du roman* (Paris, 1954), p. 19.
25 *Rome, Naples et Florence en 1817*, entry for 11 May 1817.
26 Alfieri, *Vita*, epoca quarta, ch. 1.
27 *Mélanges de littérature*, vol. 3, p. 98.
28 *Ibid.* p. 110.
29 Cf. D. H. Lawrence's introduction to his volume of poems entitled *Pansies*: 'Each little piece is a thought; not a bare idea or an opinion or a didactic statement, but a true thought which comes as much from the heart and genitals as the head.' More relevant in this connection, however, is the claim by Lawrence's one-time friend, John Middleton Murry that this definition of style is the best that has ever been formulated. See Murry's Oxford lectures of 1921 on *The Problem of Style*. Murry's own translation of the definition reads as follows: 'Style is this: to add to a given thought all the circumstances fitted to produce the whole effect that the thought ought to produce.' He adds, however: 'A more truly accurate translation, I think, would be: "the whole effect which the thought is intended to produce." At any rate the French hovers between the two meanings.' The reader will obviously choose as he prefers between Murry's translation and my own, but I believe that if Beyle had wished to convey the two meanings which Murry finds in the single word '*doit*' he would have done so more clearly. A very free translation of the whole phrase might be: 'the total effect which this thought must produce if it is to be adequately conveyed'. The last seven words would contribute, however, only to making misunderstanding impossible and I hope that my translation is clear enough as it stands.

NOTES TO PAGES 65–70

30 In, for example, an article on Italian poetry in *The London Magazine* for January 1826. See *Le Courrier Anglais*, vol. 4, p. 280.
31 In *The New Monthly Magazine* for September 1826 (*Courrier Anglais*, vol. 3, p. 154).
32 *Oeuvres intimes*, p. 568.
33 *Pensées*, vol. 1, p. 23.
34 See *Eléments d'idéologie*, part 3, *Discours préliminaire*.
35 *Oeuvres intimes*, p. 621 (11.2.1805).
36 See *Horace*, act 3, scene 6.
37 See *Andromaque*, act 5, scene 3.
38 For Beyle's debt to Reynolds see V. del Litto's *Vie intellectuelle de Stendhal*. The 'moment of repose' in *Macbeth* marked by the 'temple haunting martlet' speech is one to which Reynolds draws attention in his eighth Discourse. Beyle uses the example again in book 2, ch. 34 of *The History of Painting in Italy*.
39 See again del Litto, *Vie intellectuelle de Stendhal*. Beyle's allegation that Reynolds exaggerated his admiration for Michelangelo and that he was far more influenced in his depiction of the human form by Rembrandt, whom he feigned to disparage, is almost certainly one of his many borrowings from Knight (cf. del Litto, p. 499). William Blake makes a similar point in his annotations to Reynolds' *Discourses*: 'If Reynolds had really admired Mich. Angelo, he never would have followed Rubens.'
40 See Mill's *Autobiography*, ch. 5.
41 Beyle appears particularly as he grew older, to have had a limited confidence in the usefulness of reasoning in any discussion of music or poetry. In a dialogue, for instance, in *Racine et Shakspeare* between the Romantic and the Academician, the former talks of the moments of 'perfect illusion' which he claims are more frequent in Shakespeare than Racine. He adds, however: 'If you are dishonest or insensitive or petrified by Laharpe, [the most influential academic critic of the pre-Romantic period; he lived from 1739 to 1803] you will deny my little moments of perfect illusion. And I admit there is nothing I can say in reply. Your feelings are not something material I can extract from your heart and place under your nose to prove you are wrong... I have reached the limits of what logic is able to grasp in poetry.'
42 *De l'homme*, section 8, ch. 17.
43 Helvetius, *De l'esprit*, discourse 2.
44 There is no need to insist on the parallel with Augustan criticism in England.
45 *Lettres philosophiques*, 21. It is true that Voltaire, like Johnson, is sensitive to the kind of poetic effect of which he disapproves and, in the *Lettres philosophiques*, when writing of English poetry, he transcends his own prejudices.
46 In the *Commentaires*, in a note on Corneille's *Le Cid*, act 1, scene 6. Cf., from ch. 22 of *Le siècle de Louis XIV*, 'It must not be thought that the great tragic passions and sentiments can be varied indefinitely in a new and striking way. There are limits to everything.'
47 *Eléments d'idéologie, La grammaire*, ch. 6.
48 *Loc. cit.*
49 *Seconde lettre à M. de Voltaire*.

NOTES TO PAGES 70–86

50 *Loc. cit.* cf. Voltaire in his *Discours à l'Académie*. 'The style of Montaigne is neither pure, correct, precise or noble...'
51 Cf. the remarks attributed to Goethe by Beyle on the 'purging' of the French language in *Racine et Shakspeare*, pp. 369–70 in the Divan edition.
52 Clément, *Seconde lettre à M. de Voltaire*.
53 Hobbes on *Human Nature*, ch. 10.
54 *Quatrième lettre à M. de Voltaire*.
55 *Stendhal et le Beylisme* (Paris, 1947), p. 7.
56 *Eléments d'idéologie, La grammaire*, ch. 6.
57 *Loc. cit.*
58 *La vie de Henry Brulard*, ch. 1.
59 *Correspondance*, 4.5.1834. Cf. the opening pages of *La vie de Marianne*, where Marivaux's heroine and narrator confesses that she has no idea what 'style' means. 'Is good style the kind of style I see in books? Why then do I dislike it so often? What do you think of the style of my letters? Will it do? In any case, this is the one I intend to use.'
60 *Racine et Shakspeare*, ch. 3.
61 *Loc. cit.*
62 *Mélanges de littérature*, vol. 3, p. 430.
63 *Ibid.*, p. 431.
64 See R. G. Collingwood, *The Principles of Art*, ch. 14, section 9. The whole of this chapter corroborates Beyle's general attitude to the question of the artist and his audience.
65 See Pierre Mélèse, *Le théâtre et le public à Paris sous Louis XIV* (Paris, 1934).
66 Cf. *Rome, Naples et Florence* (the entry for 27 February 1817): 'Alfieri lacked a public. Just as generals need soldiers, so are the common people necessary to great men.'
67 Eugène Scribe, *La camaraderie*, a thinly disguised satire of Chateaubriand and his literary circle.
68 *Racine et Shakspeare*, part 1, ch. 2.
69 *La comédie est impossible* in *Mélanges de littérature*, vol. 3, p. 431.
70 *Ibid.*, pp. 432–3.
71 In a note written in a copy of *Le rouge et le noir* two years before the essay appeared, Beyle remarked that the 'society of Mme de Sévigné approved of the nonsense that La Bruyère utters on religion and government, but what an admirable judge it would have been of a scene as that between Mme de Rênal and her husband.' (See *Mélanges de Littérature*, vol. 3, p. 418.)
72 In Remy de Gourmont, *Promenades littéraires*, 2nd series, pp. 97–8.
73 *Mélanges de littérature*, vol. 3, p. 263.
74 *La vie de Henry Brulard*, ch. 9.
75 *Correspondance* (letters to Stendhal), 28.12.1805.
76 *Journal* (13.7.1810).
77 Gourmont, *Promenades littéraires*, 4th series, p. 178.
78 *Ibid.*, p. 206.
79 *Bouvard et Pécuchet* anticipates, as Mr Hugh Kenner has recently argued in his study of *The Stoic Comedians*, the novels of Samuel Beckett.
80 F. Nietzsche, *The Birth of Tragedy*, section 1 of the 1886 preface.
81 Paul Bourget, *Essais de psychologie contemporaine* (Paris, 1885), p. 325.
82 *Mélanges de littérature*, vol. 2, pp. 165–8.

83 *Molière, Shakspeare, la comédie et le rire*, p. 76.
84 See G. E. Moore, *Principia Ethica*, ch. 3, section A.
85 Similar arguments are adduced and given substantiation from a psychological point of view by I. A. Richards in the chapter on 'Pleasure' in his *Principles of Literary Criticism*.
86 In his memoir, *H.B.* (Paris, 1850), p. 12.
87 In *La Revue des deux-mondes*, 1837. Quoted by J. Starzynski in the preface to his useful selection from Beyle's writings on art, *Du romantisme dans les arts* (Paris, 1966).
88 An extraordinary claim by Lionello Venturi in his *History of Art Criticism* (New York, 1964), p. 35 is that before Stendhal 'nobody was aware that Leonardo expressed a melancholy mind in his painting'.
89 *Histoire de la peinture en Italie* (Paris, 1929 Divan edition), vol. 2, p. 361.
90 *La chartreuse de Parme*, ch. 5.
91 *Ibid.*, vol. 1, pp. 158–60.
92 *Mélanges d'art* (Paris, 1932), p. 175. See too *Promenades dans Rome* (17.3.1828): 'Jeremy Bentham helps us to understand the sense of beauty in antiquity a hundred times better than Plato and all his imitators.'
93 M. Bardeche, *Stendhal romancier* (Paris, 1947), p. 64.
94 In the *Mémoires d'un touriste* (15.6.1837), Beyle claims that Giotto would have admired Delacroix's battle scenes, but his judgment of the latter's *Massacre of Chios* in his *Salon* of 1824 is far more severe. See *Mélanges d'art*, pp. 67–71 and 168–9 in the Divan edition, for his judgments of Delacroix and David. One should mention also among contemporary artists whom Beyle admired the Neapolitan choreographer Salvatore Vigano who had 'advanced expression in every genre' and whom Beyle compares to Shakespeare. See *Rome, Naples et Florence en 1817* (10.2.1817).
95 See p. 20.
96 *Histoire de la peinture en Italie*, vol. 2, p. 111.
97 In the concluding chapter of *L'histoire de la peinture en Italie*, moreover, Beyle argues that the true 'beau idéal moderne' has still to be found.
98 *Histoire de la peinture en Italie*, vol. 2, p. 183.
99 For the method by which the *Histoire de la peinture* was composed, see Jean Prévost, *La création chez Stendhal* (Paris, 1951), pp. 120–41.
100 *Histoire de la peinture*, vol. 2, pp. 362–3.
101 *Ibid.*, p. 334.
102 In his article on Rossini in the *Paris Monthly Review* for January 1822 (*Courrier Anglais*, vol. 1), Beyle makes the point he repeats in different forms in *La vie de Rossini* and his reviews of productions of his works: '...the first composer who has the courage *not* to copy him and who abandons the various forms of *allegro* and rapid *crescendo*, to return to a slower measure and to the authentic, natural expression of the words of the libretto, will certainly see Rossini's glory fade to his own advantage...it is perhaps because of its general dash and its continual and disconcerting variations that Rossini's music never leaves any profound impression. One might say with Shakespeare that
> It is too rash, too unadvised, too sudden;

> Too like the lightning which doth cease to be
> Ere one can say it lightens...
> *Romeo and Juliet.*

In ch. 14 of his *Memoirs*, Berlioz makes a similar though far more strongly worded protest against Rossini's musical vices. He too, however, notably in the articles collected in *Les soirées de l'orchestre*, speaks with amusement, sympathy and admiration of Rossini.

103 See ch. 14 of the *Memoirs*.
104 The recommendation, like a great deal in the *Life of Mozart*, seems to have been lifted from C. Winckler's *Notice biographique sur Mozart*. See Professor Coe's excellently documented account of Beyle's musical experiences in Vienna and elsewhere in *Stendhal Club*, nos. 39 and 40, 1968. Professor Coe, incidentally, questions whether Beyle's discovery of Cimarosa was quite as sudden and early as he claims in *La vie de Henry Brulard*. See pp. 31 and 215, below.
105 See the *Lettre sur Mozart* which concludes the *Vie de Mozart*.
106 *Histoire de la peinture en Italie*, vol. 2, p. 172.
107 See del Litto, *La vie intellectuelle de Stendhal*, p. 496.
108 *La vie de Rossini*, introduction.
109 *L'histoire de la peinture en Italie*, vol. 2, p. 171.
110 *La vie de Rossini*, introduction.

NOTES TO CHAPTER FOUR

1 See p. 7, above.
2 It is commonly assumed by both historians and critics that it was Balzac who was the better historian of his time. See pp. 211–12 below.
3 See *Stendhal Club*, nos. 28, 36 and 56 (1965–72).
4 H. Marrou, *Connaissance de l'histoire* (Paris, 1954), p. 47.
5 See T. S. Lindstrom, *Tolstoï en France* (Paris, 1952), pp. 107–10.
6 *Mémoires sur Napoléon*, ch. 1.
7 Tolstoy, *War and Peace*, epilogue, II, ch. 6.
8 *Mémoires sur Napoléon*, ch. 10.
9 Tolstoy, *War and Peace*, epilogue, I, ch. 3.
10 Peter Geyl, in *Napoleon: for and against* (London, 1964), pp. 32–3, bases his severe account of the book partly on the assumption that Beyle himself published it in 1837.
11 See the autobiographical sketch of 1837, *Oeuvres intimes*, p. 1,531.
12 *Journal*, 9.2.1804.
13 See the *Lettres écrites de Méry-sur-Seine* in *Mélanges II, Journalisme* (Geneva, 1972), pp. 1–10.
14 See the final letter in the *Vie de Metastasio*.
15 *Journal*, 25.7.1815.
16 See Lord Broughton (John Cam Hobhouse), *Recollections of a long life* (London, 1909), vol. 2, pp. 45–57. Hobhouse comments: 'I have every reason to think that Beyle is a trustworthy person – he is so reported by Brême. However, he has a cruel way of talking and looks and is a sensualist...'

17 Chateaubriand, *Mémoires d'outre tombe*, 4, ch. 60 (quoted by Peter Geyl).
18 *Mémoires sur Napoléon*, ch. 1. As a corollary of this distinctly 'Roman' point of view, Beyle expressed the private conviction, just after abandoning the *Mémoires* (See *Mélanges intimes*, 2, p. 338) that it would have been better 'for the happiness of the greatest number' if Napoleon had been killed after Austerlitz, a view he admits would shock his young friend, Mlle de Montijo, the future Empress Eugénie.
19 See the essay on *Aristocracy* in *Reflections on the Death of a Porcupine*.
20 See particularly the *Vie de Napoléon*, chs. 19 to 23.
21 K. Popper, *The Poverty of Historicism* (London, 1961), p. 148.
22 *Del principe e delle lettere*, 3, ch. 9 (quoted by del Litto, *La vie intellectuelle de Stendhal*).
23 Sismondi, *Histoire des républiques italiennes*, vol. 4, ch. 25 (Zurich, 1808), quoted by del Litto.
24 C. Cordiè, *Ricerche stendhaliane* (Naples, 1967), p. 522.
25 For an extended discussion of this idea, see the fragments appended to *Rome, Naples et Florence en 1817* in Henri Martineau's edition (Paris, Le Divan, 1956, pp. 263–6) in which Beyle is paraphrasing Sismondi.
26 *Ibid.*, p. 265.
27 See especially *Rome, Naples et Florence en 1817*, pp. 279–86 and *Promenades dans Rome* (4.12.1828).
28 For the difficulties of translating *vouloir* into English, see pp. 144–5 below.
29 *Promenades dans Rome* (27.1.1828). The *carbonari* were members of a secret society dedicated to Liberalism and the unification of Italy.
30 *Journal*, 5.3.1812.
31 This is an inadequate translation of 'Personne ne *sait vouloir*...' See pp. 144–5.
32 See the introduction to Taine, *L'histoire de la littérature anglaise*.
33 Beyle's ideas of America derived to a great extent from Frances Trollope's *Domestic Manners of the Americans*, which he read soon after its publication in 1832. He also mentions Tocqueville with respect in the *Mémoires d'un touriste* (29.4.1837). Beyle's dislike of American-style democracy seems to have been strengthened partly by his misgivings concerning the pro-American faction among the French republicans of the 1830s and especially Armand Carrel, editor of *Le National*. Lucien Leuwen expresses what is probably Beyle's own view of the Utopian pro-Americanism of the period (comparable with the idealisation until recently of Soviet Russia) in his discussion with the decent idealistic republican Gauthier in *Lucien Leuwen*. See pp. 179–80 below.
34 See the portrait of Adrien Laffargue in *Promenades dans Rome* (23.11.1828).
35 See the extract from *Mémoires d'outre-tombe* quoted by H. Martineau in the Garnier edition of *Le rouge et le noir* (1960), p. 550.
36 See part 2 of *Illusions perdues* and Sainte-Beuve's essay on *La littérature industrielle* in *Portraits contemporains*, vol. 2 (Paris, 1876).
37 See the letter from Paris in the *New Monthly Magazine* for October 1826, the main argument of which is taken up in the discussion on the stage coach in ch. 1, part 2 of *Le rouge et le noir*.
38 See the *Souvenirs de soixante années* by E. Delécluze (Paris, 1862), p. 245.
39 For an extended discussion of the possible authenticity of these articles, see

Dr K. G. McWatter's article, 'Du faux Stendhal?' in *Stendhal Club*, no. 44, 1969.
40 *Vie de Napoléon*, ch. *32*.
41 An interesting defence of Félix Faure, and an attack on what he sees as Beyle's undiscriminating radical sympathies, is made by M. Jacques Félix-Faure in *Stendhal Club*, no. 13, 1961.
42 It is not always realised in Britain that the history of the right to collective bargaining is closely parallel on both sides of the Channel. The English Combination Act of 1799 has its counterpart in the legislation of all successive governments from 1789, in France, until the advent of the Third Republic. There is, of course, an excellent precedent for this prohibition of autonomous institutions within the state in Rousseau's *Social Contract*.
43 J.-P. Sartre, 'La conscience de classe chez Flaubert' in *Les temps modernes*, May 1966.
44 J.-P. Sartre, *L'idiot de la famille* (Paris, 1971).
45 *Mémoires d'un touriste*, 21.4.1837.
46 See p. 196, below.
47 *Mémoires d'un touriste*, 4.6.1837.
48 *Ibid.*, 12.9.1837.
49 *Ibid.*, Chambéry...1837.
50 *Ibid.*, 10.4.1837.
51 *Ibid.*, 12.6.1837.
52 *Ibid.*, 9.5.1837.
53 In T. Jansse, 'Stendhal et l'économie politique' in *Stendhal Club*, no. 28, 1965.
54 *Mémoires d'un touriste*, 21.4.1837.
55 *Ibid.*, especially 17.4.1837.
56 *Ibid.*, 18.5.1837 and 12.9.1837.
57 G. Rude, *Stendhal et la pensée sociale de son temps*, pp. 238–42.
58 *Mémoires d'un touriste*, 12.9.1837.
59 *Ibid.*, Marseille...1837.
60 *Ibid.*, 12.9.1837 and 12.6.1837.
61 In 'La conscience de classe chez Flaubert' in *Les Temps Modernes*, May 1966.
62 18.11.1801.
63 del Litto, *La vie intellectuelle le de Stendhal*, pp. 348–60.
64 *Leçons d'histoire*, avertissement de l'auteur (quoted by del Litto).
65 Volney, *Voyage en Syrie et en Egypte* (Paris, 1787), vol. 1, p. vi and vol. 2, p. 457 (quoted by del Litto).
66 See Doris Langley Moore, *The late Lord Byron* (London, 1961), pp. 372–95.
67 See p. 3, above.
68 E.g. 'Except for events which are very close to us, such as the conversion of the Protestants by Louis XIV's dragoons or insignificant facts like Constantine's victory over Maxentius, history is only, as they say, a fable on which men agree...', *Promenades dans Rome*, 26.10.1827.
69 In the *New Monthly Magazine*, January 1826. (*Courrier anglais*, vol. 2, pp. 413–14). See too the unfinished novel, *Une position sociale*, ch. 3.
70 *Mélanges intimes* (Paris, Le Divan, 1936), vol. 2, p. 337. Beyle here refutes Montesquieu with arguments taken from Niebuhr.

71 *London Magazine* (*Courrier anglais*, vol. 5, pp. 128–33), August 1825. This judgment is completely reversed in chapter 4 of *Souvenirs d'egotisme*, written seven years later.
72 See the introduction to *Vittoria Accoramboni* in *Les chroniques italiennes*.
73 *Connaissance de l'histoire*, pp. 284–6.
74 *Promenades dans Rome*, 5.4.1828 and *Mélanges intimes*, vol. 2, pp. 174–5.
75 *Mélanges de littérature*, vol. 3, p. 417.
76 *Le rouge et le noir*, ch. 22, part 2: the passage beginning 'Politics is a stone round the neck of literature...'

NOTES TO CHAPTER FIVE

1 *Paris Monthly Review*, June 1822 (*Courrier anglais*, vol. 1, p. 329).
2 From the essay on 'The Novel' in *Reflections on the Death of a Porcupine*.
3 *New Monthly Magazine*, December 1822 (*Courrier anglais*, vol. 1, p. 47).
4 *London Magazine*, October 1825 (*Courrier anglais*, vol. 5, p. 206).
5 *Correspondance*, 30.10.1840. In *Mémoires d'un touriste*, 27.4.1837 and 15.7.1837, Beyle mentions enthusiastically *Le curé de Tours* and *Le lys dans la vallée*, though he deplores the 'pretty neological style' in which he imagines that Balzac *rewrites* his novels.
6 See T. S. Lindstrom, *Tolstoï en France* (Paris, 1952), pp. 107–10.
7 In *Mélanges de littérature*, vol. 3, pp. 305–11 in the Divan edition.
8 See Maurice Bardèche, *Stendhal romancier* (Paris, 1947), ch. 1.
9 In the 'Avant-propos' of the *Comédie humaine*.
10 In the 'Avant-propos' itself, for instance, he suggests that Scott is poor at depicting women and love, a point made by Beyle, though Balzac adds that this was probably because Scott was at a disadvantage in being brought up in a Protestant country. In *Illusions perdues*, the dedicated D'Arthez tells the young Lucien Chardon what is wrong with his own Scott-like historical novel in terms strongly reminiscent of Beyle's (See book 2, *Un premier ami*).
11 H. James, *Literary essays and reviews* (New York, 1957), p. 152. My quotation and the slightly paraphrased translation of the letter of August 1804 are taken from James's review.
12 In an unsigned article in *The Westminster Review*, 65 (April 1856) attributed to George Eliot by G. S. Haight. See *The Letters of George Eliot* (London, 1955), vol. 7 (appendix).
13 M. Bardèche, See *Stendhal romancier* (Paris, 1947), p. 138.
14 Cf. Beyle's comment in the margin of his copy of *Le rouge et le noir* that 'the society of Mme de Sévigné approved the absurdities uttered by La Bruyère on religion and government but what an admirable judge of a scene like that between Mme de Rênal and her husband'. (*Mélanges de littérature*, vol. 3, p. 418.
15 I disagree with Middleton Murry that 'Stendhal was even less a creator of heroes than a hero worshipper.' (See the essay on Stendhal in *Countries of the Mind*) but the argument which leads him to this conclusion is one of the most intelligent I know about his writings as a whole, for all its brevity.
16 *Promenades dans Rome* (23.11.1828), vol. 3, pp. 200–2 in the Divan edition.
17 'Dark brown hair brushed low left only a tiny brow visible and in moments of anger, an air of vindictiveness...' (book 1, ch. 4).

18 The chronology of events takes no account, of course, of the Revolution of July 1830. The novel was almost entirely completed when Charles X was forced into exile. Henri Martineau in the Garnier edition of the novel provides a chronology of events according to which the action of the novel, going by Beyle's few precise indications of time, can be seen as covering a period from September 1826 to July 1831.
19 Julien is in many ways reliving Beyle's own torments with the wife of his cousin, Count Pierre Daru. See his diary for 31 May and 3 June 1811.
20 Beyle disapproved of the 'mystical' Cartesian system of the contemporary philosopher Victor Cousin but respected the man. It is possible that his thoughts on obligation which transcend the conscious self owe something to the following idea enunciated in Cousin's *Cours d'histoire de la philosophie au 18e siècle*. See, for instance, this account of the authority of Reason: 'Since Reason commands and governs me, it is superior to me and if it is superior to me, it is not me... Perhaps I shall never succeed in penetrating its essence but what I feel very well is that whenever it appears to me, I have an intuition of the immutable, the necessary and the absolute...' (pp. 30–1). A very interesting account of the philosophical significance of Julien's sense of 'duty' is offered by Colin Smith, 'Aspects of Destutt de Tracy's Linguistic Analysis as Adapted by Stendhal' in *The Modern Language Review*, vol. lı, no. 4, 1956. Professor Smith points out how Beyle, in the penultimate chapter of the novel 'moves away from the position of his ideagological mentors'.
21 Bardèche, *Stendhal romancier*, p. 264.
22 See George Sand's letter to Flaubert of 19 December 1875: 'One is a man before anything else. One wishes to find the man behind every story and every deed. That's what's wrong with *L'éducation sentimentale*, which I've spent so long thinking about...wondering why a work so solid and so well constructed should have given rise to so much bad feeling. What's wrong is the absence of *action* on the part of the characters directed towards each other or themselves. They undergo various acts and never make them their own...'
23 In his 1902 essay on Flaubert in *Notes on Novelists*, Henry James calls Frédéric 'too poor for his part, too scant for his charge...' Flaubert 'apparently never suspects either our wonder or our protest – "Why, why *him*?"' I cannot myself believe that Flaubert had not foreseen these objections. I have indicated the way in which I think they might be answered in my essay on 'Flaubert. T. S. Eliot and Ezra Pound' in *The Cambridge Quarterly*, vol. 2, no. 3, 1966.
24 In the article on *Le rouge et le noir* reprinted as an appendix to the Garnier edition.
25 *Racine et Shakspeare*, p. 308. The term is also used a great deal in Beyle's marginal notes to *Lucien Leuwen*.
26 The Penguin translator's 'people of the other sort' is a surely inaccurate guess at what Beyle means here by 'l'idée d'un public et *des autres*'. On page 159, I offer a suggestion as to how one should understand the italicised words.
27 Notably by Louis Aragon in *La lumière de Stendhal* (Paris, 1954) and Fernand Rude in *Stendhal et la pensée sociale de son temps* (Paris, 1966). Rude, it should be said in fairness, quotes several passages from *Mémoires d'un touriste* which go against his argument that ideologically Beyle was somewhere 'between liberalism and socialism'. Aragon is less scrupulous.

28 In an article in *The New Monthly Magazine* for May 1826 (*Courrier anglais*, vol. 3, p. 57), Beyle compares the young aristocrats of the 1820s who cannot openly subscribe to the liberal and Utilitarian views which their fellow-students profess as a matter of course without seeming in absurd position. Here and in *Armance*, he points out the positive disadvantages, from the point of view of social ease, of belonging to the *noblesse d'épée*.
29 Cf. pp. 63–6 above.
30 See particularly the *Discours préliminaire* and ch. 8 of *La Logique* (*Eléments d'idéologie*) in which Tracy argues against particular perceptions (or 'ideas') being replaced in discourse by conventional signs, insists that general ideas depend upon and are incorporated in particular perceptions and rejects Aristotelian logic, reducing all syllogisms to sorites. Quoting Maine de Biran, he insists that in all our thinking and speech, we should '*bear perpetually the double burden of the sign and the idea*'.
31 See G. Blin, *Stendhal et les problèmes de la personalité* (Paris, 1858), vol. 1, pp. 191–205. See also J.-P. Sartre, *L'être et le néant* (Paris, 1943), part 3, ch. 1, iv.
32 See the remarks on the style of Chateaubriand in the letter to Balzac of 16.10.1840 and *The New Monthly Magazine* for September 1826 quoted on p. 65–6, above.
33 See the remarks quoted on pp. 66–7, above.
34 In the letter to Balzac referred to on p. 2.
35 In *Molière, Shakspeare, la comédie et le rire*, pp. 197–8.
36 *Mélanges de littérature*, vol. 3, p. 87.
37 The Marquis de la Mole is the only one of the assembled noblemen plotting counter-revolution in the episode of 'The secret note' (book 2, ch. 22) to argue in favour of firmness and independence with regard to possible allies abroad. This gives the episode a relevance which it otherwise seems to lack to the rest of *Le rouge et le noir*.
38 See, for instance, the accounts of the ceremonies at the Vatican in *Promenades dans Rome* (23.4.1829).
39 In M. Imbert, *Les métamorphoses de la liberté* (Paris, 1967), pp. 580–2.

NOTES TO CHAPTER SIX

1 See *Marginalia*, vol. 2, pp. 137–45 and *Mélanges de littérature*, vol. 1, p. 143, both in the Divan edition.
2 Aristotle, *Poetics*, Everyman's Library edition, p. 17.
3 In Alain, *Stendhal* (Paris, 1935), ch. 2.
4 M. Proust, *Contre Sainte-Beuve* (Paris, 1954), p. 198.
5 Cf. pp. 122–3 above.
6 A useful history of the term and interpretation of it is given by del Litto in his introduction to the Cercle du bibliophile edition of *Souvenirs d'égotisme* (Geneva, 1970).
7 Quoted by del Litto in *La vie de Stendhal* (Paris, 1965), p. 196.
8 Foscolo, *Edizione nazionale delle opere di Ugo Foscolo*, vol. 19 (Florence, 1966). See particularly Mathilde's letters to Foscolo of 10.9.1815, 15.3.1816, 10.6.1816, 26.6.1816 and 10.8.1816.
9 A more extreme instance of the kind of intensely painful but, in its way,

privileged insight I have in mind is the motherless Gérard de Nerval's idealisation of the woman who is identified in his novels with Sylvie and Aurélia.

10 See V. Brombert, *Stendhal et la voie oblique*, pp. 118–25.
11 All my page references are to the Pléiade edition, volume 1, 1952 of the *Romans et nouvelles*; p. 1,398.
12 *Ibid.*, p. 1,401.
13 *Ibid.*, p. 1,397.
14 See Brombert's excellent comments on this in *Fiction and the Themes of Freedom* (New York, 1969), p. 184.
15 See Lavisse, *Histoire de la France contemporaine*, vol. 5, pp. 77–8.
16 In 'Sir Walter Scott et *La Princesse de Clèves*' quoted on p. 128.
17 *Romans et nouvelles*, p. 1,400.
18 Cf. pp. 169–70, above.
19 *Romans et nouvelles*, p. 1,397.
20 In M. Wood, *Stendhal* (London, 1971), pp. 115 *et seq.*
21 There is no evidence that Beyle ever read Jane Austen. A minor French novelist whom he admired is Mme de Flahaut-Souza, author of *La comtesse de Fargy*. Another is Mme de Cubière, author of *Marguerite Aymon*. (See *The New Monthly Magazine*, December 1822 and *Courrier anglais*, vol. 1, pp. 44–8.) The realistic social comedy he admired in these two authors suggests that he might have found Jane Austen even more congenial than her French contemporaries.
22 Gauthier is partly a portrait of Louis-Gabriel Gros, who taught Beyle mathematics as a boy and refused to receive payment for his lessons on the days when he would comment on the latest news and preach his Jacobin principles. Gauthier has also something of Armand Carrel, editor of *Le National*, a republican in the tradition of La Fayette rather than a follower of Blanqui, the 'Amis du peuple' and the advocates of proletarian solidarity. This, at least, can be inferred from his idealisation of the United States and from his embarrassment at the activities of the weavers whom Lucien's regiment is sent to put down.
23 Du Poirier has probably a number of traits borrowed from Beyle's friend Maurice Rubichon, who visited Civita Vecchia while the novel was being written. Du Poirier's views on the harmful consequences of abolishing the laws of primogeniture are the same as Rubichon's in his *Du mécanisme de la société*, which Beyle admired and compared with the works of Tracy and Helvétius himself. See F. Rude, *Stendhal et la pensée sociale de son temps*, pp. 209–23.
24 Margaret Tillett has suggested in *Stendhal, the background to the novels* (Oxford, 1971, p. 63) that the colonel is a rueful self-portrait and a confession of how he must have truly seemed to Mathilde Dembowski with his 'failure to understand the welcome accorded him and oblivious of his bulky girth, his common expression and his forty years...' (*Lucien Leuwen*, ch. 14).
25 Beyle had studied Raynouard's history and anthology of the troubadours and in chapter 52 of *De l'amour*, quotes several examples of courtly love. See too the appendix in which he quotes several of the judgments of the twelfth-century 'Courts of love' and finds particular interest in the question, highly relevant to *Lucien Leuwen*, 'Can true love exist between husband and wife?'

26 My own use of the term 'representative' owes a great deal to F. R. Leavis's essay on Conrad's *The Shadow Line* in *Anna Karenina and other Essays* (London, 1967), see particularly pp. 102–3.
27 Cf. pp. 96–8, above.
28 Beyle read, enjoyed and quoted *The Tempest* as an epigraph to ch. 20, book 1 of *Le rouge et le noir*; though he seems always to have preferred *Cymbeline*. Miss Tillett discusses very interestingly the influence of the latter in *Stendhal, The Background to the Novels*, pp. 84–91. Disguise and assumed rôles are, of course, very much part of the comedy here as well.
29 See J.-P. Sartre, *Les temps modernes*, May 1966, p. 1924.
30 In the *Journal des débats*, December 1831. It is to this article that Sartre is specifically referring.
31 *Romans et nouvelles*, p. 1,389.
32 For Mérimée's reaction, see the letter to Beyle of 1 December 1831 on the atrocities allegedly committed by the silk-workers in Lyon.
33 Beyle calls him 'juste-milieu', which is virtually untranslatable, i.e. an upholder of the new régime, which is neither conservative and legitimist nor revolutionary and republican. It is an illusion, a Greek communist has told me, to believe that the 'centre' parties are *ipso facto* the most 'moderate', in the sense of being the least sanguinary, and one can easily agree that, indeed, this does not follow inevitably.
34 There is no evidence that Beyle ever read Hegel and even Niebuhr, whom he admired, 'gets lost', he claims, 'among the Platonic reveries of Kant'. See *New Monthly Magazine*, February 1827.
35 See Jacques Fauvet, *La Quatrième République* (Paris, 1959), pp. 280–2, on 'l'affaire des fuites' which took place under the premiership of M. Pierre Mendès-France.
36 'Notes sur Corneille' quoted on pp. 57–60, above.
37 Cf. pp. 84, 85 and 132 above.
38 V. Brombert, *Fiction and the themes of freedom*, pp. 123–7.
39 Since the term 'human condition' originates in Montaigne, it is worth mentioning in passing that Beyle professed his admiration for Montaigne on a number of occasions and obviously preferred him to Descartes. In *Henry Brulard*, he claims that it was Montaigne, Tracy, Shakespeare and Cabanis whom he principally studied during the important period from 1800 to 1805. Lucien, after his return from Nancy (ch. 39) quotes Montaigne on the need to '*se colleter avec la nécessité*' ('come to grips with necessity'). Montaigne's concern with 'the human condition' was certainly neither foreign nor antipathetic to Beyle.
40 In G. Lukács, *Studies in European Realism* (New York, 1964), pp. 81 and 83.
41 Lukács, for example, believes that Beyle underestimates the 'revolutionary' potentialities of the proletariat and 'did not and could not see the part the proletariat was to play in the creation of a new society, nor the perspectives opened up by socialism and by a new type of democracy...' (*Studies in European Realism*, p. 83). I don't myself get this impression from the account of the attempted suppression of the weavers in ch. 27, where, as one of the lancers points out, they have 'the troops where they want them'. In failing to predict a proletarian *revolution*, furthermore, he was merely failing to predict what has so far never happened.

42 Lukács, *Studies in European realism*, pp. 72–3.
43 Bardèche, for instance, sees *Lucien Leuwen* as the novel of 'contempt' *par excellence* and Martin Turnell in *The Novel in France* puts it in the following terms: 'He [the nineteenth-century artist] was socially and intellectually out of place. The only course was for him to found a new intellectual aristocracy, a minority which lived inside society but which was at odds with every section of it. This explains Stendhal's interest in the "happy few" and Baudelaire's "dandyism". Stendhal's attitude bears a certain resemblance to Baudelaire's but in reality it was much more extreme...' (Peregrine Books, p. 141).
44 Lukács, *Studies in European realism*, pp. 78 and 80.
45 See Paul Arbelet, *La jeunesse de Stendhal*, 2 vols (1909), Arthur Chuquet, *Stendhal-Beyle* (1902) and Henri Martineau, *Le coeur de Stendhal* (1953).
46 See 'Stendhal à la recherche du temps perdu' in *Stendhal Club*, 20, July 1963.
47 Cf. George Blin, *Stendhal et les problèmes de la personnalité*, p. 570. 'One only writes one's confessions by making a confession in the present and hence a confession about the present [sic]. Thus Stendhal, who, while striving to go over once again the legacy of his former impressions, develops willy-nilly the self-portrait of the ageing consul...' Michael Wood says something similar in *Stendhal*, p. 143: 'The force of an autobiography lies not in its subjective rendering of objective occasions but in its capacity to erase just that distinction to make us attend to it as history, although we know much of it may be invented...' Both M. Blin and Mr Wood generalise about our ability to tell the truth about the past and I am personally relieved that I am unlikely ever to find myself being tried by a jury of which they are members for a crime of which I happen to remember I am innocent.
48 'Su Chateaubriand e Stendhal memorialisti' in *Annali della Scuola Normale Superiore di Pisa*, 1965.
49 Rousseau, *Oeuvres complètes* (Bibliothèque de la Pléiade, 1959), vol. 1, p. 5.
50 Compare with Proust's account of his struggle and his vision, when he has succeeded in locating the source of his memory, of 'all the flowers in our garden and in the park of M. Swann...all Combray and its surroundings', etc. with Edward Thomas's evocation of a very similar experience in his poem *Old Man*. By contrast with Proust's more famous reliving of the past, Thomas's poem has the kind of authenticity I find in *La vie de Henry Brulard*.
51 I think Etiemble is right to point out that these are not, and probably could not be, thoughts consistent with Proust's keen interest, as shown elsewhere, in the kind of 'realism' he condemns in these pages. 'Imbued, as he is, with Ruskin, seeped in the fashionable confusions of his time (encouraged by Bergsonism) between the beautiful and the sacred, the artist and the priest, between inspiration and the "moments" prized by the current mystique, between the eternity of the Platonic idea and the perenniality attributed to the work of art, it is true that Proust, appalled by the flow of time and change, will attempt to build up in his last volume the puerile hypothesis – the hypothesis, anyway – of *time* allegedly *found once more*...' (*Hygiène des lettres*, vol. 5, p. 144). One shouldn't, as Etiemble goes on to say, take any of these thoughts too literally.
52 *Eléments d'idéologie. La logique*, ch. 4.
53 Cf. p. 42, above.

54 Cf. p. 23, above.

NOTES TO CHAPTER SEVEN

1 In *Mélanges de politique et d'histoire*, vol. 1 (Paris, Le Divan, 1933).
2 For an exact account of Beyle's use of his original sources in *La chartreuse* and *Les chroniques italiennes*, see Charles Dédéyan, *Stendhal et les chroniques italiennes* (Paris, 1956).
3 Beyle seems to have been more interested in Manzoni as a poet than as a novelist and speaks on one occasion of *I promessi sposi* being over-praised, though it 'depicts extremely well the existence of the *bravi* under the Spanish government...' (*Mélanges de littérature*, vol. 3, p. 391.)
4 Quoted by Mario Praz in *The Romantic Agony* (London, 1960), p. 140.
5 See Beyle's marginal notes quoted by Henri Martineau in his edition of *La chartreuse* (Paris, Garnier, 1961), p. 528.
6 See Martineau's introduction to the Garnier edition of *La chartreuse*, p. xiii.
7 See *Morality and the Novel* in *Phoenix*.
8 See the first draft of Beyle's letter to Balzac of 16.10.1840 and the note in the manuscripts of *Lamiel* dated 25.5.1840: 'I was thinking of the death of Sandrino: that alone made me undertake the novel...'
9 For a detailed account of the religious background to *La chartreuse de Parme*, see H.-F. Imbert's *Stendhal et la tentation janséniste* (Geneva, 1970), book 3, ch. 2 and book 4 and the same author's *Les metamorphoses de la liberté* (Paris, 1967).
10 Henri Martineau includes the article in his collection of Beyle's writings in the English reviews, *Le Courrier Anglais*, 5 volumes (Paris, Le Divan, 1935). I also plead guilty to the charge of attributing it without question to Beyle in my edition of the *Selected Journalism* of Stendhal (London, 1959).
11 See too Foscolo's own letter to Fortunato Prandi of 7 May 1826.
12 L. F. Benedetto (in *La Parma di Stendhal* (Florence, 1950), part 2, ch. 3) sees the principal model for Ernest Ranuce in Francesco IV of Modena. (There was, of course, no autonomous principality of Parma in the nineteenth century.) Francesco IV saw himself as a possible ruler of an united Italy and for this reason encouraged liberalism of the nationalistic kind. In *La chartreuse de Parme*, Ernest Ranuce and his son play off the 'liberals' of Parma against the ostensibly more conservative Mosca.
13 Maurice Bardèche is the most persuasive of those who have presented this view. He describes Parma as Lilliput and Gina, Mosca and Fabrice as giants. See chs. 10 and 11 of his *Stendhal romancier*.
14 See *Racine et Shakspeare* (Paris, Editions du Divan 1928), p. 308.
15 This is not the only occasion which Beyle leaves the reader himself in sudden ignorance as to what is happening, though he will subsequently enlighten him at times, as in the course of the joke at the expense both of Mosca and the French reader in ch. 6: '...what will seem utterly improbable on this side of the Alps is that the Count would have given his resignation happily; *this is at least what he succeeded in making the woman he loved believe*...' (my italics).
Dr Giulio Lepschy has an interesting note on the 'illiterate' scribe to whom

the Prince dictates his anonymous letters (ch. 7) in *Strumenti Critici*, 12, 1970, which analyses a similar probably deliberate effect.
16 M. Turnell, *The Novel in France* (London, 1962), p. 216.
17 See one of the footnotes in *Promenades dans Rome* (1.6.1828) in which he talks of the unlikelihood of revolt in Florence: 'They still enjoy in 1829 the wise just government of the minister Fossombroni. What a difference it would make to Italy if this great man were only forty years old.' See too the detailed account of his administration in the letter to the Minister of Foreign Affairs in Paris (6.1.1834) and the letter to Count Salviati of 28.4.1831. We may be reminded of Mosca's objection to liberals like Ferrante Palla – 'They prevent us from enjoying the best of monarchies...' in Beyle's telling Salviati that Fossombroni is one of the 'gentlemen' who 'are profoundly irritated with France, whose *bad example* has disturbed the tranquility in which their old age might have otherwise followed its peaceful course...'
18 Cf. p. 110, above.
19 See Balzac's article on *La chartreuse* in *La revue Parisienne*, September 1840.
20 Notably Gilbert Durand in *Le décor mythique de la Chartreuse de Parme* (Paris, 1961).
21 See B. Croce, *Philosophy, poetry, history* (Oxford, 1966), p. 935.
22 See *Stendhal Club*, no. 5, 1959.
23 *Literary reviews and essays* (ed. Mordell) (New York, 1957), p. 156.
24 *Promenades dans Rome*, 23.11.1828.
25 Until the appearance of Professor del Litto's edition of *Lamiel* (Geneva, 1971), all editions of the novel were based on those of Casimir Stryienski (Paris, 1889) and Henri Martineau (Paris, 1928). Both Stryienski and Martineau took Beyle's first version of the novel written between October and December 1839 and, keeping only the story of Lamiel's adventures with the Duc de Myossens and the Comte d'Aubigné, inserted Beyle's second draft of the novel at the beginning. Neither offers any indication or explanation of this surgical operation.
26 Compare in the Cercle du Bibliophile edition, pp. 61–3 and pp. 305–8.
27 In his *Essai sur les sources de Lamiel* (Lyon, 1942).
28 Pp. 79–80 in the Cercle du Bibliophile edition.
29 When Josépha, one of the courtesans in *La cousine Bette*, addresses the Baron Hulot as 'mon bonhomme', Balzac tells us that this word 'addressed to a man placed so high in the administration of the state, admirably typifies the audacity with which these creatures bring down to their own level the most illustrious existences...' (ch. 19). This too, of course, can be read as a process of thought and discovery, though scarcely 'swift' and Balzac's capacity for wonder, whether real or simulated, is clearly very different from Beyle's.
30 See the account of the plight of young noblemen who feel the victims of this kind of contradiction in *The New Monthly Magazine* for May 1826 (*Courrier anglais*, vol. 3, p. 57).

NOTES TO CHAPTER EIGHT

1 Quoted by E. J. Simmons in *Leo Tolstoy* (London, 1949), p. 417, and by F. A. Ivanova *et al.* in *L. N. Tolstoy on Literature* (Moscow, 1955), p. 172.

2 See T. S. Lindstrom, *Tolstoï en France* (Paris, 1952), pp. 107–10.
3 See the *Correspondance* of Gide and Bennett, edited by L. F. Brugmans (Geneva, 1964), 28.5.1922.
4 In *Le hussard sur le toit*, the hero, Angélo asks himself at one point (ch. 2): 'What kind of figure will I cut on the battlefield? I will have the courage to charge, but would I have the courage of the gravedigger? I'll have not only to kill but know how to look at the corpses without getting upset. If one can't do that, one is ridiculous. And if one's ridiculous when doing one's job, in what else can one hope to be elegant?' This sounds like one of Julien's, Fabrice's or Lucien's inner monologues, but the word 'elegant' is betraying. Angélo's behaviour during a cholera epidemic is shown as unquestionably commendable but in their moments of serious self-interrogation, Beyle's heroes are usually less fatuous.
5 In his *Journal* (11.12.1942), Gide notes with surprise that the last chapters of *Le rouge et le noir* have a haunting quality and a depth he had failed to notice in previous readings.
6 See pp. 150–3, above.
7 See J.-P. Sartre, *L'idiot de la famille* (Paris, 1971), vol. 1, pp. 37–8 and 471–512.
8 Valéry, for instance, in a letter to Gide (5.7.1897) argues that Beyle's 'psychological theory', though poor from the point of view of 'analysis', 'gave a clear view of things and was therefore good for literary expression'. The correspondence of Gide and Valéry of this period when both were in their twenties and discovering Beyle has a freshness and pointedness lacking in their later published deliberations on his work. See, for instance, the memorable letter by Valéry to Gide of 19.4.1897, in which he claims that Beyle is the only writer he can bear to read on the subject of love.
9 *Promenades dans Rome* (17.3.1828).
10 Quoted by W. D. Williams in *Nietzsche and the French* (Oxford, 1952), p. 65. Dr Williams' book is by far the most useful guide I know to Nietzsche's reading both of Helvétius and Beyle.
11 Nietzsche, *Beyond Good and Evil*, IV, 228.
12 *Loc. cit.*
13 See pp. 48–51, above.
14 *La vie de Henry Brulard*, ch. 30.
15 See p. 152, above.

Chronological Table

Life	Work	Date of first publication of Beyle's principal writings
1783 Henri Beyle born in Grenoble, 23 January.		
1786 Birth of Pauline Beyle.		
1790 Death of Beyle's mother, 23 November.		
1796 The Ecole Centrale opens in Grenoble on 21 November. Beyle becomes a pupil on the first day.		
1799 Receives first prize in mathematics and leaves for Paris on 30 October to take the entrance examination for the Ecole Polytechnique.		
1800–2 Works in the offices of the Ministry of War before being commissioned as a second-lieutenant of dragoons. Joins his regiment and sees active service in Italy.		
1802–6 Lives on an allowance from his father, chiefly in Paris. Studies philosophy,	Begins his two comedies, *Les deux hommes* and *Lettellier* and writes his	

Life	Work	Date of first publication of Beyle's principal writings
literature, acting and English. The actress Mélanie Guilbert becomes his mistress.	*Pensées* and *Filosofia Nuova*.	
1806 After an unsuccessful business venture in Marseilles, enters the Ministry of War and leaves for service in Germany.		
1806–14 Receives rapid promotion in the Imperial service, appointed administrator of the Imperial domains in the region of Brunswick, then Inspector of the property and buildings of the Crown. Attached to the Commissariat during the Moscow campaign. Takes part in the retreat from Moscow and the organisation of the defences of Grenoble. Unsuccessfully seeks employment after the abdication of Napoleon under the new régime.	Begins the *Histoire de la peinture en Italie*, plans a treatise on 'Population, wealth and happiness' and, together with Louis Crozet, writes the notes 'On style' and the commentaries on Corneille and Shakespeare referred to in ch. 3.	*Lettres écrites de Méry-sur-Seine sur la Constitution* in the *Journal de l'imprimerie et de la librairie*, May 1814.
1814–21 Lives unemployed on his pension in Milan. Love affairs with Angela Pietragura, whom he had first met fourteen years before and with Mathilde Dembowski. Meets regularly Monti, Pellico and the contributors to *Il conciliatore*; also Byron during the latter's visit to Milan in 1816. His father dies, financially ruined, in 1819.	Begins a life of Napoleon, writes the first of his travel books and finishes *L'histoire de la peinture en Italie*. Becomes an enthusiastic reader of *The Edinburgh Review*, of Byron and contemporary Italian poetry. Takes sides in the issue of whether the language of literature in Italy should continue to be the Italian of Florence.	*Lettres écrites de Vienne en Autriche, sur le célèbre compositeur, Jh. Haydn, suivies d'une vie de Mozart, et de Considérations sur Metastasio*...Par Louis-Alexandre-César Bombet (1814). *Histoire de la peinture en Italie*. Par M.B.A.A. (1817). *Rome, Naples et Florence en 1817*. Par M. de Stendhal, officier de cavalerie (1817).
1821–30 Obliged to leave Milan, Beyle settles in Paris, travelling twice to Italy and twice to England. On the second of these trips,	Financial difficulties, after his pension is reduced, compel Beyle to live by his pen. He becomes a regular contributor to the	*De l'amour*, par l'auteur de *l'Histoire de la peinture en Italie*...(1822).

Life	Work	Date of first publication of Beyle's principal writings
he accompanies his friend, the barrister Sutton Sharpe on the northern circuit and sees Birmingham, Manchester and the Lake District. Love affairs with La comtesse Curial and Mme Alberthe de Rubempré. Friendship with Prosper Mérimée and meetings with Destutt de Tracy, Delacroix, Lamartine and Cuvier.	*Paris Monthly Review*, *The London Magazine* and the *New Monthly Review* and publishes most of what he writes. He becomes an art and music critic for the *Journal de Paris*.	*Racine et Shakspeare*. Par M. de Stendhal (1823). *La vie de Rossini*. Par M. de Stendhal (1823). *Racine et Shakspeare*, no. II. Par M. de Stendhal (1825). *D'un nouveau complot contre les industriels*. Par M. de Stendhal (1825). *Armance, ou quelques scènes d'un salon de Paris en 1827* (1827). *Promenades dans Rome*. Par M. de Stendhal (1829). *Vanina Vanini* published in *La Revue de Paris*, December 1829.
1830–6 Appointed consul in Trieste and then, having been declared *persona non grata* by the Austrian government, consul in Civita Vecchia. In 1830 seeks the hand of Giulia Rinieri in marriage, who in 1833 marries a cousin. In 1835 receives the cross of the Legion of Honour for his services to literature.	During this period, Beyle, isolated for long periods in Civita Vecchia, wrote and left unfinished *Souvenirs d'égotisme*, *Lucien Leuwen* and *La vie de Henry Brulard*.	*Le coffre et le revenant* and *Le philtre* published in *La Revue de Paris*, May and June 1830 and 'Sir Walter Scott et *La Princesse de Clèves*' in *Le National*, February 1830. *Le rouge et le noir, chronique du XIXe siècle*. Par M. de Stendhal (1831).
1836–9 Leave of absence from Civita Vecchia during which he travels through France, northern Spain and Switzerland and settles in Paris. In 1838, he is reunited with Giulia Rinieri.	A period of intense activity. Much of what he wrote during his leave of absence he published immediately. He also, however, began and left unfinished the *Mémoires sur Napoléon* and *Le rose et le vert*.	*Vittoria Accoramboni* and *Les Cenci* published in *La Revue des Deux-Mondes*, March and July, 1837. *Mémoires d'un touriste*. Par l'auteur de *Rouge et Noir* (1838). *La Duchesse de Palliano* published in *La Revue des Deux-Mondes*, August 1838 under the pseudonym F. de Lagevenais.

Life	Work	Date of first publication of Beyle's principal writings
1839–42 Returns to Civita Vecchia in August 1839. Struck down by a fit of apoplexy in March 1841. Returns to Paris, November 1841. Dies after a second stroke on 23 March 1842.	Works on *Lamiel, Suora Scolastica, Trop de faveur tue* and a revised version of *La chartreuse de Parme*.	*L'Abbesse de Castro* published in *La Revue des Deux-Mondes*, February and March, 1839. *La chartreuse de Parme*. Par l'auteur de *Rouge et Noir* 1839). Romans et nouvelles par de Stendhal (Henry Beyle) précédés d'une Notice sur de Stendhal par M. R. Colomb (1854). (This includes *Mina de Vanghel* and *Armance*.) De Stendhal (Henry Beyle) Nouvelles inédites (1855). (This includes the first published version of *Lucien Leuwen*). De Stendhal (Henry Beyle) – Correspondance inédite précédée d'une introduction par Prosper Mérimée de l'Académie Française (1855). *Vie de Napoléon* – Fragments – De Stendhal (Henry Beyle) (1876). Oeuvre posthume. – Journal de Stendhal (Henri Beyle) 1801–14 publié par Casimir Stryienski et François de Nion (1888). Stendhal (Henri Beyle) – *Lamiel*. Roman inédit publié par Casimir Stryienski (1889). Stendhal (Henri Beyle) – *Vie de Henry Brulard*. Autobiographie publiée par Casimir Stryienski (1890). Stendhal (Henri Beyle) – *Souvenirs d'égotisme*. Autobiographie et lettres inédites publiés par Casimir Stryienski (1892).

Index

Abelard, P., 126
Abravanel, E., xi, 215
Adams, R.
   Stendhal, notes on a novelist, 40–1, 47
Alain (Emile Chartier)
   Stendhal, 167
Alfieri, V., 20, 34, **54–61**, 63, **64**, 65, 66, 72, 104, 110, 112, 157, 274n.
   Cleopatra, 64
   Del Principe e delle lettere, 108
   Oreste, 55, 56, 66
   Vita, La, **54–5**, **64**, 65, 66
Amyot, J., 20
Antony, Mark, 40
Aragon, L.
   La lumière de Stendhal, 280n.
Arbelet, P.
   La jeunesse de Stendhal, 215, 271n.
Ariosto, L.
   L'Orlando furioso, 53, 66, 272n.
Aristophanes, 77
Aristotle, 36, 166, 281n.
   The Poetics, 166
d'Aubernon, Mme, 115
Austen, Jane, 142, 178, 187–8, 282n.
   Emma, 178, 187–8
   Mansfield Park, 187–8
   Northanger Abbey, 142
   Sense and Sensibility, 178

Balzac, H. de, 2, 14, 16, 43, 76, 115, **127–8**, 129, 130, 131, 154, 175–6, 177, 195, **197–8**, **211–12**, 225, 226, 233, 245, 248, 250, 253, 256, 258, 265, 276n., 277n., 279n., 286n.
   Avant-propos à la Comédie Humaine, **128**, 129
   La cousine Bette, 286n.
   Le curé de Tours, 175, 279n.
   Eugénie Grandet, 131
   Les illusions perdues, 175, 248, 277n.
   Le lys dans la vallée, 279n.
   La maison Nucingen, 195, 197–8, 211–12
   Le médecin de campagne, 177
   Le père Goriot, 131, 195, 197–8, 212
Bandello, M., 124
Bardèche, M.
   Stendhal romancier, **92–4**, 133, 145, **175–9**, 181, 211, 252, 283n., 284n., 285n.
Bassano, Il (Jacopo da Ponte), 91
Baudelaire, C., 262, 284n.
Bazard, A., 208
Beaumarchais (P. A. Caron de)
   Le mariage de Figaro, 96–7
Beauvoir, S. de
   Le deuxième sexe, 47
Beccaria, C., 110
Beckett, S., 274
Beethoven, L. van, 95
Belgiojoso, Princess, 223
Benedetto, L. F.
   La Parma di Stendhal, 285
Bennett, A., 225, 260
   Anna of the Five Towns, 225
Bentham, J., 35, 88, 89, 192, 263–5, 270n., 275n.
   A treatise of civil and penal legislation, 270n.
Bentivoglio, family of, 109
Béranger, P., 115
Bergson, H., 87, 284n.
   Le rire, 87
Berlioz, H., 95, 134, 231, 276
   La damnation de Faust, 231

INDEX

Berlioz, H. (*cont.*)
  Mémoires, 95, 276n.
  Soirées de l'orchestre, 276n.
  Symphonie fantastique, 134
Bernard, Samuel, 51
Berthet, A., 62, 138, 150, 171, 222
Besse, G., 269n.
Beyle, Chérubin, 7, 9, **18–19**, 33, 39, 169, **213–15**, 289
Beyle, Henri, *passim*
  L'Abbesse de Castro, 109–10, **222–4**, 254, 257, 291
  Armance, 4, 124, **131–3**, 158, 189, 201, 221, 256, 261–2, 281n., 290, 291
  articles in the English reviews, 13, 38–9, 41, 65–6, 79, **115–16**, 121, 123–4, 269n., 281n., 282n., 283n., 285n., 286n., 289
  Les Cenci, 221, 290
  La chartreuse de Parme, 2, 3, 43, 44, 91, 110, 111, 128, 165, 180, 191, 222, **223–54**, 257, 258, **260**, 262, 270n., 285n., 291
  Chroniques italiennes, 130, 165, **220–4**, 251, 257–8, 283n., 290, 291
  Le coffre et le revenant, 165, 290
  '*La comédie est impossible*', **74–9**, 98, 126
  correspondence, 2, **23–5**, 33, 42, 43, 44, 55, 73, 129, 154, 218, 226, 233, 257, 269n., 291
  De l'amour, 28–30, **44–8**, 121, 129, 171, 221, 282n., 289
  Les deux hommes, 54, 288
  La duchesse de Palliano, 221, 290
  '*D'un nouveau complot contre les industriels*', xi, 44, **48–51**, 61, 290
  '*Du style*', 28, 32, **64–5**, 289
  Ernestine, **129–30**
  '*La France en 1821*', 221
  Histoire de la peinture en Italie, 33, **89–94**, 95, **108–9**, 112, 122, 269n., 289
  Journal, **42**, 55, 56, 60–1, 66–7, 102, 103, 158, 218n., 291
  Le juif, 165
  Lamiel, 180, **254–8**, 262, 286n., 291
  Letellier, 4, 288
  Lettres écrites de Méry-sur-Seine, 102, 289
  Lucien Leuwen, 3, 117, 127, 134, 167, 168, **170–212**, 213, 221, 252, 256, 264, 277n., 290, 291
  Mémoires d'un touriste, 107, 114, **116–21**, 172, 220, 290
  Mémoires sur Napoléon, 13, **101**, **106**, **107**, 220, 290
  Mina de Wanghel, 130, **220**, 255, 291
  '*Notes sur Corneille*', **57–61**, 158, 201, 289
  Pensées, 28, 54, 289
  Le philtre, 165, 290
  Promenades dans Rome, **111–14**, 121, **138–9**, 286n., 290
  Racine et Shakspeare, xi, 27, 52, **73–4**, **76–7**, 79, 87, 92, 96, 146, 241, 290
  Rome, Naples et Florence en 1817, **56–7**, **59–60**, 75, 110, 224, 270n., 275n., 277n., 289
  Le rose et le vert, **220–1**, 255, 256, 290
  Le rouge et le noir, 3, 22, 23, 24, 37, **62–3**, **82–6**, 93–4, 112, 116, 118, 125, **126–64**, 165, 172, **177–8**, **183–4**, 186, 189, 201, 218, 230, 252, 255, 259, 262, 290
  Salon de 1827, 92
  '*Si la comédie est utile*', 44, **86–7**
  '*Sir Walter Scott et la Princesse de Clèves*', **127–8**, 142, 290
  Souvenirs d'égotisme, 80, **166–70**, 279n., 290, 291
  Suora Scolastica, **257–8**, 291
  Trop de faveur tue, 257, 291
  Une position sociale, **208–9**, 278n.
  Vanina Vanini, 130, 221, 290
  La vie de Henry Brulard, 2, 5, 7, **18–19**, 26, **31**, 40, 55, 73, **80**, 122, 166, **169**, **213–19**, 283n., 290, 291
  Vies de Haydn, Mozart et Metastasio, 22, **94–8**, 102, 124, 289
  La vie de Napoléon, **104**, **105–6**, 289, 291
  La vie de Rossini, 62, 95, 97–8, 110
  Vittoria Accoramboni, 124, 221, 290
  Voyage dans le midi de la France, 118, 121
Beyle, Henriette (mother of Henri Beyle), 18, 169, 213, 288
Beyle, Pauline, 20, **23–4**, 38, 39, 55, 121, 129, 218, **268n.**, 269n., 288
Beylisme, **26–51**, 88, 112, 163, 254
Bezenval, P. S., 92
Bibas, H., **150–4**, 262
Blake, W., 37–8, 66, 168, 273n.
Blanqui, A., 116, 282n.

INDEX

Blin, G., 63–6, **154**, 284n.
  Stendhal et les problèmes de la personnalité, **154**, 284n.
  Stendhal et les problèmes du roman, 63–6
Blum, L., 22–3, 25, 77, 151, 210
  Stendhal et le Beylisme, **22–3**, 25, 77, 151
Boileau (Nicolas Despréaux), 3
Bologna, 56, 109
Bonaparte, N., *see* 'Napoleon'
Boswell, J., 3
Boucher, F., 92
Bouhours, Le père, 64
Bourget, P. 23, **83–4**
  Essais de psychologie contemporaine, **83–4**
Brême, L. de, 103, 277n.
Brombert, V., 170, **206**, 209, 282
  Fiction and the themes of freedom, **206**, 282n.
  Stendhal et la voie oblique, 170, 209
Brosses, Président de
  Lettres sur l'Italie, 74
Brunswick, Duke of, 9, 105
Brutus, Marcus Junius, 55, 61, 62
Buchman, Frank, 13
Bunyan, J., 152
Burckhardt, J.
  Civilisation of the Renaissance in Italy, 112
Bussière, A., **14**
Byron, Lord, 8, 12, 15, 80, 103, **122–3**, **166–7**, 227, 289
  Beppo, 80
  Childe Harold, 15, 80
  Don Juan, 15, 80, **167**, 227

Cabanis, G., 42, 283
Camillus (second founder of Rome), 19
Canova, A., 110
Canuts, Les (silk workers of Lyon), **117–18**, **195–6**, 210
Carbonarismo, 45, 111, 130, 277n.
Carlyle, T., 49
Carné, M.
  Les enfants du paradis, 254
Carnot, L., 118
Carpani, G., 94
Carrel, A., 277n., 282n.
Cassius Longinus, Caius, 62
Catéchisme impérial, Le, 10, 267n.

Catholic Church, 8–12, 74, 110, 121, 140, 234, 236
Cellini, B.
  La vita, 124, 214
Cenci, F., 222
Cervantes, M.
  Don Quixote, 53, 81, 126, 270n.
Charles X, 10, 134, 139, 179, 280
Chartier, P., xi
Chateaubriand, F. R., **10–11**, 24, 33, 65–6, **103–4**, 105, 106, 115, 216, 269n., 274n.
  Le dernier des Abencérages, 65–6
  Le génie du christianisme, **10–11**, 33, 269n.
  Mémoires d'outre-tombe, **103–4**, 105, 216
Chuquet, A.
  Stendhal-Beyle, 215
Ciachi, Mgr, 111
Cicero, 140
Cimarosa, D., 26, 31, 95, 96–8, 187, 215, 276n.
  I nemici generosi, 97
Cincinnatus, 19
Civil constitution of the Clergy, 8
Clément, J.-M.
  Lettres à M. de Voltaire, **70–1**
Code Civil, Le, 106, 154, 236
Codrus (last king of Athens), 51
Coe, R. N., 95, 276n.
Collingwood, R. G.
  The Principles of Art, 75, 274n.
Colomb, R., 291
Comte, A., 49
Il conciliatore, 289
Concordat, 11, 21, 105
Condillac, E., 21, 34, 69, 166, 263
Condorcet, A., 20
Congress of Vienna, 232
Conrad, J., 44, 194, 283n.
  Nostromo, 44, 194
Consalvi, E., 111, 114
Constant, B., 43, 115, 127, 270n.
  Adolphe, 127
  De la religion, 43
  Journal, 270n.
Cordiè, C.
  Ricerche stendhaliane, 108, 114
Corneille, P., 20, 27, **54–61**, 63, 64, 67, 69, 112, 157, 158, 201, 289
  Cinna, **57–62**, 158, 201
  Horace, 67

INDEX

Correggio, A., 33, 91, 94, 96, 110, 112, 223
Courier, P.-L., 78, 115
Cousin, V., 43, 115, 126, 263, 280n.
   Cours d'histoire de la philosophie au XVIIIe siècle, 43, 280n.
   Du vrai, du beau et du bien, 263
Croce, B., 249
Crozet, L., 32, **57–62**, 65, 158, 289
Cubière, Marie de
   Marguerite Aymon, 282
Curial, Clémentine, 4, 290
Cuvier, G., 122, 290

Daily Worker, 13
Dante
   Divine Comedy, 55, 64, 90, 94, 107, 126
Danton, G., 148
Daru, P., 280n.
Daru, Comtesse P., 280n.
David, L., 20, 92, 275n.
Dédéyan, C.
   Stendhal et les chroniques italiennes, 285n.
Delacroix, E., 90, 92, 275n., 290
   Massacre of Chios, 275n.
Delécluze, E., 277n.
del Litto, V., xi, 1, **122**, 268n., 269n., 272n., 273n., 276n., 281n., **286n**.
   La vie de Stendhal, 281n.
   La vie intellectuelle de Stendhal, **121–2**, 268n., 269n., 272n., 273n., 276n.
Dembowski, Matilde, 45, 80, 130, **168–70**, **188–9**, 213, 235, 281n., 282n., 289
Desaix, General L., 9
Descartes, R., 32, 36, 269n., 280n., 283n.
   Discours de la méthode, 32, 269n.
Destutt de Tracy, A., **20–1**, 28, 40, 42, 46, 66, **69–70**, 71, **72**, 89, 122, 124, **152**, 166, 168, 218, 263, 265–6, 270–1n., 280n., 281n., 282n., 283n., 290
   Commentaire de L'Esprit des lois, 28
   Eléments d'idéologie, **20–1**, 66, **69–70**, 72
   La grammaire, **69–70**, 72
   La logique, **152**, 281
   Traité de la volonté, **152**, 265–6
Dickens, C., 126, 168

Diderot, D., 10, **119**, 120
   Encyclopédie, 119
   Salons, 119
Don Carlos of Naples (son of Philip V of Spain), 257
Dryden, J.
   All for love or the world well lost, 226
Dubois-Fontenelle, J., 21
Ducis, J. F., 55, 157
Dumouriez, C.-F., 118
Dupin, C., 48, 271n.
Dupont, A., 224–5, 227
Durand, G.
   Le décor mythique de la Chartreuse de Parme, 286
Durkheim, E.
   L'évolution pédagogique en France, 268n.

Eckermann, J. P.
   Conversations with Goethe, 3
Ecoles centrales, 5, **20–1**, 288
Edinburgh Review, 56, 272n., 289
Eliot, George, 47, 129
Eliot, T. S.
   'Tradition and the individual talent', **6–7**, 52, 156
Encyclopédie, 11, 119
Enfantin, P., 208
Epictetus, 93
Epicurus, 264
Etiemble, R.
   Hygiène des lettres, 284n.
Eugène de Savoie, Prince, 39
Eugénie de Montijo (Empress Eugénie), 277n.

Faenza, 109
Faguet, E., 151
Farnese, A., 171
Faubourg Saint-Germain, 13, 74
Faure, F., 33, 40, 116, 278n.
Faure, J.-F., 278n.
Fauvet, J.
   La Quatrième République, 283n.
Fénelon, F., 32
Fielding, H., 15, 126, 165
   Tom Jones, 15
Firbank, R., 228
Flahaut-Souza, Mme de, 126–7, 282n.
   La comtesse de Fargy, 282n.
Flaubert, A.-C., 117, 263

INDEX

Flaubert, G., 5, 17, **81–2**, 117, 121, 126, 135, **145–6**, 162, 192, 195, **197–8**, **211**, 225, 262, 263, 280n.
  Bouvard et Pécuchet, **81–2**
  L'éducation sentimentale, 135, **145–6**, 192, 195, 197–8, **211**, 280n.
  Madame Bovary, 17, 162
Florence, 55, 56, 64, 65, 109, 286
Florian, J.-P., 4
Foscolo, U., 45, 169, **235–7**, 281, 285n.
  I sepolcri, 237
Fossombroni, V., 245, 286n.
Fourier, C., 50, 119–20
Fournier, A.
  Le grand Meaulnes, 187
Foy, M.-S., 115
Fragonard, J.-H., 92
Francesco IV of Modena, 285n.
Franklin, B., 42, 270n.
Frederick the Great, 106
French Revolution, **8–9**, 17, 40, 43, 49, 74, 105, 112, 116, 153, 193, 210, 253–4

Gagnon, Elizabeth, 19, 54
Gagnon, H., 81
Gagnon, Séraphie, 18, 19, 39, 216
Gaulthier, Mme J., 73, 171, 184
Gautier, T., 14, 223
Genet, J., 262
Geyl, P.
  Napoleon: for and against, 276n.
Gide, A., 143, **260–2**, 287n.
  Les caves du Vatican, 143, **260–1**
  Corydon, 261
  Les faux monnayeurs, **260–1**
  Journal, 287n.
Gierke, O.
  Natural law and the theory of society, 269n.
Giono, J., 260, 287n.
  Le hussard sur le toit, 287n.
Giorgione (Giorgio da Castelfranco), 110, 223
Giotto, 275n.
Girard, A.
  Le journal intime, 270n.
Gobineau, J.-A. de
  Essai sur l'inégalité des races humaines, 113
Goethe, W., 3, 62, 131, 185, 262, 274n.

Faust, 185
Werther, 62, 131
Gourmont, R. de, 79–86
Grenoble, 1, 6, 9, 18–21, 53, 80, 116, 202, 213–14, 289
Grimm, F.-M.
  Correspondance littéraire, 120
Gros, J.-L., 282n.
Guilbert, Mélanie, 289
Guillemin, H.
  M. de Vigny, homme d'ordre et poète, 267n.

Halévy, E., 35, **49**
  The era of tyrannies, **49**
  The growth of philosophic radicalism, 35
Hartley, D., 67
Haydn, J., 94
Hegel, F., 111, 283
Helvétius, C.-A., 10, **33–44**, 48, 52, 54, **68–9**, 71, 89, 166, 195, 257, 263, 264, 265, 269n., 271n. 282n.
  De l'esprit, **33–44**, 54, **69**
  De l'homme, **33–5**, **68**
Henri IV, 38, 157, 181
Hobbes, T., 37, 71, 83
  On Human Nature, 37, 71
  The Leviathan, 37
Hobhouse, J. C., 103, 166, 276–7n.
  Recollections of a long life, 276–7n.
Hohenlinden, Battle of, 9
Homer, 54
Horace, 140
Howe, I.
  Politics and the novel, 237–42, 247
Hubert, J. D., 249
Hugo, V., 11, 13
Hume, D.
  A treatise of human nature, 41
  History of England, 41
Huxley, A., 225

Idéologues, les, 33, 35, 45, 46, 65, 129, 132
Imbert, H.-I.
  Les métamorphoses de la liberteé, 99, 163, 285n.
  Stendhal et la tentation janséniste, 285n.
Imola, 109
Ingres, D., 92
Ivanova, F. A., 286n.

INDEX

Jacquemont, V., 270n.
James, H., **6**, 118, 119, 129, 220, 236, **251–2**, 280n.
  The awkward age, 236
  A little tour in France, 118, 119
  The portrait of a lady, 220
Jansenism, 229
Jansse, L., **48**, 99, 119, 268n.
Jeffrey, F., **56–7**, 59
Jesus, Society of, 20, 115, 118, 140, 221, 229, 230, 232, 251
Journal de Paris, 96, 290
Journal des débats, 195, 283n.
Johnson, S., 3, 273n.
Julius Caesar, 100
Julius II, Pope, 111

Kant, I., 36, 88, **89–90**, 264, 269n., 283n.
Kenner, H.
  The Stoic Comedians, 274n.
Kerr, A. P., 267n.
Keynes, J. M., 48
Knight, R. Payne
  An analytical enquiry into the principles of taste, **67–8**, 98, 166, 273n.
Kutuzow, General M., 100

La Bruyère, J. de, 274, 279
Lacenaire, P., 254, 257
La Fayette, M.-J., Duc de, 168, 205, 282
La Fayette, Mme M. de
  La Princesse de Clèves, **126–8, 189, 234**
Laffargue, A., 138–9, 254, 277
Laffitte, J., 212
La Fontaine, J., 24, **66, 67**, 70, 71
La Harpe, J. F. de, 273n.
Lamarque, General M., 173
Lamartine, A. de, 4, 11, 24, **166–7**, 290
Lamothe-Langon, Baron de
  M. le Préfet, 79, 134
Lanzi, L.
  Storia pittoresca dell'Italia, 94
Latouche, H. de
  Olivier, 131
Latreille, A., 267n.
Laura de Noves, 45, 170

Lauzun, Duc A. de, 77
Lavisse, E.
  Histoire de la France contemporaine, 282n.
Lawrence, D. H., 106, 126, 127, **225, 226–7, 237, 238–9**, 270n., 272n.
  Studies in classic American literature, 270n.
  Women in Love, **238–9**
Leavis, F. R., 44, 283n.
  Anna Karenina and other essays, 44
  The Great Tradition, **283 n.**
Le Brun, Mme P., 5
Leibnitz, G. W., 36
Leonidas, 93
Lepschy, G. 285–6n.
Le Tourneur, P., 60
Ligne, Prince de, 92
Lindstrom, T. S.
  Tolstoï en France, 276n., 279n., 287n.
Livy, 40, 107
Locke, J., 21, 34, 35, 38, 46, 166
London, 111, 168, 170
London Magazine, 8, 79, 235, 290
Louis-Philippe, King, 7, 16, 118, 172, 182, 192, 199, 204
Louis XIV, 37, 73, 74, 76–7, 242
Louis XVI, 18–19
Louis XVIII, 181
Lukács, G.
  Studies in European realism, **209–12**, 283n.
Luther, M., 27
Lyon, 117–18, 195–6, 198, 210

Macaire, R., 119
Machiavelli, N., 237, 239
Maine de Biran, F., 270n., 281n.
Maistre, J. de, 49
Malthus, T.
  Essay on population, 48
Manfredi, family of, 109
Manzoni, A.
  I promessi sposi, 134, **222–3**, 285n.
Mareste, A. de, 42, 270n.
Marivaux, Pierre de Chamblain de, 73, 75, 130, 184, 221, 274n.
  Le jeu de l'amour et du hasard, 75
  La seconde surprise de l'amour, 75
  La vie de Marianne, 73, 184, 274n.
Marrou, H.
  Connaissance de l'histoire, **99–100**, 124

INDEX

Marseille, 81, 120, 289
Martineau, H., xi, 1, 215, 226, 227, 270n, 271n., 277n., 280n., 285n., 286n.
Marx, K., 43, 121, 149, 198, 210, 270n., 271n.
  The German Ideology, 43
  The Holy Family, 43
Marxism, 149, 198, 210, 270n., 271n.
Masséna, General A., 101
McWatters, K. G., 278n.
Medici, family of, 109
Mélèse, P.
  Le théâtre et le public à Paris sous Louis XIV, 274n.
Mendès-France, P., 199, 283n.
Mérimée, P., **3-4**, 42-3, **90**, 109, 117, 168, 195, 222, 283n., 290, 291
  H.B., **3-4**, 42-3, **90**
Metastasio, P., 94
Metternich, Prince K., 245-6, 249
Michaud, General C., 271n.
Michelangelo, 10, 22, 90, 92, **93-4**, 96, 111, 124, 126, 273n.
Michoud de la Tour, Mme, 62, 150
Milan, 26, 45, 80, 103, 108, 109, 122, 168-9, 170, 214, 224, 228-9, 230, 240, 245, 253, 289
Mill, J., 48
Mill, J. S., **68**, 88, **263-5**
  Autobiography, **68**
  Essay on Bentham, **263-5**
Milton, J., 56
Modena, 285n.
Molé, L.-M., 116
Molière (J. B. Poquelin), 17, 41, 54, 73, 74, 75, 77, **86-8**, 98, 241
  Le bourgeois gentilhomme, 77
  L'école des femmes, **86-7**
  Georges Dandin, **87-8**
  Le misanthrope, 17, 76
  Tartuffe, 187
Le moniteur, 122
Montaigne, M. de, 70, 265, 274n., 283n.
Montesquieu, C. de Secondat, Baron de, 2, 28, **28-9**, 37, 81, 106, 123, 129, 221, 269n., 270n., 278n.
  L'esprit des lois, **28-9**, 123
  Les lettres persanes, 221
Monti, V., 103, 289
Moore, D. L.
  The late Lord Byron, 278n.

Moore, G. E., 88-9, **212-13**, **215**, 219
  Principia Ethica, **88-9**
Morazé, C.
  La France bourgeoise, 11
Moreau, General J.-V., 9, 102
Moscow, 4, 32, 40, 103, 175, 289
Mozart, W. A., 22, 26, 42, **94-8**, 124, 126, 187
  Così fan tutte, 98
  Don Giovanni, 98, 187
  Magic Flute, 95
  Marriage of Figaro, **95-7**, 187
Murat, Caroline, 246
Murat, J., King of Naples, 103
Murry, J. M., 272n., 279n.
  The Problem of Style, 272n.
La muse française, 13
Musset, A. de, **14-15**, 75, **185**
  Confessions d'un enfant du siècle **15**
  Fantasio, 75
  Il faut qu'une porte soit ouverte ou fermée **14-15**, 75, **185**

Nancy, 175, 178-83
Naples, 257-8
Napoleon, 3, 4, 7, 9, 10, 11, 13, 21, 28, 33, 56, **100-7**, 110, 111, 112, 115, 116, 117-18, 122, **123-4**, 138, 140, 141, 147, 148, 158, 205, 210, 224, 231, 232, 236, 245, 253, 277n., 289
  Mémorial de Ste Hélène, 158
Napoleon III, 49
  Idées napoléoniennes, 49
National, Le, 127, 277n., 282n.
Nero, Emperor, 56
Nerval, G. de (Gérard Labrunie), **11-12**, 43, 281-2n.
  Les illuminés, **11-12**
New Monthly Magazine, 13, 41, 65, 271n., 277n., 281n., 282n., 286n., 290
Ney, Marshal, 102
Niebuhr, B. G., 123, 278n., 283n.
Nietzsche, F., **2**, 3, 7, 13, **82**, **85**, 86, **89-90**, 102, 112, 113, 114, 123, 261, **264**, 266
  Beyond good and evil, **3**, **264**, 266
  Birth of tragedy, **82**, **85**, 86
  Ecce homo, 13
  Genealogy of Morals, **89-90**
  Untimely considerations, **2**, 102

INDEX

Orlando, F., 216–17
Owen, R., 271n.

Paris, 33, 95, 111, 136, 145, 173, 174, 190, 213–14, 220
Paris Monthly Review, 38, 42, 275, 290
Pascal, B., 36
Paton, A. A., 6
Pellico, S., 103, 289
Périer-Lagrange, F., 268n.
Peter the Great, 106
Petrarca, F., 45–6, 109, 170
Peyrefitte, R., 228
Philip V of Spain, 257
Picavet, F.
  Les idéologues, 35, 267n.
Pietragura, A., 289
Plato, 36, 126, 283n.
Plutarch,
  Lives of illustrious men, 20, 55, 62, 107, 112, 121
Poe, E. A., 223
Polentini, family of, 109
Pope, A., 93
Popper, K.
  The poverty of historicism, 106
Pound, E., 252
Praz, M.
  The romantic agony, 285n.
Prévost, J., 4, 5–6, 53, 151, 255, 275n.
  La création chez Stendhal, 4, 5–6, 53, 151
Producteur, Le, 208
Proudhon, P., 271n.
Proust, M., 22, 135, 167, 217–18, 284n.
  A la recherche du temps perdu, 22, 135, 167, 217–18, 284n.
  Contre Sainte-Beuve, 167

Racine, J., 27, 54, 57, 67, 70, 73–4, 75, 207–8, 225, 250, 273n.
  Andromaque, 67, 73–4
  Britannicus, 207–8, 250
  Phèdre, 225, 250
Raphael, 10, 110, 177, 223
Raynouard, J.-F.-M.
  Les Troubadours, 282n.
Regulus, 39, 43
Rémusat, C. de, 16, 17, 168

Revue de Paris, La, 165, 258, 290
Revue des deux mondes, La, 14, 220, 222, 290, 291
Rey, Abbé G., 18
Reynolds, J.
  Discourses, 67, 273n.
Ricardo, D., 48
Richards, I. A.
  Principles of literary criticism, 275n.
Riego y Nunez, R. del, 51
Rinieri, Giulia, 290
Robbe-Grillet, A., 233
Robespierre, M., 30, 37, 40
Roebuck, J. A., 68
Roland, Mme M., 268n.
Roman de Renart, Le, 257
Romanticism, 10–16, 30, 52, 73–4, 76, 92, 162, 164, 183, **209–10**, 249, 273n.
Rome, 16, 110–14, 121, 123
Rossini, G., 62, 95, 96, 97, 275
Rousseau, J. J., **30–3, 34–7**, 54, 63, 65, 73, 129, 214, **216–18**, 269n., 270n., 278n.
  Les confessions, **31, 32, 33**, 34, **216–18**
  Du contrat social, **34, 36, 37**, 278n.
  Emile, **30, 32, 34, 35–6**
  Lettres de la montagne, 35, 269n.
  La nouvelle Héloïse, **31**, 73, 214
Rubempré, Mme. A. de, 23, 218, 290
Rubichon, M.
  Du mécanisme de la société, 282
Rude, F.
  Stendhal et la pensée sociale de son temps, 48, **99**, 119, 271n., 280n., 282n.
Rue Transnonain, massacre of, 117, 195, 197
Ruskin, J., 284n.
Russell, B., 212–13, 215

Saint-Cyr, General Gouvion, 240
Sainte-Beuve, C. A., 11, **15–16, 24–5, 63–6**, 71, 115, 151, 260, 277n.
  Causeries du lundi, **15–16**
  Les consolations, 16, **24–5**
  Portraits contemporains, **63–6**, 71, 115, 151, 277n.
Saint-Just, L., 37
Saint-Marc Girardin, 195

INDEX

Saint-Simon, C. H. de, 44, **48–51**, 107, 117, 120, 194, 208, 264n.
  Catéchisme des industriels, **49–51**
  Le nouveau christianisme, 49
  Le système industriel, 49
Salviati, Count, 286
Sand, George (Aurore Dupin), 145, 280n.
Santayana, G., 46
Sartre, J.-P., 117, 121, 140, **154**, 195, 197, 233, **262–3**, 281n.
  L'être et le néant, **154**
  L'idiot de la famille, 117, **262–3**
Say, J.-B., 48, 50, 264, 265
Scarron, P., 127
Scève, M., 185
Schérer, E., 20
Scott, W., **127–8**, 129, 165, 175, 176, 189, 223, 227, 233, 279n.
  Ivanhoe, 128
  Quentin Durward, 128
  Waverley, 129
Scribe, E.
  La camaraderie, 76
Ségur, P. de, 123, 279n.
  Histoire de Napoléon et de la Grande Armée en 1812, 123
Sévigné, Mme de, 76–7, 109, 274, 279
Sforze, family of, 224
Shakespeare, W., 40, **54–62**, 63, 64, 65, 66, 67, 71, 93, 95, 96, 112, 126, 134, **156–7**, 158, 159, 166, 181, 190, 215, 248, 265, 273n., 275n., 276n., 283n., 289
  Cymbeline, 283n.
  Hamlet, **156–7**, 166
  Henry IV, part one, 61, 158, 181
  Julius Caesar, **61–2**, 134
  King Lear, 248
  Macbeth, 55, 59, 67, 156, 273n.
  Othello, 59, 60, **62**, 157
  Romeo and Juliet, 276n.
  The Tempest, 190, 283n.
  Troilus and Cressida, 61, 158
Shapira, M., 61–2
Sharpe, Sutton, 290
Shelley, P. B., 12
Siéyès, E.-J., 20
Simmons, E. J.
  Leo Tolstoy, 286n.
Sismondi (L. Simonde de), 50, **108**, 271n., 277n.
  Histoire de la littérature du midi de l'Europe, 271n.
  Histoire des républiques italiennes, **108**, 271n., 277n.
  Nouveaux principes d'économie politique, 271n.
Smith, A.
  The wealth of nations, 48, 265
Smith, C., 280n.
Socrates, 93
Spinoza, B., 36
Staël, Mme de, 28, 33, 43, 67, **102**, 106, 269n.
  Considérations sur la Révolution Française, **102**
  De la littérature, 33, 43, 269n.
  Delphine, 67
Starzynski, J., 275n.
Stendhal, *see* 'Beyle, Henri'
Stendhal Club, 1 and *passim*
Strickland, G., 271n., 280n., 285n.
  Selected journalism of Stendhal (editor), 271n., 285n.
Stryenski, C., 286n., 291
Sue, E.
  Koatven, 177

Tacitus, 140
Taine, H., 2, 109, **113**
Talleyrand, Prince C.-M. de, 20, 180, 191
Talma, F.-J., 55, 157
Tascher, comtesse C. de, 257
Tasso, T.
  La Gerusalemme liberata, 42, 53, 231
Tell, William, 51
Thibaudet, A., 151
Thierry, A., 223
Thomas, E., 284n.
Tillett, M.
  Stendhal, the background to his novels, 271n., 282n., 283n.
Timoleon, 55
Titian (Tiziano Vecellio), 110, 223
Tocqueville, A. de, **16–17**, 42, 277n.
  L'ancien régime, **16–17**
  De la démocratie en Amérique, 42, 277n.
Tolstoy, L., **99–102**, **106**, 126, 127, 175, 187, 249, 259, **259–60**, 261, 266
  Anna Karenina, 175, 259

Tolstoy, L. (*cont.*)
  War and Peace, **99–102, 106**, 127, 175, 187, **259–60**
Tracy, *see* 'Destutt de Tracy'
Trollope, F.
  Domestic manners of the Americans, 277n.
Turnell, M., 52, 244–5, 271n., 284n.
  The Novel in France, 244–5, 284n.
Tuscany, Grand Dukes of, 244–5
Twain, Mark
  Tom Sawyer, 232

United States of America, 50, **114**, 116, 162, 172, **180**, 221, 277n., 282n.
Utilitarianism, **33–44**, 48, 106, 107, 110, 132, 193, 198, 246, **263–6**, 270n., 281n.

Valéry, P., 173, 287n.
Vallès, J.
  Jacques Vingtras trilogy, 149
Vasari, P.
  Lives of the painters, 94
Vatican, 9, 11, 110–11, 281n.
Venice, Republic of, 110
Venturi, L.
  History of Art Criticism, 275n.
Verlaine, P., 187
Veronese, P., 94
Vertot, R. A. de
  Les révolutions romaines, 121
Vigano, S., 275n.
Vigny, A. de, 11, **12–13**, 14, 121, 269n.
  Eloa, **12–13**, 14
Villèle, J. de, 127, 166
Villeroy, N. de, 77
Vinci, Leonardo da, 90, 92, 168, 275n.

Virgil, **38**, 44, 54, 90, 140
  Aeneid, 90
  Eclogues, **38**, 44
Visconti, family of, 109, 224
Viscontini, Matilde, *see* 'Dembowski, Mathilde'
Volney, C. de, 12, **121–3**
  Leçons d'histoire, **122**
  Voyages en Syrie et en Egypte, **122**
Voltaire, 10, 11, **27–8**, 58, 67, **69**, 70–1, 78, 93, 127, 273n., 274n.
  Candide, 27
  Commentaire sur Corneille, **69**
  Discours à l'Académie Française, 274n.
  Lettres philosophiques, **69**, 273n.
  Mérope, 67
  Le siècle de Louis XIV, 273n.
  Tancrède, 58
  Zadig, 27

Wakefield, E. G., 264
Walpole, Sir R., 166, 180
Waterloo, Battle of, 100, 103, 231–2
Wellington, Duke of, 100, 102
Williams, W. D.
  Nietzsche and the French, 287
Winckler, C.
  Notice biographique sur Mozart, 276n.
Wood, M.
  Stendhal, 177, 203, 284n.
Wordsworth, W., 68, 194, 253
Wurmser, General D., 101

Yeats, W. B.
  'The scholars', 252

Zamet, S., 51
Zola, E.
  La curée, 91